Little Business on the Prairie

Little Business on the Prairie

Entrepreneurship, Prosperity, and Challenge in South Dakota

Robert E. Wright

Nef Family Chair in Political Economy
Augustana College

THE CENTER FOR WESTERN STUDIES
2015

Publication made possible with funding by the Anne King Publications Endowment and Ronald R. Nelson Publications Endowment in the Center for Western Studies and by the National Endowment for the Humanities.

ISBN: 978-0-931170-68-3

Library of Congress Control Number: 2014951793

Number 15 in the Prairie Plains Series

The Center for Western Studies (CWS) at Augustana College is concerned principally with preserving and interpreting native and immigrant cultures of the Northern Plains. CWS also seeks to improve the quality of social and cultural life in the Northern Plains, achieve a better understanding of the region, its heritage, and its resources, and stimulate interest in the solution to regional problems. The Center promotes understanding of the region through its archives, library, museum and art exhibitions, publications, courses, internships, conferences, and forums. It is committed, ultimately, to defining the contribution of the Northern Plains to American civilization. Visit the Fantle Building for the Center for Western Studies, Augustana College, 2201 S. Summit Avenue, Sioux Falls, South Dakota, or contact CWS at 605-274-4007 • 605-274-4999 (fax) • cws@augie.edu • www.augie.edu/cws • Facebook • Twitter.

Manufactured in the United States of America

Our town was small: just five thousand residents and five thousand students. Apart from the university, there wasn't much to it except tiny family-owned shops, a funeral home, a combination steakhouse-bowling alley, and nine bars.

--May-lee Chai, *Hapa Girl* (2007)

Contents

Acknowledgments

Only one name appears on the cover of this book, and that is where the buck stops in terms of the tome's quality (or lack thereof), but many people attempted to aid this poor author along the way. I first want to thank the Augustana students who took my course in the history of entrepreneurship, especially Ian Blue, Adam Diamond, Paula Dirksen, Jonathan Emerson, Samuel Gotham, Bryan Hakeman, Brian Iverson, Brian Knight, Troy Manley, Keith Newman, Colin Raehsler, Emily Thalacker, and Blake Thompson, all of whom helped me to hone my approach in chapter one, whether they realized it or not.

Harry Thompson and the Center for Western Studies also deserve thanks for funding the study and bringing it to fruition, sometimes by offering a carrot and sometimes by brandishing a stick. Harry, an anonymous reader, and Landon Karr also saved me from numerous embarrassing malapropisms, misnomers, and other mistakes. Liz Thrond, the Center's Collection Assistant, skillfully and cheerfully guided me through the archives while Becky Folkerts, Augustana College's interlibrary loan coordinator, did yeoman work acquiring many of the distant or rare texts cited herein. Daniel Daily and Joseph J. De La Rosa helped me to navigate the newly opened William Janklow Papers at the University of South Dakota in Vermillion and Ken R. Stewart did likewise for the corporate records at the South Dakota State Historical Society in Pierre. If I were lucky enough to know half as much as Ken does about the history of business in South Dakota, this book would be twice as long, at least twice as good, and would have been finished on time. I could say the same for Stephen Cusulos, whose detailed work on ethnic businessmen in early Sioux Falls many will find meatier, if narrower, than what I offer here. Finally, Joe Kirby, Bill Peterson, and Jon Lauck also deserve my thanks for convincing me of the importance of South Dakota and its entrepreneurial business and political cultures.

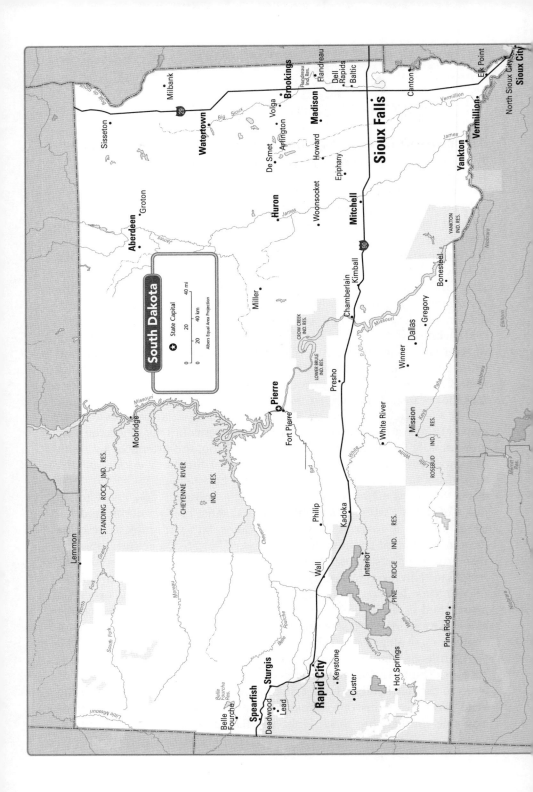

Little Business on the Prairie

Chapter 1
Entrepreneurship and the Economy

Most South Dakotans would agree free enterprise is the best economic system in the world, bar none.[1]

An orgy has erupted in South Dakota almost every August since 1938. I do not mean the sexual orgy at the annual motorcycle rally in Sturgis, I mean the orgy of entrepreneurship that surrounds the Sturgis Rally and Races, which is officially known as the Black Hills Motor Classic. During the week-long event, Sturgis, a town of about 6,000 with a long history of debauched entrepreneurship, becomes the largest "city" in the state, the temporary home of half a million Harley Davidson (and the resurgent Indian brand, which the rally's founder, J. C. "Pappy" Hoel, sold in his dealership) motorcycle enthusiasts from around the nation and increasingly the world.[2] Overnight, the town "becomes a Gomorrah of steel and hobnail boots,"[3] a place where one can get drunk, laid, and tattooed all at the same time. "It's like Mardi Gras with chrome,"[4] lots and lots of chrome. "Sturgis brings me to Sturgis," related one New Yorker. "It's the greatest place in the world."[5]

At least such is the image that rally promoters and vendors wish to convey to keep attendance up. Just a regional event until the 1960s, the rally grew rapidly thereafter and hit 300,000 to 400,000 attendees by 1990. The more who attend, the more customers for the many entrepreneurs, those from Sturgis itself as well as itinerant merchants, to relieve of their cash.[6] Some "vendors hawk brass knuckles, switchblades, and endless miles of chain"[7] while others offer "bobcat tails, bull scrotums, and fox pelts"[8] or nipple rings, harnesses, and other stuff too kinky to describe even in a book that has already used the word "orgy." Other entrepreneurs take orders for custom gas tank paint jobs while still others try to draw people to their swap meets, sled pulls, motorcycle rodeos, and tire blow-out contests. In 1995, 109 t-shirt vendors, 77 leather vendors, 96 tattoo artists, and 95 food vendors came to the event to sell their wares on the sidewalks and in rented storefronts.[9] Everywhere, "the air is filled with the gamy smell of alligator, wild boar, and venison sizzling on open grills."[10]

Sturgis became the nation's largest motorcycle rally for a number of reasons. The town's image leveraged the "bikers' sense of themselves as heirs to the hard-riding, hard-drinking, freedom-loving traditions of the Wild West," explains one scholar of American subcultures.[11] The rides available through the Black Hills, the Badlands, and Devil's Tower in nearby Wyoming are spectacular. In addition, Sturgis is near the middle of the country, east to west anyway. Perhaps most important, South Dakotans and their government know not to mess with a good thing. Law enforcement attends in force to catch people driving while intoxicated, druggies, wanted fugitives, and young women silly enough to expose their areolas, but for the most part anything goes at the rally and that really draws out the innovators. Even Rapid City Hospital has gotten into the act, running advertisements of broken arms over the caption, "We'll Develop Your Unplanned Vacation Photos." At the same time, South Dakotans let their hospitality and good sense shine through to grateful sojourners. As Robert G. Lowery of Selden, New York, reported in 1990, "there was almost no price gouging. Hotel rooms were about $75 a night, though booked for almost a year; a breakfast could be had for about $3, and the residents of Sturgis went out of their way to make us feel comfortable."[12] As a result, many remain at the rally until their money is gone.[13]

The rally is so large that it has spawned offshoots, including HOG (Harley Owners Group), which meets in Rapid City for those "rubies" (rich, urban bikers) who wish to worship their machines "without the barbarous excesses." But the main center of attraction is still Sturgis and its environs, especially sprawling campgrounds like Wild West, Hog Heaven, Covered Wagon, and the Buffalo Chip, where, it is said, "vats of beer, lakes of puke, acres of bare breasts, and billowy clouds of reefer" prepare campers for the main event, which sometimes involves a sex act with a vegetable. The Buffalo Chip has its own currency, called buffalo chips of course, its own newspaper, the *Buffalo Chip Gazette*, its own drink, the Purple Passion (grain alcohol and grape syrup, yum!) and even its own one-watt radio station. It also holds concerts with headliners like BTO, Marshall Tucker Band, Joan Jett, Steppenwolf, and other rock-and-rollers from an age gone by.[14]

Sturgis, which has been compared to Mecca or Jerusalem as well as Gomorrah, is now legendary among the biker set and even has a Harley model named for it, the Dyna Glide Sturgis, which of course is made in Milwaukee. But it is not the town or the motorcycle rally that saved South Dakota's economy and people, or even the thousands of other events and attractions that other innovators have dreamed up over the years. They are just means to an end and will change and fade with time. Rather, South Dakota's savior, with a small "s" of course, is its entrepreneurs, the men and women who start their own businesses and could replace the motorcycle rally, or any other aspect of the state's economy, if they had to, just as they have throughout the state's history and even, some scholars suspect, its prehistory.[15]

The 73rd Sturgis Motorcycle Rally drew an estimated 466,000 attendees in 2013. *Courtesy South Dakota Department of Tourism.*

A few miles away, in Spearfish, a different type of orgy, a spiritual one, has taken place every peacetime year since 1938, thanks to entrepreneur Josef Meier. The Black Hills Passion Play, which ceased operation in 2008, dramatized the final days of Jesus Christ on a stage two-and-a-half city blocks long, one of the largest outdoor stages in the nation. Two dozen professional actors and 150 extras took part in the story, which re-enacted the crucifixion on a nearby hillside. More than 10 million people, up to 6,000 at a time, viewed the spectacle. The cool, clear nights, excellent acoustics, and lack of mosquitoes, plus the welcome reception provided by nearby residents, kept the spectacle in Spearfish even after the hiatus caused by World War II.[16]

Meanwhile, 350 miles to the east, people gathered at the Minnehaha County Fairgrounds outside Sioux Falls to attend the Great Plains Buffalo Roadeo, a rally for motorhome owners. The event attracted only 2,078 motor coaches and 7,500 people and did not, thankfully says this Sioux Falls-based author, become an annual occurrence. It stemmed, however, from one of the state's many minor industries, providing a legal address for people who choose to live their lives on the nation's highways and byways (and avoid state income taxes while doing it).[17]

Entrepreneurship is not always as sexy as the Sturgis rally, as passionate as the crucifixion of Christ, or as bizarre as living one's life in perpetual travel. In fact, it is often as decidedly boring as the one bed, one bureau, one light bulb, no bathroom in the Brokaw Hotel in Bristol that Oscar Johnson, who owned a small well digging and moving company, occupied in the 1950s. Entrepreneurial enterprise—the system of political economy that encourages innovations large, small, and in-between—drives prosperity and even happiness. Without it, South Dakota would be sunk. With it, South Dakota's economic prospects are among the brightest in the nation.[18]

Flyover country. Hollowing out. Rain on the scarecrow, blood on the plow. Buffalo commons. In the 1980s, it looked like South Dakota and much of the Upper Midwest was going to suffer the same fate as the industrial Rust Belt, a crippling negative feedback cycle of economic stagnation and depopulation. In 1980, South Dakota's per capita income was just $7,800, or 18% below the national average of $9,500, and much more vitriolic than the national average due to the state's heavy dependence on agriculture. Instead of sinking into despair and bankruptcy like Detroit (the population of which is comparable to South Dakota's), however, the Mount Rushmore State rebounded strongly. Many individuals suffered during the transition, but South Dakota's economy is now thriving and not due to agricultural subsidies or oil. Today, South Dakota produces education, financial services, healthcare, and manufactured goods, not just corn and gold. Although South Dakota's countryside is strewn with abandoned farm buildings, many of the state's farms, homes, and commercial buildings are modern, its transportation infrastructure is strong, and its connection to the global telecom network is growing. Unemployment and crime rates are low, real compensation is solid, and the outlook perennially optimistic.[19] Perhaps most important of all, South Dakota is, according to business people, a "pro-business state."[20] "South Dakota may be one of the best-kept 'secrets' in the country," wrote *Entrepreneurship Press* in 2004. It is less of a secret today, but national policymakers would do well to learn more about the state's entrepreneurial enterprise system.[21]

Once considered an economic backwater at best, South Dakota has attracted capital from abroad over the last few decades and is humming along so nicely economically that some consider it a model for other states to emulate. Lessons for other parts of the nation abound but exporting the state's success is not a trivial task because state economies are a complex jumble of climate, culture, history, geography, and laws. Each state is distinctive, and not just geographically. Each state has its own past, its own legends, myths, and path dependencies. Each has its own unique blend of peoples, of individuals who decided to come, leave, or stick it out. Each has its own set of laws, not radically different from those of its neighbors in most specific cases but different enough to have significant economic impact, for better or worse.[22]

Laws can be changed with relative ease, but path dependence is notoriously immutable. A good part of South Dakota's recent economic success is linked to its past, and its people and their beliefs about their liberty. In South Dakota, entrepreneurship is not just a way to make money but a way of life. South Dakotans make lemonade out of life's lemons because they must do so in order to survive, just as their parents, grandparents, and great-grandparents did. Most are descended from the "stickers," the people who braved droughts, conflict, and grasshopper hordes and remained in the state. Two forms of selection have been at work in the state since its inception. Only the most enterprising and freedom-loving came to the state in the first place, and only the most adaptable among them stayed and faced the state's challenges while the inflexible moved away or perished.[23] The wit who once claimed that So. Dak. (its ancient postal abbreviation) was "a somewhat civilized place populated by normal people"[24] got it wrong. South Dakota was, and remains, a very civilized place populated by people extraordinarily interested in preserving their liberty—their freedom to do as they wished so long as their actions do not injure others (in any direct or obvious way). Ivy League graduate Archer Gilfillan, for example, spent almost two decades in northwestern South Dakota in the 1910s, 20s, and 30s shepherding because he relished the freedom the state, and his occupation, afforded. He remained in South Dakota during his second career as a writer-journalist and for his retirement.[25] Though few experienced as much personal freedom as Gilfillan felt, many farmers, just as animated by the desire to make what homesteader Estella Bowen Culp called "some good money" as any other American, suffered through the hard years certain that they would make more money in a different field (figuratively or literally).[26]

Aided by those twin selective pressures, South Dakotans forged solutions to difficult problems because, Gilfillan argued, South Dakota is freer than other states, and its people are "a little more unconventional."[27] Frustrated by land composed mostly of muddy gumbo and petrified wood, ranchers around Lemmon – a town in the western part of the state near the North Dakota border named after its tenacious founder George – searched for and eventually found a market for the gummy stuff, terrazzo floor pieces made by Larson Manufacturing in Brookings. Those ranchers, and thousands of other "stickers" like them, get by because they know that they will be able to keep the fruits of their labor, be it manual or mental. And that belief, which is well founded by the facts on the ground, makes all the difference in the world – literally. South Dakota's economy thrives because it is to the United States what the U.S. economy is to the rest of the world, a free port in a sea of high taxes, ubiquitous regulatory shoals, and pirates both public and private.[28]

Explaining why a few nations are rich, why they have inflation-adjusted per capita incomes above $30,000 per year, and why most are poor, with incomes below $10,000 or even $1,000 per year, proved itself a difficult task for scholars, who explored many paths, most of which led to dead ends like the failed culture-religion, geography, disease environment, and natural resource endowment hypotheses. Recently, however, a strong, though by no means yet complete, consensus has emerged that institutions are the key to the wealth question. Put as simply as possible, good institutions allow economic growth (high incomes), bad ones inhibit it, and the worst ones render mere subsistence difficult.[29]

The world is more complex than that, however, so it is necessary to elucidate the ways in which institutional quality determines economic growth with more precision. Clearly, not all governments are alike. Some do a much better job protecting their citizens' lives, liberty, and property than others do. Their relative performance can be, and has been, recorded over time via various measures like the Index of Economic Freedom. Almost invariably, governments that allow higher levels of freedom or, in other words, that tolerate lower levels of economic "slavery," perform better economically than nations with lower levels of freedom. (The exceptions to that rule are few and easily explained: even the most predatory governments can induce a short spurt of economic growth by exploiting natural resources like oil or a captive workforce.)

Freedom leads to economic growth through the incentives created for entrepreneurs, people (or companies) with a predilection for exploiting profit opportunities. Such people are so ubiquitous in every known human society, past and present, that scientists could well have labeled the species *Homo negotium inventor* (Latin for "man the business inventor," my rough translation of entrepreneur) instead of *Homo sapiens*. Alas, with equal justice mankind could also be labeled *Homo ereptor* (man the thief) or *Homo ignavus* (man the lazy). As a result, entrepreneurs come in three varieties – innovative, replicative, and exploitative – depending on the incentives they confront.

Innovative entrepreneurs are the inventors and captains of industry that drive productivity enhancements. In other words, they help people to produce more output from a given amount of inputs (or to produce a given output from fewer inputs), the very essence of economic growth. Think Benjamin Franklin, Thomas Edison, Andrew Carnegie, Henry Ford, Edwin Land, Bill Gates, Steve Jobs, Richard Branson, or Elon Musk. The most important innovative entrepreneurs introduce disruptive technologies or techniques that spur a rash of follow-up innovations by causing numerous new profit opportunities to arise. Think of the torrents of new technology unleashed by breakthrough innovations like interchangeable parts, assembly lines, airplanes, automobiles, the Internet, or mobile telephony.

Replicative entrepreneurs do not create new technologies or techniques but rather extend existing innovations into new markets, across physical space or into new niches. In other words, they introduce an existing product or service into a new territory or to a new type of customer. Like innovative entrepreneurs, they also spur economic growth but do so more subtly, by reducing unemployment or increasing the competitiveness of local markets. Many replicative entrepreneurs are self-employed individuals who cannot find employment due to cyclical downturns or structural deficiencies. Others simply enjoy the autonomy associated with running their own business. "You are your own boss, you set your own vacations," explained one South Dakota entrepreneur. "You enjoy the profits and once in a while you might get a visit from a big name," including in this entrepreneur's case George W. Bush and Barack Obama.[30] Most of the entrepreneurs discussed in Scott Shane's *The Illusions of Entrepreneurship* are replicative entrepreneurs. Without considering their salubrious effects on competition or employment, Shane concludes that replicative entrepreneurs are not major contributors to economic growth, but even this skeptic admits that they do not hinder the economies in which they operate.[31]

The same could not be said for exploitative entrepreneurs, people and companies that engage in rent-seeking and other activities that essentially divert resources to themselves without improving productivity or competitiveness. Think brutal dictators like Saddam Hussein, Stalin, or Pol Pot, organized crime figures like Tony Soprano (fictional, I know, and hence unlikely to have me whacked), and businesses that earn profits primarily through corrupt government contracts or tariffs, monopolies, or other economically stultifying policies. Exploitative entrepreneurs do provide a form of employment but the last thing that economies need are more thieves and leeches. They are essentially vampires that suck the lifeblood out of economies directly, by taking resources from others without commensurate return, and indirectly, by destroying incentives to innovate. Why work hard and smart to have your efforts ripped off by the government or some politically well-connected corporation?

It is not surprising to find, then, that in economies characterized by much freedom, some entrepreneurs will be innovative but many will be replicative and a few exploitative. As economic freedom decreases, fewer people find innovation worthwhile and more opt for replicative and exploitative strategies. In economies with low levels of freedom/high levels of slavery, innovative and replicative entrepreneurs will be few and far between because exploitative entrepreneurship will prove the easiest path to profit. In the most enslaved countries, entrepreneurs join the government and do nothing but prey upon residents and any foreigners that they can safely exploit.

Statistical evidence of the causal link between freedom and growth abounds but will not be recounted here as most readers are unlikely to appreciate fully or understand it, especially coming from an author who believes that there is more than a grain of truth to the adage that there exist three types of lies: lies, damn lies, and statistics.[32] Much more compelling evidence for most people are so-called natural experiments where nations with similar cultures, disease environments, natural resources, and so forth are arbitrarily divided and endowed with governments that permit starkly different degrees of economic freedom. After a few decades, differences in economic outcomes become palpable and always point to the conclusions suggested by the model of entrepreneurship presented above, which I call the entrepreneurship growth model or EGM for short. Think North and South Korea, East and West Germany, Haiti and the Dominican Republic, and China, which historical circumstance divided after World War II into three parts: the mainland, Hong Kong, and Taiwan. The last two parts thrived economically under political regimes that protected life, liberty, and property while the first wallowed in poverty and famines until the late 1970s when it effectively abandoned communism and allowed markets to function and some forms of private property to arise. Its economy is now the second largest in the world and will continue to grow in per capita terms so long as it continues to increase the economic freedom of its denizens.

As suggested by the natural experiments just mentioned, the EGM is a powerful model that applies broadly across long periods of time and large swathes of space. It is explicated here in full for the first time but is based on previous scholarship as well as extensive classroom discussions with Augustana College students.[33]

The EGM also applies *within* economies, both national and regional ones, though sub-economies, like that of the U.S. states, are fairly closely tethered to national outcomes. South Dakota's economy is palpably freer and more entrepreneurial than the economies of most other U.S. states and the nation as a whole. According to the Tax Foundation, South Dakota ranks second behind only Wyoming in terms of favorable tax climate for business. Its state-by-state index measures corporate, individual income, sales, unemployment insurance, and property taxes. According to the Fraser Institute, in 2011 South Dakota was, with a score of 8.1 on a scale of 0 to 10, the most economically free of all U.S. states and Canadian provinces. In addition, South Dakota has for seven years in a row ranked number one in the Small Business and Entrepreneurship Council's small business survival index, well ahead of runners-up Nevada and Texas and leagues ahead of notorious red tape states like California and New Jersey. In 2013, CNBC named South Dakota "America's Top State for Business" based on a combination of its economic performance, the cost of doing business in the state, the quality of its infrastructure, education, workforce, and overall life, its level of technology, business friendliness, cost of living, and access to capital.[34]

South Dakota is, in other words, a haven for, and incubator of, entrepreneurs. And that penchant for entrepreneurship is a very important aspect of the state's relative economic strength, which was amply demonstrated by its performance during and after the financial and economic crises of 2007-09. In December 2011, three full years after the Panic of 2008 ended, South Dakota's unemployment rate was, at 4.2%, the third lowest in the nation behind North Dakota, which continued to experience an energy boom of Albertan or Arabian proportions. (Incidentally, South Dakota's economic strength cannot be attributed to North Dakota's oil boom, the main economic effects of which are limited to northwestern North Dakota and northeastern Montana.)[35] South Dakota barely lost the second slot to Nebraska and was well ahead of fourth place, shared by New Hampshire and Vermont at 5.1%. In Mississippi, Rhode Island, California, Nevada, and, ironically enough, Washington D.C., the unemployment rate was still in double digits in late 2011. At 8.5%, the national average was twice that of the Mount Rushmore State.

South Dakota's population is not growing quite as fast as the national average, 7.9% compared to 9.7% between the last two decennial censuses, but that the state is growing at all given the hollowing out of many agricultural communities is amazing enough, and largely attributable to the 24% growth of Sioux Falls and the 14% growth of Rapid City, not to mention the prodigious growth of some of their suburbs. The population of Brandon, just outside of Sioux Falls, doubled between 2000 and 2010 and, out west, Box Elder's population soared almost 175%.[36]

South Dakota's median income in 2010 was over $48,000, just $2,500, or 5%, below the national median, a good showing given that its cost of living is 98.5% that of the national average and that it is home to five Indian reservations that rank among the nation's seven poorest counties. Nevertheless, income inequality in South Dakota is remarkably low. It is tied with Wisconsin for the lowest in the country with a Gini coefficient, a statistical measure of inequality bounded by 0 (perfect equality) and 100 (perfect inequality), of 33, a little higher than some Western European nations but lower, and hence more equal, than others, including Britain and Estonia. Nationally, the Gini coefficient is over 46 at this point and causing considerable consternation.[37]

Despite, or perhaps because of, its relative equality of incomes, South Dakota's economic performance for the decade 1999 to 2009 was ranked eleventh in the nation in a recent study by famed economist Arthur Laffer and two economists associated with the American Legislative Exchange Council. Those same three economists also ranked South Dakota second, behind Utah, in overall economic outlook. The U.S. Chamber of Commerce lists South Dakota as the fourth best growth performer in the last ten years behind energy-rich Alaska, North Dakota, and Wyoming. The Chamber also lists South Dakota second only to Tennessee in terms of favorable taxes and regulations, second in transportation, and fifth in overall infrastructure.[38]

Some attribute the economic strength of the Northern Plains to federal agricultural subsidies. Nebraska and the Dakotas receive billions in federal agricultural aid but they also receive fewer dollars from other federal sources than other states do. In 2008, for example, South Dakota received almost $1.3 billion dollars in all forms of federal assistance, or just shy of $1,600 per person, making it only the twenty-first highest federal aid recipient in per capita terms, and a far cry short of Alaska's $2,600, Vermont's $2,800, or Washington D.C.'s whopping almost $4,700 dollars per person in federal aid. In aggregate, residents of the Northern Plains do receive more in federal expenditures than they pay in federal taxes but thanks to federal government budget deficits that is true of almost all the other states too. Thank you China and Japan.[39]

A more compelling cause of the relative economic strength of the Northern Plains is rooted in the EGM. The political cultures of Northern Plains states are very friendly to economic freedom. Although long big "R" Republican, South Dakota is also staunchly small "d" democratic, so it is favorable to business interests but also effectively checks any attempted excesses. "Under God the People rule" is not just the state motto, it is political gospel.[40] South Dakota politics is extremely intimate. In 1970, the *New York Times* reported that South Dakota "remains one of those rare places where the highest political premium is still placed on kissing babies and pressing the flesh."[41] Any citizen can see the governor, generally within thirty minutes of seeking an appointment, "which makes the chief executive easier to see than most doctors."[42] The governor's door is not quite as open today, but it is hardly closed. As Eric McDonald, founder and CEO of DocuTap in Sioux Falls put it, "I feel like the state is small enough where I can probably reach out to the governor with two phone calls."[43]

To this day, South Dakotans call their politicians, even their governor and U.S. Senators, by their first names, a tradition that began in the nineteenth century. While many Republicans are social conservatives opposed to abortion and so forth, a strong libertarian thread has also long been present. [44] As South Dakota war-hero-turned-governor Joe Foss put it, his parents and many of his neighbors "took the attitude that government's main duty was to keep everybody, including itself, from interfering with the peaceful lives of ordinary citizens."[45]

Overall, South Dakota's political economy is almost Smithian, as in Adam Smith's vision of numerous, small firms competing vigorously for customers. Corporate juggernauts sometimes set up shop in the state, and have generally been warmly welcomed, but they do not dominate the local economy, which is just as well because most eventually move away or go under. And when large corporations start to behave like monopolists or monopsonists, South Dakotan politicians call for more stringent antitrust laws and get applauded for it![46] So while the state government is friendly to business, it typically does not forget that its ultimate goal is to promote the happiness of its citizens, not its corporations. And befitting the Midwest, the business culture is friendly too: "The culture in Sioux Falls is really supportive," explained McDonald of DocuTap. "Everybody will rally behind a good idea. They'll reach out to their contacts, they'll pull every string possible to help you succeed."[47]

Recent research suggests that governments that encourage entrepreneurship do so because resource endowments are so weak that they must do so merely to keep the domestic economy afloat. According to this line of thought, entrepreneurship levels in developed countries are already nearly optimal so only underdeveloped countries or areas need to stimulate additional entrepreneurship. Contrary to common assumptions, however, South Dakota's endowments are considerable. The Black Hills are chock full of resources, from metals and minerals to timber. Much of the eastern part of the state is an agricultural paradise thickly blanketed in houdek, a "heavy, deep, black loam" composed of glacial till and decomposed prairie grasses and other organic material found only in South Dakota.[48]

Even many of the state's apparent weaknesses are actually strengths. For instance, South Dakota appears landlocked – according to former South Dakota author Kathleen Norris, the state is "as landlocked as it is possible to be in North America"[49] – but actually it is bisected by the continent's longest river which connects it to international markets via St. Louis and New Orleans. Far from being remote, the geographical centers of the nation (including Alaska and Hawaii), North America, and the continent's great grasslands lie within the state.[50]

Even South Dakota's notorious weather, properly understood, is more boon than burden.[51] Comedians say that "the only predictable thing about the Northern Plains weather is that it is unpredictable."[52]

"Say what you will about our climate," another one-liner asserts, "in Dakota we say it keeps the riff-raff out."[53] In another joke, upon learning that his homestead was in Nebraska, not South Dakota, a Swedish homesteader threw his hat in the air and shouted "no more of them awful South Dakota winters."[54] One old-timer told a traveler from Boston that South Dakotans only had to buy coal eleven months of the year because July was just warm enough to "sit around with your overcoat on." In the winter, the tall-tale teller went on, a "Klondike" thermometer would freeze "to death." You walked around at an angle in the winter, he claimed, because if you walked straight your breath froze "in front of you in a solid mass that brings you to a standstill."[55] During droughts, a man hit by a drop of rain was said to have fainted from the shock and had to be revived with two buckets of dust.[56] Other wags said that "it was so dry the water had only 50% humidity" and that coyotes walked while chasing rabbits on hot summer days.[57] Similarly, during droughts, the Missouri River was said to be "too thick to drink and a mite too thin to plow."[58]

I heard variations of most of those jibes about the weather in western New York when growing up there in the 1970s and 1980s. Of course, General George Custer never likened Rochester, New York, to "a part of hell with the fires burnt out" but we now know that the general was braver than he was bright.[59] Plus, he was referring to South Dakota's Badlands in the summer. Although the temperature can jump into the triple digits Fahrenheit anywhere in South Dakota, it is usually a dry heat that most people find much more tolerable than the sauna-like climate of the summertime East. Most people find even 100 degrees of dry Dakota air tolerable.[60] Moreover, residents knew that "however hot it was during the day, the nights almost invariably were cool."[61]

South Dakota is almost as infamous as Buffalo, New York, for its snowstorms. Historic blizzards seemingly straight from the bowels of hell struck the state in 1873, 1880, 1881, 1888, 1910, 1949, and 1975. The 1949 blizzard was actually a series of storms that paralyzed the Upper Midwest for seven weeks and produced drifts 35 feet high.[62] Many lesser storms also disrupted everyday life on the Plains. One immigrant to the state in the latter part of the twentieth century remembered "long, terrible winters when the temperatures dropped to 70 below zero with the wind-chill factor, the snow drifts taller than cars, the blizzard winds that howled like a woman shrieking."[63] Most years, however, the state's denizens wished they got more snow.[64] Where it snows the most, in and near the Black Hills, the snow often melts after a short stay due to the frequent incursion of warm Chinook winds. That is not a recent phenomenon caused by global warming, either. "Contrary to the generally accepted notion," wrote one late nineteenth century settler, "the climate in the Black Hills region is not severe – mild weather often continues up to the first of December and snow does not stay on the ground long."[65] The Black Hills, a lovely but isolated cluster of hills in the far western part of the state, has a climate all its own, one that most people find delightful most of the time. In the rest of the state, winter temperatures can seem severe to outsiders but many people find the dry cold more tolerable than the humid frigidity that often encapsulates the East.[66] "The freezing point in the damp atmosphere of Chicago," one old follower told a traveler, "is worse than zero in our dry air."[67]

Moreover, the weather is often "clear, bright, sunshiny" even in January and February.[68] Again, this is not a recent phenomenon brought about by global climate change. In 1889, Frank Hagerty wrote: "The winters are cold, it is true; but the air is pure and full of invigoration, dry and devoid of any humidity during the winter months, it never penetrates and chills as does the damp atmosphere of the Atlantic states. ... Some winters there is scarcely enough snow to make good sleighing. ...blizzards are severe but fortunately are rare."[69] In fact, in addition to being known as Coyote Country, the Blizzard State, and the Windy State, South Dakota has been accurately called the Sunshine State. The area west of the Missouri River averages 250 days a year of sunshine and the "people of the prairies always get tanned" because there is no avoiding the ubiquitous sunshine.[70] "And sun! And still more sun!" O. E. Rölvaag exclaimed in his epic novel about the Northern Plains, *Giants in the Earth*.[71]

Despite the ample sunshine, South Dakota's weather can be extreme and unpredictable.[72] "Whatever the weather does in this part of the country," the shepherd Gilfillan recalled, "it does with intense and single-minded earnestness."[73] Extreme temperature fluctuations are common. In the 1880s, early pioneers recorded temperatures that ranged from 45 degrees Fahrenheit below to 112 degrees above zero.[74] Even more disconcerting, temperatures can change rapidly. "While it may have been shorts weather in the morning," travel writer Marion Head recently observed, "it can become jacket weather by lunchtime."[75] A particularly brutal thunderstorm made one homesteader wail: "Oh why do we stay in this terrible country. It is nothing but one awful thing after another."[76] The state's most intense weather, however, tends to be localized. Tornados or hail could destroy one family's farm while leaving neighbors' fields unscathed.[77] (The largest and heaviest hailstone ever recovered in the United States, an inch bigger in diameter and a third of a pound heavier than the previous records, struck Vivian, South Dakota, in July 2010.[78])

The weather in South Dakota also has notoriously bad timing. As rancher Dan O'Brien put it: "I live in a land that gets only fourteen inches of rain a year and every time you need it to be dry it decides to pour."[79] Droughts of course presented the opposite problem: rain was needed but the sky would not yield a drop. Historic droughts decimated the land and "desiccated ... dreams"[80] in 1889, 1894, 1910-11, and 1933-34 and the state has been hit by them periodically ever since, including ones in 1976, 1980, 1988, and 2012.[81]

Perhaps the best thing about South Dakota's climate is the air, which George Lemmon described as "pure, invigorating lung tonic"[82] and homesteader Estella Bowen Culp claimed "has such a delightful tang it makes you want to work."[83] British sportsman William Baille-Grohman called the state's air "dry and sparkling as perhaps none other on the globe" and claimed that "it seems to be composed not of one-fifth, but of five-fifths oxygen."[84] The seemingly unceasing wind blows so hard on the plains and prairie, it is said, that Dakotans scream at each other just to be heard.[85] According to one early wag, the wind blew so hard at times that people "could hardly keep the buttons on their clothes."[86] Another explained that "this is a great country for winds" before claiming that a straight-line gust had "tipped a passenger train off the track."[87] To this day, local weather forecasters call a day with winds in the teens "breezy." A "windy" day in South Dakota means sustained thirty-mile-per-hour winds with gusts of fifty miles per hour plus.[88] Although "it cannot be

Away from the interstates that cross South Dakota north and south and east and west, travelers can still find dirt roads that lead into the countryside. *Courtesy South Dakota Department of Tourism.*

Little Business on the Prairie

denied that our Wind on occasion momentarily oversteps the bounds,"[89] Dakota's winds tend to be straight line, not tornadic, and in addition to keeping the air fresh and pollution free, "the much objurgated wind" sweeps ridges bare so that sheep and cattle can graze even in the depths of winter.[90] The wind also tends to moderate the temperature. As one homesteader put it: "I do not agree with the person who said, 'South Dakota has only two seasons, winter and August' for the mild weather in spring and fall is almost ideal."[91]

Perhaps the most disconcerting aspect of the prairie for outsiders are the insects, hordes of them too large even for bug zappers. "The next morning," reported one newcomer, "our driveway and lawn were littered with dead insects, large ebony beetles flipped onto the backs of their charred shells, red-and-black box elder bugs scattered like pistachio shells, and unidentifiable insects that seemed to have arrived from a Hitchcock film."[92] Of course such creepy crawlers and fearsome fliers are important parts of the ecosystem, indispensable cogs in the great wheel of nature, and in their way as beautiful as the pheasants they feed and the plants they pollinate.

Before modern medicine, many people visited the Plains to restore their health and reported that the change in climate worked. After an expedition to the region in 1850, Thaddeus Culbertson claimed that he was "much stronger and have endured more fatigue than" he could "for years back." He also claimed that the climate allowed him to "sleep soundly and rise refreshed."[93] A sickly druggist moved to South Dakota "where he could breathe that pure air and get well again" while working as a shepherd.[94] Others, like Leona Wayne Huxtable, also "hoped the dry air would bring them back to health."[95]

Whatever its medicinal benefits, South Dakota's dry, clean air is also perfect for star gazers.[96] Washington Irving wrote that on the prairie "it is delightful to lie awake and gaze at the stars ... I felt this night unusually affected by the solemn magnificence of the firmament, and seemed, as I lay under the open vault of heaven, to inhale with the pure untainted air, an exhilarating buoyancy of spirit, as it were an ecstasy of the mind."[97] A century and a half later, May-lee Chai loved the way "the sky darkened and the moon rose and the stars shone like diamonds."[98] Whenever she would leave the state, Kathleen Norris missed "the night sky revealing far more stars than urban dwellers ever see."[99] The sparse population also aids star gazing because South Dakota has very little light pollution outside of Sioux Falls and Rapid City.[100]

While some visitors find the flat, open country disconcerting – on the prairie the curvature of the earth is visible, trees are few,[101] and the land appears flat enough to "shoot a cue ball from the southern boundary of the state all the way to Canada and halfway to the North Pole"[102] –

many others experienced what came to be called "prairie fever," a sense of extreme physical well-being bordering on drug induced euphoria.[103] According to young army lieutenant Francis Duncan, prairie fever "is a sweet and exhilarating feeling, absorbing for a time all recollection of the past, and killing all anxiety about the future. It is a maddening enjoyment of the present, arising from lightened spirits, and the grandeur of surrounding nature."[104] Culbertson also delighted at vistas of "wide-spread fields untouched by the artistical skill of man."[105]

Prairie fever has yet to be cured. "Whenever I return," native son Tom Brokaw has written, "I am at peace."[106] Hayden Carruth compared the prairie to Nirvana because it is "calm, serene, beautiful old age, meditative, unhurried, unafraid."[107] The prairie also renders the state's sunrises[108] and sunsets "magical,"[109] "beyond compare," as Carruth claimed, "a prairie sky being the only canvas adequate for this daily miracle, making it the marriage of heaven and earth, celebrated with a mighty harmony on Nature's color-organ."[110] Gilfillan likened the state's openness and air to its political freedom: "A great land! A free land! And, in its own way, a beautiful land. Pure, clear air; a frank, open, and friendly people; a healthful and interesting job. ... Above all, the opportunity to live his own life in his own way."[111]

This book shows how successive generations of peoples residing in that area of the Northern Plains now designated South Dakota have managed to thrive in a sometimes brutal climate and rich but uncompromising ecosystem seemingly far removed from the major avenues of world and even national commerce.[112] Chapter 2 demonstrates that entrepreneurial activities suffused the area long before the arrival of Europeans. Chapter 3 shows how vastly different systems of political economy led to vastly different economic outcomes for Native Americans and their Euroamerican neighbors. Chapter 4 describes the development of South Dakota's system of political economy from the late nineteenth century to the present. With the historical and theoretical background thus laid, the next four chapters explore, in historical context, the state's major areas of entrepreneurship today, including agriculture and food processing (Chapter 5), construction, manufacturing, and trading (Chapter 6), tourism and recreation (Chapter 7), and education, healthcare, and finance (Chapter 8). The final chapter (9) analyzes the ten biggest challenges facing South Dakota in the 2010s and beyond. If the legal and political environment remains conducive to entrepreneurship, as it likely will, the state will continue to be buffered from some types of external shocks. It can never be immune, however, from major national or international economic crises like runaway inflation. And to thrive, it must continue to balance carefully the rights of businesses with those of individual citizens.

Chapter 2
Economic Activity on the Northern Plains, 10,000 B.C.E. to A.D. 1888

When you get the feeling that the whole world can see you but no one is watching, you have come to the grasslands of North America.[1]

Native Americans were the first human inhabitants of the Great Plains and hence of the area now called South Dakota. Scholars debate exactly when or how they arrived, but humans were certainly inhabiting the region between 10,000 and 12,000 years ago, or approximately 10,000 BCE (Before the Common Era or Before Christ in older parlance). Archaeologists call the first inhabitants Paleoindians, or ancient Indians, for lack of a better name, but regardless of their appellation they are clearly identifiable as replicative entrepreneurs. Paleoindians specialized in hunting the really big game, called megafauna, that roamed the region. We know this from the work of scholars like Augustana College archaeologist Adrien Hannus, who discovered stone spearpoints and probable bone butchering flakes at a mammoth kill and butchering site at a White River Badlands location known as Lange/Ferguson. Soon after the arrival of those big beast butchers, however, the continent's megafauna, which included giant sloths, bears, lions, mammoth, horses, tapirs, beaver, capybara, armadillo, ox, deer, camel, and peccary, went extinct for reasons still unknown and much debated. Climate change, and not human predation, is currently considered the leading culprit.[2]

The so-called Archaic peoples who arose out of the Paleoindians after the megafauna extinction were more generalized foragers who killed bison (even before the aid of horses) but also lots of smaller game, including mule deer and antelope, and processed vegetable matter with specialized milling stones. With each passing millennium, more evidence of South Dakota's human inhabitants becomes available, evidence perhaps of rising populations but also of an increased likelihood of archeological sites being preserved due to the invention of caching techniques involving freezing or drying meat. Despite their entrepreneurial ways, life for the Paleo and Archaic Indians appears to have been Hobbesian, to wit nasty, brutish, and short: a third of the deceased that have been discovered were infants.[3]

During the Altithermal, a period from 7,000 to 4,500 years ago that was drier and warmer than present, human activity throughout the region declined, even in the Black Hills, which were not high enough to retain a permanent snowpack. Between 3,000 and 4,000 years ago, though, human activity in the Northern Plains markedly increased along with average rainfall and bison numbers. With the megafauna long since extinct, native peoples had only one major domesticated animal at their disposal, dogs, which served as pets, pack animals, and, when necessary, dinner.[4]

The so-called Woodland peoples who replaced the Archaics were both foragers and farmers. The rise of horticulture, or small-scale agriculture, was probably made possible by increased rainfall and climatic stability and the development of new technologies, especially pottery, which allowed for the more secure storage of seeds and crop surpluses. By about 2,000 years ago, South Dakota was a sort of middle ground between a group of people to the south and east who were largely ceramic-producing, sedentary, and horticultural, and another group to the north and west that was more nomadic and reliant on hunting and gathering, a situation that persisted for over a millennium.[5]

Contrary to common misperceptions, Native Americans were not a-economic but rather, like other peoples throughout the world, eager to improve their material condition by trading away things they did not value as highly as the goods they received in return. So the proximity of two groups that produced different economic goods created numerous opportunities for exchanges beneficial to both groups. Evidence that native groups traded shells, quartzite, chert, pottery, and other durable goods abounds. Trade in foodstuffs and contrived goods (sex, fire) is more difficult to document but can be inferred. It is possible, for example, that people near present-day Mitchell processed large numbers of bison into pemmican, a concentrated mixture of fat and protein resistant to spoilage, and exchanged it for pottery and other goods manufactured in Cahokia, near present-day St. Louis. Hide bullboats traversing the Missouri River were the most likely mode of transportation between the two manufacturing centers. Other Native groups also engaged in manufacturing, including copper goods fashioned from ores found in the Black Hills and northern Great Lakes regions, and later even rudimentary iron goods.[6]

By about a thousand years ago, eastern South Dakota was already part of a corn belt. The ancestors of the modern Arikara or Omaha lived in the region and subsisted from a combination of corn, sunflowers, squash and other domesticated plants, the gathering of wild plants, hunting, and trade. They left mounds filled with bones, beads, and lithic tools in most of the counties in the eastern part of South Dakota. These people, like those elsewhere on the Great Plains, adapted quickly to changes in the relative abundance of game. When and where bison were scarce, they adjusted to hunt pronghorn antelope or deer. They also responded to climatic changes by increasing or decreasing their horticultural activities and moving their villages and lodges accordingly.[7]

Circa 1500 A.D., near present-day Gettysburg, natives grew amaranth, beans, chenopodium, corn, squash, and sunflowers, and gathered chokecherries, hackberries, and wild plums. In addition to hunting pronghorn, bison, deer, and elk, the natives also fished, trapped small game, and, when necessary, ate their dogs. They also made awls, hoes, knives, projectile points, scrapers, and other tools and traded (or traveled) widely, into southwestern Minnesota, west central North Dakota, and both south and northwestern South Dakota.[8]

By the time of Columbus' voyages, the Native Americans inhabiting the Great Plains were generally prosperous as evidenced by the level of their material culture, the quality of the bones of their adults, and the relatively low mortality rates of their infants. Average economic output was about 400 U.S. dollars at their international value in 1990, or enough to replicate the population from one generation to the next, no mean feat. Their technology, however, lagged that of China and Western Europe, a fact that would later lead to their political subjugation and impoverishment. According to scientist Jared Diamond, Native American technology lagged because of North America's unified geography, its low population density (and hence minimal division of labor), its dearth of domesticable beasts of burden (after the megafaunal extinction anyway), and its lack of nasty, communicable diseases. Diamond's *Guns, Germs, Steel* won several major awards but some economic historians have bemoaned its material determinism. After all, North America, Australia, and other low technology areas became economic leaders after their institutions changed, suggesting that the real limit to Native technology was not geographic and biological/environmental but rather institutional.[9]

Specifically, it seems that Native Americans, on the Great Plains and elsewhere in the Americas, enjoyed secure property rights, a major component of economic freedom, for only brief periods. When and where they did, local economies flourished, populations and trade increased, and the division of labor became more complex, increasing the likelihood of scientific and technological breakthrough. In every documented case, from the Cahokians to the Inca and the Iroquois to the Aztecs, increases in wealth brought about by innovative and replicative entrepreneurs were reversed by the incursion of exploitative entrepreneurs, Native early on and European after first contact. No Native group figured out how to induce their people to concentrate on making rather than taking and trading rather than raiding, until it was too late, and European technologies and diseases had swept the continent.[10]

The most dramatic evidence of this periodic breakdown of peace and economic freedom was the massacre at Crow Creek circa A.D.1325 in south central South Dakota, where at least 486 Arikara Indians were slaughtered and their bodies mutilated by unknown assailants. The attackers may have come for wives as they spared most of the tribe's young women. The brutality with which the victims were slain – many scalped, tongues cut out, teeth broken, heads severed, bodies dismembered – and then left exposed to scavengers, however, suggests even more sinister motivations in an ethnically diverse region subjected to an extended period of drought.[11]

Peace eventually returned, however, and by A.D. 1500, a group of Oneota peoples probably ancestral to the Omaha, a Denighan or Chiiewe Siouan tribe that originated somewhere east of the Mississippi Valley, had established a community of about 480 hectares on the Big Sioux River at Blood Run on the current South Dakota/Iowa border near present-day Sioux Falls. Until its abandonment in 1714, the denizens of

The buffalo effigy incised into this catlinite tablet dates from before 1700. The tablet was used by the Oneota people to cut tobacco to smoke in preparation for a bison hunt. The image may be seen as portraying a bison giving up its life spirit for the people; alternatively, it may be understood as a bison being speared. It was found by Even Evenson on his property along Blood Run Creek and is on exhibit in the Froiland Plains Indian Gallery at the Center for Western Studies.
Courtesy Center for Western Studies.

Blood Run, as archeologists refer to it, built 275 large conical mounds, up to 800 stone circles and ovals that probably outlined houses, at least 7 large pitted Sioux Quartzite boulders, and a possible effigy mound and an earthen serpent effigy about the length of a football field.[12] According to archeologist Dale Henning, "The Blood Run villagers appear to have eaten well. Animal bone is commonplace and well preserved; articulated elements of bison, elk, and a broader range of smaller mammal bones are encountered," including butchered dog bone, fish, and shellfish and evidence of broad-based horticultural pursuits. Pipes, beads, grooved mauls, and pottery from several different groups suggest that the village was "undoubtedly an exchange center of considerable importance."[13] Sites like Blood Run reveal artifacts that were not the creations of equestrian Indians like those depicted in *Dances with Wolves* but rather were made by a sedentary or semi-sedentary people, like the Arikara, who lived in much more substantial structures than teepees.[14]

With extensive trade came indirect contact with Europeans well before indigenous peoples ever saw what Lakota speakers called Wasichu, or non-Native people. Copper and brass beads, bracelets, small iron and brass items, and other trade items appeared in the area, and disease and displaced Natives from the east soon followed. All disrupted the region's political economy.[15] By 1600, well-armed eastern groups were raiding and spreading pandemic disease "well out onto the Plains."[16] By 1700, indigenous trading networks had disintegrated into seemingly constant warfare. Between about 1650 and 1850, the Dakota and Lakota Sioux responded to Ojibway and Euroamerican incursions into their traditional lands in present-day Minnesota, the westward migration of bison herds, and the decline of the beaver fur trade by migrating into what is today Nebraska and the Dakotas, where they slowly displaced or integrated the peoples settled there. By 1750, the Lakota Sioux had crossed the Missouri River, ostensibly in search of bison. Within 50 years, with help from European epidemics, they had driven the Arikara, a tribe that had long lived along the Missouri River growing corn and other crops, hunting, and trading baskets, north into present-day North Dakota.[17]

Other native groups also felt the wrath of the Sioux, a derogatory nickname given to the loosely affiliated group by Euroamericans.[18] By 1855, Sioux lands extended, in the words of a contemporary American observer, from "the Mississippi on the east to the Black Hills on the west, and from the forks of the Platte on the south to Devil's Lake on the north."[19] Rather than a unified political entity, however, the Sioux were more like an ethnic group that shared similar languages and cultural practices. Four clusters, the Mdewakanton, Wahpeton, Sisseton, and Wahpekute, lived in southern Minnesota or extreme eastern South

Dakota near rivers or lakes. They spoke the Dakota dialect but their lifeways remained more like those of eastern woodland tribes than those of their Plains cousins. They were horticulturalists and "their produce of corn, &c., forms a valuable commodity of trade between them," according to one nineteenth-century Euroamerican observer.[20] The Yankton and Yanktonai tribes, the Nakota, settled in eastern South Dakota where they engaged in a mix of horticulture and hunting and gathering. The Teton, or Lakota, settled mostly west of the Missouri River and lived the nomadic Plains lifestyle that Hollywood later attempted to capture on film. The Teton had seven branches, the Oglala, Brule, Hunkpapa, Minneconjou, Blackfoot, Two Kettles, and Sans Arcs.[21]

Organized much like Japanese keiretsu, as layers of firms or units of production ultimately rooted in extended families called tiyospaye, Sioux groups, like Western business and municipal corporations, cooperated with their members while competing vigorously against outsiders for resources, sometimes economically (by price or quality) and sometimes militarily. (Other native tribal groups can also be conceived of as businesses, as production coordination mechanisms akin to corporations.) The keiretsu form of organization rendered individual Sioux innovative or replicative entrepreneurs (traders) within their extended families and tribes but exploitative entrepreneurs (raiders) with most outsiders. The combination proved potent for a considerable period.[22]

Direct contact between Plains Indians and Europeans did not occur until the late seventeenth century though more remote, more western parts of the Great Plains were not reached until the early nineteenth century, largely due to the expanding fur trade. Thanks to that trade, the Teton Sioux thrived between 1815 and 1850. In the peak year, 1830, they produced 26,000 bison robes, 25,000 pounds of beaver fur, 37,500 muskrat skins, 4,000 otter skins, and 150,000 deer skins. They also dealt in bison meat and tongues. The trade subsequently declined, however, due to the near extinction of some species, like the bison, and a decrease in demand for others, like the beaver.[23] By 1855, in fact, beaver were again numerous and "increasing very rapidly, and many of the mountain streams literally swarm with them. Since the days of the trapper are over, and the price of their fur has become so reduced, the inducements to hunt them are not very great, and they are allowed to multiply undisturbed."[24]

In addition to the decline of the fur trade, smallpox in the early nineteenth century ravished the Sioux, whose population plummeted from an apex of perhaps 25,000. The federal government attempted inoculations in South Dakota in the early 1830s but to little apparent effect. In August 1837, smallpox struck a Lakota war party which subsequently spread the disease again.[25] In 1850, Lieutenant Gouverneur K. Warren argued that "the Government should, by all that is humane, employ some competent person, at a proper salary, to visit them yearly and vaccinate these Indians, and thus arrest the violence of these scourges,"[26] but as late as the 1870s the government could not even prevent a smallpox outbreak among its own troops stationed at Fort Randall.[27] The Yanktonai were also hit hard by smallpox and cholera but a high birth rate helped native populations to rebound quickly. "Of all the aborigines in the Territory under consideration," a contemporary noted in 1857, "the Dakotas [Sioux] are probably the ones that have undergone the least material diminution of their numbers since their discovery by the whites. They are still numerous, independent, warlike, and powerful and contain within themselves means of prolonged and able resistance to further encroachment of the western settlers."[28] He estimated the total number of Sioux that year at 24,000; in 1880, a census showed the population stood at 27,168. Significant cultural, political, and socioeconomic damage, however, had already been suffered and proved impossible to reverse given the federal government's Indian policies, a subject taken up in the next chapter.[29]

South Dakota was part of the vast region called Louisiana claimed by France until 1762 when it ceded nominal control to Spain. Unsurprisingly, the earliest European to visit South Dakota was probably a Frenchman, Daniel Duluth, who in July 1679 visited the area around present-day Sisseton. A few years later, Frenchman Charles Pierre Le Sueur probably cast his eyes upon the falls of the Big Sioux, present-day downtown Sioux Falls, and a contemporary map shows a fur-trade trail terminating at Blood Run, the Omaha village then located there. By the early eighteenth century, about 100 French traders were said to be scattered along the Missouri River, some probably as far south as South Dakota. By 1740, French adventurers had reached Nebraska from the south. A few years later, an exploratory party descended from Winnipeg into North Dakota, down to the Black Hills, and across the western part of the state to present-day Fort Pierre. The Verendrye Monument marks the spot where they left physical evidence of their arrival in the form of a lead plate. About the same time, traders had moved into what would become the northeastern part of the state, around lakes Traverse and Big Stone. By 1755, French fur interests had established an outpost at Elk Point, near the mouth of the Big Sioux. Another post, at Flandreau, was shuttered in 1763. Other posts may also have existed but traders and trappers were not known for their literacy much less their verbosity. Moreover, French traders adopted native ways and took native brides, creating a mixed "Frindian" or Creole culture neither fully French nor fully Native.[30]

Regardless of a trader's ethnic background, to earn profits in the fur trade required both capital and entrepreneurial ability. The trade was international in scope and necessitated shipping European manufactured goods to the middle of North America and remitting furs to the best European markets in the absence of fresh commercial information. To obtain a sufficient quantity and quality of fur meant relying on a mix of white men who trapped for fixed wages and Natives who trapped to obtain ammunition, firearms, tobacco, utensils, and foodstuffs like sugar, salt, pepper, coffee, and alcohol.[31]

After seizing Canada in the French and Indian War, the British began to exert influence in what would become the American West. By 1792, three British trading companies were active in the upper Mississippi region and several independent traders of various national backgrounds traversed the state. After the Revolution, Americans took an interest in the region as well. Several were known to have visited Minnesota and North Dakota by the 1780s and two were killed by Sioux braves in 1793. The United States obtained sovereign control of the region from Napoleon, who had officially reclaimed the area from Spain before selling it to the United States in 1803 as part of the Louisiana Purchase. The following year, the famous Lewis and Clark expedition explored the Missouri River basin and discovered tribes that had clearly been trading with the British as well as the Spanish. South Dakota retains a few Spanish place names due to such interactions. In the years following, traders like Manuel Lisa maintained various temporary trading posts all along the Missouri and some of its tributaries. In 1809, Lisa and others organized the St. Louis Fur Company to help manage the trade, which was fraught with dangers ranging from raids by Teton Sioux to the rapidly shifting channels and moods of the Missouri River, which has been called the Mighty Mo, the Wide Missouri, Old Misery, and the Big Muddy due to its uncanny ability to destroy entire towns with floods and ice jams one month and to run nearly dry the next.[32]

Thomas Jefferson considered the Sioux of "immense power" and indeed they waged war against neighboring tribes with frequent success. During the War of 1812, traders on both sides tried to win and keep their affections by giving them resources directly or making exchanges favorable to the natives. The war technically ended in a tie and greatly disrupted the fur trade for a few years but soon allowed for the complete Americanization of the region. In 1817, the first permanent white settlement in South Dakota, eventually named Fort Pierre, was established, although the military's presence in the area was always light. The final few remaining British traders pulled out of South Dakota in 1823. In the 1820s, over a thousand Americans, many employed by various unincorporated "companies" or the incorporated American Fur

Company of John Jacob Astor, which exerted increasing control of the Missouri trade after Manuel Lisa's death in 1820, were engaged in the fur trade of the upper Missouri. American Fur consolidated its position in 1827 by merging with a major rival, Columbia Fur. In the 1830s, European-born or -bred entrepreneurs, like Philadelphia artist George Catlin or Swiss artist Karl Bodmer, also trickled into the region, many via the steamboat line established in 1831, to try to earn some of the needful.[33]

Provision merchants like Pierre Chouteau, Jr. (1789-1865), who ran a trading post at Fort Pierre, happily supplied them, as well as the sundry trappers, traders, and translators who traversed the region. Called the harbinger of "capitalism on the Northern Great Plains" by historian Herbert T. Hoover, Chouteau employed African Americans as cheap laborers and to interact with the Indians, who trusted them more than they trusted Euroamericans. He also employed almost all of the legendary merchants of the time: Alexis Bailly, Henry Hastings Sibley, Honore Picotte, P.D. Papin, and Theophile Bruguier. To keep competitors out, Chouteau wooed Indian leaders with lavish gifts. In the mid-1830s, Chouteau's company bought out Astor's interests in the region, which it dominated until Chouteau's death in 1865.[34]

Most of the early exchanges between natives and Europeans were conducted by barter, an inefficient means of conducting trade made possible only by the large surpluses each side gained.[35] Natives deeply desired European goods and had no other means of satiating those desires, and vice versa. According to one contemporary, competition on both sides was "spirited" because "the trade was as anxious to buy a great many furs as to buy them cheap, and the Indians knew enough to carry their peltries where they could get the most for them."[36] As late as the 1830s, a contemporary noted that manufactured goods "must be paid for in furs for there was no other currency."[37] Shell beads were a kind of native currency in some areas by A.D. 1000 but wampum, the most famous form of Native American money, served mainly ceremonial, decorative, and recordkeeping purposes and, in any event, its exchange was largely relegated to the eastern seaboard.[38]

By the 1850s, trader receipts served as a form of representative money, much like the tobacco warehouse receipts of colonial Virginia. Indians exchanged bison robes or other goods for the receipts, which they later used to buy horses, tobacco, or other goods. Later, traders issued their own trade dollars or other tokens. Payment of annuities in cash also increased the use of money in the Indian trade.[39] After Custer's defeat, one contemporary claimed, "the Indians started coming in with real money" taken from dead soldiers. "Trade at the store picked up a lot," after that, he claimed, "but the Indians didn't know a dollar bill from a ten dollar bill."[40] They learned quickly though. By 1891, Nat Salisbury could assert that "an Indian knows the value of a dollar quite as well as a white man."[41] By the mid-1890s, silver dollars and $5 and $10 paper notes were in wide circulation in South Dakota due to the payment of cash to Indians for the lands they gave up. The dearth of Indian numeracy and bilingual individuals, however, ensured that barter still occurred in informal settings, as when a Euroamerican teacher on the Cheyenne River Reservation traded pretty cloth and pins for a fox skin, pottery, and a wooden knife and spoon in the late 1880s.[42]

Some anthropologists claim that Native Americans did not understand exchange the same way that Euroamericans did, that they engaged in the mutual exchange of "gifts." An early traveler, however, saw through the façade to the underlying incentives of the native's system. "An Indian present," he explained, "is like an eastern gift, which is to be returned with compound interest." "This system," of providing gifts today in the expectation of receiving greater gifts tomorrow, "prevails to a great extent here; you would think them the most generous people in the world, and they are very generous but they get paid a great deal in the same way."[43]

By 1848, Minnesota and the Dakotas were home to about 4,000 Euroamericans. In what became South Dakota, all the Euroamericans were traders ensconced in "forts" or trading posts that bore familiar names like Vermillion, Yankton, and Pierre because the area was thought unsuitable for European-style agriculture. Despite the numerous snags and rapidly shifting channels of Old Misery, steamboats and keelboats were the preferred mode of travel into and out of the territory, although a road along the Nebraska side of the river that ran from Sioux City to Fort Randall helped when the river was too low or frozen for boats to pass. Soon after the establishment of Fort Randall in 1856, ferries across the Big Mo began to operate at the mouths of the James, Vermillion, and Big Sioux rivers. (They gave way to bridges only in the early twentieth century.)[44]

By the Civil War, however, public attitudes about the Great Plains had shifted. At first considered a "desert" peppered with an occasional "oasis," a vast stretch of "desolation and gloom" to be crossed as quickly as possible en route to Oregon, Americans slowly began to concede the region's agricultural potential.[45] Stephen H. Long's "Great American Desert" legend died hard but as successful agricultural settlements spread into northern Iowa and southwest Minnesota, South Dakota increasingly beckoned as a grassy paradise suitable for farmers and ranchers. In the late 1850s, two land companies dedicated to opening up the region formed, the Dakota Land Company of St. Paul and the Western Town Company of Dubuque, Iowa. The latter made it to Sioux

Falls first. Its attempt faltered but the movement to carve out the Dakota Territory was on.[46]

It is not surprising that corporations played such a large role in South Dakota's early economic history. The United States has been called the world's first corporation nation. Before the Civil War, the various U.S. states chartered over 22,000 corporations, far more than any other country, even the United Kingdom (England, Wales, Scotland, and Ireland combined), though British companies were larger than American ones on average. The Northeastern states (New England, New York, Pennsylvania, and New Jersey) dominated corporation formation at first, as one might expect, but by the 1830s, '40s, and especially '50s, the states of the border South (Maryland, Virginia, Kentucky) and Midwest (Ohio, Indiana, Illinois, Michigan, and Wisconsin) were all prolific incorporators that in some cases even chartered more businesses than the Northeastern states did in per capita terms (dividing by population, in other words). Before the Civil War, business corporations had even sprung up west of the Mississippi River, in Missouri, Iowa, and Minnesota as well as in the far west.[47]

Americans invaded the trans-Mississippi west from three directions, the east, via the Erie Canal-Great Lakes transportation system, the south, via the Mississippi and its ubiquitous steamboats, and the west, via the Pacific Ocean. The western route was important only to the development of California and the Pacific Northwest. The Americanization of the Northern Plains took place primarily from St. Louis and Chicago, often via Minneapolis-St. Paul or Des Moines. Cultivation had to await the last quarter of the nineteenth century, however, and was possible only after the development of agricultural innovations ranging from barbed wire to specialized or improved plows and mechanical reapers and mowers, as well as new seed varieties and dry-land farming techniques.

Most such inventions and innovations were developed elsewhere and introduced to the Northern Plains via the greatest replicative entrepreneur of all time, the pioneer farmer. Already nearly drowning in risk, the rational pioneer farmer, oft the offspring of at least one generation of pioneer, rarely had the time or the incentive to invent or innovate. He acquired existing technologies and extended them westward, sometimes successfully, other times not. The roots of the region's innovative entrepreneurial tradition must therefore be sought elsewhere. They can be located primarily in the headquarters of manufacturing, mining, railroad, and real estate companies, big corporations with big money and big ideas that opened the territory to the farmers, retailers, and other replicative entrepreneurs who followed.[48]

Of particular interest here, of course, are the early corporations of Iowa and Minnesota. Most clung close to the west bank of the Mississippi River and hence were not part of the Northern Plains. Many of the Minnesota companies were not even rooted in a prairie ecosystem. Nevertheless, the Dakotas were originally included in the Minnesota territory and the economies of both the Dakotas and Nebraska were closely tied to those of Minnesota and Iowa, both of which remain important to the Northern Plains economy to this day.[49]

Nineteenth-century Minnesota has been called a land of boosters, hustlers, and speculators but also of entrepreneurs. Fur traders, merchants, lumbermen, millers and manufacturers, and railroaders suffused the area around Minneapolis-St. Paul. Most were replicative entrepreneurs who sometimes engaged in unproductive rent-seeking activities, typically under the guise of promoting the common good. But none really controlled government resources and periodic business busts exposed the hubris of most.[50]

A steamship packet between St. Paul and St. Louis operated on a regular schedule by 1847. Minnesota's first stagecoach service began operations in 1849. Soon after, numerous bridge, ferry, steamship, and stagecoach companies formed to connect the east and west, the north and south, and agricultural and manufacturing markets. Those corporations forged the physical connections between Eastern transportation networks and the emerging frontier in the Dakotas. They also served as models that Dakotans would later use to build transportation networks of their own.[51]

The federal government established the Dakota Territory in 1861 and helped it along with the passage of the Homestead Act of 1862, which gave any citizen of at least twenty-one years of age the right to claim ownership of 160 acres of surveyed public domain merely by planting five acres, residing on the land for five years, and paying a registration fee that averaged about $30. Eventually, as demand for good land at that price exceeded supply, a lottery system was implemented and winners got to pick their parcels first. But at first demand for the land remained so underwhelming that railroads had to exaggerate the fertility of the region to get settlers, i.e., customers, to stake a claim. (For a variety of reasons, train service was much better in the late nineteenth and early twentieth centuries than it was later in the twentieth century. For example, individuals could charter their own boxcar to take their belongings to the train stop nearest their South Dakota destination. Ridership on one major line hit almost 2.5 million passengers in 1916 but dropped to 45,000 by 1953.[52])

The U.S.-Dakota War (1862) and the Civil War (1861-65) slowed the territory's development but even after the wars ended, interest in the territory remained muted, even as small settlements sprang up in Vermillion, Elk Point, Yankton, and Sioux Falls. Much of the early entrepreneurial activity in Sioux Falls and the other new towns was replicative, the expansion to the prairies of traditional businesses like banks, hotels (Yankton's first hotel was established by a Mrs. Ash by 1862), restaurants, bakeries, saloons, agricultural services companies, drug, grocery, hardware, furniture and dry goods stores, sporting goods stores, liveries, and tack and tobacco shops, as well as the shops of cobblers, gunsmiths, dressmakers, and tailors. Most important of all, perhaps, were the lumber merchants, painters, carpenters, masons, sundry smiths, coopers, and other construction workers who toiled from dawn until dusk in all seasons erecting the buildings that housed the people and the inputs needed to produce economic goods.[53]

Early Dakota Territory faced a chicken-egg problem: few Euroamericans lived there, so few Euroamericans wanted to move there. The Jeffersonian ideal of owning one's own land, of working with one's hands, of communing with/fighting against nature was alluring to many, to be sure, but was not enough to coax them that far from their comfortable homes.[54] The golden egg discovered in the far western part of the state in 1874 finally broke the impasse. The Black Hills, so called because "as they are approached from the barren, desert wastes of the Plains, they loom up in the distance as a dark range,"[55] were long suspected of harboring deposits of gold. Father DeSmet saw gold there as early as 1848 and in 1852 several prospectors who dared enter the area met death at the hands of Lakota braves. The Civil War, various Indian "troubles," and U.S. troops kept other prospectors out but continued rumors put pressure on the government to act, which it did in 1874 by sending in General Custer. The first claims were made later that year and by 1875 the rush was on. Experienced miners from California, Nevada, Montana, and Colorado came, as did adventure seeking businessmen with Harvard and Princeton degrees, former Union army generals, and bankers who had run into difficulties in the Panic of 1873 and desired a fresh start. Several prominent attorneys came too, as did scads of scoundrels.[56]

The miners themselves were entrepreneurs, of course, but so too were the businesses that got them to their destination and kept them fully provisioned. An early observer noted that "farmers, dairymen, and gardeners were doing pretty good" even if the median placer miner was not.[57] "These people must make enormous profits," a contemporary British observer opined. "The figures I have heard quoted are almost incredible. Wheat sells for 8s[hillings] the bushel of eight gallons; oats, 4s.; potatoes, 4s.; onions, 10s.; flour, 20s. per 100 lbs.; eggs, 2s. per dozen."[58] The same observer noted that the vast majority of prospectors "reaped nothing but bitter disappointment and ruin" – the vast bulk of the over 34 million troy ounces of gold ever discovered in the Hills would come out of a single mine, the Homestake – but their sweat and capital spurred the region's development almost overnight.[59]

The mining district soon spawned several boom towns, the most infamous of which was Deadwood. The town, which had more saloons and brothels than churches, also had stores, sawmills, and bakeries up and running even before it had an official government, so replicative and exploitative entrepreneurship often blended in unsavory ways. Soapy Taylor, for example, ran a sort of lottery by wrapping a few of his many packages of soap in 1, 2, or 5 dollar bills. More exploitative practices included bilking greenhorns, cock fighting and other forms of gambling like poker and keno, and prostitution. The local red light district was originally located in nearby Lead (pronounced leed because the name was related to lode, a gold vein, not to the metal lead) but it soon moved to Deadwood as mines caused subsidence of the original Lead town site.[60]

The first dance hall or "hurdy gurdy house" opened in Deadwood in May 1876 but it was soon put out of business by the Gem Theater, which an early observer called a "notorious den of iniquity." The female "employees," the observer claimed, were little more than "white slaves"[61] lured to the area with the promise of a good job and kept in line with regular beatings and the threat of being turned out penniless, a difficult fate given the region's still tenuous link to the outside world.[62] Meanwhile, in December 1876 Deadwood boosters tried to induce Congress to carve out a new territory, alternatively called "of the Black Hills," "of El Dorado," and, finally, to win over the Republican majority, "of Lincoln." Nothing became of it.[63]

A railroad did not reach Rapid City until 1886 (from Chadron, Nebraska) so people traveled in and out on horseback or via expensive and slow stagecoaches. The Medora and Black Hills line cost 10 cents a mile and was 215 miles long. With stage stations every 10 to 15 miles, a one-way trip took 36 hours. The Wyoming Stage Company took passengers and mail between Yankton and Rapid City in four days for $35 (about $800 in today's money). Like most lines, the Wyoming used Concord coaches for passengers and Conestoga wagons for freight. Both were inherently slow and costly means of transportation.[64]

Gilmer and Salisbury Stage Co. ran routes to Deadwood from Sidney, Nebraska, and Cheyenne, Wyoming, the latter in competition with the Cheyenne and Black Hills Stage Line and hostile natives. Another early transportation entrepreneur was D. T. Bramble, who ran a line from Yankton to Fort Pierre and thence to Deadwood. Beginning in May 1877, on a trail blazed by Ben C. Ash of Yankton, The Northwestern Express, Stage and Transportation Company of Minnesota ran daily from

Bismarck to Deadwood, but in 1880 it began to terminate in Pierre. It carried about 5,000 persons annually.[65]

Freight moved via covered wagon trains that consumed twelve days to three weeks depending on destination and conditions. In ideal weather, six horses could haul six tons but conditions were rarely ideal in South Dakota due to "gumbo mud, steep grades, stream fords, and snow."[66] The Sioux City and Black Hills Transportation Company was one of the largest freight companies in the Hills, employing at its height over a thousand men and wagons. It began sending wagon trains in 1875 but was soon challenged by the Witcher Company and others eager to match the bigger company, which charged men from $100 to $200 (between $2,200 and $4,400 in today's dollars) to move them and some supplies to Yankton via the Dakota Southern Railroad, thence to Fort Pierre on the steamboats of the Missouri River Transportation Company, and thence to Deadwood, Custer, or Crook City overland on the Evans and Hornick Freight Lines. The railroads, including South Dakota staples like the Chicago, Milwaukee, Saint Paul & Pacific and the Chicago & North Western Transportation Company, eventually chased them all away or into niche markets, especially after the destruction of several boats wintering at Yankton in 1881.[67]

Deadwood was a major transportation hub but it held no monopoly on vice. Since their arrival, Euroamericans had trafficked female Indians, who previously, at various times and places, had been trafficked by other natives. Prostitution and gambling were at least as old as the military forts, like the brothel and card parlor located behind the post office and sutler's store at Fort Randall. Although most Indian women were "virtuous" and some tribes marked prostitutes with the equivalent of a scarlet A, most prostitutes in the early days were native. Later, however, as the frontier advanced, "White Squaws" arrived to compete with them for customers, which increasingly meant railroad construction workers and other itinerants, including sundry drifters, grifters, hoboes, carnies, and con men. Even in the state capital, Pierre (pronounced peer), pimps and madams took most of the earnings of their workers, who were described as local girls and overflow from the divorce courts of Sioux Falls. Their customers were primarily prairie bachelors and, presumably, politicians.[68]

Prostitution in early Sioux Falls was enough of a problem to prompt Richard Dickenson, the owner of a swanky café and bakery, to propose a municipally-owned and operated brothel as a public health measure. Government ownership, he argued, would mean that both prostitutes and their johns would be inspected by a doctor to ensure that they were clean and disease-free. The place would be fireproof and liquor-free and generally take a paternalistic attitude toward the prostitutes, who would enjoy a state-protected monopoly free of "outside harlots."[69] No matter how carefully it was laid out, Dickenson's plan never quite transitioned into reality. Larger East River towns like Huron also sported brothels and gambling dens.[70]

Deadwood also did not have a monopoly on violence and unsavory characters. The most violent, lawless place in the territorial and early state periods was not Deadwood but Bonesteel, in Gregory County near the Missouri River. "It was axiomatic," wrote one Dakota historian, "that when Pinkerton Detectives were looking for a shady character they started at Bonesteel, where they usually found him."[71] Pierre also had an unsavory reputation.[72] According to a joke current around 1890, there were a few good people in Pierre: "Some argued there were fifteen or eighteen, but others said that estimate was too high."[73] By 1900, "guns were not allowed in Pierre"[74] but of course that only made it easier for criminals to ply their dastardly trades. In 1902, a confessed serial killer who murdered six men to rob them or avoid paying their wages, lurked just west of Pierre.[75] About the same time, two other men near Pierre "mysteriously disappeared and no trace of them was ever found."[76]

Deadwood and other Black Hills boom towns, like Sturgis, Spearfish and Lead, were all dangerous places too, where robbery, murder, and lynching were common. But what better could be expected of itinerant miners who got drunk at saloons with names like Bucket of Blood and the Bloody Bucket? The lack of protection of life, liberty, and property undoubtedly slowed development but the excesses were expected to be short-lived, as evidenced by the lack of long-term investment in the area by the most exploitative businesses. And the profits for other businesses were worth the risk. So after the saloons soon came grocers, tailors, and respectable hotels made of wood milled at one of the three local sawmills. As David Haxby remembered, most settlers came to start service businesses, not farms or mines. That was an exaggeration but clearly miners, ranchers, and farmers needed support from a "considerable group" of doctors, dentists, businessmen, preachers, and teachers.[77]

Black Hills entrepreneurs had to remain geographically and sectorally nimble in order to succeed because change was often rapid and complete. At its height Buffalo Gap, terminus of the Fremont, Elkhorn & Missouri River Railroad that was extended from Nebraska to the Black Hills in 1885 to help siphon off Black Hill gold and supply its miners, boasted a population of over 3,000 people, four blacksmith shops, 23 saloons, 17 hotels, two sporting houses, four general stores, two drug stores, and four Chinese laundries. After the railroad made it to Rapid City in 1886, however, the town declined and by 2010 only 126 people remained. Rapid City, by contrast, flourished with the aid of entrepreneurs who established the Rapid City Milling Company, the

Milwaukee Brewery, a cigar maker, a broom factory, several brickyards, a foundry, and a cement plant.[78]

Local economic focus could also shift rapidly. The Black Hills was at first entirely a mining district but soon people began to realize that "There's gold from the grass roots down, but there's *more gold* from the grass roots *up*,"[79] so some minor miners ploughed their profits into livestock instead of into mining implements, provisions, or Deadwood entertainments. Cattle, hog, horse, and sheep ranching soon proliferated, though early on Lakota raids could lead to the loss of up to 400 head, especially in the "luxuriant pastures" of Fall River County in the southwestern corner of the territory. Soon, the region was exporting its beeves across the nation and looked forward to entering European markets. Before the railroads moved in, big companies like the Matador Land and Cattle Company (60,000 head strong at its height) moved cattle on the hoof through "the Strip" to the railheads at Evarts on the east side of the Missouri River.[80]

Some early ranchers were salaried managers for the real entrepreneurs, British aristocrats who owned immense tracts or the organizers of joint stock corporations like the Dakota Stock and Grazing Company. Sword and Dagger, for example, ran 14,000 head on 400,000 acres; HO had 10,000 head on 360,000 acres on the Cheyenne River. Mulehead, which was established in 1912 near Bonesteel, employed 60 men to manage over 11,000 head of cattle. The ranch, which had its own electrical generating plant, cost in the range of $3 million, a pretty penny before the Great War. Other ranches had smaller but still substantial holdings.[81]

The cattlemen did better than the sheep men at first because sheep were more liable to disease and the only viable market was for their wool, not their meat. Later, however, sheep men were better able to adapt to the influx of homesteaders because their flocks were shepherded, not allowed to roam the range freely like cattle at first were. As elsewhere, sheep and cattlemen often found themselves at odds because sheep ate grass down to the roots and stunk up watering holes with their feces. Nevertheless, in some parts of the state, like the short grass country of the northwest, sheep men came to outnumber cattlemen and the two sides never went to war as they did in neighboring Wyoming.[82]

One sheep man, Myron J. Smiley, helped to keep the peace, and the safety of his 50,000 sheep, the largest flock ever recorded in the state's history, by hiring Mexican gunslingers. To induce shepherds to remain in his employ, Smiley offered anyone who stayed on for at least seven years from 300 to 400 ewes to start his own ranch. With his company headquartered in Belle Fourche, Smiley helped to establish the Belle Fourche Roundup and the U&I Sugar Beet Factory and also the obligatory local social and economic institutions like the Commercial Club, the Butte County Bank, the Elks Club, Shriners, and the Masonic Order. Smiley was also a primary stockholder in the Belle Fourche Creamery, the Smiley-Gay Hardware Company, and Belle Fourche Hospital. Other early sheep ranches, including those of Newton Tubbs and the Jones Ranch (west of Hot Springs), were much smaller outfits and their leaders were much less influential.[83]

The gold rush helped to attract attention to the entire Dakota Territory and brought in much needed cash, especially to Yankton, a major staging area. It also helped to build up the transportation infrastructure so necessary to attract permanent settlers who needed cheap transportation to move in but, more important, to move their agricultural products out. Wagons and steamboats were good enough to ship gold and even mining implements but not corn or wheat. Many of the first settlers, in fact, came to provision Indian reservations, not to ship their goods to eastern markets. The provisioning market was soon saturated, however, so what really fueled the Great Dakota Boom (1878-1887) was the renewal of railroad construction after the Panic of 1873. (Stagecoach and freight lines were not unimportant; they persisted into the twentieth century by connecting hamlets to market towns. But they could not have provided long distance freight transportation nearly as cheaply or efficiently as the rails did.)[84]

During the Great Dakota Boom, settlers claimed some 24 million acres in the area that is now South Dakota. Almost 5.5 million acres were taken up in 1883 alone.[85] By 1881, the New York *Tribune* was already

Pedro, South Dakota, no longer exists, but in 1909 this freighter was hauling cargo to the town once located between Pierre and Rapid City.
Courtesy Center for Western Studies.

convinced that the Dakota Territory should be split into two and each new state given a distinctive name because both would soon be "great, populous States."[86] Generally, the first business enterprises in a region opening for settlement were outfitters, horse dealers, and guides, i.e., people who could satiate homesteaders' immediate needs. Next came entrepreneurs who built claim shacks that could be moved to homestead sites to help pioneers meet the legal requirements of residency. Many shacks were 9 by 12 feet, made of timber, clad with rough cut timber and wooden laths, and covered with tar paper and/or horse blankets. Many other homesteaders, however, opted instead for houses composed of prairie sod. Well-built soddies were sturdier than shacks and were cooler in the summer and warmer in the winter than even balloon-framed houses. They often resembled igloos after blizzards left snow piled up to their roofs and beyond but the snow only served as additional insulation and protection from the wind. Heavy rain was the soddy's greatest weakness. Roofs and walls could collapse and they were full of creepy crawlers. Some homesteaders blessed with the right type of hill carved a dugout, a home literally dug out of hillsides or gullies like a manmade cave. Others constructed half dugouts partly dug out of a steep hill and then fronted with sod or wood. Many dugouts built west of the Mighty Mo lasted through the Great Depression. Regardless of house type, pioneers buried food in the floor to keep it cool and safe from critters.[87]

Other early entrepreneurs provided special sod-buster teams and equipment to break the virgin prairie for first plantings. While some homesteaders broke the virgin soil themselves, many with a little money to spare availed themselves of the special services to save themselves time, trouble, and backaches. Others were in it for the short haul, developing claims as little as legally possible while working fulltime as a teacher or railroader. After securing title, they sold out, generally for about $500, and then moved on, sometimes to another claim site. In most areas, entrepreneurs stood ready to buy up successful claims or to sweep in, like vultures, to pay a pittance for the abandoned claims of homesteaders who arrived with more dreams than capital or practical experience.[88]

Many homesteaders were simply unprepared for what awaited them on the frontier.[89] A Mr. Smith, an Englishman who took up a homestead near Paxton, was in the words of one contemporary, "a frail, dreamy, impractical man, about as poorly adapted to the rigors of the pioneer life as one could imagine." [90] His wife and children were new to farming, but they studied up and worked hard to keep the farm afloat. Throughout the state, but especially in the West, water was often in short supply or inconveniently located and had to be hauled in stoneboats. Traditional fuels like coal and kerosene were too expensive to ship in, so homesteaders made due with local materials: bison then cow chips, wood and lignite where available, and huge quantities of slough grass, flax, and straw. Many early homesteaders made a good side income by picking the prairies clean of bison bones which eastern factories used to refine sugar and make glue, fertilizer, buttons, china, and handles[91] but after the land was picked clean water and fuel access remained problematic and relatively expensive in terms of cash or time and effort, prompting more than a few to move on. As one poet put it:

> *Fifty miles from water,*
> *A hundred miles to wood,*
> *To hell with this damned country.*
> *I'm going home for good.*[92]

But for every person who left, several more showed up. The rate of population growth during the boom was incredible: the territorial population soared from 82,000 in 1880 to almost 250,000 in 1885. Railroad mileage grew just as quickly, surging from 399 to 4,726 in the 1880s. By 1882, Huron had eighteen daily trains bringing people and manufactured goods in and taking agricultural produce out. Unsurprisingly, speculation was rampant. Back east, Dakota town lots traded at ever higher prices, even for fictional towns like Capitola in Spink County.[93]

By the early 1880s, parts of the state east of the big river were densely populated enough to begin to support services like blacksmith, shoe, and barber shops, banks, hotels, telegraph stations, drug, hardware, and general stores, and doctors and lawyers. Ag (seed, elevators, farm equipment) and horse (stables, tack) related businesses were also increasingly common. The dry goods store and other businesses that Laura Ingalls Wilder (1867-1957) depicted in her books about De Smet were all real. Most early businesses were small scale, requiring little capital and at most a partner or two. One major exception was mills, like the six-story Queen Bee flourmill in Sioux Falls, which was constructed in 1879-81 with New York money. Many early settlers were entrepreneurs whose businesses had failed in larger, more established markets. Their initial success in virgin markets often attracted competitors until profits disappeared and commercial failures accumulated. Those with little capital cushion typically exited first, often by bankruptcy. More substantial businessmen held on longer and sometimes turned matters around but more often they moved on, to a new niche back east or some aspiring boom town further west.[94]

During the boom, the territory also attracted entrepreneurial service providers like photographers and printers. Photographer William Richard Cross, for example, ended up in South Dakota after stints in the 1860s and 1870s in Omaha and northeastern Nebraska because of his interest in Native Americans. By the late 1870s, he frequently visited Rosebud (then called Spotted Tail) to take photographs of Indians and the Badlands to sell to newspapers and stereography printers. He relocated his studio to Hot Springs in the early 1890s in order to create a large collection of Black Hills views.[95]

The first known item printed in Dakota Territory was an election notice printed by hand press in Sioux Falls in September 1858. The first newspaper came out of that same city the next year but it was abandoned during the U.S.-Dakota War in 1862, by which time Frank M. Ziebach had begun a second paper in Yankton. Soon newspapers were printed throughout the settled portions of the growing territory, in places like Elk Point, Deadwood, and Rapid City. One of the first newspapers in the Black Hills reported that "our material to print this paper was transported in the depth of winter, almost 400 miles, and brought through and into a hostile Indian country."[96] By 1881, McCook County sported not one but two newspapers, the *Pioneer Register* and the *Dakota Cricket*, which like other country papers of the era subsisted mostly on land sale advertisements. Miller (Hand County) at one point supported five newspapers.[97]

The Great Dakota Boom was an ethnically diverse movement that drew from numerous European ethnic groups plus Native and African-American populations. Immigrants into the territory included Anglo-Canadians, Austrians, Germans from Russia, Czechs, Danes, Dutch, English, Finns, French, French Canadian, German, Greeks, Hutterites, Irish, Jews, Lutheran German, Mennonites, Norwegians, Poles, Russians, Scots, Swedes, Polish, and Welsh. (By the Great War, they would be supplemented by small numbers of Arabs, Chinese, and Lebanese.) Many of the claimants during the boom were Norwegians right off the boat from the Old Country and some whose parents had settled in Minnesota, Wisconsin, and Illinois. In fact, about 13% (51,500) of the new state's people were of Norwegian descent. About a quarter of the residents of Minnehaha County were Norwegian. Most lived in the rural districts but a surprising number resided in Sioux Falls, which jumped from a population of about 2,100 in 1880, to over 5,000 just three years later, to over 10,000 in 1890, thanks to the efforts of Richard Pettigrew and others to secure multiple rail lines into the town. Other Scandinavians chose to move even further onto the Northern Plains, where they built bath/steam houses and held lutefisk feasts in places like Storla, south of Woonsocket.[98]

Most of the immigrants were replicative but some were innovative entrepreneurs. Black Sea Germans or German Russians came from Germany via the Ukrainian steppes. After moving to Russia for lebensraum (living space) earlier in the century, they fled Tsarist oppression in the 1870s. They liked Dakota's freedoms, land, and climate and settled places like Odessa, Kassel, Wagner, Wessington Springs, and Tolstoy, as well as large swathes of what became North Dakota. Some came with considerable capital accumulated during their tenure in Russia. Others worked the Great Northern Railway to save up before homesteading. They proved excellent farmers and ranchers, willing and able to work hard toward prosperity. Many were innovative. In the areas they settled, like that near Roscoe, they dominated local business. One sold Laura Ingalls Wilder "a great big fish" when she was camping near the James River in July 1894. After selling it for a dime, he came back later with two smaller fish for which he also accepted a dime.[99]

Various communal religious sects, including Dutch and Russian Mennonites and Hutterites, also thrived on the prairie.[100] Wilder reported camping near one "tribe or commune or whatever it is" that comprised seventeen quarter sections with "herds of cattle, good horses, and 300 geese."[101] She got a big pail of fresh warm milk from them in exchange for a fire mat. In Sully County, even a so-called "Colored Colony" sprang up. Charles Collins, the Irish-American editor of the *Sioux City Times*, called for Fenian colonies to be established in the territory, to be stocked initially by Irish railroad workers already toiling in the region. That never materialized, but individual Irish immigrants came in sizeable numbers, over 4,000 by 1880, and some of them settled in Garryowen, Union County, in far southeastern South Dakota.[102]

The relative isolation of the Great Plains allowed many groups to maintain their native cultures and languages. As late as the Great War, large numbers of South Dakotans could not speak or write English. Finns, Scandinavians, Russian-Germans and other groups retained much of their respective native cultures for decades. As recently as 1980, 65,000 South Dakotans still used German as a first language. Many ethnic foods are readily available in the state, especially in the larger urban centers, although sometimes they are dreadful by foreign or even New York City standards.[103]

Regardless of color, creed, or place of origin, all the newcomers had needs that urban entrepreneurs competed to fill. By the mid-1880s, for example, Yankton sported a pork plant, a woolen mill, a comb factory, a soap factory, and several breweries, flour mills, and brickyards. It even had a carbonized water facility and a flax tow mill that furnished local farmers with "a market in its territory for such waste materials as rye straw, oats straw and even corn stalks" that the mill turned into "insulation board for use in building construction."[104] Yankton became "Cement City" in 1891 because of its cement plant, which, along with the brickyard, remained in operation until the Depression. John B. Shaw, African American proprietor of the City Restaurant, offered the best ice cream in Yankton both at his ice cream saloon and by delivery cart. Yankton also sported a private bathhouse built by a Fort Randall officer who utilized his soldiers as a cheap source of construction labor.[105]

Not all innovative economic activity revolved around agriculture and manufacturing. In 1885 in Vermillion, the Bower family started a brass band staffed by seven children who for years made grocery money charging 25, 50, and even 75 cents admission to concerts held throughout the southern part of the territory. As the only brass band in the territory, they played some major gigs, including the celebration held when the Fremont, Elkhorn, and Missouri Railroad finally reached Rapid City in July 1886. The Bower's band actually toured in 1887, playing Buffalo Gap, Hot Springs, Custer, and Hermosa for $25 a gig. They continued playing together until 1895. Similarly, Emma Smith DeVoe, an important-if-too-little-studied suffragist who lived in Huron from 1881 until 1891, lectured on the suffrage circuit to make ends meet after her husband's business schemes failed. Most settlers during the Dakota Boom were farmers or petty entrepreneurs like DeVoe, not workers or capitalists. Success on the frontier was more a function of skill, work ethic, and character, than money or privilege. South Dakota was the ultimate meritocracy, a trait that would influence its political culture into the twenty-first century.[106]

Early South Dakotans also helped to develop the nation's non-profit sector. In response to perceived pricing abuses by railroads and other large corporations, farmers allied to form cooperatives designed to create working alternatives to corporate business and banking systems. Many cooperatives were established to help farmers buy goods and financial services more cheaply. They eventually established a corporation, Dakota Alliance, capitalized at $200,000, which then established additional co-ops and offered mortgages and hail insurance at cut rates. Dakota Alliance co-ops, for example, bought binder twine en masse and resold it to farmers at one-third of the regular retail price. Later, the co-ops expanded to offer a wide range of goods, from pens and watches to sewing machines and plows, at low prices. With help from South Dakota political activists like Henry Loucks and Alonzo Wardall, the co-op idea spread into North Dakota, Minnesota, and elsewhere.[107]

Even South Dakota's labor unions could be entrepreneurial. The Lead City Miners' Union was a non-profit charitable and benevolent organization chartered in 1880 to cover funeral expenses and sick pay. In 1894, it borrowed $70,000 to build a three-story building and serviced its debt by renting out the first-floor shops and the second-floor meeting hall.[108]

At its height, it seemed the Dakota Boom would go on forever.[109] Boosters of towns (the number of which increased from 6 to 310 between 1870 and 1890) and railroads calmed potential immigrants who remembered descriptions of the area as a desert by claiming that "rain follows the plow," that in other words agricultural activities *cause* rain.[110] Precipitation did appear to follow the plow, at first, and new ways of processing spring wheat considerably increased demand for South Dakota's lands. But in 1887 the rains failed and the boom, already strained by deflation, high interest rates, and high protective tariffs on manufactured goods, abruptly ended. The drought first crushed many struggling farmers and then the small businesses which had arisen to service them.[111]

As conditions worsened, some entrepreneurs of dubious moral integrity became predatory, making money by selling rainmaking services to desperately parched communities. Water witches, people who could find accessible underground water, were somewhat more respectable and successful. Schemes to fill tanks or reservoirs in wet years for use during droughts were also floated, but half a century ahead of their time. The truly helpful entrepreneurs were companies that drilled deep wells, artesian wells as they were called, that tapped the aquifer underlying much of the state. They were costly affairs, though, so there was agitation for county, state, and even federal support, the last of which the *Springfield [Massachusetts] Republican* called "a socialistic departure that would be fraught with danger to the republic." Private companies like the Artesian Irrigation Company and the James River Irrigation Company, however, stood by to sink wells in exchange for farm mortgages or to rent rigs to co-ops.[112]

By the time South Dakota became a state in 1889, Euroamericans had dramatically transformed the economy of the region from one based on the hunting and gathering of wild species owned in common by everyone in the region to one based on the private ownership of both land and the animal and vegetable resources upon it. Cattle replaced bison; domesticated chickens largely supplanted the four native species of grouse (sharp-tailed, sage, ruffed, and prairie "chickens"). That fundamental transformation allowed Euroamerican entrepreneurs to thrive but simultaneously thwarted and marginalized the ambitions of the region's native peoples, who would suffer tremendous hardships over the next century and beyond.[113]

Chapter 3
Euroamericans Ascendant, 1889-1945

The American, it seems, is a wonderful machine for making money, but he has no idea whatsoever how to enjoy it.[1]

On November 2, 1889, North Dakota and South Dakota became the thirty-ninth and fortieth states of the United States. Nobody is quite sure of the order but it doesn't matter because South (North) Dakotans are better than North (South) Dakotans in every other respect. Just ask any South (North) Dakotan. The long quest for statehood was won when it became clear to a majority of Dakotans, north and south, that policymakers in Washington "dominated" the territory instead of ruling it beneficently.[2] Thereafter, the lives, liberty, and property of South (and North) Dakotans of Euroamerican descent were protected both by the federal Constitution and a state constitution of their own creation. Despite considerable hardships at times, South Dakotans thrived, safe in the knowledge that what they worked for was theirs, to be disposed of if, when, and how they saw fit. Within the geographical confines of the new state, however, there lived a group of people with no such assurances. In stark contrast to their Euroamerican neighbors, the Lakota, Dakota, and Nakota Sioux struggled because their governments, especially the federal government but their tribal and state governments to some degree as well, reduced their economic freedom to almost nil.

Everyone knows that Euroamericans expropriated Native lands but that was not the worst thing they did, not by a long shot. Natives could have rebounded and thrived, as many landless Euroamericans did. What was far worse was that the government stripped Indians of their incentives to work hard or smart. That some still engaged in entrepreneurial endeavors, like long distance trade, is a testament to the economic vitality of their cultures. The federal government, however, essentially attempted to infantilize an entire people, to render them wards of the state, convicts in a prison without physical walls. As a result, South Dakota can be thought of not as two states (East and West River) but three, east, west, and Native. The third, composed of nine reservations (Flandreau, Sisseton, Yankton, Crow Creek, Lower Brule, Rosebud, Pine Ridge, Cheyenne River, Standing Rock), is to this day wracked by high unemployment, low wages, low educational attainment, and poor living and health conditions.[3]

After the Missouri River was opened to steamboat traffic in the 1830s and population densities increased after several smallpox epidemics ran their course, commercial intercourse between the Lakota and American traders increased. The entrepreneurial activities of the natives, however, remained limited to replicative in the economic realm and exploitative in the military and political realms. This is not to blame Natives for the injustices they have since suffered, just to point out a reason why they became increasingly marginalized. Without innovative entrepreneurs to help develop their economy, economic integration with the overall U.S. economy was a mixed blessing for the Lakota and other native groups. Had they reverted to self-sufficiency and a subsistence economy, the Lakota would have been easily defeated by other tribes or the U.S. Army. Yet trade increased brigandage (by both sides) and the flow of guns and alcohol caused societal and ecological damage palpable to this day. After the demise of the great bison herds by the early 1880s, the discovery of gold in the Black Hills, the agricultural development of the eastern Dakotas, and decades of military repression, the Lakota and other Sioux groups were relegated to reservations in agriculturally marginal areas of the Northern Plains.[4]

Economic and legal justifications for the land grab were found in the writings of John Locke, Thomas Hobbes, and others but, by the admission of some of its own officials, the U.S. government badly botched the transition.[5] "The present policy of the Government," Lieutenant Gouverneur K. Warren noted in 1855, "seems the best calculated that could be devised for exterminating the Indian."[6] Indian commissioner E. A. Hayt argued from his experience in the mid-1870s that "civilization" had "loosened" and in some cases even "broken, the bonds that regulate and hold together Indian society" but the U.S. government had failed to fill the resulting power vacuum. As a result, "women are brutally beaten and outraged; men are murdered in cold blood ... and schools are dispersed by bands of vagabonds; but there is no redress."[7] Another complained in 1880 that traders exploited Indians both on the purchase of manufactured goods and the sale of Indian wares.[8] Other agents and newspaper reporters evinced similar sentiments, rendering the common complaint that Native Americans were "disinclined to work" unsurprising.[9]

According to historian Thomas Biolsi, "during the period from about 1880 to the New Deal, the OIA [Office of Indian Affairs] instituted a mode of domination over the Lakota composed of a set of administrative technologies of power ... includ[ing] agency courts and police forces, trust restrictions on individual lands and funds, and the ration system."

Together, Biolsi argues, those technologies of power "formed an integrated system for the surveillance and control of both mass behavior ... as well as the behavior of individuals and families down to the minute details of household composition and use of land," i.e., the exact opposite of the economic freedom needed to spur entrepreneurship and economic growth.[10]

Public sentiment supported the government's harsh tactics. The Lakota had to be subjugated, it was argued, because as warriors they were simply too formidable to allow to remain free.[11] Not everyone agreed, however, with the use of military force. "Bread will do more than bayonets with the Indians," the Omaha *World Herald* editorialized in 1890, on the eve of the Wounded Knee Massacre on the Pine Ridge Reservation in southwestern South Dakota.[12]

By the end of World War I, the Indian military threat was negligible. "The Indians never cause the white people any trouble these days," homesteader Estella Bowen Culp informed a family member in 1918. "They are controlled partly through kindness and partly through fear."[13] And some, she might have added, had been co-opted, turned into entertainers by Euroamericans suddenly more enamored than fearful of Native cultural practices.[14] "That is the way I get money" explained one Lakota to a government official in 1890 who complained about the 79 Lakota employed by William F. Cody's Wild West show. According to historian Clyde Ellis, between 1880 and 1930, "thousands of Indians joined dozens of shows, exhibitions, and fairs to earn a living dancing, singing, and giving other performances."[15] They received much higher incomes than those natives who remained on reservations and, in fact, some earned as much as two-thirds of the typical Indian agents' salary.[16]

Many other natives, however, eked out a living begging scraps from slaughter houses, hunting whatever game remained, scavenging coal and wood, working odd jobs like digging graves, and thieving—by becoming exploitative entrepreneurs, in other words.[17] By the 1920s, Euroamericans tended to ignore Native Americans whenever possible, assuming them all to be, in the words of one contemporary, "dirty, lazy, and ignorant." West River they were ever present and "yet they were almost invisible."[18] From the 1890s, hundreds of young Indians annually attended the government's Indian boarding school in Flandreau. Instead of educating the young Natives, however, the school served them out to white households as domestic servants in what was called the "outing program."[19]

When the Great Depression struck in the 1930s, the Lakota were in dire straits. Relief jobs induced many to give up their traditional subsistence practices and that forced them onto the dole when the emergency jobs ended. Meanwhile, New Dealer John Collier pushed the

Indian Reorganization Act, which ostensibly would allow the federal government to slowly exfiltrate Indian Country as an imperial power. But the OIA continued to limit tribal self-government and to interfere with the day-to-day lives of Natives.[20]

The incentives of Euroamericans were vastly better, and it showed in their daily activities. Instead of being called lazy, improvident, and drunk, South Dakotans were if anything chided for working too hard, spending too little, and drinking not nearly enough. Before World War II, to be a South Dakotan, a Euroamerican one anyway, was to be an entrepreneur. In 1925, *more than three out of every five* South Dakotans owned his or her own business, be it a farm, ranch, retail establishment, or other small business or professional office.[21] Only the railroads, Homestake Mining Company, John Morrell, and a few other businesses employed significant numbers of people. Most of their employees, and those employed by smaller businesses, were aspiring entrepreneurs. "No one had to tell a Dakotan," historian Catherine Stock noted, "that it was better ... to be 'on your own' than to work for somebody else."[22] Not everyone managed to save enough to escape the wage labor force, but many did.

Consider, for example, Hamlin County, an agricultural county south of Watertown and home in the mid-1930s to 7,720 people, 5,785 of whom were in the workforce, 1,412 as farmers, 591 as laborers, 1,186 as teachers, and the rest as insurance and other agents, bakers, bankers, barbers, blacksmiths, bookkeepers, carpenters, clergy, clerks, dentists, druggists, electricians, lawyers, merchants, nurses, plumbers, shoemakers, and telegraph and telephone workers. (There were also some students, some retirees, and 55 unemployed people on the dole.) The clerks, nurses, teachers, laborers, and workers were employees, but most of the rest were self-employed and hence at least replicative entrepreneurs.[23] For that reason, some Hamlin County families were on relief but "extreme cases of poverty" were reportedly "rare."[24]

Of course some South Dakotans consciously sought the stability of a steady wage. Homesteader Estella Bowen Culp explained that her husband John preferred working as a baker to owning his own bakery because both farming and business were so precarious. "Farming in a new country was such an uncertain venture," she explained. "A business venture in a new town," she continued, "was also most uncertain" because "perhaps the new town would not develop into anything more than a trading post."[25] For every John Culp, though, there was an entrepreneurial John, like John B. Jones, Sr., a homesteader near Presho who fell into the real estate game around 1906 by selling relinquishments. He soon bought a car, moved to town, got married, and lived presumably happily until his death in 1951.[26]

Between statehood and the end of the Great Depression, South Dakota consisted of three major economic zones, each of which was peppered with small but growing urban areas. East of the Missouri River was primarily agricultural in nature, with numerous farms that produced corn, soybeans, sunflowers and other crops. Parts of the east were devoted to dairy, hog, or chicken production as well. West of the river was primarily grazing country, with fewer, larger ranches that produced cattle, sheep, horses, and goats. But it is important to realize that some corn grew west of the river and cattle could be found scattered around the entire East River region. What mattered most, even more than rainfall to some extent, was the quality of the local soil. Houdek meant farming while Chestnut group soils like Pierre shale or gumbo were extremely difficult to cultivate and hence were used to graze domesticated ungulates. The truly distinctive region was the Black Hills, where mining and lumbering predominated well into the twentieth century.[27]

The state's three regions were connected by a type of entrepreneur, the transportation entrepreneur, who would later give way to a government bureaucracy, the South Dakota Department of Transportation. Private steamships plied the rivers, especially the Missouri, while ferries, and later bridges, connected land routes. At Pierre, a big boat called the *Jim Leighton* served as a ferry from the early 1890s until at least 1902. A ferry at Chamberlain remained in operation because the bridge gave out so often. The Big Muddy could also be crossed by ferry at Sioux City. At shallower crossings, fords or plank roads built on boats were sufficient.[28]

East River received more rainfall than West River and was more densely populated because its farms were smaller than the average ranch and because it contained relatively large urban areas like Sioux Falls, Aberdeen, and Watertown, not to mention Yankton and Vermillion. The state's second largest city, Rapid City, lay in the foothills of the Black Hills, not in the ranching country. All the urban areas shared one important trait, transportation connections. Some arose solely because they were able to attract a railroad. Others attracted railroads because they enjoyed other advantages, like an existing population, a navigable river, water power, the county seat, or merely distance from other population centers. Railroads established towns like Presho in large part to provide services for passengers and freight companies over the vast distance between the metropoles of Sioux Falls and Rapid City.[29]

Within the bigger urban centers, entrepreneurs provided a variety of transportation options ranging from horse-driven taxis called hansom cabs to trolleys. By statehood, Sioux Falls City Street Railway Company (SFSRC) provided horse-drawn trolley service to the city's residents. In 1893, the company had six drivers, who each earned exactly $8.17

per week, and horses, who were paid in oats and hay (the receipts still exist). After SFSRC's demise, an electric trolley company soon arose and folded.[30]

In 1907, a serial entrepreneur and author named Frank Moody Mills, who had experience as a steamboat clerk, publisher, and electricity magnate in exotic places like Illinois, Iowa, and Michigan, established the Sioux Falls Traction Company over the objections one Mr. Jones, who claimed to have offered the city better terms. Voters thought otherwise, approving a thirty-year franchise. Mills came to Sioux Falls on the behest of his son Dan, who noted that Sioux Falls was "the largest small city in the United States without a street railway." Later, Mills also developed intercity bus lines that connected Sioux Falls to "nearby cities in adjoining states" as well as towns in southeastern South Dakota.[31]

Mills died at age 98 in October 1929, just weeks after the electric lines that powered his trolleys came down and were replaced by the buses of his sons' company, Sioux Transit. Sale of the intercity bus routes saved the company during the Depression, allowing it to squeak along in the face of bitter competition from cut-rate cabs until the war brought prosperity and profits. Sioux Falls Traction was remembered fondly then, but earlier in its existence it had been criticized for exposing the city to ridicule from outsiders after it was successfully sued for a nickel and someone complained that "the street cars of Sioux Falls present a sorry sight. ... repairs to the cars ... are badly needed. ... If the management of the Sioux Falls system is scimping [sic] on its equipment in order to pay the stockholders big dividends there is something out of whack."[32] The deplorable condition of the cars was attributed to the fact that they sat outside, exposed to "the fury of blizzards and the blistering heat of summer" even when not in service.[33] Its successor, Sioux Transit, folded in 1952.

Entrepreneurship was alive and well in the state's urban centers as evidenced by the steady churn of new businesses. Kadoka's main street, for example, was constantly in flux due to new entrants, mergers, bankruptcies, and voluntary exits. Decennial federal censuses confirm that the same can be said of Philip, Presho, and many other substantial towns. In 1907, businesses in the bustling town of Philip included the Bank of Philip, First State Bank, the *Bad River News* office, a livery and feed barn, a saloon, a hotel, a rooming house, two general stores, a small postal card shop, a drug store, a candy store, and one of the ubiquitous prairie dance halls. (Smaller towns still used people's homes for dances.)[34]

In 1910, Presho boasted of several general merchants, a building contractor, two banks, two hotels, two lumberyards, real estate agents, a bakery, a grain elevator, two jewelers, a John Deere dealer, an

International Harvester dealer, and sundry professionals, including two doctors, a dentist, an undertaker, two lawyers, and a newspaper. In 1926, Kadoka supported 46 businesses: a barber, baker, bank, hardware store, druggist, radio dealer, lumberyard, movie theater, and a combination café and taxidermy, as well as several lawyers, hotels, butchers, gas stations, road contractors, abstractors, cream buyers, pool halls, general merchants, cattle buyers, grain elevators, milliners, dress shops, auto repair garages, doctors, dentists, and real estate and insurance agents. (Bigger urban centers, like Sioux Falls, also needed garbage hauling and cleaning companies.)[35]

Kadoka was then home to six businesses run by women, including one owned by Bertha Martinksy, a Russian immigrant and single parent who settled in the town when her Badlands homestead proved less than lucrative.[36] An Orthodox Jew, Martinksy at age nineteen fled anti-Semitism at home, which was located in the Czar's notorious "Pale of Settlement." Following a stint in the Eastern European Jewish district of Des Moines, she remarried having being abandoned by her first husband, a peddler, soon after the birth of their third child. Unimpressed by her second husband, a common laborer who gave her little more than two daughters, Martinksy left for the promise of a better life in South Dakota. It was not to be, not at first anyway, as she barely scratched a subsistence from poor, dry land seven miles northwest of Interior, now part of Buffalo Gap National Grassland. She eventually abandoned the claim, which nobody would buy even for just the back taxes.

Martinksy moved her shack to Interior, where she baked bread and doughnuts that she sold to the denizens of the Pine Ridge reservation. Learning Lakota as she went, she began to sell beads and other goods out of a wagon at rodeos and powwows. Her reputation for fair dealing with the Native Americans, combined with her willingness to extend them credit, ensured their continued patronage when she moved her business to Kadoka in 1917. Her general store, which ran under the somewhat clunky slogan "if it's to eat or wear or use, get it at Martinsky's," carried clothing, dry goods, and groceries. Martinksy lived in frugal quarters at the rear of the store, which was said to smell of apricots, vinegar, and dry goods. That, and good business practices, allowed her to save up to buy a building that she leased to a creamery company, and several other properties. She also established a tourist camp that, unlike her early foray in agriculture, she was able to sell for a profit.[37]

Smaller towns naturally had fewer businesses than larger ones but even the smallest tended to have a bakery, a bank, a grocery or general store, and a hotel/saloon/café/restaurant. Grain elevators, recreation halls, liveries, and blacksmith shops or later gas stations and garages, were also early entrants. Photographers were surprisingly common, though few made much money at the trade. One who did well, Gustav Johnson of Philip, was a sort of photographic speculator, snapping pictures of quotidian scenes, printing them up, and selling them to tourists and passersby for a penny apiece.[38] For whatever reason, undertakers were latecomers to many western towns so in the 1890s many "burials had to be hurried up."[39]

Circa 1910, a hotel graced Dallas, and a restaurant served up meals in little Springview. In 1913, White River in Mellette County had two hotels, the Jones and the City Café and Hotel, visible in a post-blizzard photograph. Early hotels were typically small, often just a few rooms. The quality could be good, like a modern bed-and-breakfast, but they filled quickly during periods of unusual demand. Women owned and operated many of the smaller hotels and boarding houses and also millinery shops, confectionaries, photograph galleries, laundries, and even the odd pharmacy. For every female owner there was usually at least one hired hand, usually a "girl."[40]

Women also ran many early groceries,[41] which, it was said, "sprang up wherever there were enough homesteaders around to keep them going. Usually some farmer started one and ran it in a part of the house ... There was usually a post office at the same place."[42] Early groceries were generally just one room with a mixed stock of goods. They were not self-serve style but clerk-fetch, with everything except canned goods sold by the pound, very much like at a deli counter today. Many sold just staples, not finished products, presumably because frontier women desired to be independent and not rely on canned goods, premade clothes, and so forth. Of course budget constraints may have amplified their desire for independence. Many homesteaders were cash poor, especially when they were newly established and during the region's periodic droughts.[43] "We don't live here, we only stay/'Cause we're too poor to get away," went one song recalled by Laura Ingalls Wilder, and many a homesteader limped away from their claims in tattered clothes, worn out, and flat broke.[44]

In larger towns, grocery chain stores could be found by 1930. Red Owl Stores of Minneapolis, for example, owned stores in thirty-three South Dakota towns. By that time, chains also operated some shoe, department stores, hardware, lumber, and drug stores in coyote country.[45]

Between 1901 and 1911, the number of trade centers in South Dakota increased from 490 to 759 as every railroad siding became at least a small town with a bank, grocery, general store, and hotel.[46] Every trade center called itself a town or a city "and hoped to be the center of the universe within a few years," as one of the early residents later mocked.[47] Most, however, fell into oblivion or nearly so. The number of trade centers in the state fell back to 671 by 1921. The shift from a railroad to an automobile economy and the rise of the telephone, the radio, and the rural postal route contributed to the decline. Cars and trucks allowed people to travel longer distances to shop, even if the road system was still underdeveloped, while telephones and radios, which could be found in 44% of South Dakota households by 1930, allowed them to seek out better prices more cheaply. Rural postal routes meant that mail came to farmers instead of farmers having to go to their mail. All this spelled increased competition where only the best businesses in the most convenient trade centers, which tended to be the larger ones that offered a wider variety of stores, transportation connections, and/or government services, survived. One downside was that businesses that used to be found in just about every town and hamlet, like farm equipment parts stores, were thereafter located only in bigger towns.[48]

The number of South Dakota trade centers declined on net just one, to 670, in 1931 but the turnover rate for the 1920s was about fifty period. In other words, half of the trade centers extant in 1921 were gone ten years later, replaced by new ones. During wet, economically good years, more centers appeared than folded. During dry spells, both in terms of rain and the overall economy, more centers shriveled than sprang up. Little wonder the prairie, especially areas remote from major railroads and highways, is littered with ghost towns, places that thrived for a time but eventually, like Artesian in Sanborn County, or Argonne and Vilas in Miner County, shriveled into insignificance or disappeared entirely. By one count, in 1990 at least ninety-five such ghost towns still haunted South Dakota, but entrepreneurs turned several of them, including a former tin mining camp called Tinton in the Black Hills, into tourist attractions.[49]

Other small centers continued to cling to a tenuous existence. Incorporated in 1900, Vienna grew quickly and eventually sported the usual retail businesses (hotel, restaurant, lumber yard, various stores, and a barber shop) as well as a newspaper, the Bank of Vienna, and a dance hall. A hat maker, an undertaker, a jeweler, and a piano tuner plied their respective trades but the town was long dry (i.e., alcohol sales were prohibited). Rocked by a fire, then failure of the bank, then advent of paved highways, then the demise of small family farms, a saloon, ironically enough, is about all that is left in Vienna.[50] "The smallest towns," writer Kathleen Norris noted in the early 1990s, "have made do with so little for so long they count themselves lucky to have a post office, a gas station, a general store, and perhaps a tavern; they have no illusions that they are necessary to the farm economy"[51] but they persist because some people happily trade away convenience for less "pollution, traffic congestion, crime, employment" and so forth.[52] For some, it is "hard to give up a place where you can walk at sunrise accompanied only by the sounds of wind and meadowlarks."[53]

Unsurprisingly, then, a few towns have managed, with the aid of entrepreneurs or other key leaders, to remain small but vibrant. In 1940, Bristol had a population of 475, two new car dealerships, two banks, two hotels, four cafés, a newspaper, a movie theater, a doctor, and a creamery and various other agriculture support companies. In 2000, its population had dropped below 400, but it still had a mail-order company, a grocery co-op, two seed companies, a grain elevator, a bowling alley, and a service station operated by the Farmers Union.[54]

"Change in the business community," wrote historian Paula Nelson, "was a constant during the early years of settlement."[55] Entry, exit, and transferability were easy and cheap; people regularly bartered businesses for everything from homesteads to horses. It helped that most businesspeople were jacks (or jills) of all trades, willing and able to give up business A if business B appeared more profitable, stable, or easy. For example, the Stabler family ran a hotel, the Brule, in Chamberlain by 1889, but would later run the Wind Cave in the Black Hills.[56]

Some early entrepreneurs were flexible and ambitious enough to run several businesses at once. Charles S. Hubbard of Presho, for instance, operated a hay wholesaling operation, a livery, a bath house, and a pond that provided locals with entertainment and ice. (Before mechanical ice makers became cost effective, entrepreneurs harvested ice in the winter and stored it under ground covered with straw for insulation.) Doctors like F. M. Newman, also of Presho, practiced medicine while also owning and operating pharmacies. Barbers, like African American Richard Lamb, still practiced medicine to some degree. Maurice Cloakley, also African American, ran cleaning and portering businesses in Sioux Falls. In Artesian, Emmet Dowdell ran a newspaper, a hotel, a store, and a small farm, all at the same time. Due to the at times harsh climate and difficult market conditions, South Dakotans had to be diligent or they were bound to fail. They passed their "extraordinary work ethic" on to their children and grandchildren, so many entrepreneurs started young. After school, many kids worked pitching papers, pumping gas, and/or helping out with the family business.[57]

Most people, however, did not juggle multiple jobs at once but instead bounced between wage labor and ownership. Charles Allen, for example, was a mule driver on a wagon train, a soldier, a homesteader, and a blacksmith before becoming a newspaper reporter.[58] Tom Brick did unskilled agricultural work, then worked as a carpenter's helper, then tried homesteading, then assembled machinery in Aberdeen, then worked as a millwright in Sturgis, then tried homesteading again before bartering his claim for an automobile that he ran as a taxi in Vermillion and Yankton in 1914. For two years he was Vermillion's only policeman before buying a candy store and ice cream parlor. He sold that business to his son in 1939 and opened a liquor store. In his "retirement," Brick repaired firearms and made violins![59] He finally passed in 1979, aged ninety-eight. Serial entrepreneur Kate Reynolds, an African-American woman, ran a restaurant but then worked as a nurse and a miner before owning a boardinghouse, a timber dealership, and a dairy operation.[60]

Many early entrepreneurs were men but some were women: single women who preferred being their own bosses to wage work and married women who helped their husbands at work. A few married women even went into business themselves, owning and operating beauty or dress shops, cafés, and even appliance and department stores. Many a homestead was run by wives for weeks, months, or even years at a time while their husbands worked on the railroads or in distant towns and cities in search of cash with which to buy farm equipment. Some homesteads, up to 30% in some areas and eras, were owned and operated by single women, many of whom doubled as laundresses, missionaries, teachers, or ladies of the night.[61]

Some of the churn was just a matching issue, i.e., people looking for the occupation or business that suited them best. Some of it was just bad luck: John was a good baker but Jerry was better and the market could support only one of them. Much of it was technological, like automobiles and later tractors driving out horse-related businesses, which happened relatively early in South Dakota. Already in September 1904, the fifty-ninth car had been registered in the state and of course there were many unregistered vehicles bandying about, astonishing farmers. By the early 1910s, several automobile companies were already operating in Deadwood. The people of the Plains switched to automobiles faster than people in the rest of the country because they needed them more to shrink the vast expanses.[62] "The way of a motor-car on the prairie," one contemporary observed, "is one of swiftness."[63] As automobiles drove small hamlets and their retailers out of existence, others needed to purchase cars too just to be able to get to larger centers to shop.[64] By the early 1930s, horses were so rare that blacksmiths could not always shod them. "Hosses is a ting of de past," said one in Hettinger, North Dakota (near the South Dakota border). "Now if it was lugs ya wanted on yar tractor, I could feex ya up, but not hosses."[65]

The relatively rapid proliferation of the automobile in the plains states – South Dakota was seventh in automobile ownership in per capita terms in 1928 – brought with it significant social change (well documented elsewhere) but also a spate of entrepreneurs who sold and maintained cars or serviced their drivers and passengers. In the 1920s, for example, entrepreneurs marked out the path for the "Black and

Yellow Trail," Federal Highway 14, from Chicago to Yellowstone through the center of South Dakota. Business boosters along the route pledged to make the highway live up to its motto as the "Scenic and Safe Route" west or the "Shortest and Most Scenic Route to Yellowstone National Park." By 1923, seventy-three tourist camps were arrayed along the 1,600 mile, recently graveled trail, and the state historian was busy cooking up historic points along it to advertise, but of course Mount Rushmore would eventually become the biggest draw along the route.[66]

The impact of technological transformations suffuse the biographies of early South Dakotans. Soon after the turn of the century, Olouse Foss left the family in Jasper, Minnesota, to box, wrestle, and travel with the circus and in carnivals. He later worked as an engineer on the Great Northern Railroad and established one of the first automobile dealerships in the Jasper region. He also ran a bowling alley with a friend and of course he farmed. His son, Joe, turned his affinity for high places into a lucrative business cleaning and greasing ubiquitous farm windmills. (Windmills disappeared due to the advent of cheap fossil fuels but they are making a comeback.) While most entrepreneurial activities, including Joe's, were "merely" replicative, some were innovative. The mid- and late nineteenth century witnessed an explosion of inventive activity in both Europe and America. New contraptions ranged from silly (e.g., blushing veil, parachute fire escape, perpetual motion machine) to mundane (e.g., bottle caps, bra, player piano, Tiddlywinks) to world-altering (e.g., automobile, mechanical refrigeration, motion picture camera, pneumatic tire, radio, telephone, typewriter). Americans were avid inventors in part because they knew they could obtain patent protection relatively quickly and cheaply.[67]

South Dakotans were no different, obtaining numerous patents in the state's first few decades.[68] Unsurprisingly, many from the far western part of the state were related to mining. In late 1892, for example, Hill City resident Henry Hall filed a patent for a godevil (mining hand car and associated track pronounced "go devil") that could be more easily moved "when blasts are fired in the bottom of a mine." In 1899, Franklin Carpenter of Deadwood filed a patent for an "Improved Process of Separating Precious Metals from Their Ores" especially adapted to the "dry" or siliceous ores found in western South Dakota and central Colorado.

East River patentees, by contrast, had more eclectic interests associated with farming and urban life. In 1889, Isaac Lawshe of Sioux Falls applied to patent a "time-indicating device for musicians." Theodore Mehring of Yankton patented in 1893 an improved beer faucet attachment that prevented the "escape of gas or liquid where the bung holes are not round or have worn out." In 1894, Huron's Godfried Laube patented a gopher extermination system that involved burning sulfur in their holes, apparently the technique used some fourscore years later by Bill Murray in the 1980 movie *Caddyshack*. In 1894 Laube also patented a washing machine and the following year he received a patent for a wheel designed to prevent children's carriages from being upset by the "board walks ... commonly employed ... in the suburbs or rural districts."

In 1896, Wallace Houts of Parker teamed up with Lars Nilson of Sioux City, Iowa, to patent an improved automated telephone switchbox. That same year, Walter Gripman of Sioux Falls received a patent for a new and improved lathe attachment "designed for cutting gears, grooving taps and reamers, splining shafts, cutting T-slots in chucks, and for various other work done on a milling machine." In 1898, Elmer Gragert of White Rock in the farthest reaches of northeastern South Dakota applied for a patent for an improved crank to be used "in actuating wheels, shafts, &c." Two years later, Woonsocket's Charles Holmberg sought a patent for an improved piston engine. Abraham Lincoln Jones of Canton invented a new type of sewer pipe, one he believed would be more watertight and easier to install than the ones commonly in use in 1903.

Other patents were related to the region's climate. In 1891, for example, Andrew Ross of Sioux Falls patented a well-drilling apparatus, undoubtedly in response to the drought that was then crippling the new state's agricultural interests. Daniel Holcomb of Spink County in 1895 patented a wind wheel "whereby the wings or blades will be opened and closed automatically so that the wind will impart a rotary motion to the wheel." The following year, Ernest Bruner of Plano (near Mitchell) received a patent for tires "to be Used on Bicycles for the Purpose of Riding on Ice." In 1899, Stein and Frank Bangs of Lead patented a new type of air conditioner, "an improved apparatus for purifying and cooling air."

Other early South Dakotans received patents for an improved animal trap, can opener, combination letter opener and pencil sharpener, corn holder, coupling for buggies and wagons, cuspidor (spittoon), display stand, electric alarm, electric meter, egg tester, fire escape, locomotive engine, milk sterilizer, nut lock, pocket knife, puzzle, restaurant bill, sash fastener, semiautomatic shotgun, signal lantern, siphon, spoon, velocipede (tricycle), and sundry farming implements from corn huskers to prairie burners to wheelbarrows. And they never stopped. Since 1976, South Dakotans have been awarded over 2,300 patents from the U.S. Patent Office.[69]

The *New York Independent* noted that there was "less illiteracy in Dakota than in any New England state," so such inventiveness should not surprise readers.[70] Neither should the state's printing and publishing industry. By 1890, 558 newspapers and 28 magazines were being published in the state. Only about a dozen were dailies, however, and like many other states, South Dakota in the late nineteenth century had its own "yellow press," to wit newspapers that relied more on editorial sensationalism than hard reporting to sell papers. The first newspaper in the Black Hills appeared in 1876. By the 1920s, 96 of them were publishing west of the river, but most proved of short duration. On both sides of the river, small-town newspapers continued to come and go. Some, like the Kimball *Graphic* in 1907, were so-called "ready prints." Partially printed in Sioux Falls or even further east with national news, local editors filled the sheets with advertisements and community gossip before distribution. Despite such innovations, the number of newspapers published in the state dropped, from 329 in 1920 to 197 in 1968. By the early twenty-first century, most newspapers had disappeared for good or morphed into websites.[71]

The state was also home to so-called job printers that created business cards and so forth. The most important was located in Sioux Falls. Established in 1890 and incorporated in 1906, the company long operated as Midwest Beach Printing but early on it was known as Will A. Beach Printing. Beach moved to Sioux Falls soon after his marriage and became the bookkeeper of Fred W. Taylor's store in 1883. Six years later, Beach bought half of a small job printing business; the following year he bought out his partner and struck off on his own. By 1908, his company, which engaged in commercial printing, blank book manufacturing, engraving and lithography, and office "outfitting," claimed to be "the largest and best equipped printing house in the two Dakotas." A 1909 advertisement told prospective customers that "Success in Business is in large measure due to correctly caring for the details. The business of to-day is done by correspondence. If your business stationery is antiquated, and catalog and other printed matter poorly composed and run on the cheapest paper stocks, you are slighting the most essential details of your business." By 1935, Beach Printing was a complete photographic-lithography outfit that ran thirteen presses, two linotypes, a monotype casting machine, and twenty bindery machines. At its height, it employed fifty men and boasted an annual payroll of $75,000 per year.[72]

At the other end of the state, the Black Hills continued to be highly productive economically even though its boom days had ended before statehood. Instead of attracting itinerants who only wished to get rich, get drunk, get laid, and get out, the Black Hills by the early twentieth century was attracting substantial business interests and people who wanted to live in handsome homes. Before the automobile, people got around the region on horseback, in stage coaches, and by trolleys. A trolley that ran between Pluma, Deadwood, and Lead made fourteen daily round trips for twenty-two years before its cars were converted into cafés.[73]

The main mining region was in the north, about 100 square miles between Perry, Carbonate, and Spearfish Canyon. Gold was the most valuable resource but a variety of other elements, ores, and minerals were also exploited. Distinctive yellow, green, and pink rock used in jewelry was much sought after. Quartz was also mined for various reasons, most recently for use in laser glass, lamps, and optics. Mica from the Black Hills was used to produce sundry knickknacks but it also served a variety of other purposes, including transparent doors for stoves and vehicle axle lubricant. Mica, which was found in slabs of varying thickness, sold for about $10 per pound, enough to induce considerable speculation and innovation in the business. The first mica mine, McMackin Crown, was opened by H. E. McMackin in 1879 and produced sheet mica.[74]

Tin was first mentioned in the Black Hills in 1875 but gold fever prevented an attempt at its exploitation until ore was discovered in 1883 and won the interest of English capitalists. Tin production was begun in 1884 by the Harney Peak Tin Mining, Milling, and Manufacturing Co. and its successor, the Harney Peak Consolidated Tin Company. A dearth of good ore and disagreements between American and English stockholders doomed the concern, which was shuttered in 1893 after numerous allegations of fraud. The $3 million investment ultimately produced only $1,545 of tin. Other tin operations in the Black Hills terminated by 1904 but the region continued to spew forth other valuable commodities. Reinbold and Company, for example, shipped thirty tons of spodumene from the Etta Mine in 1898 and the Tin Queen mine produced some amblygonite. Lepidolite came out of the Bob Ingersoll mine in 1922. The southern Black Hills became the largest domestic producer of beryl in 1914. Some tungsten was also discovered and exploited for considerable profit. Feldspar mining was also important. In 1925, the Dakota Feldspar Company formed and in 1928 the Abington Sanitary Manufacturing Company did likewise. Grinding mills in Keystone and Custer were started in 1929 and 1936, respectively, to treat the crude feldspar before shipment to eastern markets. While some feldspar mining continued throughout the twentieth century, production of it, and other pegmatitic rocks like beryl, muscovite, amblygonite, and spodumene, peaked before mid-century.[75]

Gypsum was another major resource taken from the Black Hills, especially the exposed deposits on the border with Wyoming and the Spearfish formation/Red Valley, which varied in thickness from a few inches to 30 feet. It was used to make cement, fertilizer, roads, wall plaster, and floor and roof tiles but many early companies struggled to make a profit from it. Most gypsum mills went up in flames, either causing financial distress or reflecting the effect of it. By 1920, only two gypsum mills remained in operation, that of the U.S. Gypsum Company, which burned in 1915 but was rebuilt at a capacity of 150 tons of plaster per day, and the 200 ton per day mill of the Dakota Plaster Company, which was owned by local stockholders and capitalized at $150,000. It too burned, in 1916, but was rebuilt. The gypsum was of high quality, leading one analyst to conclude that the industry's problem in the Black Hills stemmed from small local markets and high freight rates.[76] Indeed, homesteader Estella Bowen Culp noted that buildings in Philip circa 1907 remained unplastered because "a train in these parts was still a novelty."[77]

The Black Hills were not thought to be a good source of timber for export out of the area in 1880, partly due to the high costs of transport. However, local concerns, like Homestake, used local trees in their operations. In the 1920s, the Black Hills became noted for its lumber, as well as for fruit farms, flour mills, brick making, creameries, canning, souvenir making, electricity generation, outdoor activities, health resorts, and even regional publishing through *Dakota Press*. Ponderosa pine, the most common tree in the Hills, grows quickly and yields a tall, straight trunk well suited to milling. By the 1980s, companies in the Hills were producing four to five billion board feet per year.[78]

A factory near Belle Fourche produced copious amounts of sugar from the tons of sugar beets grown in a nearby irrigated valley. The factory, which was five stories high and covered eight acres, daily produced 3,600 bags weighing 100 lb. each and employed up to 300 men during the refining season. Irrigation water for the beets came from the

The yard of the Warren-Lamb Lumber Company in Rapid City (c. 1950).
Courtesy Center for Western Studies.

earthen Belle Fourche Dam (Orman Dam), which blocked the flow of water from Owl Creek into the Belle Fourche River after its completion in 1911. In addition to producing sugar, the beets helped to improve soil fertility and their tops were valuable stock feed.[79]

The region's economic lynchpin, however, remained gold mining. The Homestake Mine in Lead was not just the largest gold mine in the Hills, it was the largest in the Western hemisphere and was responsible for 85% of total U.S. gold production. It relied on paternalism and innovative incentive structures to keep its workforce productive and on the job. The only major disruptions to production occurred during the lockout of 1909-10, World War I, and World War II. Lead was not a company town; Homestake operated a company store but it always faced competition. Moreover, the company paid its employees cash, not scrip, and did not coerce workers into using its store.[80]

Homestake could afford to be magnanimous because it extracted between $3 and $10 of gold per ton of ore it processed. The management was astute, purchasing nearby rivals and investing in machinery and the cyanide process on a large scale. (The cyanide plant at Pluma was small at first, but by 1900 could process 1.2 tons per day.) By 1902-3, the company had pulled $5 million of gold out of the earth and paid stockholder dividends totaling $819,000. Instead of issuing annual reports, it paid stockholders 40 cents per share ($1.50 par value) *every month*. It employed very few managers; two men supervised 600 miners. Its biggest cost was transportation; to deter theft, it shipped gold in 100 lb. ingots that were difficult to transport on horseback.[81]

Homestake also got lucky as nearby rivals were forced to close down for various reasons. The Uncle Sam Mine, for example, was shuttered in 1889 due to excess water. Ten years later, the Clover Leaf took over but it too was abandoned at 300 feet depth, again due to water. Most prospect pits turned up nothing and of those that did only a handful produced significant quantities. By the turn of the century, most had been shuttered and the rest were gone by the end of World War II. Most therefore did not reap the windfall bestowed by the devaluation of the dollar to $35 per ounce during the Depression. The few that remained were fatally wounded when the federal government closed the mines so it could turn the industry's men and machines directly to the country's military effort. A few surface heap-leach operations, like Wharf Resources, Golden Reward, and Brohm Mining, were in operation by the end of the twentieth century but their output paled in comparison to that of Homestake. By 2005, however, production at Homestake and Golden Reward was almost nil and Wharf Resources became the state's largest producer, with output of some 62,000 ounces. In 1996, sincosite (a rare vanadium phosphate), minyulite (a rare secondary phosphate mineral), and hessite (a rare silver-telluride), were found in the Golden Reward's Ross Hannibal Mine south of Lead. The sincosite was perhaps the best discovered to that time.[82]

From its earliest days, the Black Hills was also a tourist attraction. The curing waters of Hot Springs were known to the Indians and highly esteemed. In 1885, a company was formed to acquire the establishment already operating there. Soon, Hot Springs enjoyed hotel accommodations superior to those anywhere else in the state, so in addition to those seeking its curing waters, it attracted a big share of the people who came to take advantage of the state's liberal divorce laws. Out-of-staters could stay just six weeks to obtain a divorce. Sioux Falls was also noted for its so-called divorce colony, which generated considerable business for lawyers, hotels, newspapers, cafés, and other businesses. Bishop William Hobart Hare, an opponent of what he called "consecutive polygamy," finally managed to toughen the state's divorce laws in 1907-8.[83]

The region near the Black Hills also continued to produce green gold: the grasses that fed the livestock that clothed and fed large numbers of Americans (and eventually foreigners as well). Young men like Bruce Siberts bought a few dozen head, staked out on the grasslands, and made a go of it. Siberts settled in almost pristine country on Plum Creek in 1890 but by 1891 he was surrounded by neighbors "with all kinds of livestock," including dairy cows, Minnesota doggies, Texas longhorns, Nebraska shorthorns, scrub stock, "and other stuff."[84] After rustlers stole his cattle, Siberts rounded up unbranded horses in the Badlands to recoup his losses. Wild horses were common even east of the Big Mo as late as 1910; west of the river they were routinely rounded up and tamed for sale, along with wild or at least unbranded cattle. Bankrolled by his father, Siberts struggled through the tough times but most people suffered tremendous hardships until they died or gave up and moved on. Siberts eventually repaid his father the $2,400 he had borrowed and had a little money and property left over, but he was hardly wealthy. He still had some cattle on the open range but he did not know exactly where they were.[85] "I had put in three years at it," he later recalled, "and wasn't much more than even with the world."[86] National financial woes in 1893-94 made money scarce and depressed cattle prices, which hurt everybody in the region. Siberts eventually made good money by arbitraging horses and cattle, buying horses in Pierre where they were relatively cheap, then selling them for more further west. He would then buy cattle in the west where they were also relatively cheap and sell them in Pierre for a profit.[87]

In the winter of 1895-96, many ranchers were wiped out because there was more snow than usual with none of the usual warming chinooks to melt it off. One man lost 2,200 of his 2,300 head cattle herd after he ran out of winter feed. Horses, by contrast, would hoof through the snow to find feed, if necessary. Another big blizzard in May 1905 caused many ranchers to go under, much to the chagrin of their English bankers. In both years, Texas cattle were said to have suffered the brunt of the losses. By contrast, wars – the Spanish American War of 1898, the Boer War, and World War I – helped by spurring demand for both horses and cattle.[88]

By 1900, western South Dakota was filled up with cattle, horses, and sheep. Smaller ranches ran 50-100 cattle or 300-1,000 sheep and the big ones ran as many as 5,000. Everybody lived in primitive houses surrounded by a garden, a holding pasture, and hay. After a decade of hard work and luck, most of it bad, Siberts found himself in the middle, neither rich nor poor. He owned "a wagon, mower, rake, a twenty-by-twenty log house with a floor, and ... 150 horses." But he also owed a bank in Pierre $1,000 and many of his horses were too young to be marketable for another few years.[89]

The homesteading movement into western South Dakota hurt small ranchers like Siberts by denying him free and ample access to open range. But it also hurt the big ranching companies, including Oelrichs' Company, which was headed first by Harry Oelrich and then his brother Herman. In addition to running cattle, the Oelrichs established a race track and polo grounds and invited both whites and Indians to watch and wager. Harry later took the reigns of the Anglo-American Cattle Company, which was financed by James Gorden Bennett, owner of the *New York Herald*, and English capitalist J. J. Cairnes. In 1882, Anglo-American bought the TOT Ranch and its 7,000 head of cattle near Edgemont. Later that summer, it added the Bar T Ranch and its 20,000 cattle and 200 horses. Then it acquired the TAN Ranch and thereby became the largest owner of cattle in western Dakota. Not yet content, in 1888 Oelrich completed his own modern packing plant near his feeding pens. The company also constructed ice houses and dammed Horsehead Creek to ensure enough water to fill them. Best of all, the entire complex abutted a rail line. The Oelrich empire fell, however, when homesteaders came in and fenced up the open range.[90]

Other big outfits were also hurt by the homesteading movement. By 1885, Keystone Land and Cattle Company, which ran Z Bell Ranch, owned some 10,000 cattle and 500 horses. It was hurt when homesteaders claimed the best water resources in the area, forcing Z Bell's cattle to range so far in search of the essential stuff that they lost weight and hence market value. Most of the remaining big cattle outfits folded or fled after the horrible winter of 1911-12. Many smaller ranches, however, remained and many farmers kept cows for food and milk. It was said in the 1920s that all the cows in South Dakota, if placed end to end, would reach the moon and leave one to jump over it.[91]

In the early years, hard-pressed ranchers often stole from each other. According to one contemporary, "most people never bothered to eat their own beef. ... it was proper for the little men to eat beef that carried a big outfit's brand."[92] The little ranchers considered it just compensation because the big ranchers tended to take all the cattle off the range, regardless of brand, during their round ups. The big ranchers justified their clean sweeps by pointing out that legitimate small-time ranchers were often difficult to distinguish from outright rustlers, many of whom owned small herds themselves, as a sort of camouflage, then killed, butchered, and consumed or sold other's beeves. As that brazen crime grew more difficult to perpetrate, rustlers just stole calves and integrated them into their own herds. To explain his herd's surfeit of calves, one rustler alleged that twenty-one of his twenty-nine cows had twins and three had triplets! Other criminals stole milk from cows while pasturing or made off with horses, fence posts, and anything else not nailed down. Rustling still occurs today, but it is not nearly as common as it once was and is almost entirely limited to young, unbranded/untagged calves. A thief caught in Shannon County in the 1960s made news because he loaded his bovine booty into a modified house trailer but also because rustling had by then become so uncommon. Better policing helped as did the activities of the Western South Dakota Stockgrowers Association, which formed in 1892, and the South Dakota Stockgrowers Association.[93]

One might think that in a state that the federal government gave away for next to nothing, land prices would be low and tame. Entrepreneurs, however, managed to whip up speculative frenzies from time to time. Speculation in town lots could become irrationally exuberant, especially when towns vied for railroads, river crossings, and governmental ties. When Huron made a bid to become South Dakota's permanent capital, entrepreneur William T. Love sold lots there contingent on its success. The West Side Addition Company took a different approach, selling lots for $20, with $30 more due if the town became the capital. Most entrepreneurial of all was the Woonsocket Investment Company, which promised 10,000 votes in return for choice city lots. Pierre granted its wish, the company's investors went whole hog for the little town on the Missouri, and it prevailed in the contest. In other places, town-lot speculation revolved around awarding the county seat. Fraud, bribery, and lesser shenanigans helped Miller to edge out nearby St. Lawrence in the election for the seat of Hand County, much to the delight and profit of town founder Henry J. Miller and his family. Towns that lost the battles for political and transportation connections, like Vilas in Miner County, shriveled into irrelevance or disappeared completely.[94]

Agricultural property values were also subject to wide fluctuations. Good weather and good prices for crops put money in farmers' pockets, fueling booms and intense competition for rail access.[95] Bad times, by contrast, sent prices plummeting. About half of the farms west of the river were foreclosed during the 1920s, years before the Depression, because the prices of agricultural goods came off their wartime highs. A mortgaged farm was not generally a financially troubled or impoverished one but rather a thriving one. "A mortgage actually is the means of providing adequate finance," for the purchase of equipment, buildings, seed, and stock, the South Dakota State Planning Board noted, "frequently to the benefit and ultimate profit of the farm owner and operator."[96] The counties with the highest percentage of mortgaged land and the highest level of mortgages per acre, the fertile tracts in the east, far west, and southern parts of the state, also enjoyed the lowest interest rates, presumably because they were on the most productive lands. Mortgages became problematic when incomes and assess values dropped, typically due to macroeconomic fluctuations out of the control of individual agriculturalists. Most farms were well diversified; farmers often raised cows, sows, and chickens in addition to corn, alfalfa, or brome, but when prices fall, except the amount due on the mortgage, the only resort is to give up ownership and become a tenant.[97]

Boosters could also create local or short-lived boomlets. Circa 1910, for example, the Gooder Casey Land Company published an optimistic little pamphlet describing the current state and future growth prospects of southwestern South Dakota, basically from Chamberlain to the Black Hills. Replete with black and white photographs, the pamphlet described the land as "of great and lasting fertility," the wells, a mere ten to thirty feet deep, as "gushing forth," the streams as flowing from "an inexhaustible fountain," and the grasses as "the most nutritious ... in the world." "It absolutely costs nothing to raise stock here if you own your own land," the author announced, because it simply did not snow as much as reported. Moreover, the grasses made great butter that "commands the very highest price" in Boston, New York, and foreign markets. Yields, the pamphlet asserted, were "almost unbelievable." Such claims may have sounded like "fairy stories" but were based, the pamphlet claimed, on "unimpeachable evidence."[98]

Actually, many West River farmers and ranchers hired expensive crews to dig wells down sixty feet and found nothing but earth, sand, and rock and streams often went dry.[99] So water was not available "in an inexhaustible supply ... free of cost." "Heavy horses" worn out from work back East did not actually grow "as strong, healthy and valuable as any animal in your herd or barn" in a week, or ever. "The winters" were generally not as severe as depicted by outsiders but they were not "mild and agreeable" and the climate was not "positively the best of any on the American continent." The clear, dry air did help certain afflictions but simply living in South Dakota did not ensure that "hay fever, Phthisic, Bronchitis and all catarrhal affections" would dissipate "as mist before the morning sun." And, of course, there was no guarantee that "land values will advance so rapidly that it will make you dizzy to follow them."[100] In fact, when periodic droughts struck or markets became glutted, land owners reaped only lower prices, despair, bankruptcy, and out migration.[101]

Somewhat surprising, early South Dakota possessed a sizeable and important corporate sector. Early in the century, the state made a concerted pitch to replace New Jersey as the lead charter-mongering state, or in other words as the state from which large interstate corporations received their charters, a distinction now held by Delaware. South Dakota's government offered quick turnaround, low filing fees, and no taxes, but its regulatory laws and their enforcement were so lax that it soon attracted a reputation for chartering nothing but fly-by-nights, scams, and flimflams. By 1905 or so, no self-respecting corporation that sought significant public investment would consider chartering in the state. Many local businesses, however, incorporated in the state. According to federal corporate tax records, in 1910 2,151 corporations operated in South Dakota. Most were small, even by the standards of the day: three out of four had capitals of $25,000 or less and nine out of ten had capitals of $100,000 or less. Almost one in three were financial institutions, typically small unit (branchless) banks. Others engaged in agriculture, construction, manufacturing, mining and quarrying, telecommunications, trade, transportation, services, and utilities. Half were less than five years old but many had already experienced a decade or more of successful operation. Corporations, especially small banks and retailers and agricultural service providers like creameries and grain elevators, could be found throughout the state, but of course urban centers like Aberdeen and Sioux Falls attracted additional companies. The largest corporations were typically mines located in the Black Hills but several large railway, manufacturing, and utility companies also called the state home.[102]

One emerging sector where incorporation was important, but not mandatory, was telephony. Although as late as 1954 two out of every five farmhouses still did not have a telephone, early adoption rates were high because telephony helped to reduce the tyranny of the state's vast distances and the loneliness experienced by many prairie agriculturists. It also allowed farmers and ranchers to save time if they needed to discover prices or contact a vet or doctor. Numerous modest companies like Hyde County Telephone therefore sprang up and many (203 in operation in 1910) sought the legal protections and privileges that incorporation provided.[103]

The largest companies, like Dakota Central Telephone Lines, which in 1904 was "the largest business proposition in South Dakota, organized exclusively by South Dakota men and conducted with South Dakota capital"[104] were almost invariably incorporated. That company's lead entrepreneur was J. L. W. Zietlow. Despite having only one hand, Zietlow was mechanically gifted enough to build telephony equipment outside the scope of the Bell patent. By 1886-87, exchanges at Aberdeen and Columbia were already operational. The company struggled at first but its stability proved legendary as its networks remained operational even when the railroads stopped during bad weather. Due to the reliability and relatively low cost of its services, the company grew like gangbusters in 1898 and by 1904 it had 3,000 lines and hundreds of employees.[105]

Telephoning a neighbor instead of hopping on a horse, hitching up a wagon, or cranking up an automobile was so convenient that many tiny, unincorporated telephone networks also sprang up across the prairies. In 1908, for example, a preacher near Philip named Davis thought to link settlers with a barbed wire telephone line. At first the system was just a buzzer between two houses but soon farms across the whole area could communicate over real telephones. The settlers themselves set it up and maintained it and others emulated them. The quality could be good, too, as shown by the makeshift telephone company near Presho, which provided subscribers with service that allegedly "was more satisfactory in the early 1900s than" in 1955![106]

Homesteaders near Pukwana also laid their own system, bought their own phones and switches, and eventually connected to the main telephone system in Pukwana, at which point they incorporated as a mutual corporation styled the East Vega Telephone Company. The cost of the system easily repaid itself when they realized they could use the system to save money on farm equipment by using the telephone to coordinate equipment use quickly with others, rather than everyone buying the same equipment and leaving it to sit idle most of the time.[107]

Electricity provision was another area explored by early entrepreneurs. In Kadoka in 1920, for example, R. N. Rounds established a small grid powered by a generator, a battery, and a kerosene or gasoline engine. His enterprise failed in 1923 when his equipment wore out and he had not made enough profit to replace it. He started again but was permanently forced out of business when a fire destroyed his next set of inadequately insured equipment. Matters improved for Kadoka residents when Central West Public Service ran a line from a big plant in Philip circa 1930. Water was also privately provided at first. In the 1920s, for example, N. P. Nielsen supplied Kadokans with water from his own well for $.25 a barrel or fifteen barrels for $2.50. The town built a municipal water system in 1922-23 but Nielson's water was still needed as the town's system froze up in January 1924 and its well ran dry in the summer of 1925.[108]

Another early twentieth-century marvel, airplanes, came early to South Dakota, which also enjoyed a long history of ballooning. As early as 1882, daring "aeronauts" dazzled South Dakotan crowds at Independence Day celebrations, county fairs, and what not. Sioux Falls, the *Argus Leader* boasted in 1898, had attracted "some of the best balloonists of the world."[109] Many were itinerant performers from other states but Warren Albert Ward moved to Dakota Territory and set up a store in 1888 before making his first parachute jump near Kimball. Finding the endeavor more exciting and lucrative than tending his store, he began touring the state as well as Iowa and Minnesota. He died in a balloon mishap near Monroe in 1906. A number of early balloonist daredevils were women, including Hazel Keyes, who logged over 200 flights.[110]

In April 1897, Henry Heintz (1848-1918), the postmaster of Elkton, received a patent for an airship, a semi-rigid balloon powered with an engine, an early dirigible. It took him and Aurora blacksmith Frank Wulf three years to develop a prototype, which promptly crashed after leaping just eight feet off the ground. A native of Luxembourg, Heintz formed the Northwestern Aerial Navigation Company in early 1902 to build and operate airships. The company was apparently a vehicle for a bid at a prize at the Louisiana Purchase Exposition to be held in St. Louis in 1904, but Heintz and his machine never appeared.[111]

After it became clear that heavier-than-air flight was possible, airplanes came to be preferred for most activities. Ballooning remained high sport, however, and also high science. In 1908, sport balloonists from Quincy, Illinois, made national news when they got caught in a storm and ended up landing over 800 miles away, in Clear Lake, 30 miles southeast of Watertown. Later, South Dakota became something of a leader in balloon flight, a story picked up in the next chapter.[112]

The first airplane demonstration flight in the state occurred in April 1911 in Rapid City and was an act of entrepreneurship according to the local paper: "This event was of some importance. Rapid City had demonstrated that she had the enterprise to secure the first attraction of this kind ever offered in the state." The event was successful enough to induce the State Fair Board to hire the Curtiss Exhibition Company to fly "every day of the fair, morning and afternoon" during the annual September state fair in Huron, which continues to this day, though air shows have shifted to Sioux Falls. It drew huge crowds, for South Dakota that is, and enthusiastic ones. More shows soon followed, including ones in Deadwood and Yankton, and the State Fair in 1912 enjoyed record attendance. South Dakota also attracted a large number of daredevils or stunt fliers who believed that the state's air quality and climate were ideal for sensational flying.[113]

A few South Dakotans dabbled with airplanes before World War I but the war greatly added to the stock of experienced fly boys in the state. Many, equipped with inexpensive military surplus planes, became barnstormers or gypsy fliers who went, in the words of an historian of South Dakota's early aviation industry, "any place where an airplane might offer an opportunity for profit." That included providing exhibitions, rides, stunts, mock "dog fights," races, air advertising, and parachuting. Aspiring aerial entrepreneurs took off from cow pastures and cut hayfields and gradually flew farther and faster than ever before. The first nonstop flight between Minneapolis and Sioux Falls, for example, took place in July 1919. By 1920, charter flights were available at $1 per mile, twenty-five-mile minimum, out of Baird Field in Aberdeen.[114]

In 1919, Merle Hagen and Charles Ward formed the Huron Aerial Rapid Transit Company. In 1921, their company carried 500 passengers a total of 20,000 miles throughout the Dakotas, Nebraska, and Minnesota. It and others failed when pilots crashed their planes, sometimes killing both pilot and passengers, which typically numbered only one or two. Similar companies for passengers and/or freight popped up in Pierre, Volga (which boasted one of the first class "A" landing fields in the state and attracted 800 charter flights in 1921 alone), Mobridge, Ipswich, Aberdeen, and Ferney. By 1926-27, the largest companies were carrying 2,000 passengers some 40,000 miles for an average of $.25 per mile. Several companies with no fixed home base, like those of E. C. Curren of Spearfish and C. M. Larson of Dell Rapids, offered flying taxicab-like services.[115]

By 1926, South Dakota had its own airline, Rapid Air Lines, Inc. of Rapid City. Incorporated in January 1927 with a capital of $25,000, it bought a new plane for $2,500 and built the first permanent airport in Rapid City. During the March flood it ferried doctors, food, and other aid to isolated farms. It grew rapidly, increased its fleet to eight planes, and carried 65,000 passengers over 200,000 combined miles, some of them in winter with the help of ski landing gear. Profits hit 100%. Eager to open new markets, it offered aerial coyote hunting until it was outlawed. In April 1928, it bought a Ford Tri-motor for $45,000 and christened it the Wamblee Ohanka (Swift Eagle). The big bird, it was said, could carry 15 Americans or 25 Mexicans. The company's 1928 annual report revealed that it employed 12 pilots, 11 mechanics, and 20 other personnel, and suffered no crashes. One of its pilots in 1929 was S. Russell Halley, a World War I air combat veteran who a decade later would own his own airport on the outskirts of Rapid City and four planes for pilot training, sky cruises, and airport taxi service. Rapid Air moved to Omaha in 1930 to attract more passengers and to obtain an airmail contract. (No air mail routes were authorized in South Dakota until 1932.)[116]

Another early South Dakota airline was run by Clyde Ice, who piloted the carrier's only plane, a Ford Tri-Motor. Ice had been born in Miller in 1889 and got interested in aviation after attending one of the early exhibitions, first helping a pilot with his plane near Forestburg, then riding as a passenger. Soon after, he worked as a ticket seller for South Dakota barnstormer Earl T. Vance. After learning to fly by thrilling kids in the Miller area, Ice moved to Rapid City and took aerial photographs of scenic places in the Black Hills while ferrying people around the region.[117]

An aircraft assembly plant and flight school in Sioux Falls was in operation by late 1919 but it moved to Wagner in 1920 because the latter had better facilities, including a hangar. Mundale-Tennant Company, out of Sioux Falls, bought a seaplane to entertain people at the lake resorts in the eastern part of South Dakota. Its first show was at Lake Madison July 3 and 4, 1923, in which an estimated 12,000 people witnessed barnstorming staples as well as airplane water skiing. The company also sold flight instruction and dropped aerial fireworks day or night. The company wrecked the seaplane on Lake Poinsett the following year, repaired it, then sold it to another group of South Dakotans who managed to destroy the expensive craft and take the life of a student pilot. Later, Tennant formed Dakota Airlines, which added airplane sales to its litany of businesses, which included charter flights and flight instruction. A more exploitative entrepreneur, E. D. Billiter of Dell Rapids, took people up and engaged in aerobatics until they screamed to be returned to the ground for a fee.[118]

The aviation industry in South Dakota received a boost in August 1927 thanks to a visit by Charles Lindbergh. That very year, South Dakota's first female pilot, Nellie Zabel Willhite, began training in earnest. She earned her diploma from Dakota Airlines in January 1928 and five months later, after her father bought her a plane, she began making a living as a barnstormer. A member of the 99 Club, one of the first 99 women in America to become a licensed pilot, she, like other early pilots, had some harrowing experiences, including "having been shooshed up over a mile into the sky in a tornadic cloud and battling to get down, being caught in hail storms, over country I could not safely land while ice formed three-quarters inch thick on struts and leading edges of wings." But what ended Willhite's flying career was economics: "flying was a pretty expensive game" so the "depression years hit" her "and plenty hard, as they did many other pilots in this section." So she sold her airplane and worked at Renner Field as a "go-fer." She continued flying when she could, but her pilot log indicates that she had only logged 600 hours by 1934 and 700 by the summer of 1938. Her last recorded flight, in 1946, left her just shy of the 800-hour mark. As World War II geared up, Willhite argued that women could free up male pilots for combat by flying transport missions. Her application for the British Air Transport Auxiliary in early 1942 was rejected, however, due to her subpar eyesight, long-time deafness (since a bout with the measles at age two), and lack of flight hours.[119]

By 1930, South Dakota had seventeen official airports but only the one in Watertown was lit for night operations. During the Depression, one could learn to fly by taking lessons at the local airport for $64. Pilots also made money photographing farms under wheat and corn acreage allotment programs. In 1936, with Hanford Airlines of Sioux City, one could leave Omaha at 7:30 a.m. in a Ford Trimotor and arrive in Sioux Falls at 9:12, then transfer to a smaller plane and be in Huron at 10:20, or Aberdeen at 11:05, or Bismarck, North Dakota fifteen minutes past noon. But Hanford dropped Sioux Falls in 1937 because its airport was insufficient for the new, faster twin engine planes adopted by the company (which was later called Mid-Continent Airlines to reflect its growing reach). It therefore switched to the modern facilities available in Huron. Such rebuffs eventually prompted purchase and, with federal aid, development of the current airport site on North Minnesota Avenue in Sioux Falls. Passenger traffic out of Joe Foss Field, as the new airport was called, increased from 6,720 to 37,657 in 1958 to about 130,000 in 1967

Located in Renner, this airport was one of several operating in South Dakota in the early days of flying. *Courtesy Center for Western Studies.*

as the number of daily scheduled flights increased from eight to thirty-six by 1970.[120]

The Great Depression hit the Great Plains harder than it did most other parts of the country, which experienced some relief beginning with the monetary reforms implemented in early 1933. That is because the economic calamity coincided with an environmental one, the prolonged drought called the Dust Bowl. Between 1929 and 1939, all or much of the state suffered from below-average precipitation in every year except one.[121] Dust storms blinded the entire state at times, but West River was particularly devastated by the "black blizzards" of the 1930s,[122] dust storms that wags claimed were so severe they "blew away all but the mortgage."[123] Conditions were so bad at times water had to be hauled in by train. Drought affected the entire state, though conditions were somewhat better in its far eastern and far western regions. Some areas relatively unaffected by droughts, however, were wiped clean by grasshopper infestations that stripped entire fields, then tree bark, killing most of the trees, and even clothes on the line and paint off houses. The bug hordes also ate thistles, the traditional emergency food for cattle, rendering affected herds thin and gaunt.[124] Lorena Hickok, a former South Dakota resident and friend of Eleanor Roosevelt,[125] told New Deal administrator Harry Hopkins that in the "real grasshopper area ... miles and miles of fields ... look as though they had just been plowed ... the grasshoppers simply clear them off, right down to the earth, even eating the roots. ... I was in farmyards today that looked as though there'd never been even a spear of prairie grass there."[126]

Just as crop and livestock yields sank throughout most of the state due to the drought, so too did agricultural prices. (George McGovern described how a neighbor cried after he had to sell his pigs for less than the cost of transporting them to the auction during the Depression.) Farm incomes (units produced times price per unit) plummeted along with land prices (which are a function of interest rates, which were low, but also expected future income), which sank back to 1910 levels. Land that sold for $66 an acre in 1920 was worth only $17 in 1940, a 75% decrease. The average value of unmortgaged farms dropped from $11,034 to $4,920 between 1930 and 1935 alone. The percent of farms that were mortgaged dropped during the Depression, from 55% in 1930 to 45% in 1935, and average farm debt dropped from $6,069 to $5,623 over the same period. The average interest rate also dropped, from 7.1% in 1921 to 4.8% in 1935.[127]

Farmers who borrowed heavily in the 1920s, however, were doomed as prices for commodities and land plummeted in the early 1930s. Many farmers and ranchers could no longer make loan repayments so banks folded, foreclosures soared, and taxes fell into arrears. Most lenders would not and could not refinance balloon payments when they fell due because farmers and ranchers owed more than their parched land was now worth; others sought exorbitant fees and interest rates to compensate them for the extra risk.[128] Farmer equity dropped, according to the state planning board, "to a point where his title to the property is little more than a technical classification."[129] Marginal farmers and those who began the Depression heavily leveraged could not escape. For those reasons, South Dakota led the nation in distress transfers, foreclosures, and assignments to avoid foreclosure. Throughout the state, farmers tried to stop foreclosure sales altogether or worked to ensure that lenders received only pennies on the dollar.[130] Due to the foreclosures, what contemporaries thought was an "alarming increase" in corporate land ownership in South Dakota took place.[131] Where conditions were worst, west of the big river, the Depression did not hit its nadir until 1936 and the region did not fully recover until 1942, when rain and jobs finally appeared aplenty.[132]

In the meantime, South Dakotans got along the best they could, even if that meant partaking of government cheese in the form of the CCC (Civilian Conservation Corps) and the WPA (Works Progress Administration), which spent about $35 million in South Dakota between 1935 and 1938 building dams, swimming pools, and so forth. As many as two in five South Dakotans went on relief, the highest percentage in the nation, despite various price support programs, like the 1935 federal purchase of cattle "regardless of kind and weight for $26.00 each" and the sundry price supports provided under the Agricultural Adjustment Act.[133]

Such purchases were part of the government's rural rehabilitation program, which aimed to keep farmers from entering urban labor markets or soup lines. Other rehabilitation efforts provided farmers with loans of two to three years duration at 5% interest to finance seed and machinery. Rural rehabilitation alleviated conditions for marginal farmers at first but eventually it was withdrawn under pressure from bigger, successful farmers. All else equal, bigger farms did better than smaller ones because they could afford to mechanize and also suffered less waste acreage (e.g., roads, buildings) as a percentage of the total operation. Nationwide, rehabilitation did not keep farm employment up. Between 1929 and 1945, the number of farmers fell from 30.5 million to 24.4 million, or in other words from 25% to 18% of the overall population.[134]

Not surprising, West River South Dakota's rural population plummeted during the Depression as "quitters" tired of "bad luck, bad weather, bad coyotes"[135] left the state in droves, most by rail or auto but some by suicide. "Stickers" resented those who left because every defection made it that much more difficult for those who remained to make a go of it. Those who stayed were the toughest of the tough and also the most innovative. Many agriculturalists took the opportunity to acquire more land and scale up their operations. In 1920, there were approximately 18,000 farms and ranches in the west country, and average size was 806 acres. By 1940, the number of units had dropped to about 15,400 but their average size had jumped to 1,174 acres. (In 1992, only 8,000 units were still in operation but they averaged 3,000 acres apiece.)[136]

Urban businesses also used the depressed conditions to drive smaller competitors out of business. In Presho, for example, many businesses survived the Depression and a few new ones even opened, mostly at the expense of smaller, more marginal places nearby. Although not the county seat, Presho was located along U.S. Highway 16, so it got the Black Hills traffic and hence infusions of cash from tourists patronizing its gas stations, cabin camps, hotels, eateries, and service garages. The smallest towns tended to have the smallest businesses and hence were the most heavily hit. It was said that storekeepers who were also postmasters survived by monitoring the mail for customers receiving past due bill notices and cutting off their credit before it was too late.[137]

"People would take any job, no matter what, just to work and provide for their families," one survivor later recalled.[138] But there were not enough jobs for everyone. Many of those who managed to stick through it did so because their grandmother, mother, wife, sister, daughter, or other strong woman in their life dug deep and made the ends meet, as they used to say, through gardening, canning, patching, and other forms of temporizing: substituting cheaper entertainments such as reading (which was subsidized by the South Dakota Free Library Commission and often depicted strong protagonists persevering on the rugged frontier), playing horseshoes, or train watching instead of going to picture shows, buying used stuff instead of new, and bartering (e.g., meat for tractor repairs or wood for truck parts) instead of extending credit to those without ready cash. One farm wife in Potter County, for example, got her family through 1931 and 1932 by raising tomatoes that never ripened. She pickled and stored them until even all her milk bottles were full. Nobody in the family complained because six of their immediate neighbors ended up with nothing and had to subsist on the dole or pack up and head to the west coast. Another family, in Day County, ensured a crop by planting two gardens, an upland and a lowland one, planted both early and late crops, and paid careful attention to protect them from the weather and marauding critters. Many of South Dakota's women carefully canned what they were able to raise so that little would be lost to spoilage. They also increased their chicken and turkey flocks because they were tasty, could be sold or bartered for other goods, and were voracious consumers of those nettlesome grasshoppers.[139]

Social mores also adapted to the unprecedented hard times. It became perfectly acceptable to wear old, unfashionable clothes with patches, just so long as you remained "neat and clean" in appearance.[140] Most Dakotans maintained "an air of cheerfulness" through it all;[141] stories of impending revolt were untrue, the imaginings of eastern authors looking for a story, because the government's complicity in the economic side of the Depression was not yet clear.[142] At the time, South Dakotans thought God and Wall Street were to blame for the fiasco and there was no rebelling against either. Besides, most South Dakotans believed that better times were right around the corner—and those of Euroamerican ancestry were right.

Chapter 4
Governance and Growth in the Land of Infinite Variety, 1946-2015

On the last grass frontier of the cattle industry will be found the last champions of the time-tested free enterprise system and the strongest defenders of the American way of life.[1]

In the Sioux language, Dakota means an alliance or a league of friends. The state is aptly, if ironically, named. Native Americans are largely excluded from the friendly alliance, which is strongly geared toward conservative and libertarian values, pragmatism, and democracy. Though imperfect, the state government is highly democratic and has been since its inception. In 1898, South Dakota became the first state to put initiative and referendum into its constitution. Initiative gave voters the right to formulate a public policy and put it to a popular vote. Referendum gave voters the right to veto existing legislation. Although initiative was not much used in the first half-century of its existence, with only one of sixteen proposed measures being adopted, its mere existence helped South Dakotans to believe that their state government was one of, for, and by the people and that something akin to democracy was not going to perish from their state regardless of its condition elsewhere in the world. After that, usage increased and 45% of the next eighty initiated measures were approved. The state later added recall, which allowed voters to cashier elected officials, and, in 1907, direct primary, which decreased the power of political parties. In addition, female South Dakotans received the right to vote before passage of the Nineteenth Amendment.[2]

Many observers have been perplexed by South Dakota's politics and ultimately found it a jumble of "contradictory strains of self-reliance and populism."[3] In fact, the state's politics are relatively straightforward, though somewhat unique. South Dakotans of Euroamerican descent strongly believe that South Dakota's government, and South Dakota's representatives in Washington, ought to do what is best for South Dakota. Within the state, that means moderation—fiscal conservatism and efficient government, even in bureaucracies like public higher education. Within the federal system, by contrast, that means getting as many resources for South Dakota as possible. So South Dakotans send Republicans to Pierre and the White House but often send Democrats, like Tom Daschle and Tim Johnson, to Congress, where they have done a good job bringing home the bacon: dam projects, military bases, and farm subsidies have kept the state out of debt and able to pay its modest bills with relatively low levels of taxation.[4]

The state's stunningly beautiful and diverse landscape recommends the nickname "the land of infinite variety," but the state's politics would be better described as the "land of general consensus."[5] In fact, between 1889 and 1967, Republicans won 90% of all elections.[6] But "for all its conservatism," author John Gunther argued in 1947, "South Dakota is not machine run" and lobbyists were obliged to register, pay a tax, and wear name badges.[7] According to Gunther, "a favorite political maneuver is to embarrass your opponent by alleging that he does belong to a machine."[8] With the possible exception of *fin de siècle* Sioux Falls, actual corruption was minimal,[9] as two careful observers of the state's political history noted, "as a result of the small, interconnected community that exists."[10] "People like to live here because you can get things done. You pick up the phone and call someone, and it's done. You don't have to have a lot of connections," Nancy Brady of the Rapid City Hospitality Committee explained to an out-of-stater in 1986.[11]

South Dakota has had its share, and maybe more than its share, of cranks, gadflies, mavericks, and so forth but that is simply a function of its tradition of freedom of expression.[12] "It is never verboten for any South Dakotan," poet Badger Clark once asserted, "to laugh and talk as freely as he votes."[13] But allowing people to speak and respecting their views do not necessarily coincide. South Dakotans typically let people with divergent views say their piece, then promptly ignore them. According to Peder Ecker, former South Dakota Democratic party chairman, Democrats in South Dakota long experienced the same cold shoulder treatment: "people didn't regard you as a social menace or anything; they just found it hard to take you seriously."[14]

That situation changed somewhat when drought and depression caused widespread pain, and such radical groups as the Farm Holiday Association, United Farmers League, and Nonpartisan League made inroads and started to win concessions from progressive Republicans. But not until George McGovern, who hailed from a small town about fify miles almost due south of Mitchell called Avon, built up the Democratic party organization in the state in the 1960s and 1970s did Democrats provide a political check against quasi-monopoly Republican rule and break the cycle of people voting Republican because everyone else did, and always had. McGovern (1972) and another native South Dakotan (who later moved to Minnesota), Hubert Humphrey (1968), ran for president on the Democratic ticket back to back, suggesting that Nietzsche may have been right about that which does not kill you making you stronger.[15] Both men's politics had been deeply influenced by the Depression. "I learnt more about politics during one South Dakota dust storm," Humphrey admitted (ironically, given that the University of Minnesota's school of public policy bears his name), "than in seven years at the university."[16] McGovern believed he learned during the Depression that government could be helpful.[17]

Most South Dakotans, however, did not come away from the Depression with the same conclusion since they continued to distrust government pretty much as a direct function of its distance from their homes. In South Dakota, the best solutions are private and the second best are local. So they will not consolidate counties or school districts, at least not without a brawl.[18] Their preference for the local is evident everywhere in the state's political geography and history. In the 1930s, for example, Hamlin County was home to just 7,720 people living on 1,175 farms and in 8 small incorporated towns, but it had 7 high schools, 56 rural grade schools, and 11 parent teacher associations with "a fair record."[19]

South Dakotans also distrust strangers as a direct function of the relative population densities of the places from which both parties hail. As a result, people from Sioux Falls and Rapid City distrust people from Denver and the Twin Cities as much as people from Mobridge and Kadoka distrust people from Sioux Falls and Rapid City. It is no coincidence that the state capital, Pierre, is in the middle of the state, hours from any major population center.[20]

To say that there has been a general political consensus in South Dakota is not to deny that political sentiments have varied somewhat over time and place. Generally speaking, West River has been more conservative than East River.[21] It is more Posse Comitatus and John Birch Society territory. Shiloh Fairchild, for example, moved West River, though ill-suited to the lifestyle, because "he heartily damned the people who wore white collars and worked for the government."[22] In the Black Hills, people created their own governments out of nothing and they have yet to forget it. East River is more liberal and hence more likely to embrace government programs but generally is not enamored of them.[23] "If we wish to lead," one East River college professor wrote in the mid-1950s, "we must stress the development of people to the end that they, through their own initiative, may effectively identify and solve the various problems directly affecting their welfare."[24] East River is a middle ground, not entirely like the Wild West, but not as rich as the farm country of the rest of the Midwest. A strong desire for farm aid from the federal government, plus a healthy dose of Catholics, immigrants, and voting Indians, not to mention a cluster of union workers in Sioux Falls (home to three out of every five unionized workers in the state), mute its more conservative and libertarian urges. Nevertheless, East River South Dakotans are essentially Midwesterners, proud of their democratic institutions, literacy, schools, colleges, and churches. Their political beliefs differ from those in the South, the Southwest, the old Northeast, and the west coast. Their civic pride is reminiscent of classical republicanism: leaders are supposed to govern wisely on behalf of the commonweal and not in narrow or self-interested ways, a message consciously inculcated in students. With British political philosopher John Locke, they believe that government officials are their agents, or in other words their employees, and not their masters. With Thomas Jefferson, they see farmers as the consummate independent citizenry and agriculture as the most civically virtuous of all vocations. To be employed by another entails dependence, and that is no good.[25] As the Murdo *Coyote* noted in 1907, an entrepreneurial pioneer, even if young, will "within a few years ... find that he has a place in the community and has a recognized individuality which the factory hand or the small clerk can never know."[26]

South Dakota has a strong libertarian streak because it was founded by people seeking to maximize their freedom as well as the weight of their wallets. As erstwhile Chicago stenographer turned homesteader Ada Blayney Clark put it, "This opportunity of doing exactly as I pleased constituted for me one of the chief charms of the prairie."[27] Or as a booster put it in 1889, good, free land was an inducement to move to South Dakota but so too was its "favorable government."[28] After both world wars and the global depression of the 1930s expanded the federal government to unprecedented girth, people continued to trickle into South Dakota in search of cleaner air, better opportunities, and more freedom.[29]

The long-standing libertarian-conservative consensus, however, does not mean that politics in the state has always been uncompetitive. Early territorial politics were based on shifting personal alliances, not parties. South Dakota was Republican at statehood but in the 1890s a profusion of independents, Populists, and "fusion" candidates (Populist-Democrat) achieved considerable success at the polls. The state went Republican again after 1900, but the progressive wing of Coe Crawford and Peter Norbeck defeated the conservative one on numerous occasions, as in the 1912 presidential election when the state chose progressive Republican/"Bull Moose" Theodore Roosevelt over the regular Republican candidate William Howard Taft. When the Republican Party dominated state elections, competition within the party intensified, as with the recent split between the Tea Party and the old line. Interestingly, around the turn of the new millennium, less than half of the state's voters were Republican (48%) because 13% were independents or libertarians, voters who responded to the quality of a candidate and his or her policies rather than party affiliation. Except for a brief period in the early twentieth century and then again recently, party organization in the state has been relatively weak. Yet the state's voter participation rates in general elections are among the highest in the nation.[30]

The state government is *de minimis* and turnover rates are high so no powerful bureaucrats dwell in Pierre. There is little evidence in Pierre of an "iron triangle" among executive agency heads, legislative committee chairs, and private interest groups like that in Washington. The legislature is part-time, its sessions limited in length by the state constitution, and its committees are relatively weak. With a few exceptions, like Karl Mundt, Peter Norbeck, Francis Case, and Tom Daschle, the careers of most South Dakota politicians are short. Initially, governors served two-year terms and in the 1940s they were further restricted to two consecutive terms. Since 1972, governors can serve two consecutive four-year terms and can return to the governorship thereafter, as Bill Janklow did (1979-1987; 1995-2003). A vehicular manslaughter conviction and short jail term effectively ended Janklow's political career, but most important South Dakota politicians end their careers in electoral defeat. In short, as a political commentator put it in 1967, "a high degree of popular control over government officials exists in South Dakota."[31]

South Dakotans of Euroamerican origin always enjoyed a tremendous amount of economic freedom because few voters supported tough regulations and many of those laws that were passed were not, or could not be, regularly enforced. For example, when the owner of a bar in Vega, near Kimball, was asked for his liquor license, he pointed to the 30-30 rifle on the wall behind him, then to the questioner, and finally to the road out of town. Message received.[32]

By contrast, even after World War II, Native Americans continued to suffer under the virtual *dictatorship* of the Bureau of Indians Affairs (BIA). As one South Dakota BIA agent put it: "There was probably no more autocratic position under the United States government than that of an Indian agent at a remote agency."[33] U.S. Senator for South Dakota James Abourezk was right when he wrote in his memoirs that the principal enemies of the Lakota were the "federal government, which mistreats them and mismanages their resources" and anti-Indian attitudes on the part of some Euroamericans.[34] A dearth of education, work experience, and access to formal credit – all rooted in racism and government paternalism – prevented Amerindian entrepreneurs from expanding their businesses or innovating in major ways.

The Sioux understood this perfectly as shown in a missive issued by delegates to the United Sioux Tribes Conference held in Pierre in

February 1965. "In the past," they noted, "various programs have been forced on the Indian either by the Federal Government through the BIA, Congress or through the state governments without consulting the Indian people." The tribal representatives, J. Dan Howard, Frank Ducheneaux, Richard Wakeman, and Maury Baaby (as an alternate for Enos Poorbear), did not condemn all government programs but noted that "too often they have been conceived and executed as a result of political expediency or sometimes in just plain ignorance of the social and economic structure of the Indian Community." They also argued that stereotypes of Indians as lazy and irresponsible were rooted in the lack of opportunities available on Reservations. Before World War I, they noted, "South Dakota Indians were very successful cattlemen but policy changes imposed on them at the time almost completely wiped them out of the cattle business." They also noted that "in order to successfully compete in cattle, as in any other business, adequate financing must be available" but seldom was.[35]

Such treatment provided few educational opportunities for Native Americans, and many of those who were well educated did not return to leadership positions on the reservation. The end result was the worst level of poverty in the United States. Lakota culture is not acquisitive, but it is clear that most Lakota would like to improve their material condition. So they are not impoverished because they want to be, as is sometimes claimed. To this day, the Lakota suffer from a dearth of innovative entrepreneurship because, despite occasional reforms, local, state, and national governments fail to provide sufficient protection of their lives, liberty, and property.[36] "There is no more tragic aspect of South Dakota's life," as one writer put it in the early 1980s.[37]

Individual Indians knew that they did not truly own their land and were proved correct time and again. "The treaty which had determined that this territory should belong to the Indians for all time," one South Dakota BIA agent admitted, "had been broke like many former treaties."[38] In the 1950s, for example, the Pick-Sloan Missouri River dam system expropriated yet more land and cultural heritage from the natives, 550 square miles in North and South Dakota, most in the latter, and caused the displacement of 900 Indian families and the destruction of many acres of fertile, forested bottomland and untold burial and ceremonial grounds. As usual, Native people never consented to any sale and promises for compensation went largely unfulfilled. Natives on other reservations observed this and rightfully wondered why they should obtain an education or a job, much less start a business, when their property could be snatched without due process. By contrast, the Euroamerican residents of Pollock, which was also inundated by the dam system, moved their entire town south several miles. The move was funded from the proceeds of the sale of their original homes to the Army Corps of Engineers, which most believed paid residents a fair price for their properties. Their fears were merited; in 1998-99, the Mitigation Act and Governor Bill Janklow stripped another 200,000 acres from the Great Sioux Nation, and today plans are afoot to displace the residents and Native ranchers of the south unit of Pine Ridge so the area can be turned into a national tribal park and bison reserve.[39]

As a result of various land allotment and inheritance policies, Natives who own land located within reservations typically have difficulty obtaining clear title. Most tracts are so fractionated – owned by so many hundreds or even thousands of people — that they cannot be effectively developed. In addition, the over eleven million acres of Indian lands still owned in trust by the U.S. government are not available to collateralize loans. Such policies cut Native peoples off from a major source of startup capital, keeping them dependent on the government and non-Native businesses for employment.[40]

While the government no longer sent soldiers to shoot them down, it did signal that it placed low value on Indian lives by providing diets and shelter so inadequate that many Natives ended up being afflicted with tuberculosis, pneumonia, alcoholism, and depression, among other ailments. They also signaled the low value they placed on Native's well-being by ignoring domestic abuse as late as the 1970s.[41] "They must have some incentive to effort," a BIA agent realized, but he could not credibly commit to providing enough of it to motivate most Natives, who after World War I resisted the BIA non-violently.[42] They got nowhere, which radicalized a group of young people in the American Indian Movement (AIM). Violence peaked in the mid-1970s with Wounded Knee II in 1973 and the seizure of the pork processing plant in Wagner in 1975. Owned by the Yankton Sioux tribe but run by white managers, the plant had a bad reputation for mistreating its Native American employees. Two attempts to seize it, one by AIM members and a second by intoxicated teenagers, failed to change a status quo in desperate need of reform.[43]

Most Native Americans in this otherwise generally prosperous region live below the poverty line and many struggle simply to subsist. Many forgot, or never learned, how to live off the land. The Lakota people used to get everything from tatanka (bison), Belinda Joe wistfully reminded an audience at Augustana College in December 2012, but now they get it from Walmart, when they can afford to. With few formal job opportunities available, many work seasonal agricultural jobs for low wages and reap occasional windfalls dancing in festivals or appearing in Hollywood movies.[44] So many Lakota have appeared in movies that "it's not uncommon to find that a Sioux of sixty-five or older has appeared briefly in a TV show or film." By the 1970s, eighty-one movies about the

Sioux had been produced. Few Native actors, however, received much credit or praise let alone good money for their efforts.[45] Kevin Costner's 1989 hit *Dances with Wolves* was filmed in South Dakota, much of it in Spearfish Canyon west of Deadwood, and featured actual Lakota. Some Natives also landed jobs posing for advertisements during the Dakota chic phase in the mid-1980s, when Dakota Beer (a wheat beer produced by Miller) and Dodge Dakota pickups were all the rage. The 1992 film *Thunderheart*, starring Val Kilmer and Sam Shepherd, was also shot in South Dakota, on the Pine Ridge Reservation, but did not generate as much work for Native Americans as *Dances* did. Indians also generate income by leasing tribal lands to Euroamerican agriculturalists.[46]

Government policies at all levels create a vicious cycle of low expectations, high unemployment, and low wages that cannot be broken solely by economic forces. According to neoclassical economic models, the high levels of unemployment endemic on most reservations should attract capitalists eager to tap a cheap, easily replaceable workforce. It has not, however, worked out that way. In the postwar period, several businesses tried to establish factories on South Dakota's Indian reservations, most of which, then as now, were among the poorest of the poor. Some of the factories lasted for several years but all eventually failed or moved away, including a meatpacking plant, a bison ranching and slaughtering operation, and factories for making arrows, dolls, electrical circuits, fish hooks, moccasins, and shirts. The state's Employment Security Department, for example, expected big things of the Wright & McGill Fishing Tackle Company, which set up operations on the Pine Ridge Reservation in 1960. Wright & McGill is still around but shuttered its Pine Ridge facilities in 1968. It turns out that businesses do not seek low wages per se; they seek high levels of productivity, of output per dollar paid in compensation. Natives bereft of education and motivation due to government policies did not on average produce enough to justify even their low wages, so manufacturers moved on.[47]

Among the Lakota living in the Pine Ridge and Rosebud reservations in South Dakota, entrepreneurship is widespread, but the vast majority of it is nano and replicative, stemming from a dearth of employment opportunities with established companies. Small businesses owned by Lakota serve local needs for gasoline, automobile and home repair, and sundries (beers and smokes, videos, fast food) but most hire few, if any, workers and do not even have signage. Nanoenterprises such as quilting and beading wax when other forms of income, including employment and government assistance, wane. They are important endeavors in the sense that even tiny businesses can turn a meager existence into a more comfortable one. For sixteen years, Roselyn Spotted Eagle and two disabled family members lived in a cabin without running water. They often went hungry trying to subsist on disability payments and government cheese. After Roselyn was able to establish an Indian crafts business with help from the microlender Lakota Fund, however, the family was able to move to a three-bedroom trailer with running water and a washer and dryer.[48]

Others earn a decent living quilting, a craft introduced to Lakota women by Mennonite missionaries circa 1900 and since transmitted from Native women to their daughters.[49] Creative cost cutting is often key to turning a profit. After Wounded Knee II, for example, kids picked up expended cartridges and craftsmen bought them up cheap and "made 'em into breastplates and chokers, like they used to in the old days with pipe beads."[50] Some Indians sell their art, jewelry, and dream catchers near the Wounded Knee massacre memorial, which attracts tourists despite being poorly marked and a long way from good roads. In the early 1980s, eight arts and crafts companies owned and operated by Indians in South Dakota had become large enough to come to the attention of the U.S. Department of the Interior: Indian Originals, Lakota Jewelry Visions, and Tipi Shop in Rapid City, Lakota Studios in Wounded Knee, Rings 'n' Things and Tsia Crafts in Mission, Starboy Enterprises in Rosebud, and Unkowapi in Marty.[51]

That was a start, but a bare one. When the Lakota Fund began in 1987,[52] fewer than 40 businesses were in operation on the two-million-acre Pine Ridge Reservation, "and most were owned by non-Indians."[53]

Quillwork by Flossie Bear Robe is an example of reservation-based entrepreneurship, in this case the Pine Ridge Reservation.
Courtesy Center for Western Studies.

Little Business on the Prairie

Pine Ridge was so underdeveloped it had a radio station, KILI (KEE-lee) Radio, but no hotel. Big Bat's gas station, named for Baptiste "Bat" Pourier, a trader who married into the Sioux and served as an interpreter in the latter half of the nineteenth century, was the main hot spot because it looked like a non-reservation business. Big Bat, the Fourth, also owned PTI Propane south of Pine Ridge and his wife, Patty Pourier, ran it. Another successful Native-owned business at the time was Calumet Gaming, which provided assistance to tribal governments with the development of their gaming operations. The owner, Wayne Boyd, studied business administration at USD. Boyd and his brother John also owned and operated a golf course and lounge just south of Mission.[54]

Posting a classic automobile as collateral, Tim Giago was able to start a newspaper, *Lakota Times,* in Pine Ridge during the 1981 recession with the help of South Dakotan Allen Neuharth, the founder of *USA Today*. By 1999, Giago's paper had spread into Rosebud, then Cheyenne River and Crow Creek, then all the other reservations in South Dakota. Then it widened its name to *Indian Country Today* and moved into Montana, Wyoming, North Dakota and the reservations of Nebraska. Its circulation hit 125,000 and it employed forty people in Washington State, New Mexico, and Rapid City. Even though it was published weekly, it was voted the second best daily paper in South Dakota behind only the Sioux Falls *Argus Leader*.[55]

Big Bat, Boyd, and Giago were, however, the exceptions that proved the rule. The Lakota's situation is far from unique. As Hernando de Soto, the president of the Institute for Liberty and Democracy, pointed out in his 2000 book, *The Mystery of Capital: Why Capitalism Triumphs in the West and Fails Everywhere Else*, the world's poorest persons are often forced to become and remain the proprietors of nanoenterprises because they cannot obtain the credit they need to expand or innovate. They live (too often in squalor) and die (too often prematurely) in the world's barrios, favelas, ghettoes, and slums solely because they had the misfortunate of being born under a predatory regime that for selfish reasons blocks their economic freedom at every turn.[56] The EGM suggests that the single most effective way to help the downtrodden of both the Northern Plains and the less developed world is to increase economic freedom. Allow people to thrive and they will, without any direct government aid or guidance beyond the simple protection of their lives, liberties, and property. The Lakota Fund was a great start – it helped to increase real per capita income in Shannon County (using Todd County as a control) – but obviously more needs to be done and carefully. An attempt to fund reservation microenterprises in the early 1950s, for example, ended in graft, and for a variety of reasons Euroamerican-controlled banks cannot be counted on to provide Indian entrepreneurs with loans.[57]

By 2008, forty-nine Native CDFIs (nonprofit community development funds) operated across the country, and eight of them, including the first, the Lakota Fund, were in South Dakota. Lakota Fund was by then still a microlender making loans up to $500 to craftspeople but also a banker to small businesses eligible for loans up to $200,000. In addition to loans, Lakota Fund offers business planning courses and technical assistance to help entrepreneurs to expand their businesses. Its $4.1 million in loans helped to finance 325 reservation businesses and to create almost 1,000 jobs. The other South Dakota Native CDFIs, including Four Bands Community Fund, Mazaska Owecaso Otipi Financial, Sisseton-Wahpeton Federal Credit Union, and First Nations Oweesta Corporation, have also stirred Indian entrepreneurship by making loans and providing training.[58]

Loans can help, however, only when Natives have incentives to work hard and smart. What is most needed, therefore, is for government to protect the lives, liberty, and property of Natives as well as protect those of Euroamericans. Its record with Euroamericans is imperfect but far better than that with Natives. Euroamericans Art and Helen Metzinger, for example, were forced off their land, which now lies under Lake Oahe, by the Pick-Sloan project. When a James River Valley irrigation aqueduct ran through their second farm, they were forced by threat of condemnation to accept $30 per acre when they wanted more than $100 per acre, plus compensation for the gravel vein running through their property.[59] The James River Valley has been called a paradise due to its "superlative ... fertility and productiveness," but only when it received enough water.[60] Irrigation is important throughout South Dakota but especially in the James River Valley. Areas to the east expect sufficient rain and usually get it. To the west, they do not expect to receive enough rain and usually do not. In the middle, the area around the Big Jim (James River), there is uncertainty and hence more agitation for a permanent source of water.[61] In any event, the state's action certainly destroyed the incentives of the Metzingers: Helen told the state senate in 1960 that "anyone who calls this a free country as our ancestors meant it to be should hang his head in shame and despair for such alienation of rights of citizens." If thousands benefited from the projects as claimed, she queried, then why not pay a fair price for the land?[62]

The James River aqueduct project, however, was eventually blocked by a coalition of farmers called United Family Farmers (UFF), President Jimmy Carter, and tight federal budgets.[63] Called "a prime example of citizen involvement in political decision-making," UFF showed that South Dakotans of Euroamerican descent possessed genuine political power when they worked together.[64] They actually shuttered the irrigation project even though a drought was on and the project was almost wholly funded by the federal government. One turning point in the struggle was an analysis by Johns Hopkins University researchers that showed that every dollar spent on the project would return only $.54, revealing it as the type of top down, big government boondoggle that South Dakotans traditionally loathed.[65]

As noted earlier, South Dakota has been remarkably democratic since its inception. Politics in South Dakota remains an intimate affair where voters call politicians, even governors and U.S. senators, by their first names. Voters often personally know their state senators and representatives because legislative districts average only about 20,000 people. South Dakota's voters also expect New Hampshire-style personal treatment from candidates for Congress, who must traverse Texas-like distances to press the flesh in the state's over 300 communities.[66] U.S. Senator Tim Johnson admitted that "It's a fact of life in South Dakota to drive 200 miles to see 25 people."[67] That sounds a bit daft but those two dozen people matter politically because most will be landowners and entrepreneurs with significantly more pull in their communities than employees or transients can muster.[68]

Voter turnout in South Dakota is generally high by national standards because South Dakotans see voting as a duty, akin to attending church, and they believe their votes count as much as their prayers do.[69] And their votes do count in the sense that the population is so small that the chance of casting the deciding vote is, though low, much higher than in most other states. Even votes cast for president, which South Dakotans know is merely symbolic, sends a signal: we are still overwhelmingly conservative and libertarian out here and don't forget it.

South Dakotans do not put politicians on a pedestal but rather treat them like employees, which is exactly what they are in Lockean theory. They regularly keep them close to earth by calling them by their first names or, if necessary, cutting them to pieces verbally: "People around Pierre said that when the first trains arrived bringing in the politicians you could smell cow manure for several miles."[70] As a corollary, South Dakotans will vote anyone into office who they think can get the job done. In the 1960s, for example, they elected to Congress for five terms a half-German, half-Rosebud Sioux named Benjamin Reifel.[71] During the Depression, they voted into the governorship West River rancher and Democrat Tom Berry. Berry came from a family that had started ranching near Black Pipe Creek in 1912 and by the 1930s controlled a 30,000-acre cattle ranch. His background, proponents claimed, would help the state through the Depression and the repayment of the rural credit bonds. Opponents countered that Berry was illiterate, which in

South Dakota was akin to being called a leper. Responding to the rumor with humor, Berry admitted that when asked to co-sign a note (guarantee a loan) he would beg off by claiming that he could not write.[72]

Other unlikely political success stories include U.S. Senator James Abourezk (D), an attorney, and Representative James Abdnor (R), a Kennebec rancher, both of whom were sons of Lebanese immigrants. Abourezk's father, who could barely speak English, was a homesteader who sold snow cones and spices and linens from a backpack to Indians. Later, he owned a movie theater and two mercantile stores, one in Wood and one in Mission, which catered to Natives. Abourezk was born on the Rosebud reservation and grew up there speaking Arabic![73] This unlikely politician, however, appealed to voters because as Texas Commissioner of Agriculture Jim Hightower, explained: "Abourezk is not always right, Lord knows, but everyone knows exactly where he stands. He doesn't hide his true feelings behind meaningless words. He doesn't try to finesse either issues or people."[74] That's being a straight shooter and in coyote country that was much preferred to being a crooked politician with a Euroamerican background.

Women in South Dakota did not gain the right to vote upon statehood but they did win suffrage in 1918, just before passage of the nineteenth amendment. Male South Dakotans were not known for sexism. Most had seen too many females – wives, mothers, sisters, aunts, even grandmothers – toiling away in the barn or field, fetching fuel in blizzards and water during dry spells, to think of women as the weaker sex. They were also meritocrats ready to give credit where due.[75] When Susan B. Anthony visited Pierre in 1895, for example, a cattleman who listened to her admitted that "she was one of the ablest speakers I ever heard."[76] The career of early South Dakota suffragist Marietta Bones suggests why it took so long for South Dakota to award women the vote. After a defeat in 1891, which brought her into conflict with Anthony and other national suffragists, Bones joined the opposition and began to argue that voting was not a privilege but a duty and that it would be unfair to impose such a duty on hardworking farm wives and other South Dakota females.[77]

Populism was a powerful movement in early South Dakota. Later, the movement was led by Emil Loriks, president of the Dakota Farmers Union, state legislator, and Executive Secretary of the South Dakota Holiday organization, which sought to delay debt repayment during the Depression. Among other policies, Loriks pushed for a tax on gold ore at Homestake on the grounds that South Dakotans deserved a slice of the rich golden cake it was producing. Small "p" populism is still strong in South Dakota in the sense that most voters oppose big business but support small businesses like local companies and family farms. In fact, since 1974 the state has tried to enforce laws that restrict corporate farm ownership, a straw man, no pun intended, in that only 3% of farms are corporate owned and only 14% of farm output is controlled by corporations. In *South Dakota Farm Bureau v. Hazeltine*, the federal eighth circuit court declared South Dakota's anti-corporate farming laws a violation of the Commerce Clause and hence unconstitutional.[78]

Many South Dakota voters disliked most federal government initiatives implemented since the New Deal. Debt is eschewed by both the government and the people. That sounds un-American to many people elsewhere but in South Dakota limiting debt is just "common sense."[79] It is also common sense to vote people other than lawyers into the statehouse and other important positions. The state has had more than the usual share of entrepreneurs in leadership positions, including Democratic governor Richard F. Kneip (1971-1978).[80]

The state was, is, and may always remain stingy with welfare and other income-transfer programs because that is the way most citizens want it. Aid, most believe, should be provided only to those who deserve it, who got into trouble due to bad luck, not bad behavior, and who have exhausted all means of "self help." Most South Dakotans are highly religious (though generally not fundamentalist) and hence charitable but they think that aid is best dispensed locally, by churches and church-related groups, independent organizations like The Banquet in Sioux Falls, which serves three free meals a day, and individual volunteers, not the government.[81]

Government best solves certain types of problems, most South Dakotans concede, but not all problems. Take, for example, cattle branding. From 1895 until 1925, a Brand and Marks Committee was in charge of issuing and tracking cattle brands, distinctive marks that ranchers used to identify their cattle and reduce rustling.[82] The branding system was then turned over to the State Department of Agriculture but it did not understand the system well enough to do an adequate job, which understandably "caused great concern of the people the system was designed to protect."[83] So in 1937 the state created the State Brand Board, which consisted of from three to five actual cattlemen, and assigned it the task of registering livestock brands. After 1943, the government decided to outsource the task entirely to a private, non-profit corporation, the SDSGA (South Dakota Stock Growers Association), which maintained the contract for half a century. Registering brands, which requires balancing distinctiveness and clarity, was simply too difficult for salaried bureaucrats, so with prompting the state turned the function over to a group with both the appropriate experience and incentive to do a good job.[84]

Despite its homesteading origins, South Dakota by the 1930s was not a land of homeowners due to the difficulties of obtaining financing. In Hamlin County, which was very close to the state average, only 27.77% of household heads owned the homes in which they resided. Some 45% of farm operators were owners or part owners and the rest, save for a handful of farm managers, were tenants. In 1940, half of Plains farmers were tenants, typically long-term ones because short-term tenants extracted all they could from farms and invested as little as possible in them. In South Dakota, tenancy was slightly more common. The number of farms dropped from 83,000 in 1930 to 72,450 in 1940 and the percentage of tenant farmers increased from 45 to 53.[85]

"It might be hypothesized," wrote a state political analyst in the 1960s, "that South Dakota's low population density encourages individual as opposed to group action."[86] In fact, despite high tenancy and low population, South Dakota has long possessed a robust civil society. By the 1930s, Hamlin County boasted of a wide range of associations ranging from "Farmers unions, Fraternal lodges and Legion activities to the educational, extension and scout groups." The Grange was there too as were orders of the Masons, Odd Fellows, Modern Woodman, Royal Neighbor, American Legion, and Ladies' Auxiliary.[87] Sioux Falls had its Benevolent and Protective Order of Elks, El Riad Temple of Shriners, Knights of Pythias Lodge, Odd Fellows, Masons, Granite Lodge, Izaak Walton League, YMCA, Chamber of Commerce (and before that, the Commercial Club), Salvation Army, Kiwanis Club, and numerous other social clubs and benevolent societies.[88]

In the Black Hills during the 1950s, any of the many social and community groups active in the area could meet at the Covered Wagon Corral Room in the basement of a bank in Belle Fourche for only $1 per hour, all of which went to pay the security guard required by state law. Elsewhere west of the river, Presho had its Preshokiya Club, a branch of the Pierre Kiwanis Club, which sponsored a golf course, tennis courts, a recreational lake, Christmas lighting, the public high school auditorium, the night watchman, and the town basketball team. Dances were weekly affairs there, as they were in most towns statewide. Many of them were used to raise money for good causes, like fighting polio, funding the fire department, or advertising for a town doctor. Similarly, Kadoka had the American Legion, Masons, Order of the Eastern Start, Modern Woodmen of America, Royal Neighbors of America, Odd Fellows, Rebeccahs, and the Woman's Club.[89]

Kadoka also had, briefly in the 1920s, a chapter of the Ku Klux Klan. The KKK of the 1920s was an entrepreneurial and flexible version of the Reconstruction original that gained a wide following throughout much of the nation because it adapted itself to local circumstances and paid

Little Business on the Prairie

organizers handsome commissions. Equal hatred of all, except those who paid their dues, could have been its motto. It is not surprising, then, to learn that Fall River County and the Black Hills also attracted numerous recruits, or that the Dakota Klan was relatively strong in Fargo and along the Iowa-South Dakota border. It vanished quickly, but not before holding a 300-strong hooded rally in downtown Sioux Falls during the reign of Thomas McKinnon (mayor of the city from 1924 to 1929). [90] "Spasmodic applause, cheering, heckling and booing greeted the marchers" but many watched the nighttime procession "in dead silence."[91] According to the Klan's most famous historian, "the secret order was beset by the usual internal dissension, and the earth shook not where it trod."[92] The Dakota clan dissolved during the Depression. Klan membership proved too expensive, irrational, and extreme for pragmatic South Dakotans.[93] The same could be said of the next big movement, socialists, considered by most people on both sides of the river as dangerous as "mad dogs."[94] South Dakotans hated monopolies but that has never translated into a general disdain for markets as indeed logically it should not. (Monopolies are, of course, the opposite of a free market.)[95]

General William Beadle once asserted that Dakotans were "intelligent, self-respecting citizens, used to governing themselves, trained to hold meetings, to organize movements and direct events."[96] He could have added that they were also willing and able to discuss public policy. "Politics were a favorite subject of discussion," one South Dakotan recalled of the early days.[97] Public discourse remained surprisingly robust with numerous newspapers, including the Mitchell *Daily Republic* and Sioux Falls *Argus Leader*, hashing out the issues. South Dakotans also attended public lectures in droves and supported libraries as bulwarks against tyranny and oppression. A vibrant alternative media sector, including South Dakota Public Broadcasting's radio and television programming, public access cable channels, four non-profit community radio stations that operate from Indian Reservations, and five college radio stations, also encourages policy debate and/or provides a broadcast outlet for voices outside the mainstream party structures. One of those voices was a poster of Uncle Sam wearing a hat made of marijuana and telling "CORPORATE Amerikkka" to perform something anatomically impossible.[98]

In South Dakota, the American tradition of voluntarism has weakened over time but remains strong relative to elsewhere in the nation. Americans may "bowl alone," as sociologist Robert Putnam famously put it, but South Dakotans, ironically enough given their state's low population density and individualist ideology, generally do not, though these days most prefer pool or darts, leagues for which are ubiquitous.[99] South Dakotans "live apart together"; despite the low population density, many ties bind them together.[100] The state ranks first in the nation in social trust, interracial trust, civic leadership, giving and volunteering, and faith-based engagement, and fourth in conventional political and fifth in associational involvement.[101]

South Dakotans are hardly perfect, but relative to people from more urban states, they are relatively friendly and honest. Where ad hoc responses to governance problems seem insufficient, social entrepreneurs like the Chiesman Foundation for Democracy, which is based in Rapid City, have arisen and formed think tanks like the Institute for South Dakota Leadership and Protection. In 150 troubled towns, development groups arose to help fight the flight of young people and businesses out of their communities. Many were aided by the state's GOLD (Guide to Opportunities for Local Development) program, which helped communities to assess their strengths and weaknesses realistically and then to make good policy decisions. Others stemmed from a $3 million McKnight Foundation Challenge Grant (as in William L. McKnight, a South Dakota native who ran 3M from 1949 until 1966) matched by the South Dakota Community Foundation and community banks, like the Hand County State Bank in Miller, from around the state.[102]

Another source of confusion regarding South Dakota is the state government's long history of economic activism. In 1924, the state purchased a cement plant near Rapid City that employed about 150 people in its quarries, sheds, chutes, power house, crushers, hydrating and baking plant, furnaces, drying tanks, sacking, and business offices. The plant produced about 20 car loads a day and its product was "much in demand" due to its "superior quality."[103] Even Republicans supported the business, Dacotah Cement, although it could be considered, as one observer wryly put it, "an instance of state ownership of production, sometimes referred to as 'socialism'."[104] Profitable every year of its existence, even during the Depression, the plant remained politically untouchable. It was profitable because its management was not politicized, because it was surrounded by a huge deposit of limestone and other essential raw materials, and because it faced little competition within the state or in North Dakota or Minnesota. In the 1980s, South Dakota Cement, as it was by then known, was still going strong, the only government-owned cement business in the entire nation. In just eight years, it contributed over $86 million to the state treasury, not bad for a company with only 228 employees. In 2001, the state finally sold the business to a Mexican corporation for $252 million.[105]

A state-owned lignite mine located in southwestern North Dakota, by contrast, struggled due to "inefficient management."[106] South Dakota lost $174,000 when it finally shuttered the mine in 1934 but state institutions

Backed by Governor Peter Norbeck, the South Dakota Cement Plant became the only state-owned, for-profit business in South Dakota, until its sale in 2001 to GSC, a Mexican-based conglomerate.
Courtesy Center for Western Studies.

did enjoy lower energy costs while the mine was in operation. Twenty years later, economists noted that the northwestern part of South Dakota still contained lignite outcroppings that remained unexploited.[107] State-owned mortgage and hail insurance companies also ended disastrously. Begun in 1919, the hail insurance program was "actually a mutual plan operated and controlled by the state," which was out of business by 1933 because it was compulsory.[108] Farmers did not like that and hence many did not pay their premiums. The state's losses, however, were minor compared to its mortgage lending fiasco, which ended up costing taxpayers $57 million in defaults and other losses. Those experiments took place because Governor Peter Norbeck was convinced that private lenders charged exorbitant prices and that the state could save its citizens many millions by lending to them instead. Screening good from bad borrowers, though, turned out to be more difficult and costly than Norbeck understood.[109]

The state's twine factory, run as part of its penitentiary system, also ended up costing the economy big time when convicts sabotaged the works in 1919-20, leaving farmers desperate for the commodity, which was essential to the binders that grain farmers had used since the latenineteenth century. The government had started using convict labor to meet the twine demand of the state's farmers in 1909 in response to the formation of a twine trust that controlled prices. The program worked well at first, with the state's farmers buying twine some two to five cents cheaper per pound than that available from the monopoly. Quality concerns began to emerge as prison officials had difficulty keeping up with new technologies, like anti-insect additives, and market-changing events, especially the Mexican Revolution and World War I. Prisoner sabotage in 1919 and 1920 exacerbated the program's problems. John T. Belk of Henry, for example, complained that "the twine is a bad mess, much of the twine is cut." Another farmer found balls of twine stuffed with rags. He and others, like Lars Larson of the Farmers' Co-op in Bruce, demanded full refunds. Demand for prison twine fell off as farmers grudgingly paid more for more reliable commercial twine. The state eventually made some restitution to farmers in an attempt to keep the twine plant in operation. The ploy worked and the state kept the plant open throughout the 1920s, 30s, and 40s and eventually added factories for making license plates and road signs as demand for twine dropped to nothing by 1950 due to the introduction of combine harvesters.[110]

How could conservative or libertarian South Dakotans suffer such an activist government? Is the hypocrisy not palpable? In fact, no hypocrisy was involved. South Dakotans are politically pragmatic. They support whatever works and they voted for the state acquisitions by large margins. They are also intellectually humble and hence open to experimentation. So the real lesson is that when economic conditions are tough, South Dakotans are open to try new approaches, including government ownership. When it helps the commonweal, they allow state ownership to continue. When it doesn't, they shutter the operation, cut their losses, and try something else. The current experiment, one that appears to be succeeding, is for the state government to actively encourage business and economic development through a variety of targeted programs. The model, introduced and to a degree perfected by Governor William Janklow, grew out of the state's economic woes in the 1970s, which were themselves rooted in the postwar boom years.[111]

Farm incomes increased dramatically during World War II and stayed high in the postwar decades. Other Depression conditions – drought, grasshoppers, dust storms – also dissipated, though without disappearing completely. Moreover, farm incomes increased faster than the cost of borrowed money, taxes, wages, and other input costs by a wide margin. Tenancy plummeted to an all time low in 1954 and continued to trend downward, hitting 22% statewide in 1964. The favorable situation reversed around 1960 but government subsidies increased so total cash farm income continued the upward trend started in 1940. It should be noted, however, that incomes varied dramatically by county, largely as a function of the level of urbanization. In 1960, for example, per capita income in Roberts County, which contained an Indian reservation but no major town, was just $1,409 compared to $2,270 in Beadle, the seat of which was Huron, a substantial town.[112]

Despite the general boom, the countryside began to hollow out as tractors, combines, and other new equipment increasingly drove men off the farm and into urban centers. Some quit farming entirely while others became "sidewalk" farmers who lived and worked in nearby towns and commuted to their farms on weekends or during vacations or slack times at their regular work. Others became "suitcase" farmers who tended farms in several states by taking advantage of differential north-south seeding and harvesting schedules. Neither group was small; Sully County alone had seventy-eight suitcase farmers in 1952, some of whom showed the locals how to succeed with winter wheat.[113]

Some South Dakotans had used steam tractors — giant, cantankerous beasts worked by teams and often used to break virgin prairie — since the late nineteenth century. African-American John McGruder (1850-1913), for example, owned a steam tractor powerful enough to break up virgin prairie for homesteaders. Nevertheless, most South Dakota farmers continued to rely on horses until the 1920s, when new, more mobile gasoline tractors introduced by International Harvester proved themselves far easier to use than steam tractors and far more efficient than horses. They worked longer, faster, more steadily, and required only one operator. Moreover, tractors used cheap fossil fuels rather than corn or fodder, freeing up land for cash crops, a real savings after farmers switched to trucks for transportation too by not replacing horse teams as they wore out.[114]

Most farmers could afford gasoline tractors in the 1920s or '30s but not until after the Depression did they buy the mechanical beasts "with a vengeance."[115] By 1940, 55% of Plains farms, compared to just 23% of all American farms, employed at least one tractor; South Dakota farmers ranked third in the nation, just behind North Dakota and Iowa, in terms of the percentage of farmers who used tractors. By 1945, about 30% of South Dakota farmers used trucks. Mechanization allowed the Plains farmer to get out of the business of raising horses and mules and running a hotel for hired laborers and to concentrate on planting and harvesting.[116]

South Dakota ranked sixth in the nation in farm mechanization in the 1950s even as its farmers kept up with the horsepower revolution of that decade: in 1951 only 8% of tractors had horsepower greater than thirty-five but fifteen years later only 8% had horsepower less than that. The reason was that a revolution in implements was also underway as combines, six-row cultivators, and other heavy equipment became common. Farmers became more efficient but also more leveraged than ever, rendering them ever more susceptible to negative shocks.[117]

Rural electrification was largely a postwar phenomenon in South Dakota. In 1937, only 18% of South Dakota's farms were connected to the grid, but by 1950, 69% of them were. Before rural electrification, farmers used wind chargers — batteries charged by windmills – or generators for radios and electric appliances and wind- or gasoline-powered pumps to move water. The Pick-Sloan dams built along the Missouri in the 1950s and 1960s reduced electricity costs but also provided more bridges across the Big Muddy and significant economic stimulus, especially for boom towns like Pickstown. Existing towns, like Yankton, also experienced booms when the Army Corps of Engineers moved in to begin the massive, decade-long projects.[118]

After the Depression, the number of trade centers in the state continued to decline, from 635 in 1941 to 545 in 1951. Trade centers in the latter year generally consisted of at least a gas station, grocery, pharmacy, restaurant, and one or more stores that sold appliances, clothing, and furniture. The trend was toward fewer, larger trading centers due to changes in merchandising methods and the growth of chain stores and urban populations. In 1930, the largest fifteen trading centers were home to 21% of the state's total population. By 1960 that figure had grown to 35%. Over time, smaller trade centers lost their full service stores as, for example, groceries like Bohning Grocery in Harrold morphed into convenience stores frequented by locals who needed a few items quickly but who did the bulk of their shopping in larger, more distant centers. As early as 1951, more than half of the towns in South Dakota with fewer than 500 residents did not have a drug, furniture, grocery, or household appliance store or a home fuel or motor vehicle dealer, much less more specialized retailers like shoe stores, bakeries, florists, tailors, or jewelers. Two out of every five lacked a bank and one out of three had no eatery.[119]

Small towns also lost much of their social significance over the course of the 1950s and 1960s. In the beginning of the period, farmers visited town weekly to buy needed goods and services and to sell cream, eggs, and chickens for walk-around cash just as they had for generations. (Local buyers then shipped the goods to eastern markets via rail.) Farmers would then stay in town to listen to bands, watch local high school sports, attend a movie, or just fraternize. Over the years, as television replaced movies and live sports, records supplanted live music, huge, scientifically managed egg and chicken farms outcompeted small time producers, and milk processors began to pick up milk right on the farm, the need to make the weekly trip to town almost vanished, along with the robustness of the local retail sector.[120]

In the first half of the century, even towns of just a few hundred people would have two or three cafés or diners. By the new millennium, towns of that size with even a single restaurant were unusual. Most of the local drug, grocery, hardware and appliance stores, so ubiquitous at mid-century, had also dried up and blown away, outcompeted on price by big box stores in regional centers like Sioux Falls, Huron, and Rapid City and in convenience by gas station stores or lost to fires (some doubtless intentional), deaths (a few intentional), or other happenstances. Vacant lots and buildings sometimes take over, but other locations become home to a string of small businesses like antique and gift shops. Entrepreneurship levels, however, remained strong: into the late 1950s, employers and the self-employed comprised two out of every five workers in South Dakota. Moreover, proprietor's income remained a significant percentage of total personal income in South Dakota through the early 1960s. So entrepreneurship did not shrivel up and die in small towns so much as it shifted into new markets and areas, including the state's larger towns and cities.[121]

Sioux Falls and Rapid City grew the fastest, at least in absolute terms. Sioux Falls received a boost from an Army Air Force base recently chronicled by Lynwood Oyos in *Reveille for Sioux Falls: A World War II Army Air Forces Technical School Changes a South Dakota City*. Rapid City also thrived during World War II because the Army Air Force established a bomber base there. After the war, the newly formed Air Force decided to keep and upgrade the base, which was named Ellsworth in honor of World War II bomber hero Richard E. Ellsworth, who crashed his Peacemaker bomber during a training flight in 1953. Rapid City was near the center of the continent and hence safe, at first anyway, from Soviet bombers. Moreover, the area around it was thought to resemble parts of Siberia so it was a good place to practice bombing runs. From 1961 until 1964, the city was also aided by the construction of scores of missile silos in the region because South Dakota was considered "expendable from a national perspective" and its dry atmosphere was good for solid fuel rocket engines.[122] Plus, the state had a well-deserved reputation for patriotism and support for the military.[123]

In 1965, banker Art Dahl described "Rapid," as it was by then often called for short, as a trade center that "serves a large trading area extending into surrounding states. It has a diversified income from ranching, tourist, mining, lumbering, military installations, and is a wholesale distribution center. It has some manufacturing, with a large flour mill and a packing plant."[124] It was also home to the South Dakota School of Mines and even a gay bar or two at times.[125] Transportation improvements, especially paved highways, helped both great metropoles by making it easier and faster for people to visit them to work and shop. Although many counties in the state were caught up in the Good Roads movement of the 1910s, some farmers resisted so it was not until 1938 that automobiles could traverse South Dakota entirely on an oil highway, U.S. 16. By the early 1950s, however, paved roads crisscrossed the state in a dense network, especially east of the river. By 1950, the railroad network east of the James River was dense but it became less so in the west, especially in the south central and northwest parts of the state. Railroad mileage had grown almost annually from 1872 until 1940 but by 1950 was already showing slight decreases due to stiff competition from motor trucks.[126] "The keen competition between the railroads and the truckers for certain type of freight," one contemporary analyst noted, "has caused their published rates for the same commodities to be very nearly alike. The slightly higher truck rates in most instances," he continued, "can be explained by the added service offered by truckers."[127]

By the end of World War II, almost 1,000 licensed pilots lived in the state, which registered over 100 civilian aircraft. A decade later, South Dakota registered over 800 civil aircraft and licensed more than 1,100 pilots. Many were farmers and ranchers from remote areas who found that flying allowed them more opportunity to travel. Others were hired by South Dakota businesses to shuttle their personnel around the state. After the war, small aviation companies like that of fighter ace Joe Foss offered flight instruction, maintenance and repair services, charter flights, and crop dusting. Others ferried fishers and hunters to remote lakes throughout the three "Ota" states (South Dakota, North Dakota, and Minnesota).[128]

By 1950, regular commercial airliner service operated in Sioux Falls, Huron, Watertown, Aberdeen, Pierre, and Rapid City, all of which by then enjoyed "modern airport terminals."[129] In the late 1950s, United Airlines even ran a flight to Lemmon, a town of only 2,800.[130] By 1957, however, the larger trunk airlines, like Braniff, which had merged with Mid-Continental, were complaining that "the routes which cross the state are unprofitable."[131] They disappeared and an attempt by the state government to subsidize intrastate commuter air service in 1990 failed to restore service.[132] As of the time of writing (August 2014), one could fly commercially between Sioux Falls and Rapid City only via Denver or Minneapolis.

Foss, who was called "either the dumbest smart man" or the "smartest dumb man" in the state, became governor in 1955.[133] Foss pushed for improved infrastructure, especially better roads, universities, and water control systems for a state intermittently and ironically wracked by both devastating droughts and floods. The Missouri River, the worst but not only offender, flooded massively in 1844, 1881, 1943, and 1951. The glacial lakes region between Brookings and Watertown drowned in 1986. Foss created an Industrial Development and Expansion Agency (IDEA) charged with cooperating with commerce chambers and other civic organizations to attract new industries to the state and, when appropriate, he personally flew around the country trying to seal deals based on the state's high quality of life: low taxes, low crime, low pollution, and no traffic jams. (The state has always had low corporate taxes compared to its neighbors. In 1975, for example, the state corporate income tax due on $1 million in federal taxable income in South Dakota was zero, compared to $31,000 in North Dakota, $120,000 in Minnesota, $27,500 in Nebraska, and $73,800 in Iowa.) Foss also traveled the country pitching South Dakota as a tourist destination.[134]

After his two terms as governor were up, Foss joined Raven Industries, a high-altitude research balloon manufacturer that moved to South Dakota in response to Foss's IDEA program. South Dakota made sense for a number of reasons aside from its amicable weather and business climate. In addition to the state's early love affair with both balloons and aircraft, the military launched many high-altitude flights from the Stratobowl, a natural depression near Rapid City, in the 1930s, 40s, and 50s. (Steve Fossett also launched his failed global solo flight in a Rozier balloon from the Stratobowl in 1996.) The state became so enamored of ballooning that the 14,000-square-foot Soukup and Thomas International Balloon and Airship Museum was long located in Mitchell and to this day the balloons of Prairie Sky, Inc., and other companies can be seen floating above Sioux Falls or the prairie year round.[135]

Raven experienced considerably more success than the balloon museum. At first specializing in high-performance, high-altitude balloons, it began to diversify in 1960 when it started to produce fiberglass tanks and invented the modern hot air balloon. In the 1980s, its Aerostar division began making balloons, depicting characters like Raggedy Anne and Garfield, for the Macy's Thanksgiving

A test inflation of a balloon at Raven Industries, Sioux Falls, in 1963.

Courtesy Center for Western Studies.

Day parade. A decade later Raven was producing balloons, insulated clothing, and fiberglass tanks for the domestic and Canadian markets. Today, the Aerostar division also makes camouflage clothing designed to defeat optical and infrared sensors, inflatable decoy military vehicles, and high-altitude balloons designed with Google to bring internet access to millions worldwide, among other products. (When Felix Baumgartner parachuted from 128,000 feet, for example, he jumped from *Red Bull Stratos*, a zero pressure balloon built by Raven.) Other Raven divisions make precision agricultural equipment products like tractor field computers and planter and seeder controls and sundry membranes and flexible films used in agriculture, construction, and manufacturing. Still headquartered in Sioux Falls but with plants across the state and the nation, Raven in 2014 was named one of "America's Most Trustworthy Companies" by *Forbes* magazine.[136]

While Raven flourished, the 1960s, 70s, and 80s were not kind to many South Dakotans. The state was one of only two to lose population between 1960 and 1970 as agricultural consolidation continued and a decades-long brain drain commenced. With little incentive to stay on the farm, young people fled the Plains en masse for places like Minneapolis, Denver, Omaha, and even further afield.[137] "In effect," an analyst noted in 1974, "the rural areas of the Midwest have avoided poverty by exporting their youths."[138] In the 1970s, high fuel prices hurt farmers and anyone else who had to travel long distances to work, shop, or attend classes. High interest rates also hurt farmers and other small businesspeople by raising their borrowing costs. Auto and farm implement dealers, construction contractors, and furniture and appliance dealers were especially hard hit because interest rates were too high for their customers to afford.[139] As during the Great Depression, Mother Nature added to the misery with a litany of blizzards, insect infestations, and droughts, including the "terrific drought of 1988."[140]

Due to those combined pressures, many farmers temporized by sending themselves and/or their wives into town to work, an expedient that few took lightly.[141] Violet Uhden's obituary, for example, described her as a "homemaker" but then went on to state that she worked "at various jobs including Dakota Tract Industries and Earl Gust's Café in Wilmot, Dakota Poultry Processing in Watertown, and the Big Stone Canning Factory in Ortonville, MN."[142] Others went out of business after long struggles. Farm bankruptcies in the state jumped from 10 in 1979 to 338 in 1985 to 622 in 1987. Ultimately, low prices for agricultural goods and high prices for everything else were to blame, so larger, unleveraged farms made it through while smaller, highly leveraged ones succumbed.[143] Winner area wheat farmer Marie Fisher explained the problem to the U.S. Senate:

> High interest rates are making it very difficult for us to
> pay off the debts. ... Winter wheat, which is our main cash
> crop, was priced at $3.29 a bushel at Deaver-Meyer. ...
> If a farmer has a debt of $100,000, and many do now,
> and he has a loan with the Federal Land Bank where
> the interest rate is 11.75%, the farmer has to sell 3,571
> bushels of wheat to just pay the interest. Our county
> average production of wheat per acre is 28.4.... So he has
> to sell the average production from 125 acres of wheat
> just to pay the interest at today's high rate. This does
> not include payment on the principal. This also figures
> that you have an average crop each year. In my area
> of south-central South Dakota we had more poor wheat
> crops since 1975 than good crops, including 2 years of
> complete crop failure.[144]

Entrepreneurship also suffered from high interest rates because many South Dakotans were "afraid to go into business for fear that they can't make it if they have to borrow money at the prevailing interest rates."[145] Increased interest rate volatility also dissuaded entrepreneurs because they could not plan effectively as they did not know what their cost of borrowing was going to be. By 1983, the Small Business Administration's (SBA) loan portfolio in South Dakota experienced what Chester B. Leedom, the SBA's district director, called "real problems." Liquidation of small businesses with SBA loans hit 283 cases, a "significantly higher" number than just three years previously. Moreover, "quite a number of businesses that started in late 1979 and early 1980... just did not get off the ground."[146] The situation grew so dire that Bob Erkonen of Augustana College feared that significant numbers of entrepreneurs would give up and switch to wage work.[147]

Traditionally, hard times benefit the Democratic Party, even in South Dakota (e.g., the 1890s and 1930s). In the late 1970s, however, Democrats got the blame for the economy's many ills, including inflation, high interest rates, unemployment, and the farm crisis. In 1978, voters swept Republican Bill Janklow into the statehouse and two years later ousted McGovern from the Senate. Much like McGovern, however, Janklow was an economic activist, not a proponent of the hands-off approach called laissez-faire. The difference was that most of Janklow's programs paid off financially without threatening economic freedom, while McGovern's interfered with both markets and people's pocketbooks.[148]

Janklow won re-election in 1982 because voters believed his approach to state economic development was better than the Democrat's approach, not because the economy dramatically improved during his first term. In fact, nonfarm incomes were down and unemployment was up, from 3.1% in 1978 to 5.5% in 1982. Home sales were down approximately 70%, homebuilding came to a standstill, and contractors and their workers fled the state in search of employment. Meanwhile, vacancy rates in Sioux Falls were below 1% because nobody wanted to invest given the unfavorable macroeconomic climate. Also unsettling was Reagan's budget cuts, which in percentage terms (27%) cut more deeply in South Dakota than any other state in the union. But all of that was out of Janklow's control. What he could control, he handled beautifully.[149]

First was the abysmal government revenue situation. The state constitution constrains the government's budget, which cannot lawfully be run in the red (no deficits, only balance or surplus). Instead of increasing the general sales tax or instituting a personal or general corporate income tax, which was and is anathema in South Dakota, Janklow cut the budget 5%, increased the tax on Homestake — the multi-billion dollar gold mine in the Black Hills that was enjoying a resurgence due to new extraction methods and high market prices — increased excise taxes on gas, liquor, and cigarettes, and raised user fees. He also sold Missouri River water to Energy Transportation Systems Incorporated and used the money to develop the state's water resources. Down-river states, however, litigated against the deal. Nevertheless, by 1982 the state was in much better fiscal shape than neighboring Minnesota.[150]

When the railroads stopped operating in South Dakota, Janklow imposed a temporary 1% sales tax increase to fund the acquisition of key lines by the state. Cognizant of the fate of earlier state-owned businesses, he hired Burlington Northern to operate the trains instead of using state employees. Farmers and ranchers, who still relied on the rails to get their bulky products to market cheaply enough for them to earn a profit, were much obliged.[151]

So, too, were the denizens of Sioux Falls and other urban centers positively impacted by Janklow's financial reform program, which brought numerous clean, high-paying jobs into the state. Janklow's biggest coup was luring Citibank's credit card division to Sioux Falls. Unassuming Sioux Falls became a national credit card processing and call center because in 1980 Citibank decided to relocate its massive credit card operations, which included some six million MasterCard and Visa holders spread across all fifty states, to the city on the Big Sioux River. Today, an abundance of physical and human capital adapted to the credit card business keeps card issuers in the state in the same way that magnetism keeps calendars stuck to refrigerators. In 1980, however, the state enjoyed no such specific set of human capital, so it relied at first on Janklow's personal magnetism.[152]

Like South Dakota, Citibank was hurting after a decade of negative shocks, stagflation, and recession. After becoming chairman of the Federal Reserve in August 1979, Paul Volcker tried to wring inflation expectations out of the economy by raising the Fed's overnight lending rates. He also allowed commercial banks, which were losing depositors in droves, to raise the rates they paid on checking and savings deposits. Since the New Deal, the Federal Reserve had tightly regulated the rates that commercial banks could pay on deposits, effectively cartelizing them to avoid the mass panics and waves of bank failures that had rendered the Great Depression so very depressing. (About seven in ten banks in the state failed between 1920 and 1933.) The interest rate regulations, called Federal Regulation Q, rendered the banking system stable for decades but when market interest rates, driven ever higher by inflation, rose above the legal caps it caused numerous problems, especially what economists called disintermediation.[153]

Under Regulation Q and stagflation, it made sense for depositors to pull their money out of banks to invest elsewhere, like money market mutual funds, where larger returns awaited. It also made sense to borrow as much as possible in the expectation of paying back cheaper dollars later. Citibank's credit card division soon felt the pinch because it had to pay 19% for money, lend it for less than that due to state interest caps known as usury laws, and incur operating expenses of 5-6%, not to mention record default levels. At one point, Citibank's credit card operations were costing it more than $2 million dollars per week.

Rather than shutter the business, Charlie Long, on orders from Citibank CEO Walter Wriston, began looking for a state with a more favorable business climate than New York had to offer. Pinning his hopes on the Supreme Court's 1978 Marquette decision, which allowed a bank to charge any rate of interest lawful in either its location or that of its borrowers, Long identified six prospects: California, Hawaii, Rhode Island, Nevada, Missouri, and South Dakota. He eventually dropped all but South Dakota due to their distance from New York, their high costs of doing business, or the hostility of their state politicians towards the bank. Gaining the favor of state politicians was essential because, due to the Douglas Amendment of the Bank Holding Company Act of 1956, out-of-state banks had to be invited into a state before they could do business in it. Missouri held in the longest but South Dakota turned out to be the best choice overall for reasons described below. The Comptroller of the Currency approved Citibank's move in November 1980 and the Federal Reserve did likewise in January 1981. Citibank South Dakota began operations in rented space the next month and that June moved into the first of three new buildings it would construct in the city.

Soon after the move, a myth sprouted that Citibank had paid South Dakota to repeal its usury cap. The myth proliferated widely because it offered an easy explanation for Citibank's decision to invest in a state known more for harsh winters and a surfeit of ringed-neck pheasants and red-necked denizens than financial expertise. To the extent that South Dakota was known nationally in 1980, its reputation was far from savory. Just a few years earlier, the state had made national news resulting from a standoff on its Pine Ridge Reservation, known as Wounded Knee II, and the murder of two FBI agents there. That was a typical Saturday night in New York City but Russell Means of AIM was then far scarier to most Americans than any New York pimp or drug dealer. And high levels of racial tension persisted in the state, even though the American Indian Movement had moved out of the national spotlight.

The myth of South Dakota's capitulation to the emerging megabank also made for great political satire, including an infamous fake news story that claimed the South Dakota state legislature had voted to become a wholly owned subsidiary of Citicorp. According to the faux article, the state was thenceforth to be called Dakotacorp and Bill Janklow was to be its highly paid president. South Dakota's capital, Pierre, was to be renamed Wristonville. The story mortified South Dakotans, who traditionally abhorred just two things: big government and big business.[154]

In fact, South Dakota took steps to eliminate its usury cap *before* Citibank expressed any official interest in moving to Sioux Falls. The impetus for the change came from state bankers because in 1979 South Dakota banks were in the same sinking boat as Citibank, paying big money to borrow but facing the state's usury cap when they wanted to lend. Since its creation, South Dakota had looked for ways to keep borrowing costs for farmers and ranchers from going too high. Instead of solving the problem of high interest rates for riskier borrowers, the state's legislature, like many before and since, pretended to solve it by capping interest rates, first at 12%, then 10%, then 8%, at which rate it stayed from 1933 until 1970, when rising inflation and nominal interest rates made it apparent to all that the 8% cap prevented many prospective borrowers from finding willing lenders. The legislature responded to those pressures by twice increasing the cap 2% for most loans and by more for some other, inherently riskier, loan types.

Nevertheless, the state's banks were still squeezed enough on the spread between the sources and uses of their funds that their very existence was soon threatened, as was that of their business customers. Paul H. Nordstrom, president of the Security State Bank in Geddes, informed Janklow in late October 1979 that his bank could no longer lend to anyone except a handful of its very largest and best customers. The state's usury law was therefore hurting "the very class of people that it was originally intended to protect. What a paradox." Janklow responded in early November:

> I agree that the interest ceiling in its present form is causing problems for citizens and our State-chartered financial institutions. This is the end product of years of federal, congressional and executive mismanagement and inflation. I can assure you that this problem will receive careful consideration during the forthcoming legislative session.

The legislature might have simply increased its usury ceiling a few percent to buy time as it and the legislatures of other states had done previously, but Thomas M. Reardon, the founder and chairman of Western Bank in Sioux Falls, and his son T.J. Reardon, the bank's president, had a better idea, do away with the cap entirely for regulated institutions like their bank. South Dakota bankers quickly signed off on the radical idea and the lower house, which was dominated by libertarian-tinged Republicans, did too. Citibank then expressed interest in moving to the state if the law stuck and that ensured the upper house's rapid approval.

What South Dakota did do explicitly for Citibank was to change a state law that prohibited out-of-state bank holding companies from owning South Dakota banks. To get the state bankers who felt protected by that law on board, the new law allowed out-of-state bank holding companies like Citibank to form, own, and operate in South Dakota small, new banks that did not compete against existing South Dakota banks. The state's bankers acquiesced and the law passed with a large bipartisan majority.

The elimination of usury caps for regulated institutions and the bank holding company enabling legislation were necessary but not sufficient conditions for Citibank's move to coyote country. Citibank needed its card business to be pushed out of New York while simultaneously being pulled to Sioux Falls and away from Delaware. Janklow's personal magnetism was certainly part of the pull and crucial early on, but what really made the deal stick were the positive attributes of the people of South Dakota, the state government, and the city itself.

In 1980, for example, Sioux Falls enjoyed a very efficient post office while New York did not. Janklow claimed, apocryphally no doubt, that a letter sent from one borough of New York to another arrived more quickly if sent via Sioux Falls, some 1,350 miles to the west, than if sent directly across the East River. What was certainly true was that payments and other correspondence sent from most places in the country would reach Sioux Falls before they would hit New York's financial district. It has been demonstrated, Richard C. Kane of Citicorp Credit Services wrote, "that the efficiency of the U.S. Postal Service improves considerably when you are not dealing with major cities on either coast." By 1982, 32% of all the mail sent to Sioux Falls went to Citibank but the local post office's performance did not suffer.

South Dakota was also remarkably well connected to the national telephone network and to newer satellite communications technologies. The reason was that South Dakota was then home to many of America's major military assets, including nuclear bombers stationed near Rapid City and 150 missile silos peppered throughout the state's many cattle pastures and cornfields. So South Dakota had excellent, redundant communication systems, and "one of the most progressive telephone switching systems in the country," according to one banker. It was almost as fast and cheap for Citibank headquarters to call Sioux Falls as it was to call an uptown branch. Moreover, Sioux Falls was in the central time zone, an hour behind Manhattan but in the same zone as Minneapolis, Chicago, Kansas City, St. Louis, and the rest of the densely populated Mississippi basin. That also put Sioux Falls just two hours ahead of California. Perhaps most important, it was more expensive for customers from most points in the country to call New York than Sioux Falls.

Of course, there had to be somebody in Sioux Falls to pick up the phone and monitor the mail, somebody who both needed a job and could adequately fulfill its duties. Due to the farm crisis, South Dakota in the early 1980s was home to sufficient numbers of un- and under-employed men and women to meet Citibank's staffing needs. Those people were educated and smart enough to do the work and their almost accent-less voices were perfect for call-center work. Moreover, due to their religiosity, which for the most part was a genuine sort of spirituality based on service to others and not just ritualistic or perfunctory church attendance, they worked earnestly on behalf of customers. And their country upbringing rendered them extremely diligent workers. All things considered, South Dakotans were one of the nation's most productive workforces.[155]

In addition, South Dakota's government kept the tax burden light, the 48th lowest in the nation at the time. The bank franchise tax paid by Citibank in South Dakota, for example, was 6.5% of profits, compared to the 15% that prevailed in New York at the time. In South Dakota, Janklow promised, "the only hand in your pocket is your own." The state's overall business climate was then ranked eleventh best in the country and employers enjoyed among the lowest rates for worker's compensation and unemployment insurance in the nation.

The state's wage structure was also low. In 1985, for instance, Citibank reported that it paid a temp agency $5.20 an hour per worker, who received only $3.80 of that sum. The federal minimum wage was then $3.35. Some, like native son Gilbert Fite and Ben Radcliffe of the South Dakota Farmers Union, complained that Citibank viewed South Dakota as "something akin to a third world country." In fact, the state's low wages were largely a function of its entrepreneurial economy and its low cost of living. High levels of entrepreneurship, explained economist Ralph Brown in 2000, meant that proprietors' income (non-farm and farm) was higher in South Dakota than in any other state.[156] Healthcare costs were a third cheaper than in New York, too, and house prices and rents were a mere fraction of those in and around the Big Apple. Overall, the cost of living was "well below the national average," leading to the claim that "In South Dakota, it costs less to live better."[157] At about 90%, disposable income as a percentage of total personal income was higher in South Dakota than any of her neighboring states and the national average.[158] The cost of living has since moved closer to national norms, but Sioux Falls, despite having evolved into a financial center, remains "not at all like New York City," though it does have at least one New York-style restaurant downtown.[159]

Sensing a big opportunity after Citibank's move, Janklow kicked the apparatus of the state government, such as it was, into high gear. State officials kept contact notes on prospective entrants similar to those maintained by corporate sales reps. Janklow also sent bankers engraved faux wedding invitations, complete with reply cards, to "a Renaissance of Free Enterprise." Not everyone, however, liked what they saw. The Bank of New York opted for Delaware instead and Sears, GMAC, and others jilted Janklow after courtships of varying lengths and intensities. New York commercial banks Manufacturers Hanover and Chemical Bank also investigated the Mount Rushmore State but didn't come. Seattle First National and Ranier, both based in Washington state, also looked hard at South Dakota, one going so far as to buy office space in Rapid City, but ultimately stayed away. Several other banks, however, including First City Bank of Houston, First National Bank of Omaha, and Michigan National Bank, moved card operations into the Sunshine State, some into Sioux Falls but others into Rapid City or Yankton.[160] As First City Bank president David Elgena confided, his bank's move to South Dakota ultimately hinged on "the quality of the workforce the operation could attract – including wives of farmers seeking to augment a dwindling farm income and graduates of the many small colleges here. ... Residents have a strong work ethic."[161]

Detractors complained that Janklow's actions were merely part of a zero-sum game: South Dakota's gain came at the expense of New York or wherever else lost business.[162] Janklow saw the matter more clearly: South Dakota offered businesses the opportunity to move from a regulated state economy to a relatively unregulated economy. Companies made the move when more freedom was necessary to increase efficiency (and hence profits) or even to stay in business at all. So South Dakota did not cherry pick from other states but rather spurred economic growth by providing some businesses with what they needed, more leeway and lower taxes.

When the 1982 election rolled around, therefore, Janklow was well positioned to defeat the Democratic candidate, Sioux Falls businessman and state senator Mike O'Connor, who attacked Janklow as the dictatorial tool of corporate interests. With almost 71% of the vote, Janklow won the contest by the widest margin ever while most people focused on the House race, the first after South Dakota lost a Representative due to its relatively poor showing in the 1980 Census.[163]

After his victory, Janklow created a Department of State Development to further diversify the state's economy out of agriculture and tourism. He also tried, unsuccessfully, to reprise his Citibank coup by creating an opportunity for big banks to enter the national insurance market by buying a South Dakota bank.[164] In March 1983, South Dakota again teamed up with Citibank to try to circumvent financial regulations, this time the regulatory wall that separated commercial banking and insurance. A decade previously, Citibank had tried to buy into the Chubb Insurance Group but was prevented from doing so by the Federal Reserve, the main regulator of bank holding companies. For his part, Janklow was interested "to gain more jobs for South Dakota" and to "bring down the artificial economic barriers that really don't do my state or America any good." The entering wedge was again a new law, this one allowing South Dakota banks to engage in insurance activities. To gain the acquiescence of the state insurance industry, which at that time numbered over sixty insurance companies and some 750 active agents and brokers, the law stipulated that state banks active in insurance could not attempt to lure customers away from other South Dakota insurers or banks. "Let's not kid ourselves," Janklow noted in a letter to concerned insurance men, "no large national financial services company is going to risk jeopardizing its unique opportunity to do business in forty-nine other states by trying to attract even a small amount of extra business in this state." In that same letter, Bill also adroitly pointed out that if South Dakota didn't pass the legislation another state would and that it wouldn't protect South Dakota insurers from outside competition.

Interest in the new law was intense. Within a few weeks of its passage, fifteen bank holding companies had begun investigating the possibility of entering insurance markets via South Dakota. By the end of June 1983, Citicorp had purchased American State Bank of Rapid City, First Interstate Bancorp had scooped up Big Stone State Bank, and Security Pacific Bancorp had announced its intention to make an acquisition, all with the intent of beginning insurance operations.[65] Those banks were optimistic because the Federal Reserve had for some years allowed the state-chartered bank affiliates of bank holding companies to engage in any activity which they were permitted to engage in under their state charters.

This time, however, Janklow and Citicorp were up against Paul Volcker, the insurance lobby, and common sense, not antiquated state usury statutes. An article in *American Banker* by Thomas E. Wilson called the theory behind the law "utterly bankrupt, belied by the plain language of the BHC Act and the well-established principle of the law that federal law predominates over state laws when the two come into conflict." Wilson also astutely noted that "it would be extraordinarily unwise" to permit bank holding companies to engage in insurance because "it is hard to imagine two industries more incompatible than banking and insurance."

Despite renewed sarcastic references to South Dakota, Inc., Janklow and Citibank fought hard and in November 1984 received the blessing of the Department of Justice, which reasoned that "there are substantial competitive benefits to be gained from permitting banking organizations to expand into new financial activities." But in the summer of 1985 the Federal Reserve rejected Citicorp's request to enter the insurance market because, as Wilson had noted, the law clearly differentiated between banking and related activities, which were lawful for bank holding companies or their subsidiaries to engage in, and insurance activities, which were not.

Volcker was adamantly opposed to allowing Citicorp or other BHCs from buying South Dakota banks as a mechanism for entering the national insurance market. In a May 1983 speech, he argued that a conservative approach to the matter was in order because it involved "an area vital to the stability and prospects of the economy as a whole." Federal Reserve governor Martha Seger was also opposed and pointed out that because South Dakota's law prevented competition within the state it was clearly designed solely to circumvent federal law. Not surprising, the Fed blocked the initiative.

Despite that setback, the state's economy improved and diversified dramatically during and after Janklow's second term. Governmental policies, however, do not deserve all of the credit for the economic resurgence of the state or its leading city. Established by the Sioux Falls Chamber of Commerce in the 1950s, the Sioux Falls Development Foundation (SFDF) was also involved in the transformation of Sioux Falls from "prime cuts to prime rates" and from pink quartzite buildings to modern office parks. As of 2000, it owned six industrial parks. As

SFDF drew businesses away from downtown, other commercial interests, including Forward Sioux Falls, Downtown Sioux Falls, and Main Street Sioux Falls, emerged to revitalize the older parts of the city. As Sioux Falls has grown, so too has city government, which regularly annexes surrounding areas as needed so that city services, and taxes, can be extended to new housing and commercial developments.[166]

Government and private planning, however, only directed market forces that had long been working towards economic diversification, as Figure 1 shows. Somewhat different data tell much the same story, that the state's economy had been slowly shifting away from agriculture well before Janklow, the SFSD, or others pushed it. In 1965, South Dakota was home to 6,457 companies large enough to pay unemployment insurance. Of those, only 98 (1.52%) were in agriculture, fish, and forestry, while 66 (1.02%) were in mining and quarrying, 862 (13.35%) were in contract construction, 395 (6.12%) in manufacturing, 320 (4.96%) in transportation, communication, and public utilities, 3,379 (52.33%) in retail, 489 (7.57%) in finance, and 848 (13.13%) in sundry services.[167] Regional economists realized what was happening and remarked that "South Dakota, like other Midwestern states, is becoming more diversified in its economy and the result is greater urbanization with less dependence upon agriculture."[168]

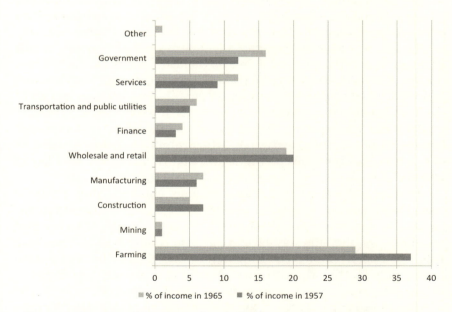

Figure 1: Sources of Income in South Dakota, 1957 and 1965. *Source: A. A. Volk,* The Economy of the Northeast Region of South Dakota *(Vermillion: Business Research Bureau, 1967), 28.*

Manufacturing had been on the increase in South Dakota since World War II, both in the form of the "expansion of established industries and the development of new ones."[169] In 1933, 348 manufacturing plants employed 4,731 South Dakotans. By 1951, approximately 500 plants employed some 10,000 people who annually turned out $100 million in products. By the early 1960s, the state had experienced a nearly 500% increase in manufacturing payrolls and value added since the war. Traditionally, South Dakota manufacturing was largely restricted to processing agricultural goods and hence entailed beef, pork, and mutton packing plants; flour mills; creameries; sugar refineries; and, in the Black Hills, sawmills and planing mills. After the war, however, emphasis shifted toward fabricating metals, assembling farm equipment, and creating building materials like cement and granite.[170]

Mining remained steady although output shifted somewhat from gold to more exotic materials like amblygonite, bentonite, beryl, beryllium, caesium, cassiterite, columbite-tantalie, feldspar, lepidolite, lithium, mica, microlite, pollucite, rose quartz, tin, tungsten, and uranium, all of which combined accounted for about half of the state's mining output in dollar terms by 1950. By 1980, the state was the nation's sixth largest producer of bentonite, which was used in bonding and water softening, and companies in Fall River County were producing some uranium and vanadium.[171]

Despite evidence that market forces were diversifying the state economy, Janklow's successor, George S. Mickelson, also took an active role in the state's economic development. Prodded by the Fantus Company of Chicago, a marketing firm that identified "critical economic trends affecting South Dakota,"[172] the Business Recruitment Council, which consisted of twenty-five members from government, industry, agriculture, and retailing charged with promoting "the business climate, quality of life, and opportunities in South Dakota,"[173] and the Business and Industry Round Table, a group composed of the Board of Regents, the Governor's Office of Economic Development, the Industry and Commerce Association of South Dakota, and Ag Unity of South Dakota, Mickelson unveiled an ambitious economic development program.[174]

Mickelson's Enterprise Initiation Program was an attempt to "build strong partnerships" among the state's leading "educational institutions, businesses and state government."[175] Mickelson's Future Fund, which was funded from residual monies in the state Unemployment Insurance Fund, and his CITE (Center of Innovation Technology and Enterprise) funded projects "based on whether or not, and how well, they related to the state's overall economic growth and development program."[176] The state also paid $1.5 million in technical assistance to local communities and small business, joint research programs with industry, and technology transfer and product development. Businesses chipped in $2 million in matching funds. The REDI Fund, a revolving loan fund for expanding industry, also helped to attract new businesses to South Dakota. Its aim was to create more "primary jobs" in the state by making loans to startups as well as funding the expansion of existing businesses and the relocation of companies from out of state. A few years later, a portion of the fund was cleaved off to form the Graduate Entrepreneur Loan Program (GELP), which provided low-interest loans of up to $50,000 to help recent high school and college graduates to open a new business. The state department of labor also pitched in, developing and then giving away more than 1,500 South Dakota Business Start Up Packages to South Dakotans interested in starting their own businesses.[177]

By 1989, an economic development finance authority allowed several enterprises to pool development bonds to lower the cost of issuance and interest charges as well. The South Dakota Development Corporation provided long-term financing to healthy and expanding small businesses. The Main Street Program helped cities and towns to implement their own economic development programs. The state also helped on SBA loans, local tax incentives, agricultural loans, industrial revenue bonds, and site location. The "Targeted Jobs Tax Credit" gave entrepreneurs up to $2,400 per year per covered worker, which included eighteen-to-twenty-two-year-olds from economically disadvantaged backgrounds, Vietnam veterans, felons, welfare recipients, handicapped persons, and SSI recipients. The state also funded free general job training called STEP (School Transition to Employment Partnership) and a Summer Youth Program that paid young people who worked for entrepreneurs. Additionally, an on-the-job training program paid half of a worker's wage during his or her training period. The FASTRACK program encouraged high school age entrepreneurs to start new businesses, in part to help stop the state's brain drain and youth emigration. The state also funded vocational-technical institutes in Sioux Falls, Mitchell, Watertown, and Rapid City and Career Learning Centers, which assisted potential workers who needed to learn "the most basic employment characteristics," in Aberdeen, Brookings, Huron, Lemmon, Madison, Pierre, Rapid City, Sioux Falls, Spearfish, and Watertown. Finally, the Job Service of South Dakota, which had 19 locations throughout the state, helped applicants and employers to locate each other.[178]

The precise effect of those programs proved difficult to assess but none was clearly a boondoggle. Not all development efforts, however, went well, and one could be called downright crappy. The state jumped when Consolidated Management Corporation promised a big payoff from mining gold out of raw sewage ash. The company shipped the ash from Minneapolis to Igloo, near Edgemont, for processing. It failed soon after cashing the last check from Minnesota but with numerous debts in South Dakota still unpaid. Worse, it never created the high income jobs it promised and it never extracted an ounce of gold from the burned feces.[179] In a scathing editorial, the Rapid City *Journal* claimed that the new state motto was "We'll Take It." Its statue of liberty would read: "Give us your heaped, huddled trash dumpsters, your straining Hefty garbage bags yearning to be free ... South Dakota – Trash Can for the Nation."[180]

If the state was burned by Consolidated Management, it was almost drowned by Energy Transportation Systems, a group of four companies that bought Missouri River water to lubricate its coal-slurry pipeline out of Wyoming's Powder River Basin. After ponying up $5 million, the company missed a payment and begged for more time so that it could find buyers of its wet, pulverized coal. Meanwhile, as mentioned previously, downstream states contested the deal. Soon after, Chem-Nuclear was close to irradiating the state with a nuclear dump but an environmental group sponsored a referendum that blocked the deal.[181]

Despite those fiascos and the dire predictions of certain prognosticators, the economy of the rural heartland stabilized in the late 1980s. Between 1987 and 1991, unemployment in South Dakota declined from 4.6-3.6% thanks to strong increases in non-ag employment, sales of trucks jumped, and construction activity increased, as did real personal income and real farm income. Ever since, starting with the 1990-91 recession, the state economy has been more stable than the national economy. Even the financial crisis and recession of 2007-09 was barely felt in South Dakota. While remote areas with low population densities still suffer, South Dakota's metro areas have continued to grow since the early 1990s, when people became attracted to the area's low taxes and crime rate and its high level of amenities for those interested in outdoor lifestyles.[182]

Several reasons for the dramatic turnaround are apparent. First, despite its economic activism, South Dakota's government remains relatively small. It grew in real per capita terms from 1980 to 1990, but in all categories except health and corrections it grew more slowly than the U.S. average. Government expenditures as a percentage of personal income actually shrank from 22 in 1980 to 18.6 in 1990, well below the national average of 19.5.[183]

Second, the state's economy, though still heavily dependent on agriculture compared to the overall national economy, continued to diversify, as Table 1 shows. The same story could also be told through the experiences of individual towns. For example, by the late 1980s, Spearfish's economy rested on six distinct "pillars": healthcare, higher

Industry	USA	South Dakota
Agriculture	2.0	13.0
Mining	1.9	1.8
Construction	4.0	3.2
Manufacturing	18.6	9.4
Transportation, Communication, and Public Utilities	9.8	8.7
Trade	16.4	17.2
Finance, Insurance, and Real Estate	18.0	20.6
Services	17.7	13.5
State-local government	8.0	7.3
Federal government	3.6	5.3
Totals	100	100

Table 1: Sources of Gross Domestic Product, US and South Dakota, 1991. *Source: Thomas F. Pogue, "Mounting Fiscal Pressures: How Can State and Local Governments Cope?" in* Economic Forces Shaping the Rural Heartland *(Kansas City: Federal Reserve Bank of Kansas City, 1996), 102.*

education (Black Hills State University), the Pope and Talbot lumber mill, several mining companies, agriculture, and tourism.[184]

Despite the changes, entrepreneurship remained strong. In a 1993 survey of family businesses in the state, researchers discovered that 40% had been formed prior to 1960. Half were still led by the founding generation but over 40% were in their second or later generation, up to six generations removed from founding. Most had started their business to achieve some measure of autonomy and half cited financial rewards as well. Only one in five indicated that they started a business because they could not find employment. Only one in twenty were going solo; almost three in four indicated that one, two, or three other family members were also involved in the business. Three in five businesses involved spouses, almost half involved children, and one in four involved brothers. Over the previous thirteen years, the companies surveyed reported increases in both sales, which jumped from an average of $2.7 million in 1980 to $5.7 million in 1993, and the number of employees, which increased from an average of twenty-three in 1980 to forty-two in 1993. Seven in ten indicated that they agreed with the claim that "SD is a business friendly state," yet over half indicated the biggest threat to the survival of their businesses was "Government regulations, taxes, etc." while only 20% felt exposed to economic fluctuation and only 14% were concerned with competition.[185] The results were telling: in some places, like Baltimore, Maryland, entrepreneurs have been known to quit in the face of overwhelming regulatory burdens imposed by their city and state governments.[186]

A study conducted in 1989 showed that South Dakota remained a small business state. Fewer than 700 businesses statewide employed more than fifty people; 60% of the state's 20,000 businesses employed fewer than five people and 90% employed fewer than twenty. Some 94% of the state's businesses had gross sales under $1 million that year. One in every three dollars of income in the state came from business proprietorship versus only 12% nationally. Some of that was due to the preponderance of farming, but even excluding agriculture, South Dakota remained a land where business ownership was important, a characteristic examined in the upcoming chapters: developments in agriculture and food processing (Chapter 5), construction, manufacturing, and trade (Chapter 6), fishing, hunting, tourism, and entertainment (Chapter 7), and education, health, and finance (Chapter 8).[187]

Chapter 5
Farming, Ranching, and Food Processing

My high school classmates from the farms were far more entrepreneurial than I realized.[1]

Agriculture is not the biggest component of South Dakota's economy and has not been for some time. By 2006, agriculture accounted for only about 7% of state product/GDP. Manufacturing contributed 11% and sundry services the balance. Agriculture remains important to the state's identity, however, and was important enough in 1985 that all 105 members of the legislature visited Washington, en masse, to lobby for agricultural subsidies. In typical South Dakota fashion, funding for much of that trip was raised privately and voluntarily by a radio station and not taken involuntarily from taxpayers.[2] The state's economy was then, and to some extent remains, indirectly "dependent upon the well-being of the farm population," upon the fortunes of which rested retailers and other components of the service sector.[3] Of course old distinctions between agriculture, manufacturing, and services no longer capture the complexity of today's increasingly diverse and globalized economy.

Any readers oblivious enough to harbor the old-fashioned notion that farmers and ranchers are pre-industrial rubes need to take a long drive through America's agricultural heartland. As they gawk at seemingly endless fields of perfectly planted corn, soybean, and wheat, gaze upon ungulate-studded pastures that stretch to the horizon, and stare amazed at the technologically sophisticated multi-million dollar machines that make food production possible on such a massive scale, they should hit the scan button on their radios. Between the sermons, the weather reports, and the country-western songs, they will hear somebody reporting prices, not of financial securities but of everything that springs forth from the earth, from orange juice to pork bellies.

Granted, most farmers and ranchers, no matter how sophisticated their businesses, behave as replicative entrepreneurs most of the time, not innovators. They use the latest and greatest technologies and techniques because if they didn't, they would soon be out of business, like the vast majority of people who came before them. In the hyper-competitive world of growing food (and fuel and raiment), an inefficient agriculturalist is soon a former farmer or a retired rancher. Intense competition can cause conservative business practices: many a farmer has refused to "bet the farm" on untested improvements no matter how promising they appear or how dire the current crisis. But competition also spurs innovation as producers look for an edge. Mostly, though, it encourages fast second movers. If the neighbor does X, and it works, you better do X next season. Farmers are famous for sharing information with each other and when they do not do so directly, their banks supply the information indirectly. The same goes for ranchers, who over the years have developed sophisticated strategies for coping with the effects of droughts and blizzards, among other shocks.[4]

The same pattern can be discerned in South Dakota's agricultural history, which provides evidence of a few first movers, some successful and some not. The former were quickly emulated by successful farmers. Failed agriculturalists either took big risks and lost or did not keep up with innovations quickly enough, only to discover that they could not produce corn or cattle as cheaply as their neighbors could. The latter can be seen as victims of railroads, weather, grasshoppers, international markets, deflation, inflation, and so forth, but in another sense they were simply failed entrepreneurs.[5]

As noted, some South Dakota agriculturalists successfully innovated. Finding just the right seed, like special strains of corn or alfalfa, and the technique best suited to one's locale could spell the difference between a comfortable living and a marginal existence. Hardy Webster Campbell of Brown County, for example, developed an eponymous system of dry farming, which included deep fall plowing, subsurface packing, and summer fallow, which helped farmers in the humidity transition zone between the James and Missouri Rivers (roughly the 98th to 100th meridians).[6] The Morrison family was also thought to have done "a lot for the settlement of the country [because] they were always out in front trying new things."[7]

Success spurred emulation. In the 1940s and 1950s, modernization, including mechanization and new methods, seeds, herbicides, fertilizers, and hybrids dramatically increased yields. In Beadle, Hamlin, Kingsbury, and Spink counties, for example, average corn yields soared from 35 to 51 bushels per acre, while oats jumped from 25 to 48 and wheat from 13.7 to 22.3 bushels per acre. Barley, rye, flax, sorghum, alfalfa, and sweet clover yields also increased. Farmers who lacked the capital, skills, time, or (due to government subsidies) the incentive to modernize soon found themselves in trouble, with costs far higher than revenues.[8]

As a group, though, agriculturalists adapted rapidly to conditions both propitious and inauspicious, so crop mixes varied over time as well as space, though corn, wheat, oats, barley, rye, flax, and various feed grasses dominated until the rise of soybeans and sunflowers. In the 1920s and 30s, for example, Hamlin County farmers shifted from primarily wheat to mixed farming of feed crops (barley, oats, corn) and dairy. Similarly, in the early 1960s sugar beet acreage increased from 6,000 to 10,000 in response to various economic forces. The movement of sunflowers and soybeans into the Winner area in the late 1990s shows that farmers remained open to new opportunities.[9]

Ranchers also readily responded to market forces. Between 1959 and 1964, the number of cattle increased from 3.3 to 4.1 million. South Dakota ranchers became more efficient during that half decade but also increased the number of cattle by shifting production from pigs and hogs (big pigs), which over that same period dropped from 2 to 1.8 million, and from sheep and lambs, which also dropped in number. In fact, wool production dropped precipitously after 1961, when it peaked at almost 16 million pounds, second only to output in 1942. Production later rebounded somewhat. In 1987, South Dakota was the fifth largest producer of sheep in the nation. Most production took place in the northwestern and eastern parts of the state.[10]

Experimentation and innovation continue to this day. By the end of 2013, for example, South Dakota was home to about two dozen or so grape wineries, which produced 105,000 gallons all told, a huge increase from the one tiny winery operating in the state in the late twentieth century. Most wineries can be found in the far eastern part of the state, extending almost as far north as Watertown, and in the Black Hills. All exist with help from federal subsidies but also innovative products. Some wineries make chokecherry and dandelion wines or sell their traditional grape wines in interesting new ways. White Headed Robin Winery in Viborg, for example, has done well selling its wine in bottles that come with collectible charms.[11] Others fortify their wine with extra alcohol, a selling point for some drinkers. Others get by with what the *New York Times* called their "homey charm."[12]

South Dakotans have also tried their hand brewing beer. In the 1910s, for example, Sioux Falls Brewing Company tried to increase sales of its Ambrosia Beer with advertising extolling the virtues of "patronizing home industry and home labor."[13] More recently, several dabbled in the microbrew craze. In 1992, two Anheuser Busch employees, Sandy Bennett and Dave Goldstone, established South Dakota Microbrewery. It posted its first profit at the end of 1995 and by the end of 1997 was producing three different labels, Buffalo Ale, Four Heads Stout, and Bismark Bock, which it sold to local pubs, colleges, restaurants, and upscale hotels.[14] It is now gone, along with a brewing company near Mount Rushmore that sold a beer called Politician's Wife, which had an intentionally bitter aftertaste.[15] Recent years have witnessed the birth of several new microbreweries, including the Gandy Dancer Brew Works at

Monks House of Ale Repute in Sioux Falls and Bitter Esters Brewhouse in Custer.[16]

The South Dakota Wheat Growers (SDWG) is another innovative organization that operates in some two dozen communities. It began operations in 1923 as a wheat pool that served growers in the Big Jim Valley. In 2000, it handled 100 million bushels of grain (also soya and corn) worth $30 million and paid dividends to some 5,000 farmer-stockholders. SDWG doesn't make anything but rather helps farmers to produce and sell by providing consulting, inputs, market know-how, and railroad shipping and storage. By 2007, SDWG had more than 3,600 active members across 37,500 square miles of some of the best wheat country in the nation. Its central storage facility could empty 500 trucks a day and load 440,000 bushels of grain in 12 hours.[17]

Innovation has also come out of the hoary bison industry. After being pushed to the edge of extinction, bison were finally domesticated in the late nineteenth century, largely through the efforts of Pete Dupree, a "half breed" Cheyenne (Sioux), and James Scotty Philip, a Scot who moved to Kansas in 1873-74 and then the Black Hills during the gold rush. Philip hauled freight before becoming a rancher and taking an Indian wife (and her land grazing rights). Later, he drilled wells around Pierre and developed some of its geothermal resources, but he remained primarily a

There are several buffalo, or American bison, ranches in South Dakota and herds in Custer State Park, Wind Cave National Park and Badlands National Park. *Courtesy South Dakota Department of Tourism.*

rancher and even organized the Minnesota and Dakota Cattle Company in 1890 with the help of Minnesota money. Meanwhile, Dupree, who did pretty well for himself as well, had started a small private bison herd. In 1901, Philip bought the Dupree herd of about ninety head of bison. By 1902, Philip had 500 head in pastures fenced in with high woven wire fences. Later, he ran 900 head, the largest privately owned bison herd in the world at the time, grazing on 10,000 acres of mortgaged range land.[18]

By rendering bison private property and not common property, ranchers like Philip created incentives to protect them. Bison products are now sold by retailers like Westside Meats in Mobridge, which sells bison raised by the Cheyenne River Sioux Tribe herd. A few ranchers also raise bison, including Dan O'Brien, in a free-range environment. O'Brien switched from cattle to bison because the latter are more adapted to the prairie, and the prairie to them.[19] He allows the bison to live "as close to a wild condition as possible," not to be "green" or "politically correct" but to maximize profits.[20] "It is the high expense-to-income ratio," O'Brien argues, "that has forever made the cattle industry tenuous."[21] In the winter of 1997-98, for example, 60,000 cattle and sheep died on the northern plains. Only one bison died, and it was run off a bridge by an eighteen-wheeler.[22]

O'Brien also kills, slaughters, and sells his own bison, which are direct descendants of Dupree's, to ensure that they are not stressed before death. Bison moved him from the brink of bankruptcy to solid solvency. In the 1980s, for example, he borrowed at 21% interest to buy cattle for $1,000 a head only to sell them for $400 each the next year.[23] "They were a sort of reverse beast of burden," bemoaned O'Brien. "*I* was carrying *them*!"[24] Today, O'Brien is able to cut out the middleman and sell directly to consumers because he found a meat inspector in Rapid City who had the good sense to realize that his procedures, while unusual today, were worthy of support. "I'd much rather do my inspecting out there in your pasture," the inspector told O'Brien, "than in a bloody, shitty, cattle-killing pen."[25] Other ranching outfits, while sticking to cattle, have also vertically integrated by growing their own feed, raising mother cows from calves, and running a slaughter plant in a nearby town.[26]

Many other farmers and ranchers, however, were too dumb or slow to make the changes necessary to keep their land.[27] That may sound mean but plenty of contemporaries reported that their bosses, husbands, or fathers were not very hard or smart workers and that some of the ladies were so frail that they needed help to "fetch a pail of water."[28] The farm crisis of the 1980s, the worst since the Depression, was driven in part by farmers and ranchers who had grown complacent, who hadn't kept reading, learning, thinking, trying, and experimenting. Hearing that between 1990 and 1997 another 20,000 farms "disappeared," many people were alarmed. In fact, the farms still exist; they were simply absorbed by more efficient operations. People who lose their farms or ranches tend to be very vocal about it. Some even write heart-rending books. Those who take over the land, however, are usually quiet. So it is not so much that the family farm is dying as uncompetitive farmers are being forced into different lines of work, a process that has been going on for a couple of centuries now.[29]

Throughout the state's history, those who made it through the rough times report having "found a way" to survive the sundry trials and travails they faced. One way was to get rid of the dead wood. Grace Fairchild, a former school teacher, moved ninety miles west of Pierre in 1902 with Shiloh, her husband of four years. Shiloh had constant, vague medical issues and according to Grace he was not a very good worker.[30] She divorced him in 1930 and he "moved into a shack of his own" so she "could now run the homestead without having a husband always around messing up things."[31] (Similarly, Lena King reported paying her husband $1,000 to "get off the place and never come back."[32]) Grace and her family were at first "barefoot and poor"[33] but eventually she expanded the ranch to 1,440 acres by having relatives homestead nearby, prove up, and then sell her the land, a tactic that other homesteaders also employed.[34] Grace, who grew up on a farm in Wisconsin where she learned to fish, spear fish, and hunt squirrels and rabbits, first with a BB gun, then a rifle, then a shotgun, also bought up land lost to relinquishments, foreclosures, and tax auctions.[35]

Such sensibility and foresight, combined with frugality, were often the difference between success and failure. Sweating the little things, like how much grass your truck destroys or how much water your cistern holds, could be the margin between life and death, survival and bankruptcy.[36] So, too, could having an extra stream of food or income, be it from gardening, beekeeping, orcharding, hunting, gathering wild fruits like plums and chokecherries, or grazing livestock on abandoned claims.[37]

Many South Dakota agriculturalists ran nano- and microenterprises in addition to their farms and ranches. As recently as the 1990s, for example, agriculturalists and other rural inhabitants put up travelers in their homes. At first most did not charge anything but later, as the countryside settled, farmers like Grace Fairchild charged for meals and a spot to sleep.[38] Similarly, Ed Eisenbraun's father "was a rancher, but also a businessman, having owned a little country store for a time" in Creighton (north of the Badlands).[39] Eisenbraun himself did the same thing, right out of his house, after bad weather destroyed his crops, again. Some, like a pool hustling Kimball farmer accordionist, worked off-farm or off-ranch out of sheer necessity, but others saw outside employment as a rational income diversification strategy. The Bower family, for example, farmed near Vermillion and made grocery money by playing band gigs. That extra income did not provide enough safety cushion, however, so the father also worked as a stonemason on area buildings and bridges.[40]

In fact, many early agriculturalists worked off the farm or the ranch for wages, especially in the winter. Since the 1970s, nonfarm income for farm families has again become important. Kathleen Norris and David Dwyer kept their ranch in Lemmon going for years by working in the local public library and saloon while doing freelance writing, bookkeeping, and computer coding. They also established a small cable-TV company and sold it for three years of blissful financial independence. In the end, they finally leased most of the ranch to family friends who needed more forage for their herds. Facing drastic reductions in corn and soybean prices in the early 1980s while their input (land, gasoline, equipment) prices skyrocketed, many farm families sent members to work off-farm on a part-time or full-time basis. In 1974, 10% of farmers reported working 200 or more days off-farm per year. By 1997, the proportion had risen to 23 percent. Most of those working farmers owned smaller, more marginal farms and identified themselves as farmers and hence fought hard to hold on, even if that meant holding down essentially two full-time jobs.[41]

Despite the seemingly dismal picture of farm life from frontier to modern times, the most successful agriculturalists have grown wealthy. Farmers worked hard but after two or three decades, an essayist declared in the 1920s, "he has now, I am assured, an immense barn, a big house, a telephone, a phonograph, a radio set, a motor-car."[42] He bought more land during the Depression, if he survived it, and thrived in the 1940s, 50s, and 60s.

By the 1980s, it was not unusual for farmers and ranchers to have half a million dollars sunk into their enterprises. As farm consolidation continued – the number of farms in South Dakota dropped from 55,727 in 1959 to 49,703 in 1964 to 34,057 in 1992 to 31,284 just five years later – average farm sizes increased from 804 to 917 to 1,316 to 1,418 acres and farm values soared to $487,039. (The average, though, obscures the fact that farms in the eastern third of the state were usually less than half the size of the average farm in the western part of East River, and that those were less than half the size of the average West River ranch.) Debt, though, was commonly about $132,000 on the Great Plains. In the late 1980s and early 1990s, booming exports to Japan, South Korea, Taiwan, and elsewhere, boosted the agricultural sector, especially producers of feed grains, soybeans, and cattle (live, meat, and hides). By the late 1990s, however, farmers were feeling pinched again, and agriculture wallowed in a recession, at least compared to the high-flying technology market.[43]

Not surprising, farm sizes, prices, and debt have continued to rise. Today, farms can be worth many millions. Some of that wealth is unfortunate from a societal standpoint because it comes from federal farm subsidies, with the biggest farms receiving the biggest subsidies. Most of what agriculturalists own, however, is well deserved. More risk must entail greater reward or nobody would farm or ranch, both of which are risky in a business and a physical sense. Crops can fail for any number of reasons and cattle can be lost due to surprise spring blizzards, heavy winter snows, calving during storms, droughts, and other natural calamities. They can break through fences and damage other people's fields and gardens. They can also kill their handlers directly by stomping them or indirectly by exposing them to delousing chemicals.[44]

Farming and ranching are not careers for the faint of heart or weak of body or mind. An old story says, in effect, if a horse gets hurt and has to be put down, the successful agriculturalist will say a prayer, shoot it, skin it, and use it as a winter blanket. Agriculturalists are not known for putting in forty-hour weeks making copies, feigning interest in spreadsheets, and conversing with colleagues around the water cooler.[45] In the late 1920s, one farmer reported, "We did not find peace on a large wheat farm. All we found was work, work, work," but even their constant toil seemed like a vacation compared to the daily struggle of dairying.[46]

Specialized agriculturalists were often among the most innovative. One, an English dandy, tromped around the prairie advertising the stud services of a large purebred Percheron, a type of French horse bred bigger, stronger, and faster than Clydesdales to pull Paris omnibuses. Others made money putting on rodeos, which were very popular West River in the 1920s but remain so to some extent throughout the state to this date.[47] A tourist in 1929 described the Belle Fourche roundup as "a gala affair. The people come there to spend money. Those running the various amusements and refreshment stands seem to understand this perfectly and render all possible assistance."[48] In 1952, the roundup was still going strong and still considered "well worth seeing."[49] Farmers also showed off their stuff and made some money in the process. In Sioux Falls in July 1960, for example, a national plowing contest was held and even attended by John F. Kennedy. He won election to the presidency that November anyway.[50]

Broom Tree Farm in Irene was an innovative attempt at turning farming into therapy. It was "a holistic renewal center" designed by Pastor Don Berheim and his wife, Helen, "to minister to clergy, to restore their physical, emotional and spiritual strength in a rural farm environment." After receiving a grant in 1990, its first guest arrived in

March 1991. By the mid-1990s, Broom Tree Farm was helping about three-score ministers per year to take a break from their stressful duties. Many found the "planned respite" helpful, calling "the environment of Broom Tree Farm … hospitable, safe, non-judgmental and hopeful." Another said, "I needed a time of healing … I bloomed and grew again" while yet another likened his time at Broom Tree to "the birthing process … I found a new world of challenges and possibilities opening up." Nevertheless, once the grant money dried up the corporation faced a series of budget deficits that fell largely on the Berheims, who took a sabbatical of their own in 1998. Early the next year, they resigned; the corporation turned over almost all of its assets to make good their back pay and rent and shuttered its service.[51]

The only activity at Broom Tree that turned a profit was the farm, which was an early entrant into organic farming, but far from the earliest. In Orland Township, Lake County, southwest of Madison, the Johnson family has been operating a large, organic farm since 1976. The man now in charge, Charlie Johnson, rotates corn, soybeans, oats, and alfalfa on his 2,800-acre spread while promoting the advantages of organic farming techniques. Organic farming may sound a little too liberal for South Dakota, but the fact is that Johnson can pretty much do as he pleases on his own land and so can anyone who wishes to emulate him. That relative freedom to innovate is one of the factors that, in the first decade of the Third Millennium, induced dairy farmers to move to South Dakota from the EU (European Union), especially Holland, where regulations were onerous, farms expensive, and milk cheap.[52]

A few of the state's most important agricultural entrepreneurs were not agriculturalists at all. In 1897, for example, South Dakota State Agricultural College professor Niels Hansen brought seeds from Siberia, including alfalfa varieties that grew at latitudes far higher than those Americans believed were possible. Hansen received numerous federal and state grants for his work at a time when governments did not regularly dole out money to scientists. He also ran a nursery in Brookings specializing in seeds that thrived in jackrabbit country; the famous

Located in Irene, the original Broom Tree Farm was an example of farming as therapy. The farm's retreat and conference center is now operated by the Catholic Diocese of South Dakota.
Courtesy Center for Western Studies.

Little Business on the Prairie

Gurney Nursery in Yankton also sold his seeds and crosses.[53] And Hansen was far from alone. "The State College at Brookings," one female farmer noted, "was to be a great help to all of us who believed in trying new things."[54] Today, companies like Hefty Seed of Baltic supply the state's farmers with high yielding seeds, soybeans in Hefty's case, that tolerate high pH soil levels, resist crop destroying bugs and diseases, and that match local climatic conditions.

Another important non-agriculturalist entrepreneur was Peter Norbeck, the future state governor. Around the turn of the twentieth century, Norbeck improved an old well drilling machine so that it could dig down 1,700 to 1,800 feet to find the aquifers that underlay much of the state. His company, incorporated in 1901, ended up buying custom rigs and drilling over 10,000 wells in South Dakota and neighboring states. His North Dakota Artesian Well Company, established in 1905 and capitalized at $40,000, drilled 710 wells between 1905 and 1909 alone.[55]

Although essentially a type of manufacturing, food processing is of course intimately related to agriculture, and its history in the state is an important and hoary one. According to a state census completed in 1947, 70% of the state's 10,300 "industrial" workers were employed in plants that processed meat, grain meal, dairy, and other agricultural products. By 1889, eighty-two flour mills, like the St. Olaf Roller Mill in Baltic, were already in operation in the state, and large creameries, breweries, and pork packing plants were churning out their wares at Yankton and Sioux Falls, "with smaller houses at Mitchell, Woonsocket and Pierre."[56]

Sometimes, processing plants sprang up near existing centers of production. Early South Dakota entrepreneurs, for example, erected grain elevators along railroad right of ways in districts where farmers were successfully growing corn and wheat. Those "prairie skyscrapers," so-called because they are usually the highest point on the prairies, are less common now, but bigger and more efficient than ever. Other times, farmers or ranchers specialized because a processor appeared nearby. The area around Sioux Falls, for example, became one of the nation's largest hog producing areas because of the John Morrell & Co. pig packing plant established there on the eve of the Great War.[57]

John Morrell & Co. began operation in England in 1827 and later spread to Ireland, Canada, and America, including Cincinnati, which was home to so many hog butchering plants that it became known as Porkopolis. Later, Morrell established a plant in Ottumwa, Iowa, and Topeka, Kansas, but by 1909 it needed another large plant in the west and settled on Sioux Falls, production at which equaled and sometimes even exceeded that of Ottumwa after an initial learning curve. It soon added cattle processing and was so successful that a bigger plant was built and put in operation by April 1911. To avoid high British taxes, the U.S. plants soon split off from the mother corporation and chartered in Maine and Delaware. World War I brought a boom and increased capacity on the hog killing floor, which was remodeled in 1922. Peak production, 2,893 hogs per day, was insufficient during the busy season, however, so the facility was upgraded again, to a capacity of 5,000 hogs per day. Reductions in hog production by local farmers caused Morrell to step up its cattle capacity and, in August 1929, to add a creamery. Early on, Morrell purchased most of its hogs and cattle directly from producers, bypassing middlemen like the Sioux Falls Stock Yards Company, which made a market in live stock from its founding in 1889 until it sold out to Swift in 1924.[58]

Labor relations were strained after the war but Morrell defeated union-led strikes in 1918, 1920, and 1921. It became somewhat more paternalistic after that by organizing sports teams and establishing an employee representation organization or "company union." In 1924, it offered workers with good attendance records a week's paid vacation and free life insurance ranging from $500 to $2,000, depending on length of service. The Depression hurt the company but World War II and the sustained postwar economic boom aided it. In 1968, most of the hogs and cattle came in from Sioux Falls' traditional catchment area, southeastern South Dakota, southwestern Minnesota, and northwestern Iowa, but ranchers and farmers from most counties east of the Missouri sent at least some beeves to Morrell's Sioux Falls plant, which Smithfield Foods eventually acquired. In Huron, Armour and Company operated a plant from 1925 until the 1980s. Other major processors included Federal Beef in Rapid City and Cimpl meats in Yankton.[59]

In 1980, the top packing companies accounted for 35% of all beef slaughtered in the United States. Twenty years later, they accounted for about 80% and purchased only 40% of their cattle in the cash market. The rest came from their own herds or ranchers under contract. In 2002, increased concentration in the meatpacking industry led to a Congressional probe, including a Senate judiciary committee hearing on the matter held in Sioux Falls. At that hearing, entrepreneur-ranchers from Belle Fourche and Watertown complained about packer domination and even manipulation of the live-cattle market.[60] Smithfield Vice President Steve Crim criticized the hearings as having "blatant political overtones just prior to an election."[61]

In 2013, a Chinese company bought Smithfield but operations in Sioux Falls continued as usual. It was not the first to succumb to frequent industry shakeouts. Dakota Pork in Huron closed in 1997, leading to a precipitous decline in the state's pork production, from over three million head in the mid-1990s to fewer than two million head in 1998. Directly and indirectly, the closure cost the local economy some 900 jobs. Dakota Poultry Processing dressed poultry, including turkeys, for retail sale. In 1973, when it could not attract enough workers to its Watertown plant, it ran a bus service from Sisseton. It survived that ordeal, plus floods, fires, and droughts, but eventually failed.[62]

Another major food processor, Manchester Biscuit, formed in Luverne, Minnesota, in 1900 but its founder, Lawrence Manchester, moved it to Sioux Falls in 1902. By 1930, Manchester was president of United Biscuit, which formed in 1927 out of the merger of Manchester Biscuit and over half a dozen other biscuit manufacturers.[63] By the 1950s, United Biscuit's Sioux Falls factory employed 400 people who made "varied assortments of appetizing crackers, cookies, and wafers." The company, which operated "in many large cities of the Middle West,"[64] shuttered its Sioux Falls plant in 1960. Fifteen years later, Interbake Foods of Canada moved into North Sioux City, employing as many as 1,100 South Dakotans.[65]

Dairy farming was long a staple in some parts of the state. In 1889, the state's farmers produced 18 million pounds of butter. Cheese production, however, proved more difficult. By the late 1880s, a cheese factory, the Crystal Spring Cheese Factory, had opened in Rapid City "and every family started to milk cows." [66] The Crystal Spring shut down in 1888, however, after just a year of operation, because most people found it more profitable to raise beef. Meat prices were better and less work was involved. Exactly forty years later, and on the other side of the state, Swiss immigrants Alfred Bonzenbach and Alfred Nef agreed to begin making cheese in Milbank's abandoned water filtration plant. Considered, wrongly, "the first institution of this kind in South Dakota" by the *Milbank Herald Advance*, the company, called Valley Queen Cheese, survived the Depression through luck and pluck. Local farmers clung tenaciously to their dairy cows throughout the downturn, and Valley Queen struck an important contract to supply Kraft Foods with cheddar longhorns and daisies (cylinders and wheels). Because ten pounds of milk produced one pound of cheese and nine pounds of whey, the company maintained its profitability by finding outlets for the whey, including butter, whey protein, lactose (milk sugar), water, and even dog food. At the time of writing, Valley Queen still made cheese for Kraft and under its own brand and its owners, Rudy Nef and family, were prosperous and generous enough to endow a professorship at Augustana College held by the author of this book. Davisco Foods International also runs a cheese factory, in Lake Norden, the motto of which is "Cheese Is Our Whey."[67]

South Dakota Soybean Processors (SDSP), a co-op that in 1995 enrolled over 2,300 growers, each of whom pledged $5,000 toward the construction of the state's first soybean processing plant, is located on the south side of Route 14 in Volga, just west of Brookings. Although about half of soybean processors had gone under or been bought up in the previous fifteen years, co-op administrator and Volga mayor Bill Riechers believed that building a plant was the right way to guarantee farmers the best return on their crop. After all, of the 90 million bushels shipped out of the state annually for processing, almost 40% was shipped back in for animal feed. Why not just process the beans in South Dakota, Riechers asked, and save on freight and middleman charges? He was right. By 2007, SDSP was owned and operated by 2,100 farmers from South Dakota and Minnesota. The plant in Volga employed sixty people and crushed 80,000 bushels per day on average, some 28 million bushels annually. It established an independent company, Urethane Soy Systems, to market value-added products like soy oil, building insulation, automotive seat cushions, and even spray-on bed liners for pickup trucks.[68]

Based in Huron, Dakota Provisions and its state-of-the art technology is owned and operated by over two-score turkey producers who in 2003 banded together to capture more economic return from their birds. Their plant, which came online in 2006, employed 500 and harvested 16,000 turkeys per day. It also cooked beef and pork products to supply the ready-to-eat meat market. At first it hired people already living in and around Huron, but soon it had to recruit immigrants and ended up setting off a migration of Karen, an oppressed minority from Myanmar (Burma), who had been previously working in St. Paul, Green Bay, Lincoln, and other U.S. communities. By 2013, more than two-thirds of the production workforce was Karen and about 170 Karen families settled in the Huron area, which saw a jump in new housing construction because of it.[69] Supervisors told Federal Reserve researchers that Karen typically "are industrious workers who learn readily on the job and turn up every day."[70]

Near Flandreau, Dakota Layers Cooperative produces chicken eggs. Its three-score employees package about 60,000 eggs daily.[71] In March 2012, its 100 farmer-investors believed the concern was doing well enough to be able to afford a donation of 10,000 eggs to Feeding South Dakota. "Our owners feel that we are obligated to give back to our community," Dakota Layers President and CEO Scott Ramsdell told members of the local media.[72]

Another important agricultural processor, though a family-owned business rather than a co-op, is also concerned with "giving back" by running the safest operation it can. Headquartered in Dakota Dunes, Beef Products, Inc., was founded in 1976 by Eldon and Regina Roth. Today, it specializes in high-quality lean beef and is a recognized leader in food safety innovation, often implementing cutting-edge safety procedures well in advance of regulatory mandates and its competitors. Tests for rare, deadly strains of E. coli cost a little more but company officials believe the added expense is well worth it. Dakota Dunes was also the home of IBP, the nation's largest beef packer and second largest pork producer. Tyson purchased the company in 2001.[73]

Numerous cooperative enterprises have been active in the state but many that expanded aggressively by taking on debt ran into problems and folded. Others, like Valley Springs, which sold corn, soybeans, fertilizer, petroleum, and feed for farmers near Sioux Falls, thrived by keeping debt levels low and customer satisfaction high. "If you take care of members," President David Kolsrud said, "new members will come in through the door. And that's what has happened."[74] Due to scale economies, however, there is constant pressure on co-ops to merge, as Fremar Farmers Cooperative of Marion and Central Farmers Cooperative of Salem did in 2007, with four in five of their members in favor of the move.[75]

Other types of businesses also process agricultural goods in South Dakota. Hayco Premium Forage, for example, was a partnership between farmers and a processing business in Sioux Falls that produced high-quality feed products for horses and cattle. It certified its products to be weed and dust free and sun-dried. Female horse owners on the East Coast were the primary market but new markets in the Pacific Rim and national parks are emerging.[76] In 1994, the Walter family of Willow Lake established Dakota Farms International to market agricultural products, including certified organic barley and barley tea, buckwheat, corn, rye, soybeans, soy flour, meal, trail mix, and wheat, both domestically and overseas. In 1997, it made its first shipment to Asia. President Tim Walter explained that the company wanted "to gain more of the end price by moving further up the supply chain."[77] At the other end of the ownership spectrum, Glanbia Nutritionals Ingredient Technologies, a $4.2 billion multinational corporation headquartered in Kilkenny, Ireland, announced in 2012 that it would replace an Angusville, Manitoba, plant destroyed by fire by building a 40,000-square-foot cereal ingredient processing plant in Sioux Falls. The site was selected because of the proximity of Sioux Falls to both flaxseed growers and efficient transportation networks and strong support from state officials.[78]

Despite all of that activity, in the 1990s South Dakota had the third highest ratio of farm output to food processing output behind only Wyoming and Montana. That means it produced much more food than it processed. Today, processing agricultural goods remains a growth industry in the state, but much rides on the continued development of biofuel technology.[79]

In 2000, Lake Area Processors Cooperative broke ground on an ethanol mill called Dakota Ethanol near Wentworth. Almost 1,000 corn growers, 98% from South Dakota, were members, each pledging at least 5,000 bushels per year in raw material. In 2013, the plant's two-score employees produced 48 million gallons of ethanol from 17 million bushels of locally grown corn. A larger plant owned by VeraSun annually produced 230 million gallons of ethanol in Aurora, near Brookings, until its failure in 2008 due to low prices and shrinking demand. Despite VeraSun's bankruptcy, South Dakota remains one of the nation's largest producers of ethanol, thanks in large part to POET, which began on the Broin family farm in Wanamingo, Minnesota, in 1983 and subsequently spread into neighboring states, including South Dakota in 1987. The Broin's plant in Scotland, South Dakota, was expanded on numerous occasions and still operates as POET's main research facility. POET's plants are environmentally friendly, spewing out nothing but fuel and quality livestock feed. POET also designs and/or manages plants for other companies, including Dakota Ethanol, Prairie Ethanol in Loomis, and the 100-million-gallon-per-year Great Plains Ethanol plant in Chancellor. It also buys methane from the Sioux Falls landfill. By 2003 it employed 560 people, including, by 2006, 150 workers at its headquarters in Sioux Falls.[80]

Chapter 6
Building, Making, and Selling

Because of men and women of imagination and drive in South Dakota, there is a successful gemstone manufactory in Lemmon, a candle-making industry in Isabel, agricultural equipment production in Salem, and an industrial crystal plant in Yankton. The little village of Lesterville has a thriving interstate smoked fish business.[1]

South Dakota's real estate prices are relatively low. Land is plentiful but not really cheap, especially where people most want to live, because it is valuable agricultural land. Developers look for the cheapest suitable land, of course, but houses are inexpensive compared to houses elsewhere largely because the state's construction industry is efficient. Steel must be brought in from elsewhere, but other building materials are available in sufficient quantities within the state: lumber from the 1,000-man lumber industry in the Black Hills, cement making materials from the Hills but multiple other locales as well, and granite from quarries in Sioux Falls, Milbank, and Harney Peak, which at 7,242 feet is the highest point on earth, between the Alps and the Rockies, that is.[2]

Gold was long the most valuable resource pulled from beneath South Dakota's earth, but sand, gravel, and granite were typically next in line in terms of aggregate value. Sand and gravel were used for construction, masonry, glass manufacturing, and roads. The granite from the Milbank outcrop was called Mahogany Granite due to its dark coloration; that from Harney Peak was tan or even flesh colored and that from Sioux Falls was pink. The pink stone, which was technically a quartzite, especially found a ready national market after the railroads came and made it cheap to haul away. The granite in Milbank, by contrast, had a narrower market at first. Dakota Granite received research help from the Business Research Bureau of USD/Future Fund to add more value to its granite, by turning it into tiles, before selling it. By the late twentieth century, due to its beauty, Milbank's granite was marketed mostly for decorative purposes and mostly internationally. In 2006 alone, Dakota Granite and Cold Spring Granite mined 257 kilotons. (To this day, Milbank's residents primarily work in the granite quarries, for the electric plant, in Rudy Nef's cheese factory, or in either of two small insurance companies.)[3] Southeastern South Dakota was also endowed with quartzite, the largest deposits "ever discovered" up to 1889.[4] They were eighty feet thick in Sioux Falls and sixty in Dell Rapids, so much, that it was shipped via rail "to the large cities for paving purposes" and employed hundreds. A contemporary called the deposits "practically inexhaustible" and indeed some are still worked today.[5]

The rocks quarried near Sioux Falls were amenable to polishing, so with the falls of the Big Sioux River nearby, a polishing industry sprang up.[6] In 1884, Drake Polishing Works began operations and at some point began polishing petrified wood from Arizona, which it sold to Tiffany of New York for further processing into jewelry, table tops, and clock faces. "As a result of this business," the obituary of one of the early polishers claimed, "the name of Sioux Falls was broadcast to fanciers of precious stones the world over. The King of Belgium of that time had articles made here of the petrified wood, and the gentry of England, France, Turkey, and many other countries were interested in it." Payroll at one point hit $10,000 per month but after some thirty-five carloads of petrified wood had been shipped to Drake's, the federal government shut down the trade. When founder James H. Drake died circa 1910, the works went down with him.[7]

Before the trees of the Black Hills became available on the prairie, entrepreneurs shipped lumber from the verdant forests near the Great Lakes. During the Great Dakota Boom, much of the lumber was brought in by Laird, Norton Lumber Company of Winona, Minnesota. Established in 1855, Laird had an extensive marketing network in the Dakotas and did a volume business. It sent sixty-seven cars of lumber to Watertown in May and June of 1879 alone. It successfully penetrated other parts of the state by following on the heels of the rail lines. Some of its agents were mere employees but others enjoyed partial ownership of the yards they managed, rendering them particularly hardworking and efficient.[8]

After World War II, South Dakota construction contractors were aided by federal building projects. The Pick-Sloan dams were manna but so too were numerous small projects spread across the state, ranging from missile silos to military ordnance depots. More important than government contracts, though, was the fact that South Dakota construction companies competed on value, not price. In many other parts of the nation, contractors bid on jobs and owners generally contract with the lowest bidder. Once on the job, however, construction contractors are near monopolists and have devised all sorts of excuses for charging owners more than the bid price through so-called "change orders." Owners who resist the increased price find their projects delayed. That is why most construction projects end up over budget or past deadline and why most construction companies are tiny and inefficient at building.[9]

A different dynamic usually prevails in South Dakota, where construction companies tend to compete more on quality and price than on their expertise at strategic bidding and change order "artistry." From the beginning to this day, South Dakota construction companies faced a competitor not usually found elsewhere, the building-moving company. It was not uncommon to move buildings in South Dakota, often considerable distances. In a place without many trees, wood buildings were too valuable to allow to rot. If moving a building intact proved too costly, it was disassembled and its lumber recycled to construct new buildings. (Foreclosed farm buildings seem to have been the exception.) After a major flood, the entire town of Vermillion was moved up the hill by entrepreneurs like Calvin Bower, who helped with the moving, and his wife Keziah, who fed the moving and construction crews. Sometimes, farm houses and barns were moved just a few hundred yards to be closer to water wells. Other times, buildings were moved large distances by train and, later, by truck. After the railroad faded from importance, many early train depots were moved miles from their original locations to serve new owners as farm buildings, artist studios, storage sheds, museums, and even private homes. When a Pick-Sloan dam made the inundation of Pollock inevitable in the late 1950s, the entire town relocated to the south and many homeowners moved their houses rather than construct new ones. Native Americans still move houses, using dish liquid to help them slide the edifices off their blocks. In 1997, Operation Walking Shield entailed moving sixty houses slated for demolition on military bases to Pine Ridge and Rosebud. Finally, just a few years ago, the recently repurposed governor's house was moved from Pierre to Rapid City, a distance of 175 miles along Route 14.[10]

South Dakota prisoners also competed against the state's construction firms by building housing appropriate for retirees in towns of 5,000 or fewer residents. Between 1996 and 1998, inmates at the Springfield and Sioux Falls prisons constructed 175 houses later moved to foundations built on site by non-prisoners in more than ninety communities across the state.[11]

South Dakota's construction companies are also relatively flexible, because they have to be. Not every town can have its own bison fencing company or its own chain-link fencing company because the markets are too thin. So many fencing companies do both, and a whole lot else besides. Moreover, because new houses are relatively cheap, they are in high demand, especially in the booming southeastern part of the state. That keeps construction companies profitable, eager to please, and in business. The endurance of South Dakota's construction companies attests to their efficiency relative to the constant turnover of construction contractors in many other states.[12]

Ronning Enterprises traces its roots to the 1880s, when Thomas C. Marson, a quartzite quarrier from Wales, settled in Sioux Falls and erected many of the city's most important early buildings and houses. D. Wayne Ronning, husband of Marson's great-granddaughter Harriet, joined the company in 1956 and started to build affordable, single family houses. The company, which is still 100% family owned, has built more than fifty neighborhoods in South Dakota and has spread into home supply, apartment building, and property management businesses as well. It was also one of the first construction companies in the region to build some components offsite.[13]

Established in 1919, the Henry Carlson Company was by the 1930s one of the largest building and construction companies in South Dakota. It built landmarks like the Veterans Administration Medical Center, the State Capital Annex in Pierre, the original Washington High School (now the Washington Pavilion), both major hospitals in Sioux Falls, the Sioux Falls Arena, Joe Foss airfield, the Minnehaha County Courthouse, and Scheels. It also owns Asphalt Surfacing Company, which does highway, street, and parking-lot repair and snow removal, and the Kyburz-Carlson Construction Company of Aberdeen.[14]

Among the many buildings designed by Harold Spitznagel is that of Augustana College's Mikkelsen Library, which opened in 1955, after a community-wide fund appeal. The wall of windows on the north side is a particularly striking architectural feature. The building was enlarged in 1980 and completely renovated in 2009.
Courtesy Center for Western Studies.

South Dakota has also been blessed with the services of several excellent architects, including Frank Charles William Kuehn, who grew up in a sod house tending cattle near Huron but longed for more. When he needed work in 1900, he took architecture classes from International Correspondence Schools of Scranton, Pennsylvania. In the half century after earning his degree, Kuehn designed some 500 buildings, including homes, churches, banks, general office buildings, hotels, and public buildings like courthouses, libraries, and schools, in Huron, Alpena, Carthage, Howard, Wessington Springs, Woonsocket, and elsewhere in the region.[15]

Born in Sioux Falls in 1896 to entrepreneurial parents, owners of the Model Bakery on South Phillips Avenue, Harold Spitznagel received a bachelor's in architecture from the University of Pennsylvania in 1925 and won two prestigious design awards in the process. After stints in Indianapolis and Chicago, where he helped to design large commercial projects for big construction contractors like Burnham Brothers, he returned to Sioux Falls in 1930 to ply his art. Over the next four decades, Spitznagel built a solid reputation based on his integrity, his manner, and, most important, his excellent design skills. It was said that he designed each building as if it were his own and that he trained his staff carefully and monitored them closely, making them "donate" ten to fifteen cents to the Christmas Party fund each time they farted or burped within earshot. Spitznagel excelled at the art-deco or "moderne style" that was so popular early in his career because of its clean, straight lines and lack of architectural detailing. After a slow start, he won the contract for Sioux Falls' municipal building, which earned his company much notoriety and other business, including Sylvan Lake Lodge in the Black Hills, a project upon which Frank Lloyd Wright declined to bid. As Sioux Falls grew, from 33,000 in 1930 to almost 41,000 in 1940, so too did Spitznagel's company and workload. Lincoln High School and scads of private residences arose from his sketches and plans, as did the Hollywood Theater, which was demolished in 1990 to make room for something newer but not necessarily better, and a new cell block for the State Penitentiary. He also designed the Huron Arena, the Sioux Falls Arena, the Ottumwa Country Club in Iowa, and over two dozen churches.[16]

In 1889, Dakota booster Frank Hagerty claimed that "Dakota's manufacturing possibilities and capabilities have been largely overlooked."[17] In the early 1970s, native son and South Dakota historian Gilbert Fite pointed out that "however much the state may have wanted to join the mainstream of America's industrial development, and however much local chambers of commerce talked about attracting industry to the state, it was not to be."[18] Both were right. If you see a hulking structure on the horizon in South Dakota it doesn't make steel or automobiles but rather soybean products (South Dakota Soybean Processing in Volga) or ethanol (one of POET's plants). To this day, South Dakota is not known for its manufacturing prowess, especially outside of food processing (milling, meat packing, dairy products), industries associated with mining, like Auric-CHLOR Corporation of Rapid City, which removed impurities from scrap gold, and western-themed niches like the bison-hide furniture made by Dakota Bison Furniture. That is because it generally does not pay to ship non-agricultural raw materials to the prairie, process them on prime agricultural land, then ship them to urban markets. Sometimes, however, it made sense to process locally sourced raw materials and then sell the manufactured product regionally. That was the general idea behind the Sioux Falls Woolen Mill established in the 1890s by Fred W. Pettigrew, which bought a small portion of the two million pounds of wool South Dakota produced and turned it into flannels, blankets, yarns, cassimeres, and tweeds for sale in the state and "other states tributary" to Sioux Falls. The factory, which was 264 feet by 264 feet, featured two sets of machinery driven by an 85-horsepower Corliss engine, a 90-horsepower boiler, and a dynamo for electric lighting.[19]

As a result of South Dakota's comparative advantage in agriculture, a number of its native sons left for careers in the East. One, Thomas Fawick, designed, built, and sold five automobiles, called Fawick Fliers, in Sioux Falls in the 1910s before heading to Iowa to build tractors. He later moved to the Twin Disc Clutch Company in Racine, Wisconsin, where, among other projects, he designed and built clutches for a new U.S. military airship to replace the Roma, which crashed in 1922 "costing the lives of most all on board." Later that very year, Fawick wrote his brother that "It was sure hard for me to get anywhere out there [Sioux Falls], thats [sic] no place for me and I'm sure you would have done better if you had left everything there and left some years ago." Fawick later moved to Akron, Ohio, where he made clutches for naval boats.[20] In the 1970s, a grateful Thomas Fawick donated jointly to the City of Sioux Falls and Augustana College full-scale bronze castings of Michelangelo's *David*, located in Fawick Park, and *Moses*, located on the college campus.

By the 1950s, however, some of the state's manufacturers found that they did not have to head East (or West, or North, or South) to make a go of it. Ed Maguire (1894-1968) of Maguire Iron Preserving Company, Inc., for example, worked out of Sioux Falls and Sioux City. Starting in the 1920s, he helped to repair and prevent rust in water towers, but in the 1950s he developed a new technology, called the Baltic Bleeder, which prevented water tank pitting not associated with rust. "This unique system," one of his promotional pieces explained, "is designed to drain out and neutralize all of the electrical charges that cause the electrochemical reaction that results in pitting attacks on the steel plates inside a water storage tank." Dozens of recommendations indicate that the technology worked as advertised; before his death, Maguire had installed the Bleeder in over fifty South Dakota water towers and scores more in Iowa, Minnesota, and Nebraska.[21]

That is not to say that South Dakota was a manufacturer powerhouse. In 1950, only 5% of South Dakota's workers were employed in manufacturing and they were not evenly distributed over the landscape. In the West North Central Region, for example, only 1% of workers were engaged in manufacturing. The far western and southeastern parts of the state, by contrast, were relatively more industrialized than the state average. In 1958, more than half of the state's manufacturing capacity was located in a dozen counties in the state's southeast corner. That was partly due to the urban nature of most manufacturing, especially the larger scale factories. In 1958, Sioux Falls, Rapid City, Aberdeen, Watertown, and Mitchell, the state's five largest cities, accounted for only 40% of the state's manufacturing establishments, but 71% of all manufacturing workers, 77% of manufacturers' payrolls, and 74% of manufacturers' value added. Food processing accounted for 64% of all manufacturing activity, printing 12%, lumber and wood 8%, and stone, clay, and glass production another 5%. All other manufacturing categories accounted for the final 11%.[22]

As Figures 2, 3, and 4 show, the number of manufacturers, the number of factory workers, and manufacturing value added grew slowly over the 1950s and 1960s but took a jump in the 1970s and 1980s, even though many endeavors proved to be only temporary boons to the economy. Litton Industries was one of about 100 businesses that moved to South Dakota from Minnesota between 1969 and 1984[23] in search of lower costs. The moves perplexed Minnesota governor Rudy Perpich, who quipped that "when you wake up in South Dakota, you're still in South Dakota" and that South Dakota was "50th in everything."[24] In fact, by some measures South Dakota had the fourth best business climate in the nation, compared to Minnesota's 48th place finish.[25] Five years later, Perpich admitted that his state was "doing so much better (now)" by reforming its business climate to be more like South Dakota's.[26] Litton, at one time the largest producer of microwave ovens in the nation, eventually went under, but blocked the sale of its Sioux Falls microwave plant, which at its peak had employed 2,250 workers in a 250,000-square-foot facility in the Sioux Empire Development Park, to French interests.[27]

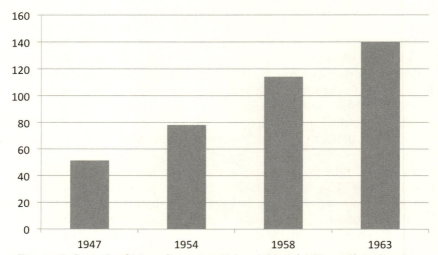

Figure 2: Growth of Manufacturing Value Added (millions $) in South Dakota, 1947-1963. *Source: A. A. Volk,* The Economy of the Black Hills Region of South Dakota *(Vermillion: Business Research Bureau, 1968), 49.*

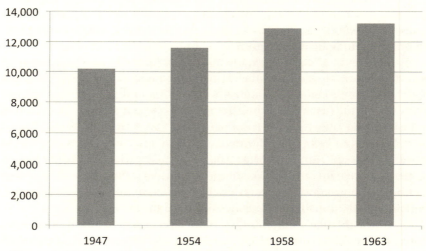

Figure 3: Number of South Dakota Industrial Workers, 1947-1963. *Source: A. A. Volk,* The Economy of the Black Hills Region of South Dakota *(Vermillion: Business Research Bureau, 1968), 49.*

In the early 1970s, Sencore, the "No. 1 Manufacturer of Electronic Maintenance Equipment" moved all of its operations from Addison, Illinois, to Sioux Falls because of the latter's productive workforce, right-to-work law, and favorable tax structure. It is still in operation in Sioux

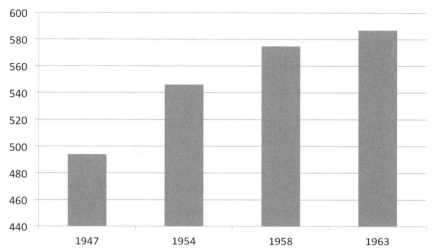

Figure 4: Number of South Dakota Manufacturing Establishments, 1947-1963. *Source: A. A. Volk,* The Economy of the Black Hills Region of South Dakota *(Vermillion: Business Research Bureau, 1968), 49.*

Falls. Grant, the largest manufacturer of motorcycle helmets in the world (including its plant in Los Angeles), also came to Sioux Falls in the early 1970s in search of productive workers and low taxes. A few years later, however, Royal bought Grant and shuttered its Sioux Falls plant.[28]

Established in 1971, Dakotah, a home-furnishings manufacturer, operated seven factories in northeastern South Dakota and boasted 400 "owner-employees." Sales of $15.7 million made it "one of the most successful firms in its market and the largest U.S. worker-owned manufacturing enterprise."[29] It is now part of Creative Home Furnishings, Inc. In 1980, though, it was just one of over 900 manufacturing firms doing business in the state. Most employed fewer than 25 people but 76 employed more than 100 workers each. Most were still ag-related: 20 meat packing and sausage plants, 15 cheese factories, and numerous creameries, poultry and egg processing plants, and flour mills.[30]

In 1985, however, accounting firm Alexander Grant & Company increased South Dakota's profile by ranking its "Manufacturing Climate" the best in the lower forty-eight states based on its low labor and energy costs, salutary government fiscal and employment policies, and labor force availability. Manufacturers took note; manufacturing increased from 8.2% of state gross product in 1977 to 9.8% in 1989. Manufacturing employment also increased, especially in rural areas close to the state's metropoles. Between 1981 and 1991, manufacturing employment in South Dakota metropolitan areas increased almost 20%, from 11,290 to 13,480, while employment in counties adjacent to metropolitan areas increased from 2,131 to 3,239, a 52% increase. More remote rural employment also increased, from 10,947 to 14,641, a 33.7% jump. All those increases were much faster than the averages recorded in other parts of the nation's traditionally agricultural heartland. Many of the new firms were micro organizations with few employees and limited prospects, but some of them, like Dakota Arms, established by gunstock master Don Allen in Sturgis in 1986, are still in business today. Dakota Arms went bankrupt after Allen died in 2003 but it was rescued in 2009 by Freedom Group, which also owns Remington, Marlin, and other marquee firearms brands. With fresh capital, machines, hand tools, and know-how, Dakota Arms employees again produced high quality rifles for African safaris and other big game hunts.[31]

According to the 1992 federal manufacturing census, over 35,000 South Dakotans statewide were employed in 889 manufacturing establishments, the value added of which amounted to $2.3 billion. Industrial machinery and equipment, food, electronic and electric equipment, and printing and publishing were the biggest manufacturing industries in the state and accounted for 58% of total manufacturing employment. The leading manufacturing counties were Minnehaha (Sioux Falls, with 187 establishments), Pennington (Rapid City, with 115 establishments), Codington (Watertown), and Union (North Sioux City), which surpassed Brown (Aberdeen) sometime after 1987. Most manufacturers, however, remained small by national standards; only seven employed more than 500 people and only thirty-one more than 250.[32]

Some of the increase in manufacturing activity in the state was due to an increase in so-called "branch" manufacturing, where manufacturers from other states moved into low-cost states to get specific processes completed on the cheap. Branch plants, like 3M's plant in Brookings, or the Bob Allen Sportswear factory, which made hunting clothing, gun cases, and tote bags in Arlington, provide employment, but according to one study they were not important sources of new entrepreneurial activity. South Dakota has no dearth of entrepreneurs, however, and its manufacturing boom has shown homegrown prowess in several non-agricultural related light industries, including truck trailers, bus bodies, boats, aircraft parts, and even surgical instruments (e.g., the $4,000 diamond scalpels produced by Magnum Diamond in Rapid City).[33]

With around $40 million in annual sales, which included exports to Canada and other foreign nations, Mitchell's Trail King Industries was by the early 1990s the nation's largest producer of specialty trailers. "We do everything they [competitors] don't want to touch," explained owner Gordon Thomsen. The company even built a 112-tire trailer capable of holding electrical transformers that weighed 600,000 pounds. Thomsen owned an ad agency and a company that produced t-shirts, caps, and other marketing items. He also bought a bankrupt Mitchell radio station and geared it up to big city standards.[34] Unlike most other South Dakota entrepreneurs, however, Thomsen didn't like the state's cold weather, so he managed his empire from Tucson, Arizona every winter. "I've got people running everything," he explained.[35]

In adjacent states, industries still largely match available natural resources. South Dakota, however, has relatively few resource-dependent manufacturing jobs.[36] That is because the state's comparative advantage is its workforce, which is productive, well educated, hardworking, and low paid. "Borne of a pioneering spirit," one piece of state boosterism claimed, "the people of South Dakota aren't strangers to hard work. If something needs to be done, South Dakotans can – and will – do it." That might sound self-serving and even corny, but anybody who has spent any time in the state knows it to be true, the occasional loafer to the contrary notwithstanding.

One might think that wages would be high in a state with relatively few, hardworking people and low unemployment rates, but that is not the case. The low pay is partly a function of the state's at-will and right-to-work/anti-union laws; South Dakota was one of the first states to enact such legislation. Although the Knights of Labor had thirty-six assemblies in South Dakota by 1890, labor unions never caught on in the state, even among its relatively large employers. Meatpacking giant John Morrell, which has a big facility in Sioux Falls, and mammoth Black Hills gold mine Homestake were, unsurprisingly, the leading lights of the right-to-work movement. Aside from railroad workers, South Dakota's industrial workers were more likely to go it alone than to pay tribute to some distant union. The only major union inroads into the state were made by the Teamsters in Sioux Falls during the Great Depression.[37]

Governor Bill Janklow loved to tell prospective entrants that South Dakota was the fiftieth best state in the nation: for crime, energy costs, and time lost due to union work stoppages. In 1985, only 27% of production workers and 11% of office/clerical workers were unionized. At-will doctrine, which states that the employer-employee relationship can be severed at any time by either party, made South Dakota an attractive place for employers, who can essentially hire and fire employees whenever they want.[38] The courts have eroded the doctrine somewhat by recognizing that employers should not be able to fire workers who reveal unlawful activities, file worker compensation claims, or refuse to commit a crime, but "it perseveres as the controlling presumption" in employment relationships in the state.[39]

Wages are relatively low in South Dakota for several other reasons as well. First, the cost of living, especially the cost of housing, is lower than in most other places. Second, the labor force participation rate is high. Women and students are more likely to work in South Dakota than in most other states, partly because employers are open to them. John Morrell and Company, for example, hired college students, struggling farmers, and just about anyone else who needed to make a buck. Men also worked second jobs, or had entrepreneurial, cash-generating hobbies. Erney Hersman, a West River ranch hand, spent his winters tying flies for fly fishers that he sold to a local fishing shop. He bought some of his materials but most, including bird skins, tufts of animal hair, and so forth, he scavenged from pasture and prairie. Others pick native grasses, sedges, and rushes to make dried floral arrangements for sale.[40]

Third, many families supplement their income by hunting and fishing. In most parts of the country, those activities are referred to as "sports," and each rainbow trout may cost $1,000 and every deer $10,000 when the total cost of harvesting them is computed. Those types of sportsmen can be found in South Dakota too, especially in the larger cities. Working families, though, will haul catfish, crappies, perch, walleye, or other delectables out of the state's many lakes and streams on the cheap. Otherwise friendly neighbors who clear snowy driveways and sidewalks, babysit, and so forth, all for free, will not divulge the location, even the county, of productive fishing holes. Ample wildlife, especially deer and pheasants, also add to family income. During the season, many a rooster falls to workers simply driving home. (It is lawful to shoot pheasants on roads and in ditches throughout much of the state.)

Many of the state's manufacturers are small or medium-sized firms. Small size allows them to move from market niche to niche more quickly than larger competitors are generally able to do. Smaller firms can and do offer appropriate training, ranging from technical training for compliance to soft skills like sales to training on new technologies, including computers, that help to drive productivity gains. That is especially true of durable goods makers, the largest manufacturing sector in the state.[41]

A productive workforce means that it pays handsomely to manufacture certain high-value products in the state, especially given its light taxes and regulations. The low cost of doing business was why Gateway moved to southeastern South Dakota in the late 1980s. The company started in Sioux City, but moved across the border to North Sioux City to take advantage of South Dakota's superior business climate. The innovative personal computer manufacturer employed about 5,000 South Dakotans in the first half of the 1990s and enjoyed revenues of over $5 billion in 1996. Unfortunately, the company's management was not committed to the region, so they later moved operations to California, suffered losses, and ended up being acquired by rival Acer in 2007.[42]

Another computer hardware manufacturer, disk drive maker Hutchinson Technology, moved into South Dakota in 1988 in search of a productive workforce. Unlike Gateway's leadership, Hutchinson, which is based in a town of the same name located west of the Twin Cities, maintained its South Dakota operations, which currently employ 550 engineers, technicians, machinists, and others in Sioux Falls.[43]

The state's low cost of doing business is also why Daktronics of Brookings is able to manufacture electronic signs and display devices for Times Square in Manhattan, Kansas City Royals' Kauffman Stadium, the Pan American Games in Winnipeg, and elsewhere around the world, including the Kuwait Stock Exchange and various Olympic games. Started by professors of electrical engineering at South Dakota State University in 1968, Daktronics' first clients included Augustana College and sundry hospitals, the U.S. Department of the Interior and the U.S. Department of Agriculture, the South Dakota and Utah state governments, Land O'Lakes Creameries, and Thompson Electric Company. Daktronics was listed on NASDAQ in 1994. Its stock price sat in the $3 per share range in early 2001 but by 2006 had increased to around $38. It subsequently dropped to around $6, but for the last few years it has hovered within a few dollars of $10 per share.[44]

Some software companies also looked to South Dakota during the tech boom in the late 1990s. Remote places like Aberdeen had talented people who would be more loyal than employees in major tech corridors and do great work for less money. They were not as cheap as programmers in India and China but they were more productive, catching the eye of TalentSoft, which was encouraged by nonprofit Aberdeen Development Corporation.[45]

Today, manufacturing accounts for over 10% of jobs and over $4 billion in annual sales. Homegrown entrepreneurs who in the past would have gravitated into agriculture or commerce now look to small-scale manufacturing to make a living. Lowell and Tami Pfleger built an embroidery business in Rapid City called Lakota Designs with the help of a timely order from the Mount Rushmore National Park Service, a Bureau of Indian Affairs grant (Lowell is part Lakota), and a bank loan with a Small Business Administration guarantee. Later an affiliate of Black Hills Embroidery (later called BHE Industries and BHE Custom Apparel), which was established in 1986, the company by 1999 employed ten to sixteen employees, depending on volume, and grossed six figures. Today, it offers innovative and affordable "image apparel solutions" for various organizations and events.[46]

Dependable Sanitation of Aberdeen is a family-owned and operated company that hauls trash for businesses, apartment owners, farmers, and residential homeowners. The company, which Myron Erickson started in 1969, is the largest privately owned waste collector in the state. It also incinerates medical waste. Also in Aberdeen is Cardinal Industries, which makes permaflex tags used to identify livestock in lieu of hide branding as well as other injection-molded parts and assemblies. Known for its quality and on-time deliveries, the company, which was started in a Minneapolis garage in 1972, can make small batches or churn out millions of units in its 40,000-square-foot facility.[47]

In Watertown, Angus Industries manufactures not beef cattle but cab enclosures for agricultural, construction, forestry, mining, and other industrial-strength vehicles such as wheel loaders, motor graders, soil compactors, feller bunchers, snowplows, harvesters, shovels, and mulchers. Its customers include John Deere, CAT, Gehl, New Holland, and other major heavy equipment manufacturers. Begun in 1988, Angus merged with Palm Industries of Litchfield, Minnesota, in 1992. The combined company opened several plants in the South before being acquired by Worthington Industries in 2011.[48]

Rainbow Play Systems was founded in Minnesota in 1985. It now has a 1.3-million-square-foot state-of-the-art manufacturing facility in Brookings. Its 500 employees build play equipment, 100 different models with 100 accessory options. The company also delivers, assembles, moves, and expands its sets, which are made of advanced plastics, milled redwood and cedar, and vinyl-coated steel. By the time of writing, the company had over 1 million installations, commercial and residential, across the globe.[49]

Another Minnesota-born immigrant, MTR Technologies, makes everything, or rather anything, that its clients need in the mechanical or electro-mechanical world. Started in 1973, the company relocated to Brookings to get closer to the research facilities at South Dakota State University. It is FAA certified for aircraft component manufacturing and sells to mega-billion-dollar corporations like Rockwell, 3M, Pitney Bowes, GE, Ingersoll-Rand, and Medtronic.[50]

Another manufacturer of note is Masaba Mining Equipment, which designs and builds bulk-handling equipment in Vermillion. Harold Higman, Jr. formed the company in 1962 as an outgrowth of his father's business, Higman Sand and Gravel. Today, the company is led by Jerad, the third generation of Higman committed to the idea of building quality mining equipment that lasts.[51]

None of this is to say, however, that South Dakota is now a manufacturing giant or threatening to become "a Taiwan on the Prairie."[52] In 2001, only 16.7% of its counties specialized in manufacturing, compared to 71.7% of the counties in Indiana and 51.5% of the counties in adjacent Iowa. In the Midwest, only North Dakota had fewer counties specializing in manufacturing, a mere 8.3%. South Dakota's manufacturing exports have been growing relatively quickly over the last two decades, mostly to Mexico and Canada, both fellow members of NAFTA, as well as to Europe, China, Japan, Hong Kong, Taiwan, Singapore, and South Korea. In 2011, however, South Dakota's manufacturers exported only $1,665 per capita, one of the lowest figures of any state. Over half a billion of the state's almost $1.4 billion of manufactured exports consisted of food products, with non-electrical machinery accounting for another $264 million. The biggest driver of manufacturing in South Dakota in the years ahead may be the cost of labor abroad. As labor costs overseas rose following the Great Recession of 2007-09, manufacturing employment in the state ticked up.[53]

What the Sunshine State lacks in manufacturing prowess it makes up for in selling. Wholesaling is prevalent but mostly confined to cities with 10,000 or more people, which account for some 60% of total business-to-business sales. By 1900, Sioux Falls had emerged as the major wholesaling center in South Dakota, southwestern Minnesota, and northwestern Iowa. One successful earlier wholesaler was Brown Drug Company, which between 1902 and 1922 supplied drug stores throughout the region with drugs and chemicals from acetanilide to tincture of cannabis to liquors to patent medicines like "Frog In Your Throat" and "Ford Brothers' Indian Oil." Brown also wholesaled other goods commonly sold by druggists, including bandages and surgical dressings, balls, baseball equipment, blank business books, brooms, brushes, combs, curling irons, doily belts (sanitary napkins sold separately), douches, "Flower Girl" and other perfumes, key rings, mirrors, nasal thudicums, pipes, pocket knives, razors and strops, sheet music, wallets, and over 700 pages of other goods.[54]

Brown Drug was closely held by its officers. It struggled a little at first, finding it necessary to obtain a $45,000 line of credit with the State Banking and Trust Company in 1906. The following year, a dispute over raising the salary of the general manager from $75 to $125 per month led to board resignations. By 1910, however, the closely held corporation began declaring 10% dividends. In 1917, the president's salary hit $10,000 per year and that of the general manager $5,200 ($433 per month). When the books were closed, per the original articles of incorporation, in 1922, the company had assets of $300,791.01 invested in accounts receivable, cash, merchandize on hand, real estate, and a truck. On the other side of the balance sheet, the company showed zero debt, a capital of $148,500, a surplus of $144,508.15, and the balance in debts it had to write off. Else Brothers in Belle Fourche, for example,

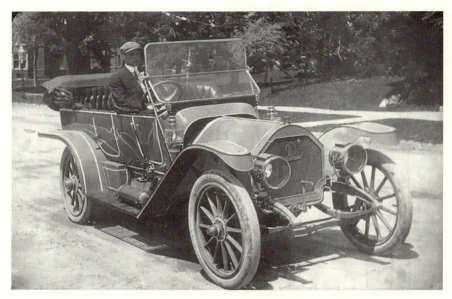

Rush Brown of the Brown Drug Company is seen in his Fawick Flyer. Brown's company was a major wholesaler of drug supplies, and Thomas Fawick was the creator of the Flyer, the first four-door automobile made in the United States. *Courtesy Center for Western Studies.*

owed it $1,150 on a note that was "past due, taken for account past due." But the debtor was "located in a farming and grazing country which has had no crop for several years. They are worse than bankrupt."[55]

Today, Sioux Falls remains the state's major wholesaling center and, indeed, was ranked as one of the nation's leading wholesaling centers (by percentage of workers engaged in wholesaling) as early as 1950. In 1967, Sioux Falls was home to 269 wholesale outfits, with aggregate sales of $485.4 million. By the mid-1970s, Sioux Falls was home to some 38 interstate trucking operations and its retail catchment area ran 130 miles to the west, ninety to the north, sixty to the east, and eighty to the south. One of its most successful wholesale businesses is JDS Industries. Begun over forty years ago, the company distributes a wide range of sporting trophies, plaques, and corporate awards out of nearly one million square feet of warehouse space nationwide, including an almost 200,000-square-foot facility at its headquarters in Sioux Falls. Nevertheless, Sioux Falls enjoys no monopoly on the region's wholesaling business. Snowmobile and winter-accessory manufacturer Polaris, for example, decided to locate its global distribution center in Vermillion, the center of its cold-weather market. In 2008, Polaris expanded its 256,000-square-foot facility in Vermillion by 50% because it found the local labor market cheap yet productive and flexible.[56]

In 1997, South Dakota was a retailing mecca, with retail sales per capita at $13,382 compared to the $9,337 countrywide average. Much of the retail trade was concentrated in urban centers, especially Sioux Falls, which has dominated East River South Dakota's higher-end service provision and retailing since the 1920s or so. In 1967, for example, Sioux Falls was home to 941 retailers, which reported total sales of $175.5 million. Nevertheless, many retailers outside of the great urban centers also thrived. For example, Walt Schramm's Schramm Furniture, Inc., off Highway 18 in Winner, lasted at least half a century and Amund O. Ringsrud's mercantile exchange in Elk Point remained in business for over seventy-five years.

Born in Norway in 1854, Ringsrud moved to South Dakota with his family in 1867. After working on the family farm and clerking in a general store in Elk Point, Ringsrud was elected registrar of deeds for Union County in 1878 and Secretary of State of South Dakota in 1889. He failed in his bid for the governorship in 1896 but had a backup, Ringsrud Mercantile Company, the mercantile exchange he had established in Elk Point in 1885 and incorporated in 1896. The business sold wheat and corn in Minneapolis among other activities.[57]

Agricultural goods retailers, like seed and ag-equipment companies, also thrived throughout the hinterland. John Deere, for example, was interested in almost every town in the state big enough to have its own name. In White Lake, for example, it contracted in 1906 with August Beutner, a married man aged thirty-nine years, to sell its plows and other farm implements. Beutner was hardly wealthy but he had a positive net worth and a good reputation for paying his bills on time, so John Deere was eager to team up with him.[58] The William Brothers in Winfred were a different story, as an agent warned that "It would be exceedingly unsafe to do any further business with them. ... We believe they are perfectly honest, but their business methods are very loose, and their ability is limited. We think it only a question of time until they are 'broke'. ... We of course, want all the profitable business we can get, but in order for it to be profitable we have got to see money in sight some time."[59]

The largest and most successful retailers and wholesalers, though, tended to cluster in Sioux Falls and, to a lesser extent, Rapid City. The state's low absolute population level and its low population density have forced its distributors of goods to businesses and individuals to get efficient, to get innovative, or to get out. Before farm families could afford their own freezers, for example, they could store meat and other frozen foods in lockers in towns like Miller and Presho, where the Nebraska-based Fairmont Food Company "sold milk and ice cream, had a poultry and egg operation, manufactured ice, and maintained a frozen-food locker."[60] It was long the town's largest employer. Before affordable electricity-supplied refrigeration, many people had their own cold storage, ranging from mere "caves" for vegetables or dairy products to full-blown ice houses. Not everyone owned such facilities, however, nor did they trust them to keep large quantities of fresh meat good and frozen.[61]

Globalization shocked many businesses throughout the nation, but South Dakota firms were relatively immune as they had already adapted to being only a small cog in the great American economic machine. Lampe Market in Huron, for example, was a vertically integrated local green producer before anybody had heard of those terms. For decades, it raised cattle on its own 900-acre farm, butchered them, and sold them in town, employing hundreds of thousands of dollars in capital and worn out, torn down farmers like Frank Bloodgood in the process.[62]

Early on, and to some extent even today, many smaller retailers stayed afloat by being generalists, selling everything they think people will pay a little more to have now rather than later from a bigger, less expensive store. The motto of Fischer Brothers in Fort Pierre in the late nineteenth century was "Everything to Eat and Wear." In Milbank, a tire store, of all things, sold Christmas toys each December. Even more desperate to attract Christmas shoppers, retailers in Gregory in 1987 made a deal with local lenders to make low-interest loans in a script good only locally until Christmas. About fifty people borrowed a total of $40,000 on those terms, promising to repay by November of the next year. Retailers also turned into landlords, renting out unneeded parts of their buildings to other businesses or even families. In 1921, for example, the O. P. Moore Grocery Company in Sioux Falls rented an office to Harold Tennant, an early aviator.[63]

Many retailers, especially established ones like Fischer's general store in Fort Pierre, and Look's Market in Sioux Falls, extended credit to customers. Some profited by charging interest, others from simply winning the business of those who were temporarily short of cash. When balances grew too high, retailers asked for customers to pay them down before they would extend more credit. In the hinterlands, such payments could be in cash or butter, eggs, or cream; nobody expected full settlement until the crops were in. In Sioux Falls, cash was already the main form of settlement by the late nineteenth century. At Look's Market, for example, customers like Joe Kirby (founder of the Western Surety Company described in Chapter 8), Bishop O'Gorman, the "Deaf Mute School," and the Dakota Penitentiary regularly took away bacon, bologna, beef steaks, chicken, corn beef, fish, goose, ham, lard, mutton, sausage, turkey, veal, and wieners but settled up monthly.[64]

Successful retailers also kept costs as low as possible. When interest rates were high, as in the early 1980s, automobile repair shops held smaller inventories of parts. That made repair times longer for customers, but kept their costs down. Automobile dealerships also stayed lean. In 1983, small dealers kept on the lot inventory worth only in the range of $500,000 to $2 million. The sixty-month auto loan became popular at that time due to high interest rates.[65] Henry Billion, "one of our outstanding and leading car dealers in the State," helped the move toward larger dealerships by combining his three, each of which had an inventory of about $1.5 million.[66] Nevertheless, one in every ten auto dealers in the state went out of business in the early 1980s recession.[67]

Retailers also kept durable goods on the shelves a long time as they could not afford to discount them. That practice hurt the state's reputation for fashion, among other things. When Senator George McGovern revealed that he bought his clothes from a shop in Huron, for example, a critic chided, "They look it."[68] Prairie retailers also had to remain open long hours to match the long days of their agricultural customers. On Saturdays, many shops stayed open until midnight or later and some even opened for a few hours after church on Sundays, years before most retailers in eastern cities thought of opening on weekends.[69]

Another key to success was to find the right market. Founded in 1956, Taylor Music of Aberdeen is still going strong today because it discovered a narrow but national niche. It has a website now, of course, but once it sent out catalogs of musical instruments to 19,000 rural schools for their bands and orchestras and took orders by mail and phone. It still refurbishes instruments so that it can continue to offer quality used products to its often cash-strapped customers. Instruments too badly broken to fix the company flattens and sells as wall ornaments. It leverages its small-town roots to sell to small-town players, who like to speak to a real, live person with a name when they call.[70]

Amerindian Mary Brandis also started her restaurant business in White River on the basis of superior customer service, providing her customers with clean, friendly service that her competitors could not match. She also stayed open longer, until midnight, except for Fridays and Saturdays when she stayed open until 2 a.m. to service the crowds after football and basketball games.[71]

Innovation in retailing even extends to ownership structure. Most small retailers are proprietorships or partnerships but when that is not possible, South Dakota's entrepreneurs turn to other forms. The Centennial Café in Harrold, for example, was owned by the Harrold Development Corporation and its thirty-five stockholders to ensure that the town had an open restaurant when it celebrated its centennial in 1986. As of August 2014, the café was still in business on South Wyman Avenue.[72]

As noted above, Sioux Falls has long been the state's most important retail and wholesale center. From Fantle's Department Store and the Shriver-Johnson Department Store, founded in the early twentieth century and located in the city's downtown, to the Park Ridge Mall completed in 1955 at 26th and Western Avenue, to the Western Mall, which in 1968 became the first major indoor shopping mall in the state, to the Empire Mall, which was the largest single-story mall in the nation when completed in 1975, Sioux Falls has led the state in retailing innovation and sheer size. Today, two interstates (I-29 and I-90) with 75-mile-per-hour speed limits make it possible for customers to travel 50 to 100 miles to shop in Sioux Falls.[73]

The state's greatest retailing strength, however, may have come from its nano-entrepreneurs, people who established small, flexible retailing outlets to meet immediate demands, like the men and women who set up impromptu lunch counters to feed stagecoach travelers and nearby ranch hands during the Dakota Boom, or the peddlers on trains who sold everything from candy and peanuts to pornography. Perhaps the most convenient retailers of all were the door-to-door salesmen for wholesale grocery Ulry-Talbert Company of Grand Island, Nebraska, hat manufacturer Portis, or various shoe manufacturers. They not only brought goods to busy people's doorsteps, unlike distance retailers (whether via catalog or internet), they allowed buyers to inspect the

Founded as a dry-goods store by brothers Charles and Sam Fantle, Fantle's Department Store became a leading clothing and household retailer in the Sioux Falls area. *Courtesy Center for Western Studies.*

goods before purchase. Laura Ingalls Wilder's husband, Almanzo, for example, financed a trip to Missouri by selling asbestos fire mats for a dime apiece, demonstrating their fire-retardant qualities whenever required. Peddlers and other retailers also had the advantage of selling goods that could be consumed immediately, not in several days or weeks. Nevertheless, catalog companies did a considerable business for those who could wait and wanted to save their pennies.[74]

The number of active retail establishments dropped from 959 in 1939 to 707 in 1954 in the West North Central part of the state, which overall saw the number of retailers drop from 8,993 in 1948 to 8,338 in 1954. The number of employees per establishment, however, doubled from .9 to 2.0 in this area and increased from 1.8 to 3.2 statewide. Likewise, the average volume of sales increased from about $11,000 in 1939 to $62,000 in 1954 for the West North Central and from $17,000 to $81,000 statewide.[75] As Figure 5 shows, the trend toward fewer retailers continued into the 1960s. Again, however, the remaining retailers were larger. Between 1954 and 1963, the average number of employees per retail establishment increased from 3.2 to 3.8 and sales jumped from an average of $81,300 to $114,300.[76]

Successful retailers had several expansion options open to them. One was manufacturing. Ivan Landstrom moved to Rapid City in 1945 and started a small jewelry store with borrowed money. The store grew and he decided to integrate vertically into the manufacture of gold jewelry. Later, he leveraged his manufacturing experience to form the Black Hills

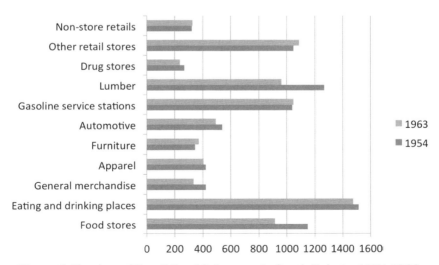

Figure 5: Number of Retail Establishments in South Dakota, 1954-1963.
Source: A. A. Volk, The Economy of the Northeast Region of South Dakota (Vermillion: Business Research Bureau, 1967), 62.

Glass and Mirror Company. Another option was to invest in higher-margin or higher-volume retailing. When a young newlywed announced to his boss that he was going to file a claim on some land near Marcus, he was told that he had "as much right to starve a woman as anyone else." Instead of farming, though, the young man ran a grocery, then used the earnings to buy a Chevrolet dealership in Rapid City. He did so well that he was able to become a bank director and enjoy a long retirement with his $100,000 fortune on deposit.[77]

Some South Dakota retailers have even invaded other states on occasion. Early in the Third Millennium, for example, Moyle Petroleum of Rapid City began building Common Cents stores, convenience stores with high ceilings and wide aisles tied to Exxon gas stations, along the Wasatch Front in Utah. But South Dakota retailers do not have to invade other states to tap their customers, they can wait until those folks willingly make the trek to them, the subject of the next chapter.[78]

Chapter 7

Entertainment, Tourism, and Outdoor Recreation

There's nothin' prettier than the upper Missouri. She's
wild and pretty like a virgin woman.[1]

Like Americans everywhere, South Dakotans have long enjoyed various forms of entertainment, after their homework and chores were done, of course. Major holidays, especially those that didn't interfere with the agricultural cycle, were especially important occasions for diversion. Even tiny towns like Dallas held elaborate Independence Day celebrations complete with merry-go-rounds, shooting galleries, and other entertainments, along with popcorn, toys, sea foam candy, ice cream, and fireworks. Dallas allegedly sponsored an hour-long fireworks show circa 1910. In that same period, Dallas also attracted a circuit Chautauqua that provided five days of cultural entertainment each summer. (Called the most American thing in America by Teddy Roosevelt, Chatauquas abounded early in the twentieth century.)[2]

The relatively large size of Sioux Falls allowed its entrepreneurs to attract more and bigger acts than the rest of the state could usually muster. Sure, Sioux Falls had its share of circuses, rodeos, and other outdoor events but where it excelled was indoors, in its numerous theaters. With names like Barrison, Coliseum, Liberty, Majestic, New Theater, Orpheum, Princess, and State, some of the city's theaters were short-lived and soon forgotten while others were of lasting importance. By 1896, Sioux Falls had gained a reputation for being a good show town as its theaters, especially the more capacious and ostentatious ones, booked many national acts in all the major categories of the day: comedies, minstrel shows, musicals, operas, plays, and vaudeville acts. Bolstered by cultured rich folk in town to obtain a divorce, local audiences proved that they were not "rubes" living in a "tank town" but intelligent and gracious viewers for whom entertainers enjoyed performing. Legends-in-the-making like comedian Jack Benny entertained audiences in Sioux Falls but so too did living legends like bandleader John Philip Sousa, violinist David Rubinoff, and singer Al Jolson.[3]

Sioux Falls, however, hardly enjoyed a monopoly on high brow entertainment. Metropolitan Opera stars sang in Aberdeen and Watertown in the 1910s. In the 1940s and 50s, over 170 different bands and orchestras played in the state. Many were composed of local musicians, but as late as the 1950s even small towns like Philip were able to attract the nationally-recognized bands of Lawrence Welk and Tommy Dorsey. The state also spawned a few bands composed of professional musicians, like the Jimmy Barnett Orchestra of Sioux Falls, that toured the entire region continually.[4]

The age of live theater and live music, like so many other cultural institutions, slowly died after World War II. Between 1958 and 1963, in fact, the number of establishments offering "amusements" declined from 425 to 398, though aggregate receipts increased from $8.6 million to $13.6 million. Conversely, the number of movie theaters dropped only slightly, from 115 to 113, but their receipts were down, from $3.8 to $3.4 million. Television was the likely culprit there. Nevertheless, movies, finally with sound and increasingly in color, saved some of the theater businesses from oblivion.[5]

When life serves up lemons, an old adage goes, make lemonade. When life serves them lemons, South Dakotans make lemonade and then sell it. When the Japanese cut off the supply of floss used in life jackets from Java's kapok trees, for example, entrepreneurial and patriotic Dakotan women collected milkweed pods as a substitute. Similarly, when Arlington, which sits at the intersection of two important highways in eastern South Dakota (14 and 81), was accidentally left off the state highway map circa 1990, local entrepreneurs organized "Put Arlington back on the Map Days," a festival that featured dances, games, races, and a town dinner. They also put out stickers, buttons, and posters proclaiming "I Found Arlington."[6]

Such events, in aggregate, are big business for South Dakota. Over a billion dollars and 30,000 jobs big. Seemingly everything that could conceivably draw in outsiders, and induce them to leave some cash behind, has been tried somewhere, some time, in the land of infinite variety. All the formal places to visit and things to do in South Dakota would fill an entire book, literally, but it would miss the impromptu, nano-entrepreneurs who have also provided entertainment to their neighbors and tourists alike. Some South Dakotans formed roving entertainment troupes that roller-skated, motorcycled, sang and danced, or did anything else to entertain folks enough to make some side scratch. Others, including a bar in Buffalo, push kitschy local memorabilia on any tourists who happen to stumble in. It, and other tourist "traps," like Buffalo Ridge just west of Sioux Falls, can be unsavory but do not literally rob visitors of anything other than their time.[7] And there are a lot of them. "No region in the country," one observer claimed in 2004, "is more a hodgepodge of historical curiosities, geological oddities and kitschy attractions than ... South Dakota."[8] "There are enough quirky things to keep you fascinated for days," a pair of tourists noted in 1986, and they were referring to a single town.[9]

Of course, some attractions fail miserably, drawing in little more than flies and cow pies. But a few catch on and attract millions – of dollars if not individuals. Many end up somewhere in between, perhaps enticing relatives who moved away and some city slickers from Sioux Falls, Rapid City, or Aberdeen or maybe attracting people from around the globe, but only in a slow trickle that may eventually peter out. Lake Preston, for example, used to host a late summer watermelon festival that was world-unrenowned but that brought in people from surrounding communities. As a last resort, just about every town in the state can attract bicyclists, boaters, campers, fishers, gamblers, golfers, and/or hunters.[10]

Some of those activities may sound impossible – South Dakota is almost 1,500 miles from the nearest ocean, notoriously flat, and habitually windy – but it is chock full of beautiful small lakes and great golf courses constructed after "golfing fever" swept the state in the 1950s. In 1963, the state even spawned a golf-equipment manufacturer, Austad, which exported its wares globally, including golf-crazed Japan. After the company transformed into a catalog and brick-and-mortar retailer, most family members sold out the catalog side of the business to Hanover Direct, which promptly ran the company into the sand like a duffer trying to get out of a deep trap with a three iron. David Austad eventually regained control of the company but its presence in Sioux Falls today is a far cry from its heyday, when it employed 600 people at a 145,000-square-foot warehouse at 10th Street and Sycamore.[11] South Dakota's thirty-eight state and four national parks are so good they have been called the region's "best-kept secrets."[12] The flat, windy prairies attract ten speed bicyclists, while the Black Hills are mountain bike heaven. Many a country hotel hangs on by providing weary fishers and hunters a place to catch some shut eye for not a lot of money.[13]

Before resorting to the great outdoors or to not-so-great casinos, though, almost every town attempts to find an edge, something unique to induce people to visit and spend time, which of course means money. Clark, for example, is South Dakota's potato capital, Redfield calls itself "the pheasant capital of the world," Brookings is "Someplace Special," and Mitchell sports the world's only "corn palace."[14] Originally built in 1892 "by an eccentric entrepreneur who had beaucoup extra corn cobs on hand," the Corn Palace, which in its current (third) iteration dates from 1921, is a big auditorium decorated with exotic colored corn.[15] It was good enough a venue to attract Lawrence Welk, Jack Benny, Roy Rogers, Duke Ellington, Bob Hope, and other "big shot" celebrities "quite often," helping to turn the town into a "busy sprawl of motels and restaurants."[16] In more recent years, the Corn Palace hosted concerts by Willie Nelson,

Glen Campbell, and REO Speedwagon, all of whom charged quite a bit more than the $1.22 it cost to see Welk in 1944.[17]

Roslyn, in the north central part of the state, is the home of the International Vinegar Museum. If you want to revisit the Cold War, Interior has a Minuteman missile museum, with its very own (unarmed) missile for you, and Ellsworth Air Force Base, just north of Box Elder, boasts a very nice warplane museum. Lake Norden is home to the baseball hall of fame, South Dakota's that is. The state has a heck of a semi-pro and minor league baseball history, one, alas, largely destroyed by television, late as it was to come to the state. In the good old days before the boob tube, small towns throughout the state sponsored summer baseball teams, often in an entrepreneurial fashion. Winner, for example, had a baseball team called the Pheasants in South Dakota's semi-pro league and financed it with community poker games called "smokers," with the house rake-off going to hire college baseball players. Even tiny towns like Toronto and Kimball managed to sponsor teams.[18] "In our towns here," a southern North Dakotan explained to a traveler from back east, "we have a Sunday game almost every week from spring to fall."[19] Moreover, the Northern League had teams in Aberdeen and Sioux Falls and the state had its own league composed of eight teams.[20]

Or maybe oversized sculptures appeal. Both Gregory and Huron sport gigantic pheasants. The one in the former weighs some 10,000 pounds while the one in the latter, erected in 1959, is over thirty feet tall. Near Montrose and within sight of I-90 is a twenty-five-ton, sixty-foot-high scrap metal sculpture of the head of a bull flanked by numerous smaller metal curiosities. Mount Rushmore is home to sixty-foot high busts of four U.S. presidents completed in 1941 by the Danish-American entrepreneur-sculptor Gutzon Borglum, who began the project in 1927. Just west of nearby Lead, the heads of all the nation's presidents can be viewed at Presidents' Park, though on a much smaller scale than at Rushmore.[21]

Also nearby, but still incomplete, is a truly massive stone carving of famed Sioux warrior Crazy Horse and the impressive Indian Museum of North America. A monument to Sitting Bull, another great Sioux warrior, sits five miles south of Mobridge, which was named for its bridge across the Missouri. The monument itself is modest, but nestled within spectacular views of the Big River and prairie over which Sitting Bull's people once claimed dominion. Since 1993, the Alliance of Tribal Tourism Advocates has been working with Dakota tribes to "provide a more diversified tourism experience for the visitors who travel to the Dakotas," including experiences like living in authentic tipis on Chief David Bald Eagle's ranch on the Cheyenne River Reservation.[22]

The petrified wood park in Lemmon was established by Ole S. Quammen early in the Depression and includes a castle-shaped museum made entirely of petrified wood. Faith calls itself the "T-rex Capital of the World" although the actual Tyrannosaurus rex discovery sites were in neighboring Ziebach County some twenty miles away.

As recently as 1987, Deadwood was a depressed rural mountain community with a burned out downtown district. Its biggest attraction was its cemetery, Mount Moriah, and the Wild West characters buried there, including Wild Bill Hickok, Calamity Jane, Seth Bullock (Deadwood's first sheriff, organizer of Teddy Roosevelt's Rough Riders, and later hotelier), Blanche Colman (the first woman admitted to the South Dakota Bar), Johnny Perrett (a Welsh gold prospector), and Henry Weston Smith (a minister killed by Indians). Money was so tight that four major brothels, protected by local businessmen, lingered unmolested until finally shut down by state authorities in 1980. Today, a revitalized Deadwood has not one but three tourist seasons. Summers are for families in search of history, rodeos, and a cool getaway; fall is for hunters looking for wild game; and winter is for thrill-seeking skiers and snowmobilers. Before World War II, Canton was the unlikely host of the longest ski slide in the nation and the scene of state, regional, and even national ski-jumping championships. Those days are long gone; Great Bear, in nearby Sioux Falls, is no match for the skiing opportunities available in the Black Hills. And every day is a good day to gamble at Kevin Costner's Midnight Star Casino or one of Deadwood's other almost two-score small-stake casinos, to eat a giant steak at Jake's, reckoned one of the best restaurants in the entire state, or to check out the 1890s architecture of many of Deadwood's buildings.[23]

One of the state's most popular, enduring, and entrepreneurial tourist attractions is Wall Drug, which is famous for being famous.[24] Wall Drug has kept tiny Wall – a West River town just north of the Badlands where Route 14 meets Interstate 90 described as "just about as Godforsaken as you can get"[25] – literally on the map while many similar towns in the vicinity have dried up and blown away. Established by Ted and Dorothy Hustead during the Great Depression, Wall Drug advertised itself via thousands of billboards, most planted seemingly in the middle of nowhere. Some of the (in)famous signs, which indicate that the complex is "only" xx,xxx miles away and offers free ice water and cheap coffee, are located abroad, at first set up by soldiers and sailors stationed in Europe and Asia and later by literally anyone who wanted to take the time and trouble. The free ice water was an early gimmick to attract customers that worked wonders for the struggling new business. According to a 1973 *Wall Street Journal* article, nearly 45% of westbound automobiles pulled into Wall Drug. By 1985, the complex boasted revenues of $5.5 million and significant positive knock-on effects. The store, the Badlands, and the highways formed a self-reinforcing magnet that soon attracted other businesses, including hotels, restaurants, and Western kitsch retailers galore. In the summer, more than 20,000 tourists a day spend some time and money in little Wall buying or doing something.[26] The only bad thing about the complex, besides its blatant "commodification" of the Old West, is that its ubiquitous signs sometimes momentarily block views of "the real Wild West, with gulches and gullies and bumpy grasslands."[27] Then again, there is plenty of that to go around.

A similar magnetic phenomenon occurred at Mount Rushmore, where four giant faces carved into the rocks brought people and their money, and entrepreneurs eager to get some of it, to a region already attracting tourists with its wild life, beautiful vistas, and respite from the scorching summer sun. Hotels, restaurants, gas stations, and sundry other attractions, some mere tourist traps, others of enduring value, soon followed, diversifying a local economy centered on Rapid City.[28]

South Dakota does not have any "George Washington slept here" attractions, not even for the historically challenged, but its entrepreneurs do leverage connections to celebrities whenever they can. A surprising number of South Dakotans have achieved global fame. Tom Brokaw, a native of Webster, left South Dakota in 1962, at age twenty-two, and went on to anchor NBC Nightly News from 1982 until 2004.[29] He attributes the state's "physical and cultural remoteness" to its denizens' predilection to "memorize almost every South Dakotan who has left the state and achieved some recognition."[30] That may be part of it, but even New Yorkers like to claim celebrities for themselves so something deeper is involved too, maybe the conviction that if somebody like Pat O'Brien, who attended Washington High in Sioux Falls and the University of South Dakota, can become famous, so can anybody from this place. For a state with a population smaller than many counties back East, South Dakota does seem to spawn numerous television stars, including Bob Barker of Pine Ridge, Cheryl Stoppelmoor (Cheryl Ladd) of Huron, Catherine Bach (Daisy Duke), who grew up on a ranch near Rapid City, and from Sioux Falls, January Jones (*Mad Men*) and Ranae Holland, the biologist on *Finding Bigfoot*. Mary Harum (Mary Hart), the host of *Entertainment Tonight* from 1982 until 2011, was born in Madison in 1950 and attended Augustana College and taught at Washington High School in Sioux Falls. More believable, she broke into the TV business in Sioux Falls after being named Miss South Dakota in 1970.[31]

The state also has a long history of temporarily harboring people who would later go on to achieve fame. African American Oscar Micheaux (1884-1951), for example, became a homesteader on the Rosebud Indian

Reservation in 1905. He later wrote, self-published, and even personally peddled autobiographical novels about his experiences. By the 1920s, he had emerged as an important independent filmmaker and, although no longer a resident of South Dakota, several of his movies, which achieved modest financial success though many critics considered them of C or "underground" quality, were set there. Ever since, South Dakota has attracted more than its share of Hollywood directors and television producers who find the state's old towns, trains, mines, reservations, and diversity of landscape irresistible. Much of *Orphan Train* (1979, starring Jill Eikenberry, Kevin Dobson, and Glenn Close) was shot in the state, for example, as was *Dances with Wolves* and numerous other Westerns.[32]

Joe Robbie, a Sisseton native and University of South Dakota Law School graduate, appeared in *Black Sunday*, the 1978 film about a terrorist attack on the Super Bowl. More importantly, Robbie was the original owner of the Miami Dolphins, including the team that won seventeen games and suffered no losses during the 1972 season. Other famous sports figures from the state include Billy Mills, a Lakota from Pine Ridge who set a world record in the 10,000 meters while winning gold at the 1954 Olympics, and Sparky Anderson of Bridgewater, the long-time manager of the Cincinnati Reds and Detroit Tigers.[33]

Authors born in, or residents of, South Dakota also abound. Black author Katherine Tillman wrote *How to Live Well on a Small Salary* (1895) and various journalistic pieces and novellas, including *Clancy Street* (1898-99), and the play *Fifty Years of Freedom* (1910). O.E. Rölvaag and Doane Robinson were other important early South Dakota authors, though the former's classic, *Giants in the Earth,* painted a picture of South Dakota as "an evil void gobbling up unsuspecting Norwegians."[34] Hamlin Garland, author of *Main-Travelled Roads, A Son of the Middle Border, Afternoon Neighbors,* and other books and poems, spent some time in Brown County and also wrote of desolation and isolation.[35]

Many famous South Dakota authors fled the state but one who stayed was Sioux Falls dentist Will O. Lillibridge, author of the 1905 bestseller *Ben Blair: The Story of a Plainsman* and a few other titles. Two years later, Yankton's Kate and Virgil Boyles sold over 100,000 copies of their *Langford of the Three Bars.* The brother-sister team also penned *Homesteaders* (1909). In 1944, Frederick Manfred published *The Golden Bowl,* which has been described as a South Dakota version of *The Grapes of Wrath.* Herbert Krause (1905-1976) was born in Minnesota but lived in South Dakota much of his life. In addition to penning novels like *Wind Without Rain* and *The Thresher*, in 1970 he founded the Center for Western Studies, the publisher of this book. Cameron Hawley of Howard won much praise for his books on the pressures of modern business life, including *Executive Suite* (1952), which sold over 400,000 copies and in 1954 became a movie and a short-lived CBS television series (1976-77). Hawley's 1955 novel *Cash McCall* was also made into a movie, in 1960. With the "democratization" of publishing in recent years, South Dakota authors have again flourished with everything from pheasant cookbooks to short stories. For example, M.J. Andersen, author of *Portable Prairie*, hails from Milbank, the "Plainville" of her 2005 story. In addition, many of the authors cited in this book are, or were, South Dakotans by birth or by choice. The editor of the collection of contemporary South Dakota poets *A Harvest of Words*, Augustana's Writer-in-Residence Patrick Hicks, whose own poetry is published by Salmon Press of Ireland, defines South Dakota writers as those either born in or at one time residents of the state.[36]

Canton, South Dakota, also spawned Ernest O. Lawrence, who received a Nobel Prize in Physics in 1939 for his invention of the cyclotron, an early particle accelerator. The scientist has two nuclear research facilities named after him (Lawrence Livermore and Lawrence Berkeley), as well as a public science education center (Lawrence Hall of Science), an award (Ernest Orlando Lawrence), and an element (lawrencium, number 103 on the Periodic Table of Elements)![37]

Another (in)famous South Dakota intellectual is Keynesian economist Alvin H. Hansen (1887-1975), who was born in Viborg and graduated from Yankton College before earning a Ph.D. at the University of Wisconsin, where he breathed a little too deeply the air of Robert LaFollette and other progressives. He then taught at Brown and the University of Minnesota before landing at Harvard, after helping the Franklin Roosevelt Administration to create the Council of Economic Advisors and Social Security. Everyone who knew him, including generations of graduate students, found Hansen "the epitome of courtesy, respect, good humor, and integrity." If his economic beliefs and public policy pronouncements were not so deeply flawed, Viborg might be able to make a little spare change from his memory.[38]

There is, of course, little money to be made from living celebrities, especially ones who no longer reside in the state, and that is most of them. The real cash cow for entrepreneurs are the state's historical figures. Frank Baum, author of the *Wizard of Oz* series of books, lived in Aberdeen where he operated a store and ran a newspaper into the ground. Aberdeen's Wylie Park/Storybook Land taps into Americans' continued love affair with the Land of Oz.[39]

The real-life Laura Ingalls Wilder, as opposed to the fictional Minnesotan on the loose television adaptation of Wilder's books, set *Little House on the Prairie* and four other books in her real hometown, De Smet, the county seat of Kingsbury. About 20,000 people per year experience "The Wilder Life" by visiting various Wilder-related sites in and about the town, set up by the Laura Ingalls Wilder Memorial Society in the 1980s. The whole experience, including the pageant, was recently included as one of the top 1,000 destinations to see in English-speaking North America. When she edited the books, Wilder's daughter Rose Wilder Lane built in an anti-New Deal storyline of self-help and individual independence, rendering the books South Dakotan in ideology as well as setting. Lane would later help to form the modern Libertarian Party.[40]

Just west of De Smet on Route 14 lies Manchester, birthplace of South Dakota's most famous artist, Harvey Dunn (1884-1952). Dunn spent most of his life well east of the Great Plains but his best work depicted prairie life and people sketched during annual visits to South Dakota in the 1930s and 40s. Much of his original prairie work, including the moving *The Prairie Is My Garden*, is housed further east on Route 14, at the South Dakota Art Museum in Brookings. Other artists of note include James Earle Fraser, who grew up near Mitchell, and Isabelle Weeks, Grace Ann French, and William Fuller, who were born elsewhere but moved to South Dakota to paint. The state's second most famous artist is Oscar Howe, a Yanktonai Dakota Sioux born on the Crow Creek Indian Reservation in 1915. After attending the Santa Fe Indian School and the Fort Sill Indian Art Center, he became a mural painter for the Works Progress Administration and then a college professor. Before his death in 1983, Howe had won almost twenty major Indian art awards.[41]

Nationally celebrated bandmaster Lawrence Welk lived in Yankton and ran the house band at radio station WNAX in the late 1930s. His famous accordion player, Myron Floren, was born in Roslyn and paid his tuition at Augustana College by selling accordion lessons. The National Museum of Music in Vermillion (formerly the Shrine to Music Museum) has an accordion, but one quite a bit older than that used by Floren.[42] As *The Economist* reported in 1999, the museum "contains one of the world's finest and most varied collections of antique musical instruments," including the incredible Witten Collection of strings and a memorable set of trombones.[43]

In short, entrepreneurs have enhanced the state's natural beauty by creating numerous man-made attractions. But the first tourists on the Northern Plains, British aristocrats, did not need anything extra to entice them. Beginning in the 1830s, they came in search of adventure, Indians, and the heads of exotic creatures, like bear, bison, elk, and mountain sheep, to hang in their parlours back home. The next wave of tourists sought even bigger heads, those of dinosaurs.[44]

The Badlands possess little in the way of mineral wealth, a fortuitous shortcoming because mines and quarries would destroy its natural beauty, which a reporter once called, "nearly beyond description, like stepping into a strange world of the future or one of the prehistoric past"[45] and its most precious asset, its "bones of old dragons."[46] By the late 1830s, the Missouri Valley, from the Big Mo's headwaters to the Big Sioux River, was known as a fossil trove. Within a decade, the first fossils had also been discovered in the Badlands, which became a favored destination for dinosaur hunters because erosion was constantly exposing old bones afresh. Alexander Culbertson came first, then John Evans in 1849, who found some giant turtle and other fossils. Soon many others followed.[47]

At first, dino hunters just took skulls that had eroded out of the earth. The discovery of an entire mastodon near Paxton circa 1910, and the increasing professionalism of the hunters, however, led to more scientific work. By the 1920s, plaster of paris or other casting systems, grids, sketches, photographs, and so forth were in widespread use.[48]

Henry Galiano of Maxilla & Mandible of Manhattan introduced the world to natural history specimens as decorative objects and thereby turned fossil hunting into the big business it is today. The most lucrative type of fossil hunting, dinosaur hunting, is centered in the American West, including Colorado, Utah, Wyoming, and Montana, but the Badlands have a big advantage due to the constant erosion naturally occurring there. Hoteliers, like the owners of the Raptor's Nest Inn, are happy to add to the reputation of the region and some even claim that fossils function as an "alternative currency" in Harding County.[49]

Launched in 1995, Triebold Paleontology makes a business of digging up prehistoric critter skeletons and assembling them into whole animals that can be displayed in museums or the headquarters or homes of the biggest bidders. Triebold also runs the Rocky Mountain Dinosaur Resource Center, a for-profit museum in Woodland Park, Colorado. The Black Hills Institute of Geological Research in Hill City, a five-block town near Mount Rushmore, also does a dinosaur business by selling and renting casts and some original fossils. It might get $100,000 for a good specimen of a duck bill or similar dinosaur, but that works out to as little as $1 per hour when all the costs, including financing, are counted, as it takes many years to move from discovery to final sale. In nearby Custer is In the Beginning Fossils, started by Diana Hensley.[50] In the northern Hills, Walter Stein runs PaleoAdventures for families and offers "part science, part fun," including dinosaur hunts, as well as more scientific endeavors.[51]

The entire dino-hunting industry received a big boost thanks to the dinosaur named Sue. At the time of her discovery, only eleven other Tyrannosaurus rex skeletons had ever been unearthed and, at 90% complete, Sue's skeleton was by far the best. She sold at Sotheby's auction for $7.6 million, far more than any previous fossil dinosaur had ever culled. Full-time dinosaur "boneheads," like Bob Detrich of Buffalo, were heartened, but the market is only so big. About fifty commercial fossil dealers are now in business, but only a handful are fully staffed.[52]

For those who like their old bones a little fresher, Hot Springs boasts mammoth and other prehistoric mammal megafauna remains that rival the La Brea Tar Pits of Los Angeles. Mammoth number 61 was recently discovered and boosters were offered $100 tax-deductible bricks to help the Mammoth Site museum to expand.[53]

"Our Midwest offers few endpoints of interest for tourists," Faye Lewis complained in 1971. "Most of them consider it a wide monotonous area to be traveled through, at all permissible speed, to the more scenic areas on either side."[54] South Dakota, especially west of the river, is one of those more scenic areas but its current popularity has as much to do with entrepreneurs as it does its natural beauty. In fact, South Dakota's modern tourism industry grew directly out of early boosterism, or in other words out of attempts to attract permanent settlers.[55] The Gooder Casey Land Company wanted to attract permanent settlers who would purchase their land, but their 1910 pamphlet read like a tourist brochure:

> There is something here to interest each individual nature. To the sportsman, the mountains furnish a countless number of deer, antelope and wild turkey. The streams are filled with delicious mountain trout. To the lover of majestic scenery a trip over the Crouch Line Ry., from Rapid City to Mystic will thrill the traveler with a delight, such as they have never known before. To the artistic natures we present one veritable flower garden blended with sturdy pines, picturesque hills, dizzy canyons and sweet singing birds. No spot on earth will so interest, amuse and invigorate you as will Pennington County, South Dakota.[56]

As that description suggests, the state's stunning natural scenery was a major draw, one with more legs than old dinosaur or mammoth femurs possessed. One town even named itself Scenic as "a laconic understatement to describe the landscape that surrounds the town," as author Ian Frazier put it. "The immense horizontals stretch all across and around, the long, low buttes and pastel badlands varying endlessly under open sky."[57] In 1910, the Black Hills were featured, somewhat ironically, in Clifton Johnson's *American Highways and Byways of the Rocky Mountains*.[58] The scenery of the Black Hills Johnson called "ruggedly attractive" and suffused with "many picturesque villages in the valleys."[59] Similarly, *Clason's Green Guide* asserted that "a more delightful place for the summer tour could not be imagined … Good main trunk highways will be found between the principal towns," and opportunities for outdoor amusement abounded.[60]

By 1920, complete rail tours of the Black Hills were available and tourism was already important to West River towns like Kadoka, where up to one in four workers toiled in the rail, gasoline, and auto-repair businesses or at Camp Joy, which in 1926 became the first fee-based tourist camp in the state. Four more such camps popped up in Kadoka in the 1930s. In the Black Hills, the water baths at Hot Springs, Latchstring Inn in Spearfish Canyon, Pierre Lodge (a sort of early timeshare), and scattered dude ranches were attracting business by the 1920s.[61] Soon, "people all over the Hills, especially in the larger cities" were, according to one observer, "fast awakening to the realization that good parks play a tremendous part in the development of their localities. Spearfish, Sturgis, Rapid City, and Deadwood were the first to realize the value of service to their visitors" and Sturgis had the best.[62] In the 1910s, numerous municipal parks and campsites had sprung up and were offered free to tourists; the camps would pay for themselves via increased sales taxes and land values, it was believed. Most were shut down in the 1930s, however, when they attracted unemployed vagrants instead of spendthrift tourists. The state soon learned to profit directly from tourists by taxing what all tourists needed: food, lodging, and entertainment.

With the proliferation of municipal parks and campsites, private entrepreneurs also entered the business, providing more amenities, but for a fee. Their sites, which came to be known as tourist camps, were the precursors of the motel, or hotels that specialized in attracting motorists. By the 1920s, as railroad travel began to give way to automobile travel, tourist camps, most with private cottages, hot showers, swimming pools, and the like, dotted the South Dakota landscape along major roads and in the Black Hills, where elaborate resort camps intended as destinations in and of themselves sprang up.[63]

In 1927, President Calvin Coolidge chose to summer in South Dakota's Black Hills in order to enjoy nature and the area's "mild and even" climate.[64] His high profile visit further increased the state's growing reputation as a vacation hot spot. Coolidge's trip proved a boon for the new Black Hills Transportation Company, which transported not freight but passengers in tour cars with convertible tops that held over a dozen sightseers.[65]

Tourism continued to grow in the 1930s, despite the Depression, as people looked for cheaper travel destinations. Camps in places like Sturgis cost just 50 cents per car per night and included lights, shower baths, toilets, firewood, and other amenities. For the better heeled, cabins could be had for a buck a night. People came from all over the state, nation, and world to the parks and also the new hotels. By the end of the 1930s, tourism was the state's second largest industry, behind only agriculture.[66]

Despite their name, the Badlands were a big draw. "The White River Badlands are readily accessible," Cleophas O'Harra wrote in 1920. "Many of their features may be observed with pleasure and satisfaction from a Pullman window. Well-travelled wagon roads connect the better known passes and these give opportunity through much of the year for delightful automobile drives. Off-the-road places may be reached by saddle or in pedestrian boots."[67] The town called Interior provided the best access but "there are facilities at every station and at some of them they are nearly or quite as good as at Interior," O'Harra claimed.[68] "The Badlands are strange, and inspirational and good," he concluded.[69] Well, if you did not have to live there. The Badlands are very bad indeed, alternately too hot, too cold, too windy, too dry, and then dangerously wet, and all within the course of a few hours.[70] According to General Custer, they were "a part of hell with the fires burnt out."[71] For many, however, they possessed a strong and strangely alluring quality. The famous architect Frank Lloyd Wright, for example, described them as "a distant architecture, ethereal, touched, only touched, with a sense of Egyptian."[72]

In the east, Hamlin County, especially its Lake Poinsett, was by the Depression "considered one of the superior recreational localities for

The unique land formations caused by erosion in Badlands National Park in western South Dakota attract visitors from all over the world.
Courtesy South Dakota Department of Tourism.

years past, where fishing, boating, and bathing could be enjoyed."[73] The county's lakes dried up somewhat in the drought years but the cabins, dance and pool halls, and parks remained. All the county lacked, the state and county planning boards claimed, was a golf course and that problem was rectified not long after.[74]

Tourism was a nice fit for the state because South Dakota's culture genuinely effuses kindness to strangers. Throw the need to earn cash on top of it, and South Dakotans turned, as one writer put it in 1920, "accommodating to the point of urgent hospitality."[75] Another writer, in 1929, noted that "the people are courteous" in Rapid City, especially during the "tourist season."[76]

South Dakota is also chock full of archeological sites, mostly Amerindian but also a few from the fur-trading, bison-slaughtering days. Prehistoric Amerindian rock art, for example, can be found in the Black Hills. In the eastern part of the state, numerous Indian mound sites remain, including Sherman Park in Sioux Falls proper, Blood Run on its outskirts, Spirit Mound near Vermillion, and the Fort Thompson Mounds. More could probably be done to increase tourism to archeological sites, including the one enclosed by the Archeodome in Mitchell.[77]

Native Americans also sell their culture, or rather a stylized version of it. Donald F. Montileaux, an Oglala Lakota who moved to Rapid City at age five after being born in the Indian Health Hospital on the Pine Ridge Reservation, employs the traditional Sioux flat style and colors in his major works and then develops such associated items as prints, greeting cards, and book publications. Recently honored as an inductee into the South Dakota Hall of Fame, he also sells his ledger art at such shows as the Northern Plains Indian Art Market, sponsored by Sinté Gleska University, and the Artists of the Plains Art Show and Sale, sponsored by the Center for Western Studies, both held in Sioux Falls. The South Dakota State Historical Society Press published his illustrated children's story *Tasunka: A Lakota Horse Legend* in 2014.

It is not a coincidence that Montileaux vends his art in the state's largest city. Its hoteliers, restaurateurs, and gas stations are happy to cater to the needs of tourists headed to other parts of the state, but it has less to offer in terms of natural beauty, though Falls Park and the gorges near Garretson, both found in the verdant Big Sioux River Valley, offer brief diversion. Unable to compete head-to-head with Rapid City and the Black Hills for tourist dollars, Sioux Falls and the rest of southeastern South Dakota has turned itself into something of a cultural mecca, replete with art and book festivals and musical concerts.[78]

The impressive falls of the Big Sioux River in the state's largest city, Sioux Falls, can best be appreciated from Falls Park.
Courtesy South Dakota Department of Tourism.

After World War II, the state's tourism industry found tremendous aid with the completion of two interstates (I-90 and I-29) and the artificial lakes created by the dam projects on the Big Mo.[79] In 1950, about 1.5 million out-of-state tourists, aided by "a fleet of sight-seeing buses, with convertible tops"[80] expended about $66 million in the state, "drawn by such attractions as Mount Rushmore National Memorial near Keystone, Spearfish Canyon, the extensive fossil forest at the foot of Matias Peak, the Stage Barn Crystal Cave near Piedmont, and the Wind Cave near Hot Springs."[81] In the 1950s, up to three quarters of the state's tourist industry rested on Rushmore, which one author called "one of the state's most valuable assets."[82] In the 1960s, advertisements in the *New York Times* stressed the state's other attractions, proclaimed the state the "Land of Wonder," and asked,

> *Ever heard a Sioux war cry? You can, in the thrilling, chilling re-enactment of Custer's Last Stand, staged in a great mountain-walled amphitheatre. The eerie moonscape of the Badlands, the age-old Passion Play, gold mines and ghost towns, the unforgettable majesty of Mount Rushmore – South Dakota is packed with vacation pleasures for all the family. Enjoy rodeos, great fishing, folk plays and festivals, mountain-splendored highways, Old West hospitality. Ski lift. Mail coupon. FREE! New full color 36-page Vacation Brochure, picturing and describing – with maps – 21 scenic auto trips in South Dakota. Mail Coupon Now.[83]*

The number of hotels operating in the state dropped from 700 in 1958 to 684 in 1963, but receipts increased from $13.3 million to $17.65 million over that same period, a boon to the state's coffers. Eventually, the state placed a 1% levy on the gross receipts of hotels, campgrounds, motor vehicle rentals, visitor attractions, recreational rentals and services, and spectator events.[84] By the early 1960s, everyone knew that tourism was important to the state's economy, and "many and varied estimates of its importance" were bandied about but nobody had yet made a "concentrated effort ... to establish its size and economic importance."[85] By the middle of the decade, however, solid numbers became available. In 1965, about 829,000 out-of-state highway travel parties, consisting of 2,856,000 persons who spent $54.2 million, visited the state. The aggregate expenditure was even broken down by category: $19 million went to car expenses, $17 million to food, $11 million to lodging, and the rest to sundries. Half the tourists visited the Black Hills, almost a quarter visited the southeast, a few less checked out the northeast, and most of the balance went to the great artificial lakes on the Missouri.[86] With 1.5 million visitors, Mount Rushmore was the biggest draw, with the Badlands second at 1.1 million visitors. Wind Cave attracted 886,000, though most chose to stare at the bison above ground rather than to explore what has been called "the most complex 3-D ... cave in the world."[87] Jewel Cave counted only 57,000 visitors, but that still made it the fourth biggest attraction in the state. Many visitors were from the Midwest, but in 1990 alone Mount Rushmore drew in over 160,000 Canadians. Foreign tourists were especially welcomed because they spent considerably more money on average than Americans did.[88]

The most popular attractions were all publicly owned by then, but the big money was in food, lodging, shopping, and side attractions, like water parks and safaris. Interestingly, some of the biggest public attractions had been begun by entrepreneurs who found that they could not make a go of it for various reasons. Wind Cave, so called because of the wind that emanates from its entrances, formed tens of millions of years ago.[89] Its 30.5 miles of explored routes as of 1979 made it the fourth largest cave system in the U.S., but it still has not been fully explored yet because of its "real Swiss cheese spongework" structure, which continues to form "down deep."[90] The initial developers were entrepreneurial families named Stabler and McDonald. The latter family, which was comprised of poor Quakers, arrived first and made the cave more accessible while collecting and selling interesting bits of the cave to specimen collectors. The Stablers followed in 1891 to run a hotel and provide cash for the cave improvement effort. They increased tourist traffic in the early 1890s by manufacturing publicity stunts that included "petrified men" and psychics and improving the local infrastructure with a stage line, post office, and hotel. Many visitors to the spa at nearby Hot Springs were lured over as well. The cave and its sundry side operations could have turned into a profitable business but ownership disputes between the McDonalds, the Stablers, and the South Dakota Mining Company led to lawsuits, management changes, and the death of the elder Stabler. By 1901, the government controlled the cave entrance; it became a national park two years later.[91]

Some twenty miles to the Northwest, fourteen miles west of Custer off U.S. 16, is Jewel Cave, another famous Black Hills cave system initially developed by entrepreneurs. It was probably first encountered by Euroamericans about the same time as Wind Cave, but access was not improved and commercially exploited until 1900, when the Michaud brothers, Albert and Frank, filed a mining claim and began improving the passageways for tourists. From the main passages and rooms they extracted only unattractive minerals like iron, manganese, and chert, leaving behind beautiful jewel-like calcite crystals. From side pockets, however, they removed the crystals for samples and for sale. In 1908, jealous onlookers persuaded Theodore Roosevelt to declare the cave a national monument, but his presidential proclamation did not allocate funds to develop the site and stated that it was "subject to prior claims." In 1927, the Jewel Cave Corporation was formed and received a contract to operate the cave as a commercial tourist enterprise. It operated until 1939, when the National Park Service finally took complete control of the cave after paying $300 to Albert Michaud's widow to relinquish her claim.[92]

Numerous but only slightly less spectacular caves remain in private hands. Wonderland Cave, which is southeast of Deadwood on Route 385, boasts a reflecting pool and a forty-foot stalactite fence among other notable features. Rushmore Cave and Sitting Bull Crystal Cave both sport numerous fossils embedded in their walls. Black Hills Caverns, just four miles west of Rapid City, hosts underground weddings in its seventy-five-foot-high-vault. (Half the couples probably end up wishing they had opted for the so-called bottomless pit feature of the cave instead.) Thunderhead Falls, ten miles west of Rapid, offers visitors an underground waterfall.[93] "Here, in the southwest corner of the state," wrote a reporter in the 1980s trying to explain why he deviated from his tight itinerary to spend extra time in the Black Hills, "are two national parks, a national monument, a national memorial, a national forest, one of the country's best-known state parks, as well as other national and historic attractions that could keep a visitor occupied for several weeks."[94]

Even South Dakota's vaunted fisheries and hunting grounds were to some extent the products of entrepreneurship, public and private. South Dakota's numerous lakes, rivers, sloughs, and other waterways have teemed with fish for as long as we have written records. Unfortunately, members of the Lewis and Clark Expedition considered fish as a source of food, not science, so they recorded little of value. An 1857 study, however, found two dozen species of fish in the state's waters and undoubtedly missed the sunfish, redhorse, suckers, and catfish later found in West River ponds.[95] The state's fisheries received little systematic study until late in the nineteenth century but early commentators noted that Dakota's waters abounded in "fishes of many varieties."[96] Pioneers recall that "many fish" lived in the James and other rivers, enough that a few people with a good net "would catch a bushel of a fish at one drive."[97] A sampling and collection study conducted in 1892 and 1893 revealed 69 species inhabiting the state's waters. When the Department of Game and Fish surveyed the state's waters in 1925, it documented 81 species and physically netted all but nine of them. In a study conducted from 1955 to 1958, some 48 different species were discovered in the Vermillion River alone. Inhabiting the state's waters in 1962 were 93 species, 87 of which were considered native and six introduced. Northern pike, catfish, crappie, sunfish/bluegill, sauger, walleye, yellow perch, black bass, drum, and carp were all widespread by the 1960s, though changes in ichtyofauna due to environmental changes – some man-made, like the introduction of exotics, the transplantation of native species, agricultural run-off, mining tailings, and damming, and some natural, like droughts — meant that fish ranges and densities were in almost constant flux.[98]

In 1907, the Missouri River was described as the only "river with a personality, habits, dissipations, a sense of humor, and a woman's caprice; a river that goes traveling sidewise, that interferes in politics, rearranges geography, and dabbles in real estate; a river that plays hide and seek with you today and tomorrow follows you around like a pet dog with a dynamite cracker tied to its tail."[99] By the 1910s, many South Dakotans wanted to dam the damn river but intra- and interstate politics defeated them time and again, and the projectors lacked sufficient capital to forge ahead on such a huge project without outside funds.[100]

The big dams built on the Missouri River in the 1950s with federal money tamed the unruly beast to a large extent. In addition to rendering property along the river more secure (before the reservoirs, it was said, farmers of bottomland never knew if they were going to harvest corn or catfish), the Pick-Sloan project also purposely created extensive boating, ice racing, camping, and swimming facilities, along with 2,350 miles of shoreline. It also eventually enhanced fishing and hunting opportunities. The projects at first hurt the river's ecosystem, however, rendering it less fertile for both fish and fowl well downstream.[101] In 1955, for example, Gerald Jauron noted that "the hunting on the Missouri River from Sioux City to Omaha has been the worst in years."[102]

By the 1970s, however, Mother Nature and some prudent management had produced a liquid, man-made garden of fishing Eden. "These lakes are alive with hungry fish waiting for a nervous, hurrying tourist from the big city to catch them," reported James Robinson in

1974.[103] By the 1980s, South Dakota's "Great Lakes" were thriving, drawing anglers from across the Midwest. In one ten-day period in summer 1991, over 100,000 people visited the Lewis and Clark Recreation Area just west of Yankton. Most hailed from Omaha, Sioux City, and Sioux Falls, but they all spent money locally while recreating, which often entailed trying to get a big catfish (blue or channel), sauger, or walleye at the end of their lines. In 1998, two state records fell, one for flathead catfish (56 lbs.) and the other for paddlefish (93 lbs.), to anglers fishing the boundary waters just downstream from the dam.[104]

The trout-infested waters of the Black Hills were also man-made, the product of stocking and management, not natural fecundity. In 1887, a French traveler noted the absence of trout in the state's western waters, but by the 1920s millions of trout swam in the waterways of the Black Hills, some of which (reportedly freshly stocked and prevented from stealing away by secret weirs) were caught by President Calvin Coolidge during his vacation there in 1927.[105] The stocking programs and publicity stunts worked. In 1929, a visitor reported that "during our visit to the Hills we see fishermen practically in every part of every stream from the interior of the tourist camps to the headwaters in almost jungles."[106]

Nobody stocked the Black Hills with game (several species, including elk and bison, had to be reintroduced), but entrepreneurs did provide the outfitting services required by wealthy Easterners, like Charles Edward Rushmore, who came so often they named a mountain after him that later became rather famous. Euroamericans never saw the Hills or the Plains in their pristine state; only the first human visitors some 10,000 B.C.E. witnessed a truly virgin landscape. But the amount and variety of game they encountered was truly prodigious by later standards because Native Americans had been fair stewards of the state's animal and vegetable resources, more because of their low population densities than their hunting and foraging practices, the environmental friendliness of which have been somewhat exaggerated. (Native Americans sometimes made use of entire bison but other times they ate just the tongue or the unborn calf inside. Euroamericans wasted bison too, but they used every part of their cattle. The difference was that they owned the latter, a point I will return to shortly.)[107]

When Lewis and Clark explored the Missouri River Valley in the early nineteenth century, prominent mammals included antelope, beaver, bison, blacktail deer (in the Black Hills), coyote, mule deer, porcupines, prairie dogs, rabbits (cottontail and jack), skunks, whitetail deer, wolves, and grizzly bears. The last mentioned beast was extirpated in South Dakota circa 1890, but continued killing people to the end. Wolves had haunted South Dakota for at least half a millennium and continued to dwell in the Hills until the early twentieth century when their cattle depredations induced ranchers to exterminate them. Bobcats and mountain lions roam the Black Hills to this day in huntable numbers, and are sometimes seen east of the Big Muddy. Lynx were once present too. They went extinct locally and were not re-introduced. Neither was the black ferret or the wolf, but the rest of the mammals that inhabited the Black Hills at the time of Euroamerican settlement live there today.[108]

Later travelers also saw black bears in the Black Hills, bighorn sheep in the Badlands, and elk as far east as the Missouri River and occasionally beyond. Badgers, gophers, marmots, marten, mink, mountain goats, otters, squirrels, and weasels also inhabited the area that eventually became South Dakota. Raccoons, by contrast, apparently followed the frontier line into the state. Coyotes were already present but thrived in the world created by the settlers, despite repeated attempts to exterminate them. They were so numerous in the early twentieth century that one bored cattle man trapped $150 worth one winter, averaging between two and three per day. The only dangerous creature more common was the rattlesnake.[109]

Despite the big populations of coyotes, foxes, snakes, and other predators, rabbits were plentiful most times and places. A cottontail was relished as "at all seasons of the year a most toothsome morsel. When rolled in corn meal and fried in butter till there is a brown crust over him, he is warranted to make a vegetarian suffer total amnesia of the principles."[110] The much larger jackrabbit, by contrast, was ubiquitous but generally considered only emergency food for humans and even dogs. That did not stop entrepreneurs from making a buck on the big bunnies. Jackrabbit chases, or coursing, took place west of Huron beginning in 1893. Hundreds of men and hounds, some from as far away as England, participated in the events, which were relished due to the open ground and the high quality and speed of the quarry, which were chased down by the hounds rather than shot. What they did with the carcasses, I know not, but today many a dead jackrabbit transmogrifies into the mythical jackalope with the help of bored taxidermists and small-antler sheds.[111]

Turkeys were common in the Hills and the river valleys further east. Along with rabbits and sage grouse, they could even be found in the Badlands. (The author personally saw a large flock twenty miles south of Wall in 2011.) Crows, doves, bald and golden eagles, passenger pigeons, dusky grouse, sharp-tailed grouse, prairie hen, partridge, and quail, along with numerous lesser bird species, were also present in sizable numbers, many even in prehistoric times as revealed by the fossil record.[112]

Waterfowl were plentiful too.[113] "The numerous lakes and marshes were the breeding places of myriads of wild fowl, including swan, geese and ducks," noted one traveler to the region in the 1830s.[114] In the 1880s, "ducks, geese, and brant" crowded the region's "sloughs and streams."[115]

In the early 1900s, flocks of ducks and geese were still large enough that the air was "sometimes fairly blue with them" in the James River Valley.[116] Almost everybody hunted them, for the meat, the challenge, or both. Canada and snow geese, trumpeter swans, and sundry ducks remained widespread and numerous. (Archeological sites confirm that trumpeter swans have lived in the Missouri Valley since at least the late pre-contact period.)[117]

Entrepreneurs made South Dakota a legendary place to hunt but only after almost wiping out several species that were owned in common and therefore subjected to heavy hunting pressure. Economists call that problem the tragedy of the commons, tragic because in the absence of binding conservation laws or social mores, individuals have an incentive to exploit resources held in common at an unsustainable rate. Most infamously, bison were hunted to the edge of extinction by Natives, Americans, and European travelers, like English sportsman Sir St. George Gore, until entrepreneurs rendered them private property and hence had an incentive to protect them from further unsustainable depredation.[118]

The key reforms were the assertion of property rights over the land by people and corporations and over game animals by the state, once its writ extended into the hinterlands. For most species, hunting opportunities are better today than a century ago because of management and privatization. That is certainly true of bison, which a century ago were almost extinct but today can be hunted in limited numbers. The Cheyenne River Sioux Tribe, for example, offers trophy bison hunts, as does the state government, which also sells a few non-trophy permits.[119]

A century and more ago, matters were very different. Market hunters came from Minneapolis and Chicago to shoot waterfowl in northeastern South Dakota, where the skies were darkened by migrating wildfowl. The market hunters traveled by horse and buggy and shot cases of shells each day, shipping the dead ducks and geese to city markets, sometimes in-state but mostly not, for a buck a bird.[120] Those hunters were about the harvest, not the hunt, so they used four-gauge shotguns with long barrels that could "throw buckshot point-blank two hundred yards."[121] The Migratory Bird Law of 1913 finally reigned the market hunters in, opening the way for modern sport hunting. By the 1930s, over 7,000 federal migratory bird stamps were annually sold in South Dakota, more than in New York, Iowa, California, North Dakota, and most other states.[122]

Market hunters (and bored wagon passengers and drivers) also targeted prairie chickens, which were tasty treats, except in the hands of one unskilled cook who managed to make them taste like "a fried shoe."[123] "A nice fried prairie chicken," one fellow in the know told a traveler, "is something worth talking about. It's a far greater delicacy than any farmyard fowl." "This is fine country for prairie chickens" one early denizen of the James River Valley noted, "and hunters come from everywhere to shoot them."[124] Indeed, contemporaries used "chicken hunts" to entice friends to visit and business clients to call.[125] As hunting pressure mounted, however, the birds became "shyer and shyer," necessitating the use of a "well-trained dog."[126] Each professional hunter, armed with the "latest and most effective guns and ammunition" and helped by the "best trained dogs," could bag a score or more birds a day. One Iowan claimed to have killed over 3,000 prairie chickens in a single season. That kind of carnage could not long continue and the number of birds on the Northern Plains slipped, so governments began to regulate the take by instituting seasons, daily bag limits, and restrictions against the sale of wild game.[127]

Early on, however, poaching was common, especially by so-called "pot hunters" who shot game to keep their families fed. Almost all early farmers and ranchers supplemented their diets and incomes by hunting, fishing, and trapping. In the early 1920s, for example, a young Joe Foss used his Remington .22 rifle to keep his family's table laden with pheasant and rabbit.[128] One family near Paxton killed prairie chickens "in season and out. Out of season we referred to them as 'prairie ducks,' a species not mentioned in the game laws, or in any ornithology text. Game wardens were unknown to us, personally. Officialdom seldom penetrated this far from its offices. None of us went hunting for sport, anyway, only for a refreshing change from our ham and bacon meals."[129] Near Montrose in the 1880s, there were "a great variety of wild birds, such as 'prairie chickens,' ducks and geese. ... These birds," recalled one inhabitant, "often became a factor in our family menu when meat was scarce."[130] West River, one homesteader cried when her husband managed to miss "six grouse that lighted in some brush not far away."[131]

In the winter, prairie chickens flocked into groups of fifty or so and posted sentries so they were very difficult to shoot. In the late summer and early fall, however, they were good sport and, along with quail, were quite numerous.[132] "During the heat of the day," painter Frederic Remington noted in an 1894 article, "the chickens lie in the cover of the grass at the sides of the fields, or in the rank growth of some slough-hole, but at early morning and evening they feed in the wheat stubble." Dogs found them and pointed. "Prairie chickens are not difficult" to shoot, Remington claimed, echoing others who said they flew "almost in a straight line, like a clay pigeon," but nevertheless he still witnessed many "clean misses."[133]

The tasty, testy birds attracted "carloads and planeloads of hunters from Omaha, Des Moines, Chicago, and neighboring areas."[134]

Remington described the scene on one South Dakota-bound train car in 1894, which included a former army officer and some Harvard boys along with "numerous setter-dogs, while all about were shot-gun cases and boxes labeled 'Ammunition.'"[135] Sharptailed grouse, the breast of which was considered "white and very delicious," also attracted the attention of some of this new breed of hunter, the so-called sport hunter or sportsman, who hunted for fun and to renew his sense of agrarian masculinity.[136] Grouse were most prevalent in the Missouri River Valley, especially west of the river, but were nowhere numerous, however, and hence could not support large numbers of hunters, even sporting ones more interested in the pursuit rather than the actual bagging of game. Four-year population cycles also hurt the sport but by no means eliminated interest. In 1969, 20,400 hunters bagged 96,300 of the birds. Before some combination of parasites, reduced habitat, and hunters rendered the native birds too sparse to hunt, however, entrepreneurs had introduced a new game bird to the state, the ringnecked pheasant.[137]

The ringnecked pheasant was a native of Asia, not Europe or America, though they had been successfully introduced into Western Europe, including the British Isles, two millennia ago. Attempts to introduce European varieties into New England and New York in the eighteenth century failed. In the 1870s, the word "pheasant" was sometimes used in the American West to denote what we today call a partridge or a ruffed grouse, but true "brilliantly plumaged" pheasants were not introduced into the United States until 1881, when a U.S. emissary returned from China with some that "wonderfully multiplied" on the prairie near Albany, Oregon. Before 1905, fewer than 500 pheasants had been introduced into the Northern Plains and most introductions had failed. Between 1905 and 1918, however, thousands of adult birds from various locations domestically and overseas were released, at first by private individuals and later by the state, and birds were raised and hatched from eggs. The most famous shipment came in 1915, in a ship aptly called the *Minnehaha*, which imported 16,000 pheasants from England. Some 2,000 of those birds apparently made their way to South Dakota, where they were banded and released. These birds, and another 5,000 purchased and released by the state during the Great War, joined with the remnants of the earlier releases to propagate the millions of pheasants spread around the central and eastern parts of the state through local capture and release programs. Where they thrived, where habitat was suitable, pheasants were captured and used to stock other likely locations nearby. Once a significant range had been established, the birds were allowed to flourish without further stocking by the state, though individuals continued to stock their own properties as they saw fit. Today's South Dakota ringneck, therefore, is not wholly

Chinese, but rather a mix of Chinese, Mongolian, Japanese, and English strains.[138]

Pheasants proved to be tasty table fare, fecund, and remarkably adapted to local conditions. They quickly spread throughout the eastern part of the state and even well west of the Big Mo.[139] By the late 1920s, pheasants were said to thrive "throughout South Dakota,"[140] and by 1929 the "Pheasant Dining Room" at the Game Lodge in the Black Hills had 33 mounted pheasants "standing, flying, and alighting."[141] The first hunting season opened in 1919. By the late 1920s, 1.5 million pheasants were harvested every year on a sustained basis, about 20 million all told between 1919 and 1941. Farmers in Huron demanded their extermination because pheasants ate crops, but others sought to increase their local populations because the prolific birds also ate prodigious quantities of crop-destroying insects in the spring. Moreover, even during the Depression, sportsmen were willing to pay to hunt them, though not as much as they are willing to pay today in inflation-adjusted dollars.[142] That was because of the nature of the birds themselves: not too bright but, as a South Dakota game warden once put it, "really, really good at what they do, and that's getting away. ... They run. They sit. They flush in your face and cackle at you."[143] "The poignant beauty" of the South Dakota countryside also kept hunters coming back according to hunting expert Steve Grooms.[144] The friendships that developed between hunters and their "guides," locals who helped hunters to find lodgings and permissions, also kept hunters coming back for more, year after year. The Hansens of Hitchock, for example, hosted a group of hunters from Anderson, Indiana, every year from the mid-1950s into the 1990s. Another group near Salem has been at it, with some turnover in membership, for over sixty years.[145]

The introduction of pheasants into the state went so well that in the late 1920s the state game department introduced another invasive species, the Hungarian partridge, which was expected "to provide good shooting within a few years."[146] The partridge took well to certain parts of the state but most hunters did not take to the partridge, which can be overly difficult to bag even if the birds are found because they flush hard and at long distance. That was why private individuals were not involved in their introduction, as they had been from the start with the ringnecks.

During the Depression, pheasant numbers increased dramatically because relatively little of the state was under the plow. In 1933, the worst year of the Depression, towns close to "good pheasant ranges advertised accommodations for hunters and in some instances even met the out-of-town sportsmen with brass bands."[147] After the drought finally broke in 1934, incomes throughout the eastern part of the Midwest soared, and so too did pheasant bookings in South Dakota, which remained parched due to a lack of both water and money.[148] By 1936, South Dakota was thought to have the "best natural pheasant conditions of any State, the birds being so abundant that game wardens spend a large part of their time preventing commercialization and guarding against 'bootlegging' of birds across the State boundaries."[149]

Pheasant populations increased further in the early war years because of advantageous weather and other conditions. Due to large numbers of birds and a shortage of hunters and shells, the 1942 hunting season was extended through February and then March 1943.[150] The pheasant population grew so large that in 1944, when it topped 16.7 million, farmers paid boys to "go out in the grain fields to tramp on eggs in pheasant nests."[151] The following year, South Dakota shipped hundreds of the birds to feed the officers and crew of its namesake battleship, the remnants of which are on display in a park in Sioux Falls. In 1944, many birds and few hunters spelled a season that stretched from late September to the end of February, with a daily bag limit of ten birds, up to five of which could be hens. Despite attempts to literally stomp them out, pheasant populations hit thirty to fifty million in eastern South Dakota in the 1940s. By the early postwar period, the state game department was earning so much from licenses – one dollar from residents and $20 from nonresidents, a hefty sum (over $200 in 2013 dollars) that 40,000 hunters were willing to pay annually — used the extra revenue to purchase public hunting lands for pheasant, waterfowl, and other hunters.[152]

Reflecting on the Depression and war years from a perch in the late 1960s, one biologist claimed that "pheasants never had it so good."[153] That may have been, but the boom years for hunters came in the decade following World War II, when the annual pheasant harvest averaged three million, or ten roosters per every 100 acres of prime range. That was despite three horrible winters in the late 1940s when storms took the lives of over 50% of the state's pheasants.[154] Right after the war, United Airlines began offering a "Hunters' Special" to whisk hunters from Boston, New York, Philadelphia, Washington, Toledo, Detroit, and Chicago to the Dakota Ring Neck Lodge near Aberdeen. "The hunters," a *New York Times* reporter claimed, "would be walking behind the dogs the next morning" on this all-expense-paid jaunt.[155] It made sense to head west because upland game hunters in the east had been lamenting the "pheasant situation for years."[156] Flying off to the state just to hunt seemed a little trivial, however, after a plane carrying a prominent Virginia physician and his brother to the pheasant promised land crashed in heavy fog in West Virginia.[157]

Local entrepreneurs also capitalized on the pheasant boom. All around the pheasant range, towns like Aberdeen held fall festivals with

The pheasant, South Dakota's state bird, draws thousands of hunters from across America and abroad. *Courtesy South Dakota Department of Tourism.*

names like "Golden Pheasant Day," and every town had to have at least one business, usually a bar, with pheasant or rooster in the name. One of them, the Pheasant Bar and Lounge in Winner was, unlike the two local movie theaters, still in business at the end of the century. U.S. Senator James Abourezk worked as a bartender in the Pheasant before moving down the street to the Stockman's Bar, another of Winner's four drinking establishments, which included the Peacock Bar.[158]

The state government nearly killed the birds that laid the dollar-laden eggs in 1947, however, when it banned nonresident waterfowl hunters altogether and restricted out-of-state pheasant hunters to just ten days of hunting, ten days after the locals could start shooting. "Many a non-resident hunter," a newspaper reporter pointed out, "will find himself paying rent on hunting grounds on which he cannot hunt."[159] But the shooting was simply too good to pass up, especially for the rich and famous. In 1948, big-league baseball players John Lindell (Yankees), Enos Slaughter (Cardinals), Dizzy Trout (Tigers), and Joe Gordon (Indians) gave the state a big boost when they were photographed with their shotguns over a pile of fine looking, but thoroughly dead, South Dakota roosters. The photo-op was part of Huron's "Baseball Pheastival" held each fall when big league all stars played minor league all stars and then went out pheasant hunting the next day. Governor George T. Mickelson (not to be confused with his son George S., who also served as governor, almost half a century later) also took to the field for a photo-op replete with shotgun, vest, and two roosters dangling off his belt. In the early 1950s, the state lengthened the season in certain East River counties but cut daily limits to two roosters in some places. Non-residents were forbidden to ship more than fifteen cocks home. Pheasant populations remained relatively high and steady through 1956, when almost 130,000 out-of-state hunters descended on coyote country, up from 90,000 just a few years before.[160] Pheasant numbers, however, eventually declined off their legendary highs, when they numbered between twenty and fifty million and were said to be "so thick ... that nobody can possibly miss."[161]

In addition, by 1959 competitors – game preserves that stocked pheasants – had popped up in forty-one states and were starting to erode the state's market share even though many of the preserves were deemed artificial and expensive. Hunting was by then a $2 billion a year industry, with fifteen million active hunters (14.5 million of whom were male), a 50% increase since World War II. The state responded in 1963 by regulating South Dakota's own preserves liberally. (Today, scores of regulated preserves across the state enjoy extended seasons, liberal bag limits, and other perks that allow them to compete nationally for hunters that are not hesitant to blast stocked birds.) In the meantime, many relatively well-heeled sportsmen still made the trip to the "promised land," some 68,000 in 1963, and harvests stayed around 3 million a year in the early 1960s before dropping in 1965, allegedly because the state eliminated bounties on foxes, a major predator.[162] According to state biologists, however, bounties had "never accomplished predator control in South Dakota."[163]

Owing to the pheasant's tremendous economic value to the state, the causes of its population surges and declines were intensively studied. Pheasant numbers declined because of blizzards, corn chopping and fall plowing, herbicides, fertilizers, pesticides, an increase in alfalfa acreage, more livestock grazing, mowing too soon, cover diminution, an increase in the number of predators, cold or dry spring weather, too much hot weather at hatching time, and disease. (Though it must be recognized that pheasants are remarkably free of disease unless stressed by other shocks like loss of habitat, fertilizer, or bad weather.)[164] In March 1966, for example, a blizzard killed 85% of the pheasants in the north central part of the state while blizzard kill was "practically non-existent from 1954 to 1959."[165] According to biologists, however, most mortality occurred in the spring and summer, though it was then more difficult to see and hence to document. Late springs were more deadly than blizzards and short droughts because molting and breeding occur in the spring, when food resources are scarce and fat reserves are depleted from the winter, putting the birds on the razor's edge. Of course, multiple shocks hit the birds the hardest. From fall 1963 to fall 1964, for instance, the number of birds plummeted from about 10 million to just 5.3 million due to a cold April followed by a scorching May and June.[166]

What the state's game managers learned early on is that, with market and pot hunters mostly relegated to history and a roosters-only rule firmly in place, sport hunting pressure is *not* a major source of pheasant population fluctuations. "HABITAT AND WEATHER ARE KEYS TO GAME ABUNDANCE," as one researcher adamantly put it in 1967.[167] The best habitat was farmland that was only 50-75% cultivated, with plenty of shelter and limestone, which helps hens to produce ten times as many eggs as those without access to lime. Newer, more intensive farming practices that included planting crops right to the fence, mowing roadsides, and draining wetlands, were the main reason why pheasant populations declined according to scientific accounts like those of Carolyn Burks, which pointed to the importance of the quality and diversity as well as the quantity of cover.[168]

Hunting is not a major factor in populations because predators, whether feathered, furred, or in blaze-orange vests, fluctuate with pheasant numbers. They go where the most birds are, always leaving a few roosters and more hens around to reproduce the next spring. Even if exterminated locally because of bad weather and bad luck, during good years pheasants from other areas will fan out in search of cover and hence naturally re-populate any area with suitable supplies of water, food, nesting, and hiding places.[169]

The rooster-only rule promulgated in 1946 helps to maintain pheasant numbers because only one rooster is needed to mate every eight, ten, or more hens, up to fifty by one estimate. That means that up to 90% of cocks can be shot without impacting the next year's hatch. Moreover, when the ratio of roosters to hens drops toward one to three, roosters, which have nasty talons and dispositions, will outcompete hens for food and shelter and hence actually reduce the overall population. Shooting roosters, then, essentially saves hens (and makes for happier roosters, one suspects) and hence helps to increase population levels. (That is, if hunters can tell the difference between the sexes. In 1965, hunters reportedly mistakenly killed one hen for every 4.5 cocks they bagged.) Biologists also point out that pheasants cannot be "saved" from one season to the next. Birds not harvested by hunters typically fall victim to something else. So the most heavily hunted counties, like Miner (where I do most of my hunting), are also those with the best pheasant densities.[170]

Finally, raising and stocking pheasants is a losing proposition, especially for governments, and South Dakota's officials have been intelligent, or frightened, enough to never try the experiment. Pheasants

Little Business on the Prairie

are wild creatures, not chickens, and do not respond well to enclosed conditions. Captive roosters have to be hooded or they will tear each other to shreds. They will also kill and eat hens with even minor wounds. They therefore cost over $8.00 per *bagged* bird even in the late 1960s, before the Great Inflation, and run to $20 per *released* bird (not all of which are harvested) today.[171]

Even after the rooster hunters' heyday ended in the early 1960s, the state's legendary status as a "pheasant-hunting state" continued to grow, thanks in part to some timely publicity.[172] In 1970, for example, a political pundit covering politics in the state noted in the *New York Times* that "from the steps of the state house one can see pheasant hunters moving through fields not five blocks away."[173] In 1979, New York Yankees manager Billy Martin made national headlines when he allegedly struck a marshmallow salesman in a Minnesota hotel after pheasant hunting in South Dakota. Pheasant hunting made national news again the next year when former presidential nominee and Senator George McGovern was not allowed a resident license because he had spent too much time out of the state. He lost re-election that fall by a substantial margin.[174]

Of course, no amount of publicity would have helped if the state lacked birds. By the mid-1980s, the state's pheasant population sat between three and four million. In the late 1980s, pheasant populations continued around four million birds, but hunting in South Dakota was still better than anywhere else, including Iowa, which lost pheasants when their habitat was reduced due to the rise of industrial farming methods. Eventually, conservation programs, like CRP, helped to improve pheasant numbers in South Dakota and the good publicity continued. On the *Tonight Show with Jay Leno*, Vice President Dick Cheney joked that the "undisclosed locations" that he frequented to avoid terrorist threats after the 9/11 attacks included good species and places to hunt, like pheasants in South Dakota, ducks in Maryland, and quail in Texas. During his reign in office, Cheney actually took annual pheasant hunting trips to South Dakota but thankfully waited for a quail hunting trip in Texas to accidentally pepper a friend in the face with bird shot.[175]

By the late 1990s, pheasant hunting brought into the state $50 to $60 million per year. While the percentage of Americans who hunted dropped from about ten in 1955 to just four in 2005, the number of pheasant hunters in South Dakota has increased from the long-term average of about 130,000 to almost 180,000 by 2005. By 2002, for the first time since 1919, nonresident hunters outnumbered residents. How was South Dakota able to buck a sustained, nationwide trend?[176]

The details of the highly regulated pheasant season, including its start in mid-October, its length (until early January), its shooting times (afternoons only early in the season), and bag limits stemmed from a combination of tradition and cunning calculation designed to maximize the experience for hunters without unduly distressing the birds, not all of which have matured by early November, before which most kills are made. The bag limit (now three, but at various times two to five) is actually designed more to protect hunters' egos than the species because, as noted above, it is almost impossible to overhunt cocks. The notion is that a hunter who gets his limit of three is happier than one who bags four birds under a limit of five. At about an hour per bird in the best conditions, the three-rooster limit also leaves hunters plenty of time to head into town to spend some money.[177] As geographer Christopher Laingen put it, "pheasant hunting is to South Dakota what golfing is to Scotland," and worn-out hunters are no better than worn-out golfers at spending money.[178]

Since the 1950s, South Dakota, especially the area around Huron, has been known as the "Pheasant Hunting Capital of the World" and, as noted, the state's economy still gets a notable boost from the cagey critter.[179] In 2007, for example, 181,000 hunters shot two million pheasants and added an estimated $219 million, or .65% of the state's GDP, to the state economy, buying everything from ammunition to freezer lockers for their birds. Little wonder the state put two symbols on its commemorative quarter, Mount Rushmore and a rooster with a trophy-length tail.[180]

But the ringneck, which is also the official state bird, is simply the most famous of the state's wild game. Cottontails, crows, deer (whitetail and mule), doves, ducks, geese, grouse, partridge, prairie chicken, quail, squirrels, snipe, turkey, and a wide variety of varmints and furbearers were taken in large numbers by hunters after the war and up to the present, and to some extent native upland birds were protected by the emphasis placed on hunting the immigrant.[181] In 1952, one author made several assertions that held throughout the rest of the twentieth century and into the twenty-first:

> South Dakota is best known for its pheasant hunting. ...
> The State also offers mountain big-game hunting, and
> some excellent goose and duck shooting. There is every
> kind of fresh-water fishing—trout in mountains streams;
> pike, bass, and other game fish in the lakes; and catfish
> in the Missouri and tributary rivers.[182]

He could have added turkeys as well, especially West River and in the Black Hills, where Merriams are abundant and easy to hunt.[183]

Doves were a little different. Hunting them was banned in the state from 1972 until 1981. By 1986, the hunters were back: some 20,000 of them bagged about 350,000 of the super-agile four-ounce birds, out of a breeding population of about 20 million statewide. Outfitters cashed in on shot-shell purchases because the little guys are ubiquitous but difficult to hit: even good shots are happy with a 50% takedown rate. Entrepreneurs like Joe Jensen, Rich Converse, and Doug Converse cashed in, too, turning 880 of their 3,500-acre spread, Dakota Dream Hunts, into a shooting preserve.[184] "We got tired of farming fence line to fence line and not making any money while at the same time we watched the game disappear," Rich Converse confided to a reporter in 1986.[185]

After the big dams changed the face of central South Dakota into one with lots of corn and lots of open water, geese started "shortstopping," wintering there instead of flying further south as they had for untold millennia. Instead of the 32,000 geese that used the river corridor in 1953, by the 1990s hundreds of thousands of honkers were counted within 30 miles of Pierre at the peak of the migration. Big numbers opened up big opportunities for farmers willing to dig pits along the edges of their fields and invite goose hunters in to pound the ravenous birds, charging from $10 per goose to $75 per day. The state also opened up land along the river to hunters. Hotels and outfitters also cashed in, though the state kept strict limits on the number of nonresident licenses sold. Despite being hunted further north than they traditionally had, the geese thrived under the new conditions because it meant less flying and hence less stress and caloric loss and, in the end, larger broods.[186]

In fact, all the state's game species have become big business. By the 1850s, hunting and fishing guides were prominent in New York's Adirondack Mountains so South Dakotans clearly did not invent outfitting. They brought the industry, however, to a new level. From the state's beginning, out-of-state hunters were lured in, lavished with attention, and brought back time and again by successful hunts and memorable experiences. Hunting excursions became so common by 1946 that a guidebook dedicated to the state's pheasant shooting opportunities was published. Cottages and lodges for duck and geese hunters also proliferated in the glacial lakes region in the northeast part of the state, where 46 waterfowl per square mile could be found. By the 1920s, Watertown's Lake Kampeska attracted thousands of fishers and other tourists annually. Although not as famous as the Black Hills, South Dakota's lake country attracts a large number of recreational tourists and is still home to many outfitters, including the Glacial Lakes Hunting Resort near Watertown, which advertised full-service hunts for groups of two to twenty in the *New York Times* as late as 2000. It is still in business and business looks good as the sport has seen an influx of new, affluent hunters aged 25 to 45 who think nothing of dropping thousands on gear and expeditions to far-away places like South Dakota just to bag a few birds.[187]

Today, every hunter, from the rich and famous to the poor and obscure, can find just the right hunting package to suit him- or herself, from barebones self-guided access to prime, private, fair chase pheasant habitat to preserves that "almost hand feed the birds to the gun" to luxurious ranches with eye-popping per diems and opportunities to hunt several species in a variety of ways as well as to land giant walleyes or a bucket of perch or crappie.[188] Those who would rather just fish, ride horseback, and take pictures of stunning scenery can bunk up at western ranches, like the RRR in Keystone.[189]

The biggest strides were made during the 1980s, when more farmers began charging hunters, especially ringneck chasers, upon learning that some farmers had earned more from hosting pheasant hunters than from growing crops or raising stock. Innovations have followed ever since. Long gone are the days when hunters would pay to hunt private land by giving the landlady some portion of the birds they harvested (typically, it was claimed, the older, tougher roosters, or the ones that several hunters blasted simultaneously at close range, which were more lead than meat). The trend towards paying for land access actually began with deer hunters in the West River area of the state in the early 1970s, a good half-century after it began in Texas, by an outfit called Dakota Safaris. From there, commercialization spread east and to pheasants. By 2000, as many as 100,000 pheasant hunters during opening week alone pumped $100 million into the state. That included lodging, food, and so forth but also payments to access private land, be the charges per gun/day or per bird.[190]

In addition to aiding retailers and hoteliers, hunting and fishing provides opportunities for taxidermies, companies that "stuff" trophy game animals from fish to pheasants. In Sioux Falls, for example, from 1941 until 1975 Walter A. Heldt ran a taxidermy business as well as a tanning company that made "beautiful custom-made deerskin products," like gloves, rugs, and coats, as well as products made from the skin and fur of the antelope, badger, bear, beaver, bison, bobcat, cow, coyote, fox, goat, lion, lynx, marten, mink, moose, muskrat, raccoon, seal, sheep, tiger, and wolf. He displayed numerous mounts in the broad windows of his store, in which he also sold fishing bait, guns, and other sporting goods, including expensive items like boats.[191]

Hunting, like other forms of tourism, is not an unaltered benefit to the state. Some hunters only road hunt, i.e., drive down dirt roads looking for roosters or other game to pick off. They can no longer "shoot pheasants in South Dakota while driving an automobile," at least not lawfully, but overanxious hunters sometimes shoot too close to homes and livestock.[192] "They seemed to be shooting just to be shooting," remembered one resident. "Just to make loud noises ... outside our house."[193] Others hunt intoxicated, which is especially dangerous when mixed with road hunting. Hunters can lawfully shoot over private property at game animals that originated on public road right-of-ways, an intrusion on private property rights tolerated in a state strongly favoring property rights because, as the South Dakota Supreme Court held in 2006, the cost and inconvenience to landowners is minimal compared to the economic benefits that hunting brings to the state.[194]

Of even more concern is the connection between hunting tourism and sex trafficking. Most hunters come to enjoy the sport and maybe have a few drinks with friends, but some come looking for sexual encounters, as well. They pay for the experience but many of the females engaged in the trade are underage and/or forced into the business. The vast majority of South Dakotans do not take kindly to slavery, especially sexual slavery, and are taking steps to ameliorate the problem but much work remains to be done.[195]

Chapter 8

Education, Health, and Finance

It was banking that built the states of North and South Dakota. It was banking money that financed the stockgrower, the merchant and the miner of those early days, even as it has down the years that have intervened to the present day. It was the public-spirited banker who helped the young towns to grow into the splendid cities of today.[1]

For all the state's mineral, vegetable, hoofed, and winged wealth, the bulk of its income is generated in the service sector, from lowly retail jobs to highly paid doctors and scientists. The state's large service sector is diverse and entrepreneurial to the core. And it all begins with education.[2]

Education and extractive industries like mining, farming, and ranching may not seem to easily mix, but they did in early South Dakota.[3] "Zeal for learning," wrote an early state historian, "has characterized the South Dakotan from the earliest period." Even French fur magnates like Manuel Lisa and the Picottes sent their mixed-blood children to St. Louis for a formal education. Fort Randall had a school by 1857. In 1862, the territorial government established common schools and what would become the University of South Dakota. After food, water, and shelter were satisfactorily provided, schools always went up first in a new community, along with the church.[4] As Mr. Hardy said in Annie Fellows Johnson's "Washington's Birthday at Hardyville" (1889), "Thank goodness, they [the town's otherwise lazy founders] *did* put up the church and schoolhouse."

In 1904, South Dakota employed 4,800 teachers in 4,100 schools where 132,000 students attended classes. Most were one-room schools, but they should not be dismissed since prevailing pedagogical practices, especially low teacher-student ratios and peer tutoring practices, were arguably better than those employed today. Many who attended the little prairie schools later attested to their quality.[5] Irene Mortenson Sargent, for example, recalled that "the teachers we had were really dedicated and we did have some great teachers."[6] The State still had 2,338 one-room schools in operation as late as 1960 and at least one, near Freeman, lasted into the 1990s.[7]

By the 1960s, most one-room schools were for the lower grades only. By high school, most students were in larger institutions encompassing large districts. Those who could not commute daily due to long distances, poor roads, and/or the lack of an available automobile boarded with families in town, often in exchange for doing household chores like cooking and cleaning. The system worked tolerably well until deadly contagions swept the area, as in Philip in 1918, when several students at the high school perished. (The pandemic of that year, the so-called Spanish flu, also took several lives near Howard.) Open enrollment policies rendered public schools somewhat competitive and home schooling was a viable option for many families. Parents could hire tutors or teach their children themselves. Some chose to do so for the entire curriculum, while others hired itinerant instructors to teach their children specific subjects or skills, like how to play the piano or other instruments.[8]

In 1920, the illiteracy rate in the state was only 1.7%. In the early 1950s, the state still boasted one of the lowest illiteracy rates in the nation. Throughout the postwar period, South Dakotans, like their neighbors in Minnesota and Iowa, graduated high school at a higher rate than the national average. South Dakota's four-year college degree attainment rate, however, lagged a little, largely due to West River attitudes about diminishing returns to higher education and concerns about high interest rates on student loans in the early 1980s.[9]

In 1889, the state was described as having "an excellent public school system with ample funds."[10] Nobody would argue that South Dakota's public schools continued to receive "ample" funds but a good case could be made that they have received "sufficient" funding. In 1990, the state expended on education only 86% of the U.S. per capita average but the schools were unusually efficient, producing excellent results on budgets that appeared downright niggardly to outsiders. Small-government Midwesterners would not have it any other way.[11] In 1991, in response to national calls for educational reform, South Dakota initiated a "Modernization Project," not to catch up, but to continue to produce "favorable results" as measured by scores on standardized tests, like the Stanford achievement tests of fourth, eighth, and eleventh grade students.[12]

Public schools achieved so much with so little because education was never considered the exclusive bailiwick of the government. Successful sheep rancher M. J. Smiley, for example, wanted more than anything for his children to receive "a good education and learn how to run some business successfully."[13] So in addition to their schooling he set his boys up in the pony business so they would learn how to buy, sell, and maintain assets and to keep accounts. Such activities became more formalized over time. In the 1990s, almost 20% of South Dakota elementary schools surveyed teamed up with local businesses to help students better to understand the importance of what they were learning in school to employment later in life. One school even set up a bank, complete with tellers and loan officers. Another allowed students to compete for start-up grant money for their own nano-businesses.[14]

Many parents "made great sacrifices to get their children educated" and educated well.[15] Grace Fairchild got all of her children except two through South Dakota State College in Brookings.[16] "When I look back now and see how the children managed to get an education," Fairchild said, "I feel very proud."[17] The Morrison family also saw four children graduate from South Dakota State.[18] Another family near Howard got all six children through high school during the Depression. The effort cost the family a patch of land on which back taxes were owed and "several good Insurance policies."[19] Even a preacher's widow living in the small town of Toronto (between Brookings and Watertown) managed to get five of her six children through college, including the University of Minnesota and St. Olaf. The sixth became a banker instead.[20] Expectations were as important as finances for such families. "Dad came from a family where his parents valued education," reported one West River woman, "and that attitude would also permeate our home. All of us were expected to take school seriously."[21]

Private philanthropy helped too. Homestake and its major shareholders gave liberally to education and established a library in Lead. It did so to attract family men to work the mines because they tended to be more stable employees than bachelors. There were no private schools in the area at the time so the children of the mine's superintendents attended too. As a result, in 1897 Lead paid teachers $67.50 per month when the average in urban eastern South Dakota was just under half that, $33.[22]

The state's educational system remains impressive to this day. Almost 92% of its high school students graduate, compared to the national average of 84.1%. In 2006, the state ranked eleventh in the nation in the percentage of twenty-five-year-olds who have completed high school. And they are ready to work: few manufacturing companies expressed the need to conduct remedial training. South Dakota also ranked highest in the nation in computers per student thanks to a 1997 initiative that included having (non-violent) prison inmates wire schools for the Internet. Although the project ensured that the state would be connected to the emerging information superhighway, the state did not make technology education a graduation requirement, potentially limiting the impact of the computers on students and employers.[23]

South Dakota's system of higher education is also relatively efficient. As New York University professor Richard Richardson noted, "South Dakota, unlike most other states, has successfully moved toward greater centralization and made decisions unheard of elsewhere – such as closing an institution."[24] South Dakota also asked its colleges and universities to achieve cost savings by cutting low-enrollment programs, consolidating administrative functions, and improving business practices. Its biggest fault, according to Richardson, is that it lacks a network of comprehensive community colleges, instead concentrating on technical schools. Two of the state's institutions of higher education, the University of South Dakota and Augustana College, are consistently ranked among the best liberal arts colleges in the Midwest.[25] "The quality of the University of South Dakota," Gilbert Fite wrote in the early 1970s, "is undisputed. The graduates of the university have done well in nationwide competition. The university has turned out professional people of the highest quality and at low cost."[26]

So, too, has Augustana College. Established in 1860 in Illinois as the Augustana Seminary, the Norwegian, as opposed to the Swedish, contingent moved to Canton in the late nineteenth century and Sioux Falls in 1918, where it merged with the Lutheran Normal School, established in 1889. By 1962, Augustana was considered "a very fine institution and the largest private college in the state."[27] In the early 1980s, it housed a small business institute that worked with the SBA to help businesses employing fewer than ten people.[28] Senator Larry Pressler lauded the institute for "doing a good job in research. As has been pointed out, 90% of our business community here in South Dakota would be classified as small business."[29] Like Augustana, Dakota Wesleyan University and the University of Sioux Falls are known for their small class sizes, good tuition rates, and a great liberal arts education. The state has also been home to numerous technical schools and for-profit colleges, including Nettleton Commercial College in Sioux Falls.[30]

Scholars of entrepreneurship usually think of education as a type of infrastructure necessary to the creation of entrepreneurs with sufficient knowledge and skill to compete in local, state, regional, national, or global marketplaces. In South Dakota, however, the business of education has also led to innovative pedagogical approaches and products. South Dakota educators, for example, have long been interested in teaching spelling more efficiently. In 1913, W. Franklin Jones, the head of the University of South Dakota's Department of Education, published *Concrete Investigation of the Material of English Spelling with Conclusions Bearing on the Problem of Teaching Spelling*. The thin volume sought to answer the question, "What is the matter with our spelling teaching?" with empirical research conducted on actual students. The author concluded that more time should be spent teaching fewer words, specifically the ones most commonly used by students of different grade levels and about three-score words that most students consistently misspell.[31]

Born in Depression-era Aberdeen, James King graduated from Aberdeen High School before attending college at the University of Colorado and the Ohio State University School of Optometry. He returned to Aberdeen briefly before moving to Rapid City with his wife in 1961 to practice optometry with Leland Michael. Together, the pair created the MKM Reading System for use with children who had difficulty learning to read due to visual or other problems. MKM sold its systems throughout the nation and even internationally. In 2007, King moved to Sioux Falls, where we had lunch together several times to discuss his MKM business. Very accomplished in his profession and once a guest on *The Tonight Show with Johnny Carson*, King exuded confidence and remained hopeful that his reading system would become even more popular in the future. Dr. King died in April 2012, not quite an octogenarian. His research, as important as it was, was but a small part of the medical research being conducted throughout the state, but primarily in Sioux Falls at Sanford Research and at Avera Research Institute.[32]

Hard work and a generally clean environment have always rendered South Dakotans relatively fit. South Dakota, for example, was second only to Kansas in the percentage of its young men found healthy enough to participate in the Great War.[33] "I don't think that we ever called a doctor," claimed one homesteader.[34] It was a good thing, too, because the state's earliest healthcare providers lagged the scientific frontier as folk remedies gave way to the quack potions and dangerous treatments (e.g., mercury purges and bloodletting) typical of nineteenth century Euroamerican medicine. The smallpox vaccination was a helpful advance but little else improved on what the Natives could do.[35]

In 1885, the territorial legislature passed a law for licensing physicians. Six years later, the new state government created a board of health, which checked that putative doctors possessed both a medical degree and a good moral character. The license, however, was to *practice* medicine, not to actually help people. Preventive medicine remained an afterthought, even in the 1930s when scarlet fever, rheumatic fever, and other serious maladies ravished a countryside where it was still not common for people to wash up or brush their teeth daily and where long hours and poor communication and transportation networks made it difficult to summon doctors quickly, especially in the winter. As late as the early postwar period, polio and other outbreaks could decimate communities or at least cause the cancellation of social events like dances and rodeos.[36]

The most controversial figure in early South Dakota medical history was undoubtedly Father William Kroeger, a medical entrepreneur who died in Epiphany in 1904 after an eleven-year medical career in South Dakota. At the height of his business, Kroeger served between 300 and 400 patients at his "sanitarium" each week, and thousands of people purchased the products of his Father Kroeger's Remedy Company.

The standard story is that Kroeger had been born in Cincinnati in 1853, where he became a doctor. Then he was ordained in 1880 and took charge of Saint Vincent's Church in Elkhart, Indiana. In 1893 he moved to South Dakota for health reasons. The area he settled needed both a doctor and a priest so he provided both services, which got him in trouble with Bishop Thomas O'Gorman, who demanded that Kroeger practice one profession or the other. Kroeger appealed to Rome but lost, so he gave up the priesthood. German immigrant Louise Mentele served as his nurse and pharmacist and her father, Anton Mentele, provided the famous cancer cure Kroeger later sold to thousands. Many customers believed Kroeger's cures were literally miraculous. Most of his patients hailed from South Dakota, Iowa, and Minnesota but some came from overseas. Few complained and some claimed to have been completely healed.

So much for the standard story. It turns out that Kroeger held no medical degree. He had been a priest in Indiana but also a businessman who apparently fled his creditors. The Catholic community in South Dakota accepted him because the state was short of priests. Kroeger, though, was foremost a businessman, one of many patent medicine purveyors in an $80 million per year industry. In 1900, competitors lurked everywhere, in Sioux Falls, Sioux City, and even nearby Mitchell. Unlike those of his competitors, however, Kroeger's concoctions were not chock full of alcohol and opium; he was never investigated by the American Medical Association. Kroeger also pioneered the use of X-ray machines to diagnose ailments.

Kroeger's business was highly vertically integrated. He owned his own medicine production factory, which even made its own boxes. He also owned the hotels in Epiphany where people stayed while being treated, and even owned the buggy lines that connected Epiphany to rail stops in Canova and Alexandria. When Kroeger took over the water and electrical plants and the bank, Epiphany essentially became a company town. In 1902, assessors valued the entire town at $22,400, $18,900 of which Kroeger owned! Not that the town held all his assets; he died reportedly worth between $175,000 and $250,000. Epiphany still exists but it shriveled after Kroeger's death and today is mostly known for the path leading to and from its church to the Coon Hunter Inn. It is not clear that Kroeger actually healed anyone but his treatments were relatively inexpensive and apparently did not cause serious complications.[37]

At about the same time that Kroeger ruled Epiphany, religious hospitals, like Sacred Heart in Yankton and St. Luke's in Aberdeen, began operations. By the 1920s, over two score communities throughout the state had hospital service, a number that peaked at seventy-four in 1955. Along with country physicians, community hospitals provided most of the healthcare services delivered in the state in the first half of the twentieth century. By 1949, Sioux Falls, especially its McKennan Hospital, was a regionally important center for healthcare. By 1960, one in every five doctors in South Dakota were located in the state's eastern metropolis. As early as 1940, one in every four specialists practiced there and by 1967 one in every three did so, in part due to the success of the Van Demark Clinic, which specialized in the treatment of bones, joints, and tendons.[38]

South Dakota ranked as low as the twenty-seventh healthiest state in the nation in 1999 but its average life expectancies for both men and women remained well above national averages. More recently, South Dakota ranked as the twentieth healthiest state in the nation, dinged largely because of the aging population of its rural hinterlands and its large, and largely unhealthy, Native population. In 2013, Sioux Falls was ranked the ninth healthiest city in America by *Prevention Magazine* because its residents' self-reports revealed them to be the healthiest *feeling* people in the nation, even though they may eat too much chislic and too many gravy-soaked, country-fried steaks. The city's extensive bicycle path and parks systems, in addition to the outdoor lifestyle so common to the state's denizens, may explain the discrepancy. Of course, even relatively young, health-conscious residents of coyote country, especially those exposed to mines and pesticides, can still get gravely ill and need healthcare services, too.[39]

Sioux Falls and Rapid City remain the state's two largest medical centers. The eastern metropolis has long been home to two major medical systems, Sanford, which until recently was called Sioux Valley Hospital, and Avera McKennan. In 2000, the former system had 3,100 employees and the latter 2,300. In the 1980s, the state government told the Bank of New York that Sioux Falls provided the best medical care between Rochester, Minnesota (home of the world-famous Mayo Clinic) and Denver, Colorado. In 1985, Sioux Falls Surgical Center increased competition between the two hospitals yet further, leading several economists to call for a system of managed competition throughout the state.[40] In 1990, U.S. Senator Tom Daschle claimed that anyone who could make it to Sioux Falls for treatment received the "finest" healthcare "in the country, perhaps in the world."[41] Rapid City Regional, which Daschle called "the best," still dominates the west.[42] (Veterans and Natives have their own health networks, both of dubious quality.)[43]

Until recently, healthcare costs in South Dakota have been relatively low. As recently as 2004, outsiders marveled that "the health care system is excellent and affordable with the average cost per day at half the national average."[44] Cost and access, however, have presented problems at times. In the early 1990s, entrepreneur Dan Stroh sold his business when his insurance costs skyrocketed, from $350 to $1,000 per month for just four employees. (His liability insurance also soared, from $2,500 per year to $12,000.)[45] Today, full implementation of the Affordable Care Act ("Obamacare") similarly threatens small businesses but its full impact is yet far from clear.

Between the state's two metropoles lies a vast region that has been underserved since the demise of the country physician after World War II. Many people in the rural districts have insufficient health insurance and live many miles from treatment centers. Traditionally, state aid has been low and the quality and price of rural healthcare provision irregular. More recently, however, the expansion of the big-city networks has improved both the quality and quantity of services available in the hinterlands. By 2005, 63,000 people worked in the healthcare industry in South Dakota, 8.9% of the state's total workforce, and more than the 7.7% national average. The $2 billion per year business included the highest number of medical centers per capita, 6.4 per 100,000. The state also boasted 5.78 beds per 1,000 people, twice the national average.[46]

South Dakota, especially the Sioux Falls area, has also developed an extensive system of nursing homes and other elder-care facilities. Good Samaritan and other elder-care providers attract people from the region, which outside of the urban centers is aging rapidly (from 3.3% of the population 65 or older in 1910 to over 13% by 1980 to almost 15% in 2013), who want to stay close to friends and family. It also attracts older people from other parts of the country looking to stretch their retirement dollar by moving to relatively low-cost facilities. Everyone knows that most aged individuals do not like cold weather, but climate is not as big a barrier as it may at first appear. As noted in the introduction, South Dakota's climate is often delightful. During the winter, which admittedly can be six months long and extremely challenging, retired seniors can brave the elements if they want to, or watch the wind and snow from the comfort of their cozy facilities.[47]

Higher education and healthcare are currently combining in exciting ways. Founded in Maryland in 1998 to produce antibodies for humans in genetically engineered cattle, Hematech early in the third millennium opened a 20,000-square-foot lab and office in Sioux Falls to aid its partnership with the University of South Dakota's School of Medicine.

Sanford purchased Hematech in 2013. Similarly, the South Dakota Technology Business Center (SDTBC), a 38,000-square-foot business incubator, opened in Sioux Falls in 2004 to help create a biotech cluster in the Vermillion-Sioux Falls-Brookings I-29 corridor.[48] To date, it has "graduated" 18 companies, including Alumend (née PhotoBioMed), which develops "innovative medical products based on a platform tissue bonding technology."[49]

South Dakota is also developing other high tech industries. Dakota State University in Madison had an Enterprise Development Center, which served as an early incubator for companies like Dakota Automated Systems, LaserTech, and Galley Proof, all tech start-ups. South Dakota State University boasts a research park run by SDSU Growth Partnership, Ltd., where professors and graduate students meet with businesses to help solve their technology problems. Intelligent Community Forum named Mitchell a Smart21 Community in 2012 and 2013, one of just twenty-one communities from eight countries and six continents so honored for transforming their local economies through broadband access, digital literacy, precision farming, and other high-tech innovations.[50]

Indeed, Aberdeen, Brookings, Madison, Mitchell, Rapid City, Sioux Falls, and other South Dakota communities have spawned or succored numerous high-tech companies over the years. One of South Dakota's earliest high-tech connections is the USGS Earth Resources Observation and Science Center (EROS). Established near Baltic and Garreston in 1973 to be near the middle of the continent and away from interference from radio and television signals, EROS collected information from Landsat satellites and used it to provide users with geologic, topographic, and hydrologic information, including photographs that it sold to the military and the public (to the tune of $3 million by 1975).

Located near Garretson, the Earth Resources Observation and Science (EROS) Center houses one of the largest computer complexes in the Department of the Interior. Its collection of remotely sensed data, such as images of the earth, supports the U.S. Geological Survey's Climate and Land Use Change Mission Area. *Courtesy U.S. Geological Survey, Department of the Interior.*

It came to the Sioux Empire because the Sioux Falls Development Foundation, led by David Stenseth, raised about $500,000 in three weeks to buy land for the center. To seal the deal, the Foundation also financed the main building and signed it over to the government via a buy-back lease agreement. A government center that employed about 400 people directly, EROS also generated almost 500 private-sector consulting jobs and gave the state entré into the telecom and computer markets.[51] By 1986, more than half of the center's employees were "scientists with advanced degrees" who enjoyed not having "to battle bumper-to-bumper traffic every day or contend with pollution," as they would have had to do in Houston or San Francisco.[52] In the late 1980s, South Dakota was a contender in the race to attract a federally-funded supercollider for atom research because of its low costs. The fancy contraption, however, was never built.[53]

Established in 1902, Hurley Telephone Company later moved to Sioux Falls and became the telecom services company PrairieWave. After purchasing Black Hills FiberCom of Rapid City in 2005, PrairieWave was able to extend its network from Minnesota and Iowa throughout South Dakota and into Montana. Acquired in 2007 by Georgia-based Knology, the company offered many of the denizens of South Dakota something that few Americans enjoy, a choice in cable-based telecommunications company. Wow!, a Colorado company privately owned by Avista Capital Partners, acquired Knology in 2012.[54]

Circa 1990, South Dakota was home to many freelancers who did word processing and other clerical tasks from home or small business offices. A decade later, South Dakota, like many other places, was overrun with internet companies building web pages and so forth. A shakeout occurred but what emerged from the dust was stronger, like Computer Doctor, a South Dakota-based company that franchises out computer repair. Most South Dakota computer geeks remain self-employed nanoentrepreneurs but a few have grown sizeable companies. Professional Mailing and Marketing, for example, allowed companies to outsource their mass mailings. Its competitive advantage came from an intimate understanding of the U.S. Post Office, for which the CEO was formerly a high-level employee. LodgeNet Entertainment, which provided telecom services to hotels, wedded South Dakota's high-tech tendencies with its tourism industry. Founded as Satellite Movie Company in 1980, it became known after its 2012 bankruptcy as SONIFI Solutions. Although under new ownership and headquartered in Los Angeles, its primary operations center remains in Sioux Falls.[55]

To protect its agricultural heritage and its tourism and outdoor recreation sectors, South Dakota was long wary of attracting too many people and too many old-fashioned "smokestack" industries. The education, healthcare, and high-tech sectors provide numerous high-paying, low environmental-impact jobs but they can grow only so large and are to some extent interrelated and hence vulnerable to the same shocks. The financial sector has also created "good" jobs and helped to diversify the state economy and could do much more in the future.

South Dakota evokes images of the Badlands, cattle, and verdant fields, not of financial services. But from the beginning, the state was home to numerous banks and other financial institutions. During the fur-trade era, St. Louis-based fur companies were the area's bankers. Instead of hauling cash upstream, the company kept account books of wages and purchases and settled accounts only in St. Louis. Anyone who accumulated coin buried it in the ground for safekeeping. Pierre Narcelle had $30,000 to $60,000 in gold and silver squirreled away at any given time. The technique was generally safe, but Felix Duboise lost $45,000 worth of buried coins, along with his wife and four children, and 600 head of cattle, when a massive flood tore through his trading post.[56] During the gold rush and the Dakota Boom, the first two signs in many frontier towns read "saloon" and "bank." Nearly all the state's early important businessmen, from miners to cattlemen to retailers, were associated with at least one bank.[57]

Pennington County Bank, Rapid City, is an example of the boom-and-bust cycle in South Dakota banking. Although the bank was rebuilt after a fire destroyed it in 1914, it went broke in 1932.
Courtesy Center for Western Studies.

In 1869, L. D. Parmer established a private bank in Yankton with a capital of $1,000. It prospered for a few years before attracting competition in the form of Peter Wintermute's private bank, which formed in 1872, and the First National Bank of Yankton, which began operations the following year. Parmer's bank failed in 1878 and paid $.40 on the dollar to creditors. In 1873, E. E. Otis established the first bank in Sioux Falls but it soon failed, as did the Bank for Savings established in 1874. By 1904, however, Sioux Falls had six strong banking institutions with $600,000 in aggregate capital. One of those was Minnehaha National Bank. Established in 1885, the bank is still in operation as First National Bank in Sioux Falls and takes pride in its local ownership and management. Like many community banks, First National is relationship rather than transaction driven; it thrives because it knows the local area, economy, and people as well as any other financial institution, if not better.[58]

Another important Sioux Falls bank was the Union Savings Association, which was established in 1894 by George Abbott, a serial entrepreneur born in New Hampshire in 1858. After graduating from Phillips Academy, Abbott worked and ran businesses in Colorado, North Dakota, and Minneapolis. In 1891, he moved to Sioux Falls to run the Co-operative Loan and Savings Association, a three-year stint that proved wildly successful as he was able to increase the institution's assets from $10,000 to over $600,000 and to pay members $150,000 in dividends while suffering only one mortgage foreclosure.[59]

Abbott's new bank proved just as successful. By 1910, the Union Savings Association had assets of $1.25 million and had financed the construction of over 3,000 homes in South Dakota, Minnesota, and Oklahoma. Regulators lauded Abbott as "a strong building and loan man" who made "the association what it is, one of the largest, strongest and most reliable building and loan associations in the North."[60] Investors concurred, calling Abbott "not only a man of unquestionable integrity and financial standing, but ... a man of exceptional business ability."[61] The loan portfolio was conservative (50% loan-to-value, or LTV) so defaults were rare and did not cause losses.[62]

By 1910, Abbott appeared poised to embark on a new undertaking, the expansion of the Equitable Fidelity and Title Guaranty Company of Brookings into a major statewide or even nationwide enterprise. "With such a Company," the president of the Equitable argued, "it would be possible to do a nice line of work in other lines than the usual surety business, as for instance, burglary insurance in Towns of one thousand and over, is an extremely profitable business and considered pretty safe." "We have a large number of Agents and Agencies here and in Minnesota," Abbott enthusiastically responded, "and these people could doubtlessly act in behalf of both companies to the mutual advantage of all concerned."[63] Later, however, Abbott would offer only a personal investment in the venture, claiming that he was too busy to help manage the concern.

The Bank of Vermillion began as a private bank in 1875 but it received a federal charter in 1891. In 1937 it became a member of the National Bank of South Dakota. The bank, which was started by Darwin Inman of New York, took deposits, made loans, and sold drafts on major cities. Although like other early banks, it consisted of little more than a safe, a counter, a set of scales, and a handful of account books, its loans helped pioneer farmers to acquire land, start-up tools, and seed. It also helped them through grasshopper plagues and various other fluctuations in farm income.[64]

The First National Bank of Deadwood was established in 1878. In 1935, it merged into the First National Bank of Lead, which began life as Samuel N. Wood & Co. in 1879. First National Bank of Lead, which had established a *de novo* (brand new) branch in Hot Springs in 1934, also acquired the Bank of Spearfish (née Stebbins Fox and Co., est. 1882), Butte County Bank of Belle Fourche (est. 1891), and Reclamation State Bank of Newell (est. 1910) before it changed its name in 1938 to the First National Bank of the Black Hills (FNBBH). The following year, FNBBH gobbled up the Commercial Bank of Sturgis (est. 1903) and added it to its branch system.

In 1929, FNBBH fell under the control of Northwest Bancorporation (aka Banco), a so-called "group bank," or loose bank holding company, due in large part to the efforts of Robert E. Driscoll, Sr., who some referred to as "Mr. Black Hills." Born in Central City in the heart of the hills in 1888, Driscoll graduated from Lead High School before heading east to Michigan and Harvard for his B.A. and M.A. degrees, respectively. He then returned to the Black Hills, where he served several banks before joining FNBBH. A stalwart Republican and president of the South Dakota Bankers Association, Driscoll was active in several non-financial companies, including A. C. Johnson Hotel, American Colloid, Bald Mountain Mining, Hearst Mercantile, and Western Airlines.[65]

Another important early banker, James Halley (a telegrapher in 1877), went on to become president of the First National Bank of Rapid City (née Lake, Halley and Paterson, est. 1881), which in 1929 also became affiliated with (acquired is a little too strong a term) Banco and later established a branch in Philip. Northwest also affiliated with (purchased controlling interests in), and helped to build, branch networks in other parts of South Dakota. In 1929, it affiliated with the First National Bank (née Codington County Bank, est. 1880) and the Citizens National Bank (est. 1885), both of Watertown, and merged them in 1933. In 1930, Northwest affiliated with the First National Bank of Aberdeen, which subsequently purchased banks in Britton, Groton, Hecla, Milbank, Mobridge, and Redfield. It turned the acquired banks into branches, sometimes after updating their facilities. Its new branch building in Mobridge, for example, was designed by Aberdeen architect Clarence L. Herges and considered an "urbane and functional" space in which to conduct "all of the many jobs connected with banking."[66]

Northwestern Bank also made inroads into the Sioux Falls market by affiliating with Security National Bank and Trust, the product of the 1919 merger of Security National Bank of Sioux Falls (est. 1914) and State Bank and Trust Company (nee State Banking and Trust Company, est. 1890). Within a few years of its affiliation with Banco, Security National built a branch network by acquiring the First National Bank and Trust of Chamberlain, the deposits of the First National Bank of Pukwana, the New First National Bank in Dell Rapids, Northwestern National Bank of Madison, the National Bank of Huron, Brookings County Bank, and Northwestern Bank of Gregory. Later, the institution, renamed Norwest Bank of Sioux Falls, expanded into Lake Preston, Mitchell, Parker, and Springfield as well.[67]

Banco gave its member banks considerable local autonomy while simultaneously augmenting their access to capital and expert advice on the more technical aspects of banking and taxation, while providing their customers with more sophisticated banking services like foreign exchange and wire transfers. "Every member of the Northwest Bancorporation group," early acquisition announcements explained, "retains its separate character in every respect; it retains its state or national charter, is subject to state or federal examinations, maintains its own capitalization, its own staff of officers and handles all its business just as before becoming a member of the group. Membership in the group adds a very strong and valuable contact. ... [locals may] become shareholders in their own bank and other leading banks and trust companies of this territory, through ownership of stock in the Northwest Bancorporation." South Dakotans did indeed partake of the profits of the group by owning shares in Northwestern. In 1966, for example, Melvin and Gene Banck of Sioux Falls owned 16 Banco shares, Anna and Lois E. Christen of Huron owned 75, and Minnie Elrod of Hot Springs owned 819 shares, just a few of numerous examples that could be adduced.[68]

Most early South Dakota banks, however, remained unit (independent, branchless) banks until well into the twentieth century. Already by 1887, Dakota Territory was home to 62 national and 232 private banks. By 1904, 326 commercial banks operated in the state. In 1910, according to federal tax records, 531 commercial banks operated in the state. By the 1920s, more than 700 banks were in business. The state had many banks because of its various legal restrictions against branching. The unit banks that resulted were small and to some degree monopolized their local markets.[69] Assured of profitability, they did not take big risks, prompting one early chronicler to observe "there has been but little of the spectacular in South Dakota banking."[70] Most of the shenanigans took place in the Black Hills, where one "bank" created a "safe" made of pine boards painted black to look like cast iron. It took gold from miners on deposit until the "bankers" fled with their pine safe one dark night. But that was when the Black Hills was still a lawless district. Thereafter, regulations presumably rendered it difficult for rogues or rascals to engage in banking in the state.[71]

The small size and limited geographical distribution of unit banks' assets, however, left them vulnerable to economic shocks. When trouble struck, as during the Panic of 1893, they generally behaved as "conservative" banks should, by restricting lending and replacing "impaired capital," even though drastic drawbacks in credit availability spelled the end of nascent manufacturing and transportation companies in Sioux Falls and elsewhere in the state. During the Great Depression, many bankers lost their entire savings trying to rescue their banks. Some even left their personal deposits in their banks when they closed so that they would suffer along with other depositors. When the bankers and their communities had insufficient savings to replace capital destroyed by the prolonged downturn, banks folded or sold themselves to larger, healthier concerns like Banco.[72]

Conservative bankers earned profits by charging interest rates commensurate with the risks they assumed. Many charged 10% interest on agricultural loans. Ranchers and farmers hated them for it, but given the rate at which agricultural enterprises failed, the rate was justified and successful ranchers and farmers could well afford it. When the risks were too high, or too difficult to measure, conservative bankers did not lend at all. Circa 1900, for example, the state's banks would not lend on horses because they were too easily stolen or killed. They did, however, lend on cattle as collateral. Private banks and those chartered by the state could make mortgage loans but those chartered by the federal government, the so-called national banks, could not. So as late as 1920, most mortgage loans were extended by individuals eager to earn interest and have a chance at taking over a neighbor's land in the event of default.[73]

Despite their conservative ways, many early South Dakota banks failed in the 1920s and 1930s. Some were plagued by bank robberies, others by troubled agricultural loans. Hoary practice had been to lend on renewable notes on the basis of reputation instead of on a sound business plan. Bank failures brought nothing but hardship. When two banks in Kadoka failed in the 1920s, Otto Sharon, the fifty-two-year-old local postmaster and a key stockholder in both banks, took the train to Wentworth and hanged himself in the stockyard there. Before formation of the FDIC during the New Deal, depositors lost much of their money. Existing borrowers still had to repay or suffer foreclosure; potential borrowers suffered if new lenders did not understand their business. It was said, for example, that big bankers in Minneapolis did not understand ranching. One allegedly asked how quickly a herd composed of twenty steers (castrated male cattle) would grow![74]

When banks and private lenders receded in the 1920s, the state stepped into the gap, with the disastrous results related in Chapter 3. "It was at this point," a commission later explained, "that the insurance companies entered the field as a principal source of farm loans in South Dakota."[75] As Figure 8 shows, all types of lenders, except the federal government, receded in the face of the Depression. After the Depression, banks originated most mortgage loans but then sold them to other banks, insurers, pension funds, or the new Federal National Mortgage Loan Association (later privatized and called Fannie Mae).[76]

The poor performance of the unit-banking system during the 1920s and 1930s induced branching reforms as well. Beginning in 1933, South Dakota began to allow state and national banks to branch in towns with more than 3,000 residents. Thanks to those and other reforms, the state's banking sector, like the nation's, thrived for decades after World War II. One of the state's leading bankers during that period was A. E.

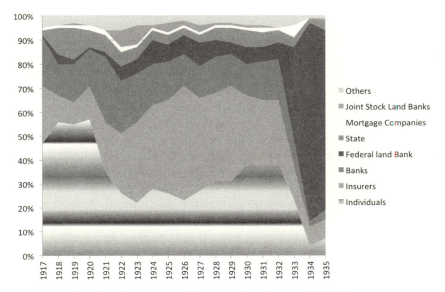

Figure 6: South Dakota Farm Mortgage Lenders, 1917-1935. *Source: South Dakota State Planning Board,* Mortgage Status of Farm Land in South Dakota *(1938), 9-10.*

Dahl, who became a banker by taking a bookkeeping job at the First National Bank of Toronto in 1917, just as the tiny bank was transitioning from big paper ledgers to a Burroughs posting machine.[77] The contraption was hand operated but, Dahl later recalled, a "big improvement over the pen and ink method."[78] After a stint in the navy during the Great War, Dahl went back to the bank where he was made assistant cashier, a director in the bank, and the proud owner of ten shares paid for with a $1,700 stock note. (In other words, Dahl borrowed the money for the shares from the bank itself and then pledged those shares as collateral for the loan!) The bank was not very well run. In addition to lending too much to its own employees, it lent too much during the wartime real estate bubble and bought too many of the notes of a poorly run bank in Garretson and another in North Dakota. Then it foreclosed on hogs that had already been sold. When its local competitor, the Farmers Exchange Bank, closed, depositors ran on Dahl's bank.[79]

Dahl ran from the failing institution too, right into a legal apprenticeship. He passed the bar in March 1927 but did not make much money so he went to work for the new Citizens State Bank of Castlewood in nearby Hamlin County in 1927. He began to innovate by lending on automobiles on installments and also monthly installment mortgages, instead of the quarterly or annual interest-only mortgages then common. The new bank also invested in industrial bonds but sold out just after the stock market crash for only a small loss.[80]

Dahl made vice president and became a director. Although the bank was doing as well as could be expected given the Depression, he decided to take a patronage job as a bank examiner. He had to close many banks, typically the smallest ones, including one in Waverly with only about $62,000 in deposits. New banking laws enacted during the Depression made it possible for Dahl to form a new national bank in Rapid City, the Rapid City National Bank ($100,000 capital), using the (good) assets of a failed bank as collateral. Dahl's bank may have been the first in the state to open a personal loan department that made loans with monthly installments to salaried men for automobiles and personal needs. It was also one of the first to buy a Recordak for microfilming checks. It did well enough at first to buy out the distressed Hermosa State Bank in 1936.[81]

Dahl's bank also grew organically, by treating customers equitably, not harshly interrogating them, and not taking too much collateral or exacting other tribute. "If you treat one customer well," Dahl believed, "he sends more business to the bank."[82] Dahl also believed in advertising and did it more than any of his competitors, via both newspaper and radio. The bank provided full financial statements and an annual report to customers and stockholders to show that it had nothing to hide. Unlike other banks, Rapid City National also kept very good information about accounts, occupations, previous loans, and so forth on cards, which allowed it to provide prompt, efficient customer service.[83]

By 1939, Dahl's bank employed 16 and held 2,847 checking accounts, 1,125 savings accounts, 145 time certificates, 2,365 loans, 516 safe deposit box accounts, and deposits of almost $2.6 million. Although Dahl was constantly innovating and the bank was growing, some directors complained that Dahl was "too conservative" compared to the First National Bank of Rapid City. Dahl's policies, however, kept Rapid City National in great shape. By the end of 1943, Dahl's bank had suffered losses on just $8,000 of the $17.7 million in loans it had made and service charges provided much-needed additional income.[84]

Dahl's bank was innovative itself but of course its most important role was in bankrolling other innovators. "Many of the prominent people in Rapid City," Dahl later recalled, "were small borrowers with small means in the earlier days of our bank. We extended credit to many of them and it was profitable for them and for our bank."[85] Dahl was particularly eager "to make loans to young men who are energetic and know how to handle money."[86] His bank essentially engaged in what would come to be called microfinance. "Many people with low incomes are better credit risks than others with large incomes who have a spending appetite beyond whatever they make," he explained. "Young people often start in the personal loan department and grow to where they have large credits in our commercial loan department."[87]

South Dakota's regulatory system was imperfect, as all are. The banking commission, for example, was composed of three bankers, some of whom looked out for his own interest and those of his friends rather than the public's by peeking at a competitor's books or denying the charter application of a potential competitor. Nevertheless, it did try to minimize bad banking practices, first by imposing double liability on bank stockholders. When that failed because most stockholders paid scant attention to their banks' activities, it made directors personally responsible for any excess loans they made over established limits and for paying dividends on phantom profits. Sometimes bank directors personally had to pay six figures to settle suits.[88]

The best regulator, Dahl understood, was proper governance and incentives. He and other officers bought shares in the bank so that most of their net worth was tied up in the institution.[89] That made them work hard to minimize embezzlement by carefully selecting new employees, monitoring employees' spending habits, running random audits, introducing "controls to detect wrong-doing early," and paying "a living salary so" employees could "live decently" without resorting to theft.[90] In 1958, Dahl added outside directors at the behest of regulators but used them mainly to "bring to the bank an outside viewpoint" and additional information on borrowers.[91] In 1964, the directors and their families owned 66.8% of the bank's outstanding stock. Employees and the profitsharing fund owned an additional 7.6%. The policies apparently worked because in its first fifty years the bank paid dividends every year except the first.[92]

Unfortunately, much of Dahl's time and talents were spent sidestepping silly state regulations instead of making his bank more efficient. When the bank constructed a drive-in counter in their parking lot, for example, Dahl decided to connect it to the main building by a tunnel lest regulators consider it an illegal "branch." When the bank wanted to form actual branches, it at first had to charter new banks because the Comptroller of the Currency and the State Banking Commission wrongly held that "a branch bank could not be opened within the city of the parent bank." After much agitation, it was finally determined that that rule held only in places with fewer than 15,000 inhabitants, a size that Rapid City had long since surpassed.[93]

Then the banking commission tried to stop Dahl's bank from branching across county lines or more than fifty miles from its headquarters, citing a rule that it had recently concocted. The supreme courts of both South Dakota and the United States sided with the bank, holding that the state banking department had no authority to pass such a rule. So Dahl's bank, now called American National Bank, was able to move into Hot Springs and Sturgis in the early 1960s.[94]

Thanks to bankers like Dahl, total deposits in the state increased from $42.8 million in 1940 to $359 million in 1960. By 1965, South Dakota had just thirty-three national banks operating thirty-five branches, 140 state banks operating thirty-six branches, and several "group" or informal bank holding companies as well. The biggest of those was Banco, which owned four banks that operated twenty-three branches. The second biggest was First Bank Stock Corporation, which consisted of seven banks operating eight branches. Dahl's American National Bank and Trust was third. Dahl died in November 1977, just a few years before the Citibank revolution described in Chapter 4.[95]

After South Dakota eliminated its usury cap in 1980, some borrowers began to complain that bankers were profiting too much at the expense of small businesses. In 1983, the U.S. Senate held a hearing at Augustana College to investigate. Augustana Business Professor Bob Erkonen testified, as did Professor Jerry Johnson of the University of South Dakota, who pointed to the negative effects of high interest rates on small business and farmers.[96] Local bankers countered that the high rates were justified by high risks and that the banking situation in Sioux Falls and eastern South Dakota more generally was "extremely competitive."[97] Entrepreneur Bob Elmen agreed, noting that he did most of his "borrowing in Sioux Falls because for many years going 300 miles in any direction would cost us 1% more—Rapid City, Fargo, Lincoln."[98] Elmen at that time operated "about 50 very small firms in five States" and borrowed at just above the prime rate. According to Senator Pressler, Elmen was "one of the most successful and respected businessmen in this region ... probably in the top 10."[99]

Burdette Solum, a farm boy turned banker, tried to ensure that banking in northeastern South Dakota remained competitive as well. After graduating from South Dakota State in Brookings, he got into banking and by the 1980s managed the show in the Watertown region for Norwest Bank South Dakota, an outgrowth of the old Northwest/Banco group bank established in 1929. Solum knew that for his bank to thrive, the communities it served also had to thrive. That meant helping agriculturalists but also entrepreneurs trying to diversify the economy: his bank lent $15 million of its $60 million loan portfolio to farmers and ranchers. Regardless of the economic sector of their activity, applicants had to establish the three C's of credit – character, collateral, and capacity – before Solum, who still reviewed larger loan files, would lend to them.[100]

With the relaxation of interstate branching restrictions in the 1970s and 1980s, Norwest became a so-called superregional bank that by the mid-1990s owned eighty-eight commercial banks serving sixteen states, including South Dakota, where it bought up unit banks until consolidating them as branches of the bank holding company Norwest Banking Association in 1984.[101] Norwest was one of the nation's largest and most profitable banks thanks to what observers called its "superb financial ratios." CEO Richard Kovacecich said its goal was to "be regarded as one of America's great companies," a bank able to "outlocal" the big boys and outsize the locals. That approach ended in 1998, when Wells Fargo, one of the largest bank holding companies in the nation, acquired the bank.[102]

As in its earlier history, however, South Dakota remained home to numerous locally owned and controlled banks, some of considerable note. In 1999, for example, First Dakota National Bank of Yankton became the first bank in the nation to gain preferred lender status from the Department of Agriculture's guaranteed loan program. Preferred status allowed the bank to submit minimal loan information to the USDA, allowing the bank to respond to the loan applications of farmers and ranchers within fourteen days. Only banks that had a 3% or lower loss rate on thirty or more guaranteed loans over the previous three years were eligible for the program. At the time, First Dakota had $300 million in assets, about a third of which was loaned out to farmers and ranchers.

Established in 1872, First Dakota had assets of just over $1 billion at the end of 2013.[103]

Dacotah Banks of Aberdeen turned fifty in 2014. Now a financial holding company, Dacotah owns insurance agencies and title companies and has assets north of $1 billion. It has thirty-two locations, 400 employees, and 40,000-plus customers, many agriculturalists. It has tried to find a sweet spot: large enough to meet its customers' borrowing needs but small enough to handle their special circumstances. It grew through acquisitions and *de novo* branch formation and invaded North Dakota as well, beginning with the 1999 purchase there of Rolla Holding Co., Inc., a two-bank holding company worth $80 million.[104]

First Western Bank was also owned and run by South Dakotans. It serviced twelve communities from eighteen locations in the Black Hills and Badlands. It started in 1976 when Paul and Donna Christen purchased banks in Wall and New Underwood, and then expanded into Sturgis, Belle Fourche, Custer, Edgemont, Hot Springs, Spearfish, Hill City, and Deadwood over the next two decades. In 2009, First Interstate Bank, a $7.5 billion bank established in Billings, Montana in 1916, took it over.[105]

Beresford Bancorp, a bank holding company based in the state, had $550 million in assets and more than twenty branches spread throughout South Dakota, New Mexico, Texas, Nevada, and the Midwest by 1999. Headed by Frank Farrar, governor of South Dakota from 1969 until 1971, Beresford specialized in acquiring and fixing troubled community banks. "Those small banks in those small communities," he explained, "allow people to get credit to become entrepreneurs and to build new enterprise."[106] By the end of 2013, its assets sat just shy of half a billion dollars and its return on equity was a respectable 8.3%.[107]

South Dakota also spawned various non-bank financial institutions, including insurers, most small. Between 1950 and 1960, South Dakota's FIRE (finance, insurance and real estate) sector grew 43.6%, faster than the 40.4% national average. The number of FIRE workers jumped from 3,900 in 1950 to 6,450 in 1962, and total income from FIRE companies soared from $7 million in 1929 to $39 million in 1961. Total life insurance in force also increased dramatically, from $610 million in 1951 to $1.6 billion in 1961.[108] Expansion and change has characterized the sector ever since.

Prairie States Life of Rapid was acquired by Laurentian Capital Corp., an insurance holding company based in Florida, in 1985. Dakota Mutual Life formed in 1906 in the Black Hills. It moved to Watertown and demutualized in 1909. A private company called Sammons Enterprises purchased it in 1958 and moved it to Sioux Falls. Today, the company is called Midland National Life Insurance Company and it remains headquartered in Sioux Falls. Employees now own a large percentage of the company, so it is conservative and focused on the long term, hence its A+ rating from insurance watchdog A. M. Best. Other Midwest insurers, like Bankers Life (now Principal Financial Group) of Des Moines, Iowa, also sold life insurance in South Dakota. The Bankers Life agent in central South Dakota in the 1930s was A. E. Nickelson, a giant man who squeezed into his Model-T Ford along with a keg of corn mash that he used to start conversations and keep them going, especially before Prohibition ended.[109]

Western Surety out of Sioux Falls also sold life insurance, but only for a few years in the late 1970s and early 1980s. During the rest of its existence as an independent joint-stock corporation, Western Surety sold bail, contract performance, fidelity, immigration, public official, saloon, and surety bonds. It was highly successful because it concentrated on profitability, not large size. Although it eventually spread into adjacent states, then California, and finally most of the country, it grew slowly by remaining conservative in its underwriting practices. If the person or business to be bonded appeared to represent a substantial risk, Western

The Syndicate Building at 8th and Main in Sioux Falls was the home of the Western Surety Company from 1909 until 1958. A family-owned insurance business, Western Surety was for many years the nation's leader in the field of small, miscellaneous fidelity and surety bonds. In 1992, the Kirby family sold the company to CNA Surety but the surety business is still conducted in Sioux Falls. *Courtesy Center for Western Studies.*

Surety turned the applicant away. It was able to attract independent agents to sell its products by providing them with top-notch customer service. In an era when a week was considered quick turnaround, Western Surety's model was "Everything is answered the day it is received." For about fifteen years it also incentivized its agents, which at one point numbered 42,000, with bonus coupons. To process so much information so quickly, Western Surety employed numerous people in its Sioux Falls headquarters, and at times was among the city's largest employers. In 1963, it began to automate its information processing with an IBM mainframe. Always a step ahead of the competition in terms of innovation, the company, which had been established by Joe Kirby in 1900, continued to thrive. In 1992, however, the managers decided to sell out to Sam Zell because the stock of the once closely-held company had diffused over the years via stockholder estates and sales and they feared loss of control. In 1997, Zell sold the company to CNA Financial in Chicago.[110]

Risk Administration Services, Inc. (RAS) was founded in 1989 to help employers reduce losses and improve productivity by improving workplace safety and helping workers who are injured to recover as quickly and fully as possible. Out of its headquarters in Sioux Falls and an office in Apple Valley, Minnesota, it helps nearly 3,000 employers handle workers' compensation issues in South Dakota, Minnesota, Nebraska, and Iowa and writes $45 million in workers comp policies annually.[111]

Debt collection also thrives in South Dakota in part because of the state's relatively strong creditor protection laws. Skills and techniques developed in South Dakota can then be applied nationally. Aman Collection Service of Aberdeen, for example, specialized in collecting from graduate students who had not yet started repaying their college loans. The key, the company discovered over three decades, was locating the students and counseling them correctly. Wells Fargo eventually purchased and then shuttered the business.[112]

Increasingly, the line between financial and nonfinancial companies has blurred. The Hegg Companies in Sioux Falls, for example, specializes in hospitality management, real estate, and brokerage and calls itself a "private equity real estate firm." Founded as a farmland real estate agency in 1945 by P. Ode Hegg, the company expanded operations in the 1960s with help from Hegg's son, Peter P. Hegg[113]

South Dakota also has a sizable and growing trust business, especially so-called dynasty trusts or South Dakota trusts, which are basically mechanisms for dodging some estate taxes. The trusts are perpetual investments that spin off only interest to heirs, thereby protecting them from the full brunt of estate taxes. "Properly drafted and funded," Daniel Worthington and Peter M. Williams wrote in 1997, "the South Dakota Trust literally transforms any insurance trust into a perpetual family tool for wealth preservation and asset protection."[114] Available in only three states, only one of which (South Dakota, of course) has no state income tax, dynasty trusts generate significant fees for South Dakota entrepreneurs like Pierce H. McDowell III, president of South Dakota Trust Company, which has billions of dollars of assets under administration. State laws further boost demand for South Dakota trusts by cloaking them in secrecy and thereby protecting them from creditors and former spouses. The coup, however, was not nearly as important to the state and its residents as the credit card industry coup has proven itself: only about 100 South Dakotans are needed to run the dynasty trusts, which raised a mere $1.2 million for the state's coffers in 2012.[115]

In 1889, L.E.Q., writing for the New York *Tribune*, claimed that South Dakota "has passed its experimental stage. It is no longer the home of saloon-keepers and gamblers."[116] That pronouncement was more than a little premature. The history of gambling in South Dakota is legendary and not limited to Deadwood. The Plains themselves seem to beckon risk-takers by offering a small chance of bliss and a large chance of dying in a blizzard or in some other horrible way. Native Americans wagered on indigenous ball games like bandy and billiards. Pierre and other towns had plenty of places for cowboys to lose all their money at blackjack or some other game of their choice, including craps, faro, and roulette. Gambling, in the form of live games of poker, craps, and blackjack, was alive and well in the mid-twentieth century in taverns like the Pheasant Bar in Winner. When a reporter from the *Sioux Falls Argus Leader* caught two Republican officeholders gambling away in a backroom, however, the state cracked down on live games. Today, only three types of gambling are legal in the state: tribal, Deadwood "small stakes," and video.[117]

Few people realize that gambling remains an important business today, and state government and many students want to keep it that way. Pierre is second only to Reno in terms of dependence on gambling revenues, most of which are earmarked for education, yet there are no big casinos in South Dakota, even on the Indian Reservations. Several of the ten tribal casinos are flourishing but remain trivial affairs compared to competitors in Las Vegas, Atlantic City, or even the tribal casinos located close to large urban centers like Minneapolis and New York.[118]

In Deadwood, the hub of the state's non-Native gambling industry, the definition of "small stakes" was increased from $5 to $100 per play in 2000, when the total volume of wagering in the town was about $500 million. By 2007, it exceeded $1 billion even though gambling halls were deliberately kept small. Gambling is big business in the state not because of large casinos, or Deadwood, but because of ubiquitous, tiny gaming halls. Taverns, restaurants, and even gas stations have casinos, computerized monstrosities with pitiful paybacks (80%). By 2010, over 8,200 machines in some 1,400 locations were in operation. First authorized in 1989, video lottery was defended at the polls in 1992, aligned fully with the state constitution in 1994, and defended again at the polls in 1996, 2000, and 2006. In addition to padding the state's coffers (to the tune of $110 million in 2007) and ensuring that most poor people stay poor, video lottery has generated hundreds of millions of dollars in revenue for entrepreneurs like Hub Music and Vending, Sodak Gaming, and Concorde Gaming Rapid that operate casinos or sell video lottery machines and services.[119]

Chapter 9
The Ten Biggest Challenges Ahead

Even if you're on the right track, you'll get run over if you just sit there.[1]

If you ever meet Sioux Falls entrepreneur Mark Nelson, hear about his company called Maximum Promotions (which for almost thirty years produced promotional materials like banners and vehicle magnets and rented U.S. flags, big ones), or read his 2009 self-published book *The Spirit of an American Entrepreneur*, it will be difficult to deny that the good types of entrepreneurship—innovative and replicative—are alive and well in South Dakota.[2] But that does not mean that South Dakota is in the clear because as any denizen of the Great Plains will explain, a storm may loom just over the horizon and strike the prairie in a flash and with a bang. The state's small size will always render it, as economist Ralph Brown wrote, subject to, if not "dominated by forces beyond its control."[3] Long-term trends linked to structural changes in the economy, like the slow replacement of family farms with corporate ones, will likely continue, laws to the contrary notwithstanding.[4]

Robert Karolevitz called his South Dakota history textbook, published in 1975, *Challenge*. He obviously did not mean that the state was "challenged" in the modern sense of the word, to wit what people of Karolevitz's generation would have called "handicapped." Rather, he meant that the state's abilities and resources had often been tested. Everyone faces such tests, he knew, but the implication was that South Dakota's tests had been more frequent and pressing than the challenges faced by most other states. In fact, it was once suggested to change the state nickname to the Challenge State but thankfully that notion was jettisoned because it would probably have frightened away tourists.[5]

South Dakota no longer seems so challenged, in any sense of the word. As pointed out in the introduction, the state has overcome most of the obstacles it has faced. Its leading city, Sioux Falls, transformed itself from prime cuts to prime rates, "from a mid-sized Midwestern agricultural town to a nationally recognized urban growth success story."[6] The city and the state should not, however, grow complacent. (South Dakotans are, as a rule, too modest to warn of hubris.) In a rapidly changing world, the state needs to maintain its best features and continue to improve its worst as it will be tested again, probably several times, before its bicentennial (2089) or even its sesquicentennial (2039).[7]

In fact, the only constant in the state's economic and business history is change. In the 1870s, steamboats were all the rage, but a decade later steamboats and stagecoaches were almost extinct, replaced by railroads. A century later, many miles of railroad track had been ripped up. Horses gave way to tractors in the blink of an eye. While old businesses folded, new ones sprang up, many with roots in unexpected places like Asia (pheasants), Idaho (birthplace of Gutzon Borglum, creator of Mount Rushmore), and even outer space (EROS).[8]

Prognostication is a notoriously difficult proposition. "South Dakota in 2010," predictions made by the Business and Industry Round Table in 1988, proved only vaguely on mark.[9] It is safe to say, however, that the ten challenges described below will prove important to the continued happiness of South Dakotans present and future. Readers may find some more important and pressing than others, but I believe that all need to be carefully considered by policymakers, businesses, and citizens.

1. State image: In 1889, state boosters complained that "Dakota is in the same latitude with some of the most prosperous and populous states of the Union, yet dense ignorance or prejudice exists in the East concerning not only the resources but the climate of the great territory."[10] The state's image is better than it used to be, but it still needs improvement if the tourism sector, which has stagnated at times in the past, or even the high-tech sector, is to grow robustly and continuously.[11] And image is sticky. "Once an image or perception of a state has been established," as Darrell Butterwick pointed out, "it takes an enormous amount of work and energy to change."[12]

Strange as it sounds, many Americans who dwell on the coasts are unsure of South Dakota's "whereabouts."[13] "In the minds, or imaginations, of the people living on or near the nation's coasts," wrote John R. Milton in 1977, "the Dakotas are very much alike – if they exist at all."[14] According to Professor Milton, of the University of South Dakota, "a Danish family arriving in New York in 1975, on its way to visit relatives in South Dakota, talked to an employee in a restaurant in the Big City who knew where Copenhagen was but had never heard of South Dakota."[15] Not that South Dakota has a big following overseas. "Much of the world," a business group complained in 1988, "does not know that South Dakota exists."[16] Others claim that it must be a myth because "people know people who say they know people who come from there," but there is about as much concrete evidence of its existence as there is for Bigfoot (which is occasionally spotted in the state, believe it or not).[17] Celebrity correspondent Mary Hart claimed that as recently as the 1960s many Scandinavians believed that cowboys and Indians still roamed the area, shooting each other, and a corporate reporter in the 1970s swore that a Pennsylvania woman making a site visit for a sewing business got off the plane and immediately "wanted to see the Indians!"[18]

D. L. Flyger of Freeman claimed in 1998 that "most people have no idea where South Dakota is even located."[19] After pitching a project on Wall Street circa 2000, one South Dakota entrepreneur recalls, one of the venture capitalists observed that "for a southerner" the entrepreneur did not "have much of a southern accent!"[20] Scholars sometimes invoke the state's name as synonymous with an unappealing place to live, as Hans-Peter Kohler does in his article subtitled "Could Silicon Valley Be in South Dakota?"[21] "The Dakotas are looked on by many," Tom Brokaw wrote in 2002, "as largely empty tracts of land, remote and all but uninhabitable."[22] No wonder so many conflate North and South Dakota. "North Dakota, South Dakota – to some New Yorker living in Connecticut, what was the difference? ... How the hell would I know?"[23] More than once, "Bismarck, South Dakota," has been mentioned on the national news. Sioux Falls has also been accused of being in North Dakota and Fargo in South Dakota.[24] South Dakotans need to get the word out that South Dakota is the land of entrepreneurship, while North Dakota is the emerging energy giant.

2. Energy independence: Speaking of energy, South Dakota needs to increase its energy independence. The state is almost devoid of fossil fuels. There is a little lignite within its borders but the coal ended up mostly in Wyoming and the natural gas in North Dakota. What South Dakota has plenty of is renewable energy: water sources have been exploited since the end of the Pick-Sloan era and the biomass (e.g., ethanol) industry is growing, but the state has barely begun to tap its solar, geothermal, and wind energy potential. As noted in the introduction, it can get cold in South Dakota but it is usually sunny and the wind almost never stops blowing, especially in the western two-thirds of the state. The state was recently ranked as enjoying the fourth best wind power potential in the entire nation and as early as 1889 people have called for it to be harnessed as it "sweeps over the prairies."[25] Dakota, Lakota, and Nakota tribes could tap the wind, one of the few resources left to them, were it not for their distance from major energy markets. The Rosebud Sioux Tribe's Owl Feather War Bonnet Wind Farm, a 30-megawatt facility, has met some success and could portend future growth. Entrepreneurial initiative on the household/farm side, where transmission costs are trivial, has been minimal. Time was when everyone had a wind mill. They are making something of a comeback, as are earth homes, the modern equivalent of homesteaders' dugouts, but much remains to be done. As for large-scale energy projects, transmission costs have been daunting and capital has been lacking.[26]

3. Access to financial capital: A dearth of capital, in the sense of access to long-term funding for major projects, has been a long-running complaint in South Dakota. "Because of the lack of venture capital and technical expertise," complained business analysts in 1988, "minimal industrial development has taken place in South Dakota."[27] Several years later, the situation was unchanged and entrepreneurs in the state received "negligible venture capital investments."[28] Today, some venture-capital firms are beginning to pay attention to entrepreneurs from the state, and loans are available from community and regional banks but more and cheaper funding sources would of course be a big boon. The state's image holds it back to some extent, but so too does the sense that its recent economic rebound may be fragile. The Dakota Boom fizzled, as did the prosperity of the Great War and postwar eras. The Great Depression and the farm crisis of the 1980s seem to outsiders to be the state's default condition. It is not entirely their fault as the state is still emerging from its rural past. Only in 1990, seventy years after the nation overall, did more than half of the state's population live in "urban" jurisdictions, i.e., in places with more than 2,500 residents, and it remained the fifth most rural state in the nation. The state often ranks dead last in federal research monies, a level not likely to change after the National Science Foundation learned that it could not fund a DUSEL (Deep Underground Science and Engineering Laboratory) in the old Homestake Mine after all.[29]

4. Environmental quality: A dearth of capital is why it is so important for the state to maintain, or better yet improve, its environmental quality. Due to its relatively large agricultural and tourism sectors, South Dakota is more vulnerable than most other states to climate changes, at least those not associated with rising sea levels. (Its lowest point is 294 meters above sea level, well higher than even the most pessimistic forecast.) For that reason alone, it has been argued, the state ought to facilitate carbon sequestration (carbon capture and storage) within the state by clarifying subsurface property rights.[30]

The thought that global climate change might increase the number or severity of natural disasters frightens many South Dakotans, who have suffered from floods, blizzards, cyclones, and ice storms.[31] Dams have tamed the Big Muddy to a great extent but flooding elsewhere occurs regularly. From settlement of the Black Hills until 1938, fourteen floods struck Rapid City, several of which led to loss of life. Entrepreneurs were not allowed to try to fix the problem because the federal government asserted control. Citizens warned the Army Corps of Engineers that their knowledge of local conditions "based as they are on long residence in this vicinity, cause us to believe that a reoccurrence of these floods is sure to come and would cause tremendous loss of property and life." The Corps' response proved inadequate: in 1972, a flood in Rapid City claimed more than 225 lives and destroyed over $100 million in property. Forty percent of the city's buildings were completely destroyed and another 30% damaged. In addition, 1,300 mobile homes and 5,000 vehicles were severely damaged or totaled. In good South Dakota style, the *Rapid City Journal* exhorted the region's inhabitants to "convert disaster into opportunity."[32] According to geographer Neil Ericksen, the worst of the 1972 disaster could have been avoided and damage and loss of life could have been substantially mitigated at low cost, but nobody wants any repeats, much less even more destructive catastrophes, especially droughts and their concomitant scourges—fires and grasshoppers.[33] Yet, in 2011 a combination of record snowfall in the Rockies and heavy spring rains caused devastating floods in the Missouri River Valley.

South Dakota is vulnerable to invasive species. A beetle that is destroying pine trees in the Black Hills has not hurt tourism, yet, but it has already dented the lumber industry. Similarly, chronic wasting disease (CWD) appeared among captive and free ranging elk and free ranging deer populations in the Black Hills. Although most hunters were unconcerned, continued spread of CWD or other diseases in game animals could threaten hunting tourism in the state. Potentially more devastating to hunting tourism was a proposed change to the definition of wetlands that could have led to the destruction of the state's prairie potholes, temporary or seasonal wetlands that millions of migratory waterfowl depend upon for nesting and feeding.[34]

Loss of grassland to farming means more crop income, but less income from hunters. Markets are best positioned to determine such tradeoffs. Loss of grassland to bugs or fire, by contrast, would mean less crop *and* diminished tourist income, a double whammy that could hurt the state's budget and its ability to provide public services efficiently, so some regulation is appropriate. Aesthetics are increasingly important to home values. Many people want to live where they can gaze at natural scenery and easily access attractive recreational opportunities, and many rate those attributes above economic opportunity, at least in surveys. This suggests that it would be unwise to pursue economic development opportunities that negatively impact air or water quality or increase population or traffic densities. Those who want South Dakota to industrialize have obviously never been to Cleveland, Gary, or Trenton.[35]

Many areas of the state, including scenic orgies like Custer County, lack zoning, creating the potential for future clashes as residents fight over the right to see distant hills or even just the flat horizon. Balancing those amenity rights with the traditional right to do with property as the owner sees fit may disrupt property rights and values, the exception of pheasant hunting notwithstanding. The Highway Beautification

Act, which threatened to cut off federal highway money if small-town businesses did not get rid of their billboards, is a trickier issue but ultimately not that important in a state with more land than businesses that need to advertise.[36]

The state's regulation of the mining industry, though not as important since Homestake closed early in the new century, has been lauded for balancing the "economic benefits of a healthy mining industry, while maintaining proper environmental protection."[37] Many of the state's other industries would benefit if a similar balance could be struck and maintained.

5. Treatment of Native Americans: The extreme poverty suffered by many of South Dakota's Native Americans also injures the state's image and its access to capital. Although the federal government is ultimately responsible for the immiseration of the nation's Native peoples, South Dakota has done little to alleviate their situation and at times exacerbated it. In 1974, for example, state attorney general candidate and future governor Bill Janklow stated that "the only way to deal with the Indian problem in South Dakota is to put a gun to the AIM leaders' heads and pull the trigger."[38] Even more disconcerting is that he won the election.

Before Pine Ridge finally got a depository institution, Lakota Federal Credit Union, in late 2012, residents had to drive sixty miles or use

Native American culture is celebrated at powwows and festivals throughout South Dakota. *Courtesy South Dakota Department of Tourism.*

Little Business on the Prairie

high-cost lenders. Backed by Lakota Funds, the credit union will accept direct deposits of Social Security checks. South Dakota's government should have helped to establish state-chartered credit unions on all its reservations decades ago.[39]

The state government could do more to help improve business conditions on the reservations in the state. Although there is still a painfully long way to go to achieve parity, the material condition of Native Americans has improved somewhat in recent years, as evidenced by the increasing population (up over 9,500 between 2000 and 2010) and incomes.[40] A number of Indian entrepreneurs have been mentioned in this book, and some of them have high praise for the state government. Lisa Little Chief Bryan, for example, claims that "the governor's office in the State of South Dakota has been wonderful for my business. They promote my product at every function that they do. They serve my fry bread; they tell people about it. Sometimes when you're in a bigger state with a bigger population, you tend to get lost. ... What tends to happen in South Dakota is that people know who you are. They promote you. You're kind of like a big, large family."[41]

Most Native Americans, however, remain outside of the state family. As recently as 2006, only about 5% of the work-age population in the Rosebud and Cheyenne River reservations were engaged in formal entrepreneurial activities and more than half of all businesses operating on or near those reservations were owned by non-Natives. Numerous replicative unregistered nano-enterprises owned by Natives operate in the underground economy, as is typical in Third World nations with chronic double-digit unemployment and little public confidence in government authorities, but few innovative or scalable enterprises exist, though interest in entrepreneurship among Natives has been trending upward since the mid-1990s. Receiving small liquidity loans from micro-finance lenders helped many beaders, quilters, nano-retailers, and others to escape the deepest recesses of poverty but in and of themselves are insufficient to transform local economies, in part because it takes Natives significantly more time and money to register businesses than it takes non-Natives, something the state could surely help to rectify. Many Natives still report difficulty obtaining loans, and Indian construction contractors often must remain small because they cannot obtain the surety bonds required on larger projects, public or private.[42]

Billy Mills, an Olympic gold medalist in the 10,000 meter, became an entrepreneur because his dad owned a barbershop and a restaurant on the Pine Ridge Reservation.[43] Most Natives, however, did not have close relatives or friends who were entrepreneurs. The state could try to break the negative feedback cycle that limits Native entrepreneurship. The dearth of Native entrepreneurs makes it difficult for Indians to try because "there's no one to go to, to ask how it's done" as Monica Terkildsen of the Lakota Fund put it.[44] "Because so few Indians own their own businesses," another Native noted, "there are very few mentors to train others or to pass on information about owning your own business."[45] Formal studies have also concluded that a lack of entrepreneurship in one generation impedes it in the next. (Meanwhile, in South Dakota's Euroamerican community, entrepreneurship begets yet more entrepreneurship.)[46]

Where tribes have done well developmentally, tribal governance has been non-predatory and political power has been sufficiently checked. The Mescalero Apache Tribe, for example, improved its economy by first changing its constitution to promote, in the words of Wendell Chino, "more stability." Chief Phillip Martin of the Mississippi Choctaw also credits constitutional reform for his tribe's relative economic success, which includes enough automobile subassembly, plastics manufacturing, printing, and electronics manufacturing jobs for every tribe member who is willing and able to work. Similarly, economic conditions on the Flathead Reservation in Montana improved after constitutional reforms reduced tensions between rival tribes. Tribal corporations have done best when not subjected to political oversight. Again, the state government could help here, not paternalistically but in partnership with Natives looking to improve tribal governance and hence entrepreneurial incentives.[47]

6. Immigrants: Recently, Hispanics, East Asians (Chinese, Burmese, Vietnamese and others), Pacific Islanders, Russians, Balkans, Africans, African Americans, Middle Easterners, and Asian Indians have begun immigrating to South Dakota, particularly its biggest cities. Many South Dakotans welcome these people and indeed are instrumental in their choosing to come to a place that is still overwhelmingly Euroamerican. They know that America is a nation of immigrants and that new, young blood can help to keep the state's economy vibrant as the Euroamerican population stagnates and ages. Others, however, do not like the newcomers and wish them gone.[48]

South Dakota is a less bigoted place than outsiders may assume because the prevailing ethos is so meritocratic. Although gays must confront widespread and deeply ingrained religious beliefs as well as the usual prejudices against their sexual preferences, they live openly in the state to the extent that they can accept gradual change. Such toleration is not new. French traveler Edmont Mandat-Grancey claimed, for example, that in the 1880s and 90s black cowboys were considered perfectly equal to white ones.[49] In the 1880s, people near Huron actually debated questions like "Resolved that the Indian received more injustices than the Negro."[50] The hotels in Hot Springs brought black people from Chicago to work because of their experience.[51] Early in the twentieth century, members of a Chinese family that moved to Pierre were called "chinks" and their daughter, Tocky, was not allowed to attend the local school, but the parents later moved to Deadwood and "made good in a store there."[52] By the late 1920s, lesbians enjoyed a thriving, if circumspect, culture in the Deadwood area and probably elsewhere in the state. "We never felt discriminated against," one later claimed.[53]

In 1961, backpackers from Des Moines, Iowa, vowed never to vacation in South Dakota because of "racial discrimination" there, especially in Rapid City bars. Governor Archie M. Gubbrud responded by asserting that "there is less racial discrimination in South Dakota than anywhere else in the world." Many would argue otherwise but discrimination is notoriously difficult to measure. Clearly, however, the state was not on the forefront of the civil rights movement as it long allowed segregation of African Americans and/or Native Americans. When the Harlem Globe Trotters played in Yankton in the 1930s, for example, they slept in the showroom of an auto dealership or camped in Forester Park. When Louis Armstrong, Cab Calloway, Ethel Waters, and other black entertainers visited Sioux Falls, they slept in the homes of black residents, or after 1930, in the Booker T. Washington Center. Older South Dakotans may remember 'Indians not welcomed' signs in the 1950s and even more recently; Native Americans had their own bars.[54] "The appearance of any actual Negro caused a minor stir," Tom Brokaw recalls, but "more out of curiosity and ignorance than hostility."[55] Such treatment was not unusual at the time, however, even in northern states, and South Dakota was not a recalcitrant holdout on civil rights. In fact, it was the twenty-ninth state to pass a nondiscrimination law for transportation, hospitality, amusement, and hair-cutting businesses. It also had a long history of allowing black entrepreneurs, like Louise Mitchell, to own and operate their own businesses, a beauty school in Mitchell's case.[56]

In 1979, a Chinese man with a blonde wife and their two kids moved to Vermillion, where locals stared at them. The newcomers laughed, thinking the stares were directed at their New Jersey license plates.[57] "Later," one of the children admitted, "it wouldn't seem so funny. The stares made me feel as though I'd forgotten to put my clothes on. I could feel their gaze rub across my skin. After men started driving by our house to shoot, after our dogs were killed, it wasn't funny at all."[58] Locals apparently believed that the father "was a white slaver. He must have somehow kidnapped my mother and forced her to marry him."[59] When the couple hired two young Lakota to rake leaves, the neighbors warned them that "the Indians are just waiting for their chance to break into your home and bleed you to death. They've done it before."[60] One might expect better in a college town, but the University of South Dakota was the same institution where a visiting Jewish professor was asked publicly if he was ready to "accept" Jesus Christ as his "lord and savior."[61]

Most South Dakotans are less xenophobic now because the economy is humming and Wounded Knee II is, for them, a distant memory. An environmental coalition called the CIA (Cowboy and Indian Alliance) is an interesting example of how much conditions have changed. Nevertheless, many Euroamericans still resent newcomers and some even give voice to their resentment. It would be a mistake, however, to drive the recent immigrants away. South Dakota is a land of immigrants; even the Lakota are recent arrivals in the 10,000 plus years of human occupation of the region. The new immigrants, like the old, are not drawn primarily from other societies' castoffs but rather from the ranks of their most enterprising. Many, like Sadiya and Dawit Daba of the Shalom Ethiopian Coffee House, come with entrepreneurial instincts and aspirations that can further invigorate the state's economy by increasing its diversity.[62]

7. Economic diversity: The lesson from the recent bankruptcy of Detroit, once a great city with a population several times that of all of South Dakota, is not to be a one trick pony. Agriculture is great but farm crises could strike again due to any number of plausible causes. Contrary to received wisdom, short-term fluctuations in agricultural output do not much stress the non-agricultural sector. Long-term declines, like those experienced in the 1880s, 1930s, and 1980s, however, are certainly destructive. Places that have been able to rebound from the destruction of a major sector, like Pittsburg (steel) and Baltimore (shipping), have had other bases of economic strength upon which to draw, including a major *private* university, something of which the state has long felt the lack, and a healthcare system.[63] "The strength of our economy is diversity of income in the community," banker Art Dahl wrote in 1965, "much more perhaps than in most communities."[64] He was right then and ever since South Dakota's economy has grown increasingly diverse. It has not one but three major private healthcare systems but, alas, it still lacks a major private university. The state's university system is adequate to good, but it remains vulnerable to economic downturns that shock the state budget, which must always balance or run a surplus. Besides, by almost all measures private universities produce more and better research than even the best public ones. In the 2014 *U.S. News and World Report* rankings, the best public university, Berkeley, ranked twentieth overall. The University of South Dakota ranked 190th, eleven places higher than South Dakota State, but both were well ahead of almost 100 universities that were too poor to rank or have their rank published.

The high cost of getting into and out of the state remains a barrier: airfares are high and connection hubs are limited and seemingly ever changing. In the 1970s and 80s, airlines offered direct flights out of Sioux Falls to New York and Los Angeles as well as Chicago, Denver, and Minneapolis. Along with the added convenience of more direct flights to important cities, the state needs lower airfares so that people can come and go as needed, without busting their budgets to do so.[65]

8. Government efficiency: South Dakota's state and local governments need to maintain or better still to increase their efficiency. That does not mean slicing public services and lowering taxes; rather, it means finding ways of providing quality services, desired by the public, at the lowest possible cost.[66] The Sioux Falls Area Chamber of Commerce was established in 1936, not to reduce taxes but to help the state maintain "a balance of reasonable tax levels and adequate public infrastructure."[67] Thanks to democratic processes and institutions, like the Chamber, the state's conservative-libertarian voters have done a decent job of maintaining a seeming oxymoron: efficient government. But politicians naturally want to borrow and spend, so eternal vigilance remains as important today as in Thomas Jefferson's era.[68]

Keeping taxes in check is important, but so too is identifying the proper sources of government revenue. In 1985, Grant Thornton, a Chicago-based public accounting firm, ranked South Dakota the best state in the nation on the basis of twenty-two factors like wages, union membership, government debt, taxes, welfare spending, and energy costs. Just two years later, the Corporation for Enterprise Development, a Washington think tank, ranked South Dakota forty-ninth because it believed the state's tax system was unfair. Some echo its complaints today because the state government's revenue still primarily comes from user fees and real estate, sales, and excise taxes, not corporate or personal income taxes. Some landowners complain bitterly about real estate taxes. More effort should be made to educate people about the tax implications of buying houses and other real estate, but it also needs to be made clear that renters pay their share of real estate taxes too, albeit indirectly. Taxes on food, especially unprocessed ones, should be cut or eliminated to reduce the regressivity of the sales tax. If critics of the current tax system gain traction, the state may lose one of its most attractive features, its lack of a state income tax, in the name of an abstraction. Thankfully, imposition of a state income tax seems unlikely in the near future and should remain so as long as the government continues to be relatively efficient and limited in scope.[69]

One area in which the government could improve its efficiency is in crime prevention and punishment. In 2000, the Sioux Falls police successfully clamped down on "Loopers," teens who drove around and around the city's downtown on weekend nights, but at the same time the incidence of organized and drug crimes rose in the state, and not just on the reservations. Sex trafficking has also become more commonplace, exacerbated by two of the state's most lucrative attractions—the Sturgis motorcycle rally and hunting—even though the brothels in Deadwood were finally shuttered in 1980. A drunken bus driver, school violence, teenage drinking, and even gang rapes were not unheard of in the 1980s and illicit drugs like meth have, if anything, made conditions worse.[70] Not all that long ago, Falls Park in Sioux Falls was overrun by "transients, drug dealers and delinquents."[71] And the homeless, who numbered 601 in Sioux Falls one night in August 2001, are more likely to commit crimes *and* to be victims of them. An entrepreneurial culture that blocks, or seems to block, the aspirations of some entrepreneurs is bound to create some exploitative entrepreneurs. The state still boasts of one of the lowest crime rates in the nation but it also has relatively few law enforcement officers per square mile and is more accessible to organized urban criminals than are Alaska, Montana, and Wyoming.[72]

One way to decrease the need for law enforcement is to revise the penal code. Like the federal government, the state tends to imprison people for victimless crimes, such as drug possession, and to keep them in prison long after they have ceased being serious public safety risks. Stints in jail serve mainly to turn potheads into seasoned criminals. Decriminalizing marijuana would be helpful because it would immediately turn many exploitative entrepreneurs – jail bait—into innovative and replicative ones, as is now occurring in Colorado.[73]

9. Balancing interests: South Dakota's government has sometimes been extravagant in its desire to be seen as friendly to business. Creditors have much more power in South Dakota than in most other states. While that helps to attract lenders and other businesses to the state, if taken too far, as it might have been in the case of wage garnishments, for example, the government risks driving citizens (taxpayers/workers) away. No amount of prairie fever, low taxes, and so forth can compensate people being ripped off by collection agencies, voracious bank holding companies, large auto dealerships, and the like. Creditors' rights should not be paramount anymore than debtors' rights should be. Rather, South Dakota's lawmakers need to strike a just balance.[74]

10. Entrepreneurial spirit: All of the state's other nine challenges impinge in one way or another on its tenth, the incentives of its citizens to continue to engage in legitimate entrepreneurial pursuits, whether innovative or replicative. Although not as ubiquitous as it once was, entrepreneurship remains strong in South Dakota, in part because incorporation remains relatively easy and cheap.[75]

Entrepreneurship is better supported educationally than ever. Start-ups can obtain help on business plan review, education, networking, and venture-capital acquisition from the Enterprise Institute in Sioux Falls, Brookings, and Yankton, Genesis of Innovation in Rapid City. South Dakota Small Business Development Centers across the state, the USD Business Research Bureau in Vermillion, and Dakota State University's Small Business Innovation Research program in Madison. In addition, business incubators in Sioux Falls and Rapid City provide space and additional assistance. Nevertheless, more could be done, particularly in public schools K through graduate school, to help people become self-employed, start their own businesses, and, most important, become innovative thinkers, regardless of their race or gender.[76]

Entrepreneurship in South Dakota was never an entirely male activity. In the early 1980s, for example, Carolyn Chai, wife of a former university administrator, opened a photography studio in Vermillion. She developed film and did wedding shoots to help the family get through some rough times. Today, women are more directly engaged in South Dakota's entrepreneurial culture than ever. By 2004, majority women-owned firms accounted for 17,833 (26.2%) of all privately-held firms in the state, in both rural (population less than 2,500) and nonrural (population greater than 2,500) areas, an increase of 45.6% from 1997. In addition, 54.5% of South Dakota companies were at least 50% female owned; 19,282 of them, 28.3% of all privately held firms in the state, were owned by married couples. Most were replicative: they actively sought out under-served areas or competed solely by providing higher service levels, like being friendlier. Just over a third, 33.6%, were engaged in retail trade, 23.4% provided professional services, 8.4% provided healthcare and social assistance, and 5.6% finance or insurance. The rest were engaged in a hodgepodge of wholesale trade, construction, manufacturing, entertainment, and real estate activities.[77]

Only 25% had gross sales greater than $100,000, which is not surprising given that most focused on local and regional markets. Only 8.2% competed for business nationally and a mere 1% internationally. Yet satisfaction was high. By 2004, distance from major centers was no longer a disadvantage as communication and financial networks were readily accessible from anywhere in the state (outside of the reservations). In fact, over half of female rural entrepreneurs felt that the rural setting of their business was at least moderately positive, due to a lower wage bill and also a lower cost of living.[78] As Lisa Little Chief Bryan, who runs several businesses in White River, a town of about 800, explains, "expenses would be higher to operate my business out of one of the [Twin] Cities because of the rent, the wages and a lot of the problems there."[79]

Over half also reported that being female had at least a moderately positive impact on their businesses. The keys to success, they reported, were hard work, prior experience, strong support systems, and efficient financial management. A follow-up econometric study, however, could not link any of those traits to success, perhaps because the goal of most female entrepreneurs was to help others, contribute to and add diversity to family income, and create a sense of accomplishment, not to maximize profits.[80]

The outlook for entrepreneurship in South Dakota is good because entrepreneurship tends to self-replicate. Both businesses and citizens recognize that entrepreneurship can make a positive difference in their communities.[81] Unemployment is low but, paradoxically, there are plenty of qualified applicants for most jobs because if it suits them, South Dakotans will readily trade up to a better job, work multiple jobs, re-enter the workforce, or return to the state after a stint elsewhere. In 1985, for example, Citibank had 22,000 applications on file, 10,000 from "former South Dakotans who wish to return."[82] And people from other states are again willing to move to South Dakota. After decades of losing people both before and after the Depression, the trend reversed in the 1990s, when over 20,000 people moved into the state on net. The Sioux Falls area, especially, was able to create a virtuous cycle of real estate development, new businesses, demand for labor, and successful recruitment even from distant cities, which then fueled additional real estate development and another turn of the cycle. Taxes remain low: South Dakota is the only state with no corporate income tax, no personal income tax, no personal property tax, no business inventory tax, and no inheritance tax.[83] It also possesses "some of the lowest unemployment insurance costs in the nation" and "one of the lowest worker compensation rates in the country."[84]

Most South Dakota companies are small by international, national, and even regional standards, but that is not always a disadvantage, especially in today's global economy. Smaller companies tend to be more nimble and therefore better equipped to respond rapidly to changing domestic and world markets. Large companies continue to have more clout and more ability to tap economies of scale, but smaller ones tend to have more local knowledge or much more sensitivity to their customers and clients, which can be a decided advantage. Small machine manufacturers, for example, have morphed into quasi-consultants, not just selling machines but also helping clients to buy the right ones. Some have even started doing the manufacturing themselves, on contract.[85]

None of this is to say, however, that the Commons proposed by Professors Frank and Deborah Popper of Rutgers University is a completely harebrained idea, as much as some South Dakotans would like to see the idea tested in New Jersey first.[86] In fact, the notion of returning West River to nature was born during the Great Depression when a federal official suggested that both Dakotas be abandoned as "submarginal."[87] To protect the East from dust storms, people spoke of growing a huge shelterbelt stretching from Canada to Texas, similar to one started in the Ukraine in the 1880s, west of the river.[88] The winner of a contest explaining the meaning of photos of abandoned farms and ruined fields popularized the idea by writing, "No plow land. Keep grass. Buffalo eat. Indian eat buffalo ... no ask relief."[89] The big shelterbelt never came to be, but during the Depression many small shelterbelts were planted and the state started planting one million trees a year beginning in 1947. Prodigious annual tree planting continues in the state thanks to the Arbor Day Foundation and Enterprise Holdings, but the global economy's voracious appetite for corn, invigorated with federal subsidies for ethanol, again threaten to turn the state into a dusty desert.[90]

Since the drought of 1910-11, when West River counties lost up to 50% of their populations to bankruptcy and despair, parts of West River South Dakota have been returning to their natural state as a result of economic forces, and more would revert if it were not for payments from Social Security, the Veterans Administration, and the Department of Agriculture. By the 1990s, over half of the income of farmers in the far western part of the state, north and south, came from various agricultural program payments. South Dakota entrepreneurs would quickly learn how to turn a buck or two from the Commons, much as they already leverage the state's existing federal grasslands and other natural resources.[91]

The state's biggest challenge will be spreading its entrepreneurial spirit and institutions to the rest of the nation. The economic future of the United States is not necessarily bleak, as when other erstwhile economic superpowers, like Holland, Britain, and Japan, continued to be comfortable even as they receded into stagnant unimportance. America's economic future, however, hardly appears bright, especially as the nation's overall economic freedom rating continues to drop in both absolute and relative terms. South Dakota's economy is tethered to that of the nation, so it is imperative to fire up the national economy before it drags the state down with it. That means that South Dakotans must convince their countrymen to mend their ways much as when Governor Janklow tricked Perpich into liberalizing Minnesota's sclerotic political economy.

Notes

Chapter 1

1 Congress, Senate, Committee on the Judiciary, *Ensuring Competitive and Open Agricultural Markets: Are Meat Packers Abusing Market Power?* 107th Cong., 2d sess., 23 Aug. 2002, 22.

2 W. Hampton Sides, *Stomping Grounds: A Pilgrim's Progress Through Eight American Subcultures* (New York: William Morrow and Co., 1992), 156-60; Carlton L. Bonilla, "A South Dakota Rendezvous: The Sturgis Motorcycle Rally and Races," *South Dakota History* 28, 3 (1998): 123-43; Betti VanEpps-Taylor, *Forgotten Lives: African Americans in South Dakota* (Pierre: South Dakota Historical Society Press, 2008), 4; Patricia Schultz, *1,000 Places to See in the USA and Canada Before You Die* (New York: Workman Publishing, 2007), 659-60.

3 Sides, *Stomping Grounds*, 155.

4 Schultz, *1,000 Places to See*, 659.

5 Bonilla, "A South Dakota Rendezvous," 132.

6 Daniel Krier and William J. Swart, "The Commodification of Spectacle: Spectators, Sponsors and the Outlaw Biker Diegesis at Sturgis," *Critical Sociology* (May 2014), 1-21; Sides, *Stomping Grounds*, 156-62.

7 Sides, *Stomping Grounds*, 155.

8 Ibid., 167.

9 Sides, *Stomping Grounds*, 155, 173; Bonilla, "A South Dakota Rendezvous," 134.

10 Sides, *Stomping Grounds*, 167.

11 Ibid., 156.

12 Robert G. Lowery, "Motorcyclists Find South Dakota Warm," *New York Times,* 3 Sept. 1990.

13 Bonilla, "A South Dakota Rendezvous," 129; Sides, *Stomping Grounds*, 157-58.

14 Sides, *Stomping Grounds*, 158-60.

15 Ibid., 156-57.

16 Schultz, *1,000 Places to See*, 658-59; Mary Craig, "The Black Hills Passion Play at Spearfish, South Dakota," (M.A. thesis, University of Wyoming, 1952); Shebby Lee, "Traveling the Sunshine State: The Growth of Tourism in South Dakota, 1914-1939," *South Dakota History* 19, 2 (Summer 1989), 199; *Clason's So. Dakota Green Guide*, CWS.

17 Michael Demarest, "In South Dakota: The Motor Homers Gather," *Time,* 7 Aug. 1978.

18 Tom Brokaw, *A Long Way from Home: Growing Up in the American Heartland* (New York: Random House, 2002), 37.

19 Ibid., 10-11

20 Business and Industry Round Table, *South Dakota: Final Report* (Oct. 1988).

21 Entrepreneur Press, *How to Start a Business in South Dakota* (New York: Entrepreneur Media, 2004), 13.7.

22 Benno Wymar, "Foreign Investments and South Dakota," *South Dakota Business Review* 55, 3 (Mar. 1997), 1, 4-8.

23 Dorothy Schwieder, *Growing Up with the Town: Family and Community on the Great Plains* (Iowa City: University of Iowa Press, 2002), 159; Mae Urbanek, *The Uncovered Wagon* (Denver: Sage Books, 1958), 61; Grace Fairchild and Walker D. Wyman, *Frontier Woman: The Life of a Woman Homesteader on the Dakota Frontier* (River Falls: University of Wisconsin-River Falls Press, 1972), 40; South Dakota State Planning Board and Hamlin County Planning Board, *Economic and Social Survey of Hamlin County* (Brookings:

Central Office, 1937), 2, 30; Paula M. Nelson, *The Prairie Winnows Out Its Own: The West River Country of South Dakota in the Years of Depression and Dust* (Iowa City: University of Iowa Press, 1996).

24 As quoted in James Marten, "'We Always Looked Forward to the Hunters Coming': The Culture of Pheasant Hunting in South Dakota," *South Dakota History* 29, 2 (Summer 1999), 95.

25 Archer B. Gilfillan, *Sheep: Life on the South Dakota Range* (St. Paul: Minnesota Historical Society Press, 1993), xxv, 267-72.

26 Estella Bowen Culp, *Letters from Tully: A Woman's Life on the Dakota Frontier* (Boulder: Johnson Books, 2007), 126-27; Michael Johnston Grant, *Down and Out on the Family Farm: Rural Rehabilitation in the Great Plains, 1929-1945* (Lincoln: University of Nebraska Press, 2002), 24.

27 Gilfillan, *Sheep*, 270.

28 Urbanek, *The Uncovered Wagon*, 16-17; Kathleen Norris, *Dakota: A Spiritual Geography* (New York: Ticknor and Fields, 1993), 11; South Dakota Board of Regents, *Foundation for the Future: The Future Fund* (1989), 8, 12.

29 For an overview, see William Easterly, *The Elusive Quest for Growth: Economists' Adventures and Misadventures in the Tropics* (Cambridge: MIT Press, 2001).

30 Mark Nelson, Paul Higbee, and Ken Steinken, *The Spirit of an American Entrepreneur: Succeeding in Family Business* (Sioux Falls: Mark Nelson, 2009), 8.

31 Scott Shane, *The Illusions of Entrepreneurship: The Costly Myths that Entrepreneurs, Investors, and Policy Makers Live By* (New Haven: Yale University Press, 2008).

32 Those interested in the statistics, however, can consult James Gwartney, Robert Lawson, and Joshua Hall, *Economic Freedom of the World: 2013 Annual Report* (Montreal: Fraser Institute, 2013) or earlier or later versions of that work.

33 Daron Acemoglu and James A. Robinson, *Why Nations Fail: The Origins of Power, Prosperity, and Poverty* (New York: Crown, 2012); William Baumol, Robert Litan, and Carl Schramm, *Good Capitalism, Bad Capitalism, and the Economics of Growth and Prosperity* (New Haven: Yale University Press, 2007); David Landes, Joel Mokyr, and William Baumol, *The Invention of Enterprise: Entrepreneurship from Ancient Mesopotamia to Modern Times* (Princeton: Princeton University Press, 2010); Benjamin Powell, *Making Poor Nations Rich: Entrepreneurship and the Process of Economic Development* (Stanford: Stanford University Press, 2008).

34 Todd Mitton, "The Wealth of Subnations: Geography, Institutions, and Within-Country Development," (Working Paper, Mar. 25, 2013); Paul Caron, "2012 Business Tax Climate: Chilliest in Blue States," *TaxProf Blog*, 26 Jan. 2012; "South Dakota is Friendliest State for Small Business, Again," *Sioux Falls Argus Leader*, 12 Dec. 2011; Raymond J. Keating, *Small Business Survival Index 2009: Ranking the Policy Environment for Entrepreneurship Across the Nation* (Oakton, VA: Small Business & Entrepreneurship Council, 2009); Scott Cohn, "Set It In Stone! South Dakota Is 2013 Top State for Business," *CNBC,* 9 July 2013.

35 Dulguun Batbold and Rob Grunewald, "Bakken Activity: How Wide is the Ripple Effect?" *Fedgazette* (July 2013), 14; Rob Grunewald and Dulguun Batbold, "Bakken Stands Out in Comparison with Other Shale Drilling Areas," *Fedgazette* (Jan. 2014), 13-15.

36 U.S. Census.

37 Robert Wuthnow, *Remaking the Heartland: Middle America Since the 1950s* (Princeton: Princeton University Press, 2011), 263; South Dakota, Governor's Office of Economic Development, "Cost of Living"; Entrepreneur Press, *How to Start a Business in South Dakota*, 13.4; Branko Milanovic, *The Haves and the Have-Nots: A Brief and Idiosyncratic History of Global Inequality* (New York: Basic Books, 2011), 178.

38 Arthur B. Laffer, Stephen Moore, and Jonathan Williams, *Rich States, Poor States: ALEC-Laffer State Economic Competitiveness Index* 4th ed. (2011), 11, 17, 48, 90; U.S. Chamber of Commerce and the National Chamber Foundation, *Enterprising States: Recovery and Renewal for the 21st Century* (2011) , 16, 20, 25, 108.

39 Brookings, Metropolitan Policy Program, "Counting for Dollars: State and District of Columbia."

40 M. Lisle Reese, ed., *South Dakota: A Guide to the State* 2nd ed. (New York: Hastings House, 1952), vii.

41 B. Drummond Ayres, Jr. "Politicians in Dakota Are Still Just Folks," *New York Times,* 30 Oct. 1970, 48.

42 Ibid.

43 "Best Small Cities for Startups," *Bloomberg Businessweek.*

44 Sheryl Gay Stolberg, "Chasing a Coveted Democratic Prize Across the Plains," *New York Times,* 24 Oct. 2004, N22; Peter Pagnamenta, *Prairie Fever: British Aristocrats in the American West, 1830-1890* (New York: W. W. Norton and Co., 2012), 69.

45 Joe Foss and Donna Wild Foss, *A Proud American: The Autobiography of Joe Foss* (New York: Pocket Books, 1992), 16.

46 Congress, *Ensuring Competitive and Open Agricultural Markets*, 22-23, 36-37.

47 "Best Small Cities for Startups," *Bloomberg Businessweek.*

48 Catherine Bampoky, Luisa Blanco, Aolong Liu, and James E. Prieger, "Economic Growth and the Optimal Level of Entrepreneurship," Working Paper, 17 July 2013; Frank Hagerty, *The Territory of Dakota: The State of North Dakota; the State of South Dakota* (Aberdeen: Daily News Print, 1889), 79; Gooder Casey Land Co., *Southwestern South Dakota: A Booklet Descriptive of the Country Along the New Extension of the C. M. & St. P. Railway Between Chamberlain and the Famous Black Hills* (Chamberlain, S.D., 1910?); Professional Soil Scientists Association of South Dakota, *Soil, the Basis of Life: Houdek, South Dakota's State Soil* (June 1999).

49 Kathleen Norris, "South Dakota: The Long Mile," in *These United States: Original Essays by Leading American Writers on Their State within the Union*, ed. John Leonard (New York: Thunder's Mouth Press, 2003), 408.

50 Brad Herzog, *Small World: A Microcosmic Journey* (New York: Pocket Books, 2004), 53; John Milton, *South Dakota: A Bicentennial History* (New York: W. W. Norton and Co., 1977), 3; Hayden Carruth, "South Dakota: State without End," in *These United States: Portraits of America from the 1920s*, ed. Daniel H. Borus (Ithaca: Cornell University Press, 1992), 336; Herbert T. Hoover, "South Dakota," in *The American Midwest: An Interpretive Encyclopedia*, ed. Richard Sisson, Christian Zacher, and Andrew Cayton (Bloomington: Indiana University Press, 2007), 46.

51 Richard Maxwell Brown, "The Enduring Frontier: The Impact of Weather on South Dakota History and Literature," *South Dakota History* 15, 1 (Spring 1985): 26-57.

52 Dan O'Brien, *Buffalo for the Broken Heart: Restoring Life to a Black Hills Ranch* (New York: Random House, 2001), 207; Milton, *South Dakota: A Bicentennial History*, 5.

53 Norris, *Dakota: A Spiritual Geography*, 26.

54 Fairchild and Wyman, *Frontier Woman*, 87.

55 Clifton Johnson, *Highways and Byways of the Rocky Mountains* (New York: MacMillan Co., 1910), 275.56 Harry F. Thompson, ed. *A New South Dakota History* 2nd ed. (Sioux Falls: Center for Western Studies, 2009), 227. See also Fairchild and Wyman, *Frontier Woman*, 36.

57 Fairchild and Wyman, *Frontier Woman*, 36.

58   As quoted in Michael Lawson, *Dammed Indians: The Pick-Sloan Plan and the Missouri River Sioux, 1944-1980* (Norman: University of Oklahoma Press, 1982), 4 and also in Robert Schneiders, *Unruly River: Two Centuries of Change Along the Missouri* (Lawrence: University of Kansas Press, 1999), 23.

59   Bahman Dehgan, ed. *America in Quotations* (Jefferson, North Carolina: McFarland & Co., 2003), 52.

60   Reese, *South Dakota*, 9; J. D. Irving, S. F. Emmon, and T. A. Jaggar, Jr., *Economic Resources of the Northern Black Hills* (Washington: Government Printing Office, 1904), 23; Schwieder, *Growing Up with the Town*, 3.

61   Lewis, *Nothing to Make a Shadow*, 19, 90. See also Johnson, *Highways and Byways*, 275.

62   Steven J. Bucklin, ed., "'Pioneer Days of South Dakota': The Memoir of Frank Bloodgood," *South Dakota History* 29, 2 (Summer 1999): 141-44; Milton, *South Dakota: A Bicentennial History*, 89; Martha Shirk and Anna Wadia, *Kitchen Table Entrepreneurs: How Eleven Women Escaped Poverty and Became Their Own Bosses* (New York: Westview Press, 2002), 109.

63   Chai, *Hapa Girl*, 145.

64   David Garoogian, *Weather America: A Thirty-Year Summary of Statistical Weather Data and Rankings*, 2nd ed. (Lakeville, Ct.: Grey House Publishing, 2001), 1,645.

65   Laura Bower Van Nuys, *The Family Band: From the Missouri to the Black Hills, 1881-1900* (Lincoln: University of Nebraska Press, 1961), 83.

66   Irving, Emmon, and Jaggar, *Economic Resources of the Northern Black Hills*, 23; Henry Newton and Walter P. Jenney, *Report on the Geology and Resources of the Black Hills of Dakota, with Atlas* (Washington, D.C.: Government Printing Office, 1880), 22-37; Edmont Mandat-Grancey, *Cowboys and Colonels: Narrative of a Journey Across the Prairie and Over the Black Hills of Dakota*, trans. William Conn (Philadelphia: J. B. Lippincott Co., 1963), 119; Carrie E. Gray-Wood, "Resource Perceptions in the Black Hills of Custer County, South Dakota: Fifty Years of Change," (M.A. Thesis, South Dakota State University, 2007), 11-12; D. L. Flyger, "An Invitation to South Dakota," *Countryside and Small Stock Journal* 82, 2 (Mar./Apr. 1998), 43.

67   Johnson, *Highways and Byways*, 275.

68   Gooder Casey Land Co., *Southwestern South Dakota*; Garoogian, *Weather America*, 1,646.

69   Hagerty, *Territory of Dakota*, 58.

70   Robert Karolevitz, *Challenge: The South Dakota Story* (Sioux Falls: Brevet Press, 1975), v; Gooder Casey Land Co., *Southwestern South Dakota*; John Oswald, *Printing in the Americas* (New York: Gregg Publishing Company, 1937), 457; Norris, "South Dakota: The Long Mile," 410; Shirley Cochell and George Beine, *Land of the Coyote* (Ames: Iowa State University Press, 1972), 1; Reese, *South Dakota*, vii; Gilbert Fite, "South Dakota: Some Observations by a Native Son," *South Dakota History* 4, 4 (Fall 1974), 457; Schwieder, *Growing Up with the Town*, 1; Lewis, *Nothing to Make a Shadow*, 28.

71   As quoted in Brokaw, *A Long Way from Home*, 14.

72   Herbert T. Hoover, "South Dakota: An Expression of Regional Heritage," in *Heart Land: Comparative Histories of the Midwestern States*, ed. James H. Madison (Bloomington: Indiana University Press, 1988), 189.

73   Gilfillan, *Sheep*, 88.

74   Irving, Emmon, and Jaggar, *Economic Resources of the Northern Black Hills*, 23; Lynus Kibbe, "Early Recollections of the Son of a Pioneer Newspaper Man of South Dakota and Dakota Territory," *South Dakota Historical Collections and Report* 25 (1950): 327.

75 Marion Head, *South Dakota: An Explorer's Guide* (Woodstock, VT: Countryman Press, 2009), 14.

76 Culp, *Letters from Tully*, 98.

77 Paula M. Nelson, *After the West Was Won: Homesteaders and Town-Builders in Western South Dakota, 1900-1917* (Iowa City: University of Iowa Press, 1986), 36-37.

78 "Record Hailstone Plunges into South Dakota Town," *Bulletin of the American Meteorological Society* (BAMS), Oct. 2010, 1,346.

79 O'Brien, *Buffalo for the Broken Heart*, 161.

80 Nelson, *After the West Was Won*, xv, 129.

81 Milton, *South Dakota: A Bicentennial History*, 89; Peter Carrels, "South Dakota Farmers Reject a Free Lunch," in *Reopening the Frontier,* ed. Ed Marston (New York: Island Press, 1989), 119, 124; "Drought in South Dakota Brings Big Increase in Disaster Claims," *New York Times,* 14 Sept. 1980, A59

82 August Schatz, *Longhorns Bring Culture* (Boston: Christopher Publishing House, 1961), 26.

83 Culp, *Letters from Tully*, 177.

84 As quoted in Pagnamenta, *Prairie Fever*, xvii.

85 Lewis, *Nothing to Make a Shadow*, 29; Van Nuys, *The Family Band*, 76; Schwieder, *Growing Up with the Town*, 3; Nelson, *After the West Was Won*, 37.

86 Johnson, *Highways and Byways*, 250.

87 Ibid., 265.

88 Norris, *Dakota: A Spiritual Geography*, 21.

89 Carruth, "South Dakota: State without End," 335.

90 Gilfillan, Sheep, 16.

91 Culp, *Letters from Tully*, 131.

92 Chai, *Hapa Girl*, 94.

93 John Francis McDermott, ed., *Journal of an Expedition to the Mauvaises Terres and the Upper Missouri in 1850 by Thaddeus A. Culbertson* (Washington: Smithsonian Institution, 1950), 37.

94 Fairchild and Wyman, *Frontier Woman*, 50.

95 Ibid., 60, 80-81.

96 Business and Industry Round Table, *South Dakota*.

97 Pagnamenta, *Prairie Fever*, 58.

98 Chai, *Hapa Girl*, 64.

99 Norris, "South Dakota: The Long Mile," 417.

100 Norris, *Dakota: A Spiritual Geography*, 1; Norris, "South Dakota: The Long Mile," 411.

101 Bruce Siberts and Walker D. Wyman, *Nothing but Prairie and Sky: Life on the Dakota Range in the Early Days* (Norman: University of Oklahoma Press, 1954), 113-14; Norris, *Dakota: A Spiritual Geography*, 128; Glenda Riley, "Farm Women's Roles in the Agricultural Development of South Dakota," *South Dakota History* 13, 1 (Spring 1983), 84-85.

102 Holger Cahill, *The Shadow of My Hand* (1956) quoted in Dehgan, *America in Quotations*, 52.103 Pagnamenta, *Prairie Fever*, xvi.

104 As quoted in Ibid.

105 McDermott, *Journal of an Expedition to the Mauvaises Terres*, 41.

106 Brokaw, *A Long Way from Home*, 13.

107 Carruth, "South Dakota: State without End," 334.

108 Riley, "Farm Women's Roles," 107.

109 Schwieder, *Growing Up with the Town*, 1; Chai, *Hapa Girl*, 56.

110 Carruth, "South Dakota: State without End," 335.

111 Gilfillan, *Sheep*, 272.

112 John E. Miller, *Looking for History on Highway 14* (Pierre, S.D.: South Dakota State Historical Society Press, 2001), 59-60; Culp, *Letters from Tully*, 37.

Chapter 2

1 Dan O'Brien as quoted in Norris, "South Dakota: The Long Mile," 409.

2 Donald Parker, "Early Explorations and Fur Trading in South Dakota," *South Dakota Historical Collections and Report* 25 (1950): 1-4; Kathleen Pickering, "Articulation of the Lakota Mode of Production and the Euro-American Fur Trade," in *The Fur Trade Revisited: Selected Papers of the Sixth North American Fur Trade Conference*, ed. Jennifer Brown, W. J. Eccles, and Donald P. Heldman (East Lansing: Michigan State University Press, 1991); George Frison, "Clovis, Goshen, and Folsom: Lifeways and Cultural Relationships," in *Megafauna and Man: Discovery of America's Heartland*, ed. Larry Agenbroad, Jim Mead, and Lisa Nelson (Hot Springs: Mammoth Site of Hot Springs and Northern Arizona University, 1990), 100-101; Larry J. Zimmerman, *Peoples of Prehistoric South Dakota* (Lincoln: University of Nebraska Press, 1985), 52; J. M. Adovasio and David Pedler, "The People of North America," in *North American Archaeology*, ed. Timothy R. Pauketat and Diana DiPaolo Loren (Malden, MA: Blackwell Publishing, 2005), 30-55; Dale R. Henning, "The Evolution of the Plains Village Tradition," in *North American Archaeology*, ed. Timothy R. Pauketat and Diana DiPaolo Loren (Malden, MA: Blackwell Publishing, 2005), 161; L. Adrien Hannus, "The Lange-Ferguson Site: A Case for Mammoth Bone-Butchering Tools," in *Megafauna and Man: Discovery of America's Heartland*, ed. Larry Agenbroad, Jim Mead, and Lisa Nelson (Hot Springs: Mammoth Site of Hot Springs and Northern Arizona University, 1990), 86-99; L. Adrien Hannus, "The Lange/Ferguson Site -- An Event of Clovis Mammoth Butchery with the Associated Bone Tool Technology: The Mammoth and Its Track," (Ph.D. diss., University of Utah, 1985); R. Dale Guthrie, "Late Pleistocene Faunal Revolution – A New Perspective on the Extinction Debate," in *Megafauna and Man: Discovery of America's Heartland*, ed. Larry Agenbroad, Jim Mead, and Lisa Nelson (Hot Springs, SD: Mammoth Site of Hot Springs and Northern Arizona University, 1990), 42-53; Paul S. Martin, "Who or What Destroyed Our Mammoths?" in *Megafauna and Man: Discovery of America's Heartland*, ed. Larry Agenbroad, Jim Mead, and Lisa Nelson (Hot Springs, SD: Mammoth Site of Hot Springs and Northern Arizona University, 1990), 109-10; Zimmerman, *Peoples of Prehistoric South Dakota*, 30; Donald Grayson and David Meltzer, "A Requiem for North American Overkill," *Journal of Archaeological Science* 30 (2003): 585-93.

3 Lauren W. Ritterbush, "Drawn by the Bison: Late Prehistoric Native Migration into the Central Plains," *Great Plains Quarterly* 22 (Fall 2002): 259-70; Donna C. Roper, "Documentary Evidence for Changes in Protohistoric and Early Historic Pawnee Hunting Practices," *Plains Anthropologist* 37, 141 (1992), 353-66; Frison, "Clovis, Goshen, and Folsom," 103-7; Zimmerman, *Peoples of Prehistoric South Dakota*, 52-53; E. SteveCassels, *Prehistoric Hunters of the Black Hills* (Boulder: Johnson Hills, 1986), 31-42; Zimmerman, *Peoples of Prehistoric South Dakota*, 35.

4 Cassels, *Prehistoric Hunters*, 47-58; Zimmerman, *Peoples of Prehistoric South Dakota*, 30.

5 Zimmerman, *Peoples of Prehistoric South Dakota*, 2, 62; Cassels, *Prehistoric Hunters*, 64-76; Kerry Lippincott, *A Late Prehistoric Period Pronghorn Hunting Camp in the*

Southern Black Hills, South Dakota: Site 39FA23 (Pierre: South Dakota Archaeological Society, 1996).

6 P. Shawn Marceaux and Timothy K. Perttula, "Negotiating Borders: The Southern Caddo and Their Relationships with Colonial Governments in East Texas," in *American Indians and the Market Economy, 1775-1850,* ed. Lance Greene and Mark R. Plane (Tuscaloosa: University of Alabama Press, 2010), 87, 89, 92; Bradley J. Birzer, "Expanding Creative Destruction: Entrepreneurship in the American Wests," *Western Historical Quarterly* 30, 1 (Spring 1999): 45-46, 50-51; Henning, "Evolution of the Plains Village Tradition," 164; Landon Karr, Alan Outram, and L. Adrien Hannus, "Open-area Excavations at the Mitchell Prehistoric Indian Village, South Dakota (A.D. 1000-1150): New Interpretations of Site Function from Interdwelling Areas," *Journal of Field Archaeology* 36, 4 (2011): 281-88; Timothy Pauketat, "The Forgotten History of the Mississippians," in *North American Archaeology,* ed. Timothy R. Pauketat and Diana DiPaolo Loren (Malden, MA: Blackwell Publishing, 2005), 200; Robert Schneiders, "Missouri River," in *The American Midwest: An Interpretive Encyclopedia,* ed. Richard Sisson, Christian Zacher, and Andrew Cayton (Bloomington: Indiana University Press, 2007), 1,355; Irving, Emmon, and Jaggar, *Economic Resources of the Northern Black Hills,* 94.

7 Henning, "Evolution of the Plains Village Tradition," 162, 167; Zimmerman, *Peoples of Prehistoric South Dakota,* 77; John R. Bozell, "Fauna from the Hulme Site and Comments on Central Plains Tradition Subsistence Variability," *Plains Anthropologist* 36, 136 (June 1991), 229-52; John R. Bozell, "Culture, Environment, and Bison Populations on the Late Prehistoric and Early Historic Central Plains," *Plains Anthropologist* 40, 152 (1995): 145-63.

8 John Coleman, "The Missouri Valley of South Dakota: Its Human Geography at Euroamerican Contact," (Ph.D. diss., Indiana University, 1968): 86-116.

9 Angus Maddison, *The World Economy: A Millennial Perspective* (Paris: OECD, 2002), 28 (Table 1-2), 46 (Table 1-9a), 264 (Table B-21); Ola Olsson and Christopher Paik, "A Western Reversal Since the Neolithic? The Long-Run Impact of Early Agriculture," University of Warwick Working Papers Series No. 139 (June 2013).

10 Zimmerman, *Peoples of Prehistoric South Dakota,* 74.

11 P. Willey, *Prehistoric Warfare on the Great Plains: Skeletal Analysis of the Crow Creek Massacre Victims* (New York: Garland, 1990); Pauketat, "Forgotten History of the Mississippians," 190-91.

12 Henning, "Evolution of the Plains Village Tradition," 174-75.

13 Ibid., 175.

14 Diana M. Lawrence, et al, "Mitochondrial DNA of Protohistoric Remains of an Arikara Population from South Dakota: Implications for the Macro-Siouan Language Hypothesis," *Human Biology* 82, 2 (Apr. 2010): 157-78.

15 Zimmerman, *Peoples of Prehistoric South Dakota,* 123-24; Henning, "Evolution of the Plains Village Tradition," 175-76, 179-80.

16 Henning, "Evolution of the Plains Village Tradition," 174.17 Henning, "Evolution of the Plains Village Tradition," 178; Allyson Brooks, "Anticipating Mobility: How Cognitive Processes Influenced the Historic Mining Landscape in White Pine, Nevada and the Black Hills of South Dakota," (Ph.D. Diss., University of Nevada, Reno, 1995), 66; Jerome A. Greene, *Fort Randall on the Missouri, 1856-1892* (Pierre, S.D.: South Dakota State Historical Society Press, 2005), 2-3; Nelson, *After the West Was Won,* 2-3; Herbert Schell, *History of South Dakota* 4th ed. (Pierre: South Dakota State Historical Society Press, 2004), 17-18.

18 Norris, *Dakota: A Spiritual Geography,* 127.

　　　　Little Business on the Prairie

19 Gouverneur K. Warren, *Preliminary Report of Explorations in Nebraska and Dakota, in the Years 1855-'56-'57* (Washington, DC: GPO, 1875), 47.

20 Ibid., 51.

21 Bruce Forbes, "Introduction," in *Blue Star: The Story of Corabelle Fellows Teacher at Dakota Missions, 1884-1888*, ed. Kunigunde Duncan (St. Paul: Minnesota Historical Society Press, 1990), xiii.

22 Lance Greene and Mark R. Plane, "Introduction," in *American Indians and the Market Economy, 1775-1850*, ed. Lance Greene and Mark R. Plane (Tuscaloosa: University of Alabama Press, 2010), 10, 17.

23 Cody Newton, "Business in the Hinterlands: The Impact of the Market Economy on the West-Central Great Plains at the Turn of the 19th Century," in *American Indians and the Market Economy, 1775-1850*, ed. Lance Greene and Mark R. Plane (Tuscaloosa: University of Alabama Press, 2010), 67-70; Schell, *History of South Dakota*, 50; Greene, *Fort Randall on the Missouri*, 3-4; McDermott, *Journal of an Expedition to the Mauvaises Terres*, 37.

24 Warren, *Preliminary Report of Explorations*, 91.

25 Annie Abel, ed. *Chardon's Journal at Fort Clark* (Pierre: Department of History, State of South Dakota, 1932), 128, 140, 319, n. 507; Greene, *Fort Randall on the Missouri*, 6.

26 Warren, *Preliminary Report of Explorations*, 51.

27 Greene, *Fort Randall on the Missouri*, 113.

28 Warren, *Preliminary Report of Explorations*, 51-52.

29 Warren, *Preliminary Report of Explorations*, 47-48; Will G. Robinson, "Report of the Commissioner of Indian Affairs, 1880," *South Dakota Historical Collections and Report* 32 (1964), 441; Pagnamenta, *Prairie Fever*, 81; Robert J. Miller, *Reservation "Capitalism": Economic Development in Indian Country* (New York: Praeger, 2012), 29-30; Howard Lamar, *Dakota Territory, 1861-1889: A Study of Frontier Politics* (New Haven: Yale University Press, 1956), 31-32.

30 Schell, *History of South Dakota*, 24, 30; Newton, "Business in the Hinterlands," 67-70; Parker, "Early Explorations and Fur Trading," 5-211; Miller, *Looking for History*, 159-62; Michael Strezewski, "'These Indians Appear to Be Wealthy': Economy and Identity During the Late Fur-Trade Period in the Lower Great Lakes," in *American Indians and the Market Economy, 1775-1850*, ed. Lance Greene and Mark R. Plane (Tuscaloosa: University of Alabama Press, 2010.)

31 Herbert T. Hoover, "The Arrival of Capitalism on the Northern Great Plains: Pierre Chouteau, Jr. and Company," in *South Dakota Leaders: From Pierre Chouteau, Jr., to Oscar Howe*, ed. Herbert T. Hoover and Larry J. Zimmerman (Vermillion: University of South Dakota Press, 1989), 6-10; Bonilla, "A South Dakota Rendezvous," 127; Schell, *History of South Dakota*, 51.

32 Strezewski, "Economy and Identity," 21; Carlos M. Fernandez-Shaw, *The Hispanic Presence in North America from 1492 to Today* (New York: Facts on File, 1991), 179-80; Miller, *Looking for History*, 166; Lamar, *Dakota Territory, 1861-1889*, 30; Schell, *History of South Dakota*, 32-36, 51; Schneiders, *Unruly River*, 23, 28-29; Pagnamenta, *Prairie Fever*, 13; Carruth, "South Dakota: State Without End," 332; Head, *South Dakota: An Explorer's Guide*, 113; Hoover, "South Dakota," 46; Laura Ingalls Wilder, *On the Way Home: The Diary of a Trip from South Dakota to Mansfield, Missouri, in 1894* (New York: Harper & Row, 1962), 28; Lawson, *Dammed Indians*, 4.

33 Miller, *Looking for History*, 167-70. Schell, *History of South Dakota*, 53-54; Jocelyn Wills, *Boosters, Hustlers, and Speculators: Entrepreneurial Culture and the Rise of Minneapolis and St. Paul, 1849-1883* (St. Paul: Minnesota Historical Society Press, 2005), 22; VanEpps-Taylor, *Forgotten Lives*, 29.

34 Hoover, "Arrival of Capitalism," 1-13; VanEpps-Taylor, *Forgotten Lives*, 14, 21, 23-25, 35.

35 Wills, *Boosters, Hustlers, and Speculators*, 11.

36 As quoted in Parker, "Early Explorations and Fur Trading,"197.

37 Ibid., 210.

38 Kenneth M. Ames, "Tempo and Scale in the Evolution of Social Complexity in Western North America: Four Case Studies," in *North American Archaeology*, ed. Timothy R. Pauketat and Diana DiPaolo Loren (Malden, MA: Blackwell Publishing, 2005), 68; David Murray, *Indian Giving: Economies of Power in Indian-White Exchanges* (Amherst: University of Massachusetts Press, 2000), 116-40; Miller, *Reservation "Capitalism"*, 20, 24.

39 McDermott, *Journal of an Expedition to the Mauvaises Terres*, 52, 83; Will G. Robinson, "Board of Indian Commissioners Report, 1880," *South Dakota Historical Collections and Report* 32 (1964): 498; Miller, *Reservation "Capitalism"*, 12, 24; Mark R. Plane, "'Remarkable Elasticity of Character': Colonial Discourse, the Market Economy, and Catawba Itinerancy, 1770-1820," in *American Indians and the Market Economy, 1775-1850*, ed. Lance Greene and Mark R. Plane (Tuscaloosa: University of Alabama Press, 2010), 42; Will G. Robinson, "Our Indian Problem," *South Dakota Historical Collections and Report* 25 (1950), 362.

40 Will G. Robinson, "Recollections of an Adventurous Life as Told by Dennis Moran to Will G. Robinson," *South Dakota Historical Collections and Report* 24 (1949), 129.

41 As quoted in Clyde Ellis, "Five Dollars a Week to Be 'Regular Indians': Shows, Exhibitions, and the Economics of Indian Dancing, 1880-1930," in *Native Pathways: American Indian Culture and Economic Development in the Twentieth Century*, ed. Brian Hosmer and Colleen O'Neill (Boulder: University Press of Colorado, 2004), 195.

42 Siberts and Wyman, *Nothing but Prairie and Sky*, 84; Fairchild and Wyman, *Frontier Woman*, 38-39; Kunigunde Duncan, *Blue Star: The Story of Corabelle Fellows Teacher at Dakota Missions, 1884-1888* (St. Paul: Minnesota Historical Society Press, 1990), 85-86.

43 McDermott, *Journal of an Expedition to the Mauvaises Terres*, 71.

44 Wills, *Boosters, Hustlers, and Speculators*, 35; McDermott, *Journal of an Expedition to the Mauvaises Terres*, 9-12, 37; Schneiders, *Unruly River*, 33-35, 45-59; Greene, *Fort Randall on the Missouri*, 29, 46; James M. Robinson, *West from Fort Pierre: The Wild World of James (Scotty) Philip* (Los Angeles: Westernlore Press, 1974), 327.

45 Lamar, *Dakota Territory, 1861-1889*, 32-33.

46 James D. McLaird, "From Bib Overalls to Cowboy Boots: East River/West River Differences in South Dakota," *South Dakota History* 19, 4 (Winter 1989): 480; Lamar, *Dakota Territory, 1861-1889*, 33, 35, 41-42; Linda Hasselstrom, *Roadside History of South Dakota* (Missoula, MT: Mountain Press Publishing Co., 1994), 151; Gary D. Olson,"Norwegian Immigrants in Early Sioux Falls: A Demographic Profile," *Norwegian-American Studies* 36 (2011), 48; Kenneth Elton Hendrickson, Jr., "The Public Career of Richard F. Pettigrew of South Dakota, 1848-1926," (Ph.D. diss., University of Oklahoma, 1962), 1-90.

47 Robert E. Wright, *Corporation Nation* (Philadelphia: University of Pennsylvania Press, 2014).

48 Culp, *Letters from Tully*, 7, 32-33; Don L. Hofsommer, "Boosterism and Townsite Development Along the Minneapolis & St. Louis Railroad in South Dakota," *Journal of the West* 42, 4 (Fall 2003): 8-16; James F. Hamburg, "Railroads and the Settlement of South Dakota During the Great Dakota Boom, 1878-1887," *South Dakota History* 5, 2 (Spring 1975): 165-78.

49 Wills, *Boosters, Hustlers, and Speculators*, 11-12.

50 Ibid., 3-4, 9.

51 Ibid., 21, 30, 64.

52 Lamar, *Dakota Territory, 1861-1889*, 52-62; Thompson, *A New South Dakota History*, 225; Betti Carol VanEpps-Taylor, *Oscar Micheaux Dakota Homesteader, Author, Pioneer Film Maker: A Biography* (Rapid City: Dakota West Books, 1999), 34-35; Nelson, *After the West Was Won*, 8; Hofsommer, "Boosterism and Townsite Development," 8-16; Donovan L. Hofsommer, "The Watertown Express and the 'Hog and Human': M&StL Passenger Service in South Dakota, 1884-1960," *South Dakota History* 3 (Spring 1973): 127-55; Cochell and Beine, *Land of the Coyote*, 11.

53 VanEpps-Taylor, *Forgotten Lives*, 33; Doris Weatherford, ed., *A History of Women in the United States: State-by-State Reference* (Danbury, Conn.: Grolier Academic Reference, 2004), 4:405; Olson, "Norwegian Immigrants in Early Sioux Falls," 48, 71-72; Schwieder, *Growing Up with the Town*, 34; Culp, *Letters from Tully*, 88-89.

54 Nelson, *After the West Was Won*, 15-16; Lewis, *Nothing to Make a Shadow*, 70-71.

55 Newton and Jenney, *Report on the Geology and Resources*, 2; Gray-Wood, "Resource Perceptions in the Black Hills," 10.

56 Brooks, "Anticipating Mobility," 62-64; Joseph H. Cash, *Working the Homestake* (Ames: Iowa State University Press, 1973), 5-7; VanEpps-Taylor, *Forgotten Lives*, 70-71; Robert E. Driscoll, *The Black Hills of South Dakota: Its Pioneer Banking History* (New York: Newcomen Society in North America, 1951), 16-17.

57 Siberts and Wyman, *Nothing but Prairie and Sky*, 12.

58 Mandat-Grancey, *Cowboys and Colonels*, 106.

59 James J. Norton, "Gold in the Black Hills, South Dakota, and How New Deposits Might Be Found," *Geological Survey Circular* 699 (1969), 1, 10; Irving, Emmon, and Jaggar, *Economic Resources of the Northern Black Hills*, 55; Mandat-Grancey, *Cowboys and Colonels*, 120.

60 VanEpps-Taylor, *Forgotten Lives*, 73-74, 80; Mark Dugan, *The Making of Legends: More True Stories of Frontier America* (Athens: Ohio University Press, 1997), 111, 114-23; John S. McClintock, *Pioneer Days in the Black Hills: Accurate History and Facts Related by One of the Early Day Pioneers* (Deadwood, S.D.: John S. McClintock, 1939), 65-67; VanEpps-Taylor, *Oscar Micheaux Dakota Homesteader*, 46; Ian Frazier, *On the Rez* (New York: Farrar, Straus, and Giroux, 2000), 209-10; Cash, *Working the Homestake*, 61.

61 McClintock, *Pioneer Days in the Black Hills*, 65-69.

62 Siberts and Wyman, *Nothing but Prairie and Sky*, 10; McClintock, *Pioneer Days in the Black Hills*, 70.63 "Lincoln Territory (South Dakota)," in *Declarations of Independence: Encyclopedia of American Autonomous and Secessionist Movements*, ed. James L. Erwin (Westport, CN: Greenwood Press, 2007), 84-86.

64 Jesse Brown and A. M. Willard, *The Black Hills Trails: A History of the Struggles of the Pioneers in the Winning of the Black Hills* (Rapid City: Rapid City Journal Company, 1924), 461; Hyman Palais, "A Study of the Trails to the Black Hills Gold Fields," *South Dakota Historical Collections and Report* 25 (1950): 221; Hamburg, "Railroads and the Settlement of South Dakota," 166-67.

65 Brown and Willard, *The Black Hills Trails*, 460; Lewis Crawford, *The Medora-Deadwood Stage Line* (Bismarck: Capital Book Company, 1925); J. Leonard Jennewein, "Ben Ash and the Trail Blazers," *South Dakota Historical Collections and Report* 25 (1950): 300-305.

66 Robinson, *West from Fort Pierre*, 47.

67 Brown and Willard, *The Black Hills Trails*, 458-6; Palais, "A Study of the Trails to the Black Hills Gold Fields," 217-219; Miller, *Looking for History*, 164; Charles W. Bohi and H. Roger Grant, "Country Railroad Stations of the Milwaukee Road and the Chicago & North Western in South Dakota," *South Dakota History* 9, 1 (Winter 1978): 1-23; Schneiders, *Unruly River*, 60, 64-65.

68 Pagnamenta, *Prairie Fever*, 51; William W. Sanger, *The History of Prostitution: Its Extent, Causes, and Effects Throughout the World* (New York: Harper and Brothers, 1858), 374, 377, 384; Alan Gallay, *The Indian Slave Trade: The Rise of the English Empire in the American South, 1670-1717* (New Haven: Yale University Press, 2002), 28-29; Greene, *Fort Randall on the Missouri*, 28, 36, 105-6, 113, 137; VanEpps-Taylor, *Forgotten Lives*, 37-38; Siberts and Wyman, *Nothing but Prairie and Sky*, 10, 32, 143-15; Cochell and Beine, *Land of the Coyote*, 153-55; Neal Peirce and Jerry Hagstrom, "South Dakota: State of Reluctant Change," in *The Book of America: Inside Fifty States Today* (New York: W. W. Norton, 1983), 564.

69 "Plans and Laws Governing a Red Light District," Richard W. Dickenson Papers, CWS.

70 Jennifer M. Ross-Nazzal, *Winning the West for Women: The Life of Suffragist Emma Smith DeVoe* (Seattle: University of Washington Press, 2011), 14.

71 VanEpps-Taylor, *Oscar Micheaux Dakota Homesteader*, 34.

72 Siberts and Wyman, *Nothing but Prairie and Sky*, 142.

73 Ibid., 44.

74 Ibid., 145.

75 Fairchild and Wyman, *Frontier Woman*, 12-13.

76 Siberts and Wyman, *Nothing but Prairie and Sky*, 68.

77 VanEpps-Taylor, *Forgotten Lives*, 72-73; Mandat-Grancey, *Cowboys and Colonels*, 279; Hendrickson, "Public Career of Richard F. Pettigrew," 34-35; Robert J. Casey, *The Black Hills and Their Incredible Characters: A Chronicle and a Guide* (Indianapolis: Bobbs-Merrill Co., 1949), 148, 253; James Abourezk, *Advise and Dissent: Memoirs of South Dakota and the U.S. Senate* (Chicago: Lawrence Hill Books, 1989), 19; Casey, *The Black Hills and Their Incredible Characters*, 148; Brown and Willard, *The Black Hills Trails*; McClintock, *Pioneer Days in the Black Hills*, 72-73, 76; Siberts and Wyman, *Nothing but Prairie and Sky*, 50; Catherine Stock, *Main Street in Crisis: The Great Depression and the Old Middle Class on the Northern Plains* (Chapel Hill: University of North Carolina Press, 1992), 45; Lewis, *Nothing to Make a Shadow*, 148; Wuthnow, *Remaking the Heartland*, 4.

78 Frazier, *On the Rez*, 141-42; VanEpps-Taylor, *Forgotten Lives*, 78.79 Newton and Jenney, *Report on the Geology and Resources*, 317.

80 Mandat-Grancey, *Cowboys and Colonels*, 286, 345; Brown and Willard, *The Black Hills Trails*, 482-84; McClintock, *Pioneer Days in the Black Hills*, 77-79; Schatz, *Longhorns Bring Culture*, 17; Ike Blasingame, *Dakota Cowboy: My Life in the Old Days* (New York: G. P. Putnam's Sons, 1958), 7-9, 15, 37, 316.

81 Pagnamenta, *Prairie Fever*, 210, 259, 270, 273; Robinson, *West from Fort Pierre*, 94; VanEpps-Taylor, *Oscar Micheaux Dakota Homesteader*, 42; VanEpps-Taylor, *Forgotten Lives*, 119; Van Nuys, *The Family Band*, 137-39, 185.

82 Gilfillan, *Sheep*, 15; Schatz, *Longhorns Bring Culture*, 137-38; Jami Huntsinger, "Pioneering Black Hills Sheepman: Myron John Smiley," in *South Dakota Leaders: From Pierre Chouteau, Jr., to Oscar Howe*, ed. Herbert T. Hoover and Larry J. Zimmerman (Vermillion: University of South Dakota Press, 1989), 260-61.

83 Charles Roegiers and Sandy Weeldreyer, "South Dakota Sheep," *South Dakota Business Review* 47, 2 (Dec. 1988), 5; Huntsinger, "Pioneering Black Hills Sheepman," 261-62, 266; Schatz, *Longhorns Bring Culture*, 136-37.

84 VanEpps-Taylor, *Forgotten Lives*, 55; Brooks, "Anticipating Mobility," 67; L. A. Poth, *Transportation Rates, Products Transported, and Trade Barriers Important to South Dakota* (Vermillion: University of South Dakota, 1950), 11; VanEpps-Taylor, *Oscar Micheaux Dakota Homesteader*, 31-33, 40; Siberts and Wyman, *Nothing but Prairie and Sky*, 19; R. Alton Lee, *Principle Over Party: The Farmers' Alliance and Populism in South Dakota, 1880-1900* (Pierre: South Dakota State Historical Society Press, 2011), 8-9; Miller, *Looking for History*, 8; Culp, *Letters from Tully*, 63, 68-69.

85 Olson, "Norwegian Immigrants in Early Sioux Falls," 45.

86 "North and South Dakota," *New York Tribune,* Feb. 20, 1881, 6.

87 Pagnamenta, *Prairie Fever*, xv; Nelson, *After the West Was Won*, 1, 7, 13, 28, 30; Riley, "Farm Women's Roles," 92-94; Hasselstrom, *Roadside History*, 77; Siberts and Wyman, *Nothing but Prairie and Sky*, 20, 74; Fred W. Peterson, *Homes in the Heartland: Balloon Frame Farmhouses of the Upper Midwest, 1850-1920* (Lawrence: University Press of Kansas, 1992), 48-60; Fairchild and Wyman, *Frontier Woman*, 47; Lewis, *Nothing to Make a Shadow*, 93; Nelson, *The Prairie Winnows Out Its Own*, 145.

88 Thompson, *A New South Dakota History*, 226; Nelson, *After the West Was Won*, 42-50; Culp, *Letters from Tully*, 121; VanEpps-Taylor, *Oscar Micheaux Dakota Homesteader*, 34-35.

89 Culp, *Letters from Tully*, xiii, 3, 8, 10, 187-89, 196, 231; Philip S. Hall, *To Have This Land* (Vermillion: University of South Dakota Press, 1991), 10; VanEpps-Taylor, *Oscar Micheaux Dakota Homesteader*, 45.

90 Lewis, *Nothing to Make a Shadow*, 67.

91 Robinson, *West from Fort Pierre*, 155; Nelson, *After the West Was Won*, 33, 53-54; Urbanek, *The Uncovered Wagon*, 11; Bucklin, "Memoir of Frank Bloodgood," 146; Francie Berg, *South Dakota: Land of Shining Gold* (Hettinger, ND: Flying Diamond Books, 1982), 146; O'Brien, *Buffalo for the Broken Heart*, 70; Milton, *South Dakota: A Bicentennial History*, 105; Daniel Herman, *Hunting and the American Imagination* (Washington: Smithsonian Institution Press, 2001), 205.

92 Hasselstrom, *Roadside History*, 229.

93 Thompson, *A New South Dakota History*, 227; Lee, *Principle Over Party*, 11.

94 Culp, *Letters from Tully*, 13, 20; Kibbe, "Early Recollections of the Son of a Pioneer Newspaper Man," 316-25, 344-47; Miller, *Looking for History*, 55-56; Olson, "Norwegian Immigrants in Early Sioux Falls," 48-73; Hendrickson, "Public Career of Richard F.Pettigrew," 101-2; Wills, *Boosters, Hustlers, and Speculators*, 49-61, 65; McClintock, *Pioneer Days in the Black Hills*, 189-90.

95 Lynn Marie Mitchell, "William Richard Cross, Photographer on the Nebraska-South Dakota Frontier," *South Dakota History* 20, 4 (Winter 1990): 81-95.

96 Oswald, *Printing in the America*, 457-58.

97 Miller, *Looking for History*, 104.

98 VanEpps-Taylor, *Oscar Micheaux Dakota Homesteader*, 46; VanEpps-Taylor, *Forgotten Lives*, 10; Nathan Brenneise, Hardships Blessings Opportunities: A History of the Brenneise Family (1979), CWS; Hoover, "South Dakota: An Expression of Regional Heritage," 194; Phillips G. Davies, "Touring the Welsh Settlements of South Dakota, 1891," *South Dakota History* 10, 3 (Summer 1980): 223-240; Olson, "Norwegian Immigrants in Early Sioux Falls," 45-47; Hendrickson, "Public Career of Richard F. Pettigrew," 91-99; Reese, *South Dakota*, 77-78.

99 Shirley Fischer Arends, *The Central Dakota Germans: Their History, Language, and Culture* (Washington: Georgetown University Press, 1989), 33, 35-42; George Rath, *The Black Sea Germans in the Dakotas* (Freeman, SD: Pine Hill Press, 1977), 109, 133-36; Lee,

Principle Over Party, 10; Norris, *Dakota: A Spiritual Geography*, 126; Wilder, *On the Way Home*, 20-21.

100 Reese, *South Dakota*, 78; Weatherford, *A History of Women*, 4:406-7.

101 Wilder, *On the Way Home*, 20.

102 Wilder, *On the Way Home*, 22; VanEpps-Taylor, *Forgotten Lives*, 102; Kerby A. Miller, "In the Famine's Shadow: An Irish Immigrant from West Kerry to South Dakota, 1881-1979," in *Fleeing the Famine: North American and Irish Refugees, 1845-1851*, ed. Margaret Mulrooney (New York: Praeger, 2003), 124-26.

103 Hoover, "South Dakota: An Expression of Regional Heritage," 186, 200; VanEpps-Taylor, *Forgotten Lives*, 10; Reese, *South Dakota*, 76; Head, *South Dakota: An Explorer's Guide*, 21; Chai, *Hapa Girl*, 69-71, 106-8.

104 *Lewiston Daily Sun*, 29 July 1922.

105 VanEpps-Taylor, *Forgotten Lives*, 56-57, 113; Greene, *Fort Randall on the Missouri*.

106 Van Nuys, *The Family Band*, 61, 87-88, 130-33, 223; Ross-Nazzal, *Winning the West for Women*, 4-8, 14-59; Stock, *Main Street in Crisis*, 44-45.

107 Lee, *Principle Over Party*, 7, 27, 29, 36-37, 188-89; Lamar, *Dakota Territory, 1861-1889*, 233; Steven Piott, *Giving Voters a Voice: The Origins of the Initiative and Referendum in America* (Columbia: University of Missouri Press, 2003), 18

108 Cash, *Working the Homestake*, 37-38.

109 Hamburg, "Railroads and the Settlement of South Dakota,"168-69; Peter Carrels, *Uphill against Water: The Great Dakota Water War* (Lincoln: University of Nebraska Press, 1999), 4.

110 Hasselstrom, *Roadside History*, 18; McLaird, "From Bib Overalls to Cowboy Boots," 480; Brown, "The Enduring Frontier," 29.

111 Lee, *Principle Over Party*, 9, 12, 15; Kibbe, "Early Recollections of the Son of a Pioneer Newspaper Man," 339.

112 Carrels, *Uphill against Water*, 1; Robert Amerson, *From the Hidewood: Memories of a Dakota Neighborhood* (St. Paul: Minnesota Historical Society Press, 1996), 290-98; Linda Hasselstrom, *Windbreak: A Woman Rancher on the Northern Plains* (Berkeley, CA: Barn Owl Books, 1987), 232; Berg, *South Dakota: Land of Shining Gold*, 145; Bucklin, "Memoir of Frank Bloodgood," 146; Marc Cleworth, "Artesian-Well Irrigation: Its History in Brown County, South Dakota, 1889-1900," *Agricultural History* 15, 4 (Oct. 1941): 195-201.113 VanEpps-Taylor, *Forgotten Lives*, 118; Lester D. Flake, John W. Connelly, Thomas R. Kirschenmann, and Andrew J. Lindbloom, *Grouse of Plains and Mountains: The South Dakota Story* (Pierre: South Dakota Department of Game, Fish and Parks, 2010).

Chapter 3

1 Mandat-Grancey, *Cowboys and Colonels*, 116.

2 Lamar, *Dakota Territory, 1861-1889*, 268-69.

3 Albert White Hat and Travis Whirlwind Soldier, "Panel V: Revitalizing Economies, Preserving Cultures & Protecting the Environment: Striking the Balance in South Dakota & Indian Country," *Great Plains Natural Resources Journal* 7, 1 (Fall 2002): 62-63; McLaird, "From Bib Overalls to Cowboy Boots," 454-91; Norris, "South Dakota: The Long Mile," 414; Hasselstrom, *Roadside History*, 4-5.

4 Bucklin, "Memoir of Frank Bloodgood," 125-26; Raymond Orr, "The Reservation of Common Secrets: Pain and Profit in the Making of the American Indian World," (Unpublished ms., 2014); O'Brien, *Buffalo for the Broken Heart*, 67; Kathleen Ann Pickering, *Lakota Culture, World Economy* (Lincoln: University of Nebraska Press, 2000),

2-5; George Kolbenschlag, *A Whirlwind Passes: Newspaper Correspondents and the Sioux Indian Disturbances of 1890-1891* (Vermillion: University of South Dakota Press, 1990), 3-8.

5 The most complete and nuanced view that I have seen is Stuart Banner, *How the Indians Lost Their Land: Law and Power on the Frontier* (Cambridge, MA: Harvard University Press, 2005); Hall, *To Have This Land*, 3-7.

6 Warren, *Preliminary Report of Explorations*, 52.

7 Will G. Robinson, "Digest of the Report of the Commissioner of Indian Affairs, 1877," *South Dakota Historical Collections and Report* 32 (1964): 260.

8 Robinson, "Board of Indian Commissioners Report, 1880," 498.

9 Robinson, "Digest of the Report of the Commissioner of Indian Affairs, 1877," 268, 271, 385; Kolbenschlag, *A Whirlwind Passes*, 20-23.

10 Thomas Biolsi, *Organizing the Lakota: The Political Economy of the New Deal on the Pine Ridge and Rosebud Reservations* (Tucson: University of Arizona Press, 1992), 3.

11 Warren, *Preliminary Report of Explorations*, 49.

12 Kolbenschlag, *A Whirlwind Passes*, 10.

13 Culp, *Letters from Tully*, 207.

14 Nelson, *After the West Was Won*, 87.

15 Ellis, "Five Dollars a Week," 185.

16 Ibid., 194, 199.

17 Schatz, *Longhorns Bring Culture*, 47; Abourezk, *Advise and Dissent*, 10; Cary C. Collins and Charles V. Mutschler, ed., *A Doctor among the Oglala Sioux Tribe: The Letters of Robert H. Ruby, 1953-1954* (Lincoln: University of Nebraska Press, 2010), 52; Dale Peterson, *Storyville USA* (Athens: University of Georgia Press, 1999), 213; Shirk and Wadia, *Kitchen Table Entrepreneurs*, 110.

18 Schwieder, *Growing Up with the Town*, 140.

19 Brenda J. Child, *Boarding School Seasons: American Indian Families, 1900-1940* (Lincoln: University of Nebraska Press, 1998).

20 Biolsi, *Organizing the Lakota*, 126, 137-38, 142, 150-62

21 Stock, *Main Street in Crisis*, 42.

22 Ibid., 13.23 South Dakota State Planning Board and Hamlin County Planning Board, *Economic and Social Survey*, 36.

24 Ibid., 38.

25 Culp, *Letters from Tully*, 73.

26 "J. B. Jones Stays On to Become Leading Land Agent Here," *Lyman County Herald*, 25 Aug. 1955.

27 Douglas Chittick, *Growth and Decline of South Dakota Trade Centers, 1901-51* (Brookings: South Dakota State College, Rural Sociology Department Bulletin 448, May 1955), 26; Nelson, *After the West Was Won*, 11; Hagerty, *Territory of Dakota*, 96.

28 Siberts and Wyman, *Nothing but Prairie and Sky*, 87; Fairchild and Wyman, *Frontier Woman*, 10; Nelson, *The Prairie Winnows Out Its Own*, 103; Culp, *Letters from Tully*, 9-10.

29 Schwieder, *Growing Up with the Town*, 33; Michael P. Conzen, "Understanding Great Plains Urbanization Through the Lens of South Dakota Townscapes," *Journal of Geography* 109 (Jan.-Feb. 2010), 3-17.

30 Graham Russell Gao Hodges, *Taxi!: A Social History of the New York City Cabdriver* (New York: New York University Press, 2007); Sioux Falls City Street Railway Company, Box 2, Bessie Pettigrew Collection, CWS.

31 David M. Smith, "Mills Family Closing 45 Years of Transit Service Here," *Sioux Falls Daily Argus-Leader*, 14 Sept. 1952.

32 Obituary, *Sioux Falls Argus Leader*, Oct. 21, 1929; "A Five Cent Lawsuit," *The Press*, Sept. 1912; *Sioux Falls Journal*, n.d. p. 3, Frank Moody Mills Collection, CWS.

33 David M. Smith, "Mills Family Closing 45 Years of Transit Service Here," *Sioux Falls Daily Argus-Leader*, 14 Sept. 1952.

34 Schwieder, *Growing Up with the Town*, 38, 48-51; Culp, *Letters from Tully*, 122-26; Bucklin, "Memoir of Frank Bloodgood," 136; Fairchild and Wyman, *Frontier Woman*, 84-85; Norris, *Dakota: A Spiritual Geography*, 138.

35 Schwieder, *Growing Up with the Town*, 39-40; Nelson, *The Prairie Winnows Out Its Own*, 80-81; VanEpps-Taylor, *Forgotten Lives*, 63.

36 Nelson, *The Prairie Winnows Out Its Own*, 80.

37 Orlando J. Goering and Violet Miller Goering, "Keeping the Faith: Bertha Martinsky in West River South Dakota," *South Dakota History* 25, 1 (Spring 1995): 37-48.

38 Nelson, *The Prairie Winnows Out Its Own*, 44; Fairchild and Wyman, *Frontier Woman*, 84; Lewis, *Nothing to Make a Shadow*, 31; Rath, *Black Sea Germans in the Dakotas*, 108-9; Miller, *Looking for History*, 185, 187-88.

39 Siberts and Wyman, *Nothing but Prairie and Sky*, 123.

40 Lewis, *Nothing to Make a Shadow*, 23, 141; Nelson, *After the West Was Won*, 31; Kolbenschlag, *A Whirlwind Passes*, 15-16; Stock, *Main Street in Crisis*, 54; Schwieder, *Growing Up with the Town*, 47; "Earl Roberts in Business Since 1909," *Lyman County Herald*, 25 Aug. 1955; Maurine Hoffman Beasley, "Life as a Hired Girl in South Dakota, 1907-1908: A Woman Journalist Reflects," *South Dakota History* 12, 2 (Summer 1982): 152-53.

41 Weatherford, *A History of Women*, 4:405.

42 Fairchild and Wyman, *Frontier Woman*, 112.

43 Culp, *Letters from Tully*, 21; Abourezk, *Advise and Dissent*, 15-16; Nelson, *The Prairie Winnows Out Its Own*, 45-46.

44 Wilder, *On the Way Home*, 6; Cochell and Beine, *Land of the Coyote*, 12.45 Edwin J. Perkins, *Wall Street to Main Street: Charles Merrill and Middle-Class Investors* (New York: Cambridge University Press, 1999), 1-2, 100-26; Stock, *Main Street in Crisis*, 155-56.

46 Miller, *Looking for History*, 119-21; Chittick, *Growth and Decline, 1901-51*, 11.

47 Siberts and Wyman, *Nothing but Prairie and Sky*, 11.

48 Chittick, *Growth and Decline, 1901-51*, 12; Paul H. Landis, *The Growth and Decline of South Dakota Trade Centers, 1901-1933*, Bulletin 279 (Brookings: South Dakota State College of Agriculture, 1933), 4, 14, 20, 24-25, 32-33; Nelson, *The Prairie Winnows Out Its Own*, 93, 110; Miller, *Looking for History*, 38.

49 Chittick, *Growth and Decline, 1901-51*, 12, 28, 34-37; Landis, *Growth and Decline, 1901-1933*, 3, 10-14; Hamburg, "Railroads and the Settlement of South Dakota,"176; Conzen, "Understanding Great Plains Urbanization," 3-17; Donald C. Miller, *Ghosts on a Sea of Grass: Ghost Towns of the Plains* (Missoula, MT: Pictorial Histories Publishing Company, 1990), 182; Karolevitz, *Challenge: The South Dakota Story*, 182-206; Yvette Cardozo and Bill Hirsch, "A Midwinter Night's Dream," *South Florida Sun-Sentinel*, 19 Jan. 1986, 1J.

50 Herzog, *Small World*, 58.

51 Norris, *Dakota: A Spiritual Geography*, 53.

52 Robert F. Karolevitz, "The Human Dimension," in *Communities Left Behind: Alternatives for Development*, ed. Larry R. Whiting (Ames: Iowa State University Press, 1974), 22-27.

53 Norris, "South Dakota: The Long Mile," 416.

54 Kenneth P. Wilkinson, "Consequences of Decline and Social Adjustment to It," in *Communities Left Behind: Alternatives for Development*, ed. Larry R. Whiting (Ames: Iowa State University Press, 1974), 47-48; Brokaw, *A Long Way From Home*, 20.

55 Nelson, *After the West Was Won*, 83.

56 Nelson, *After the West Was Won*, 90; Nelson, *The Prairie Winnows Out Its Own*, 81; Schwieder, *Growing Up with the Town*, 41; U.S. National Park Service, *Wind Cave National Park, South Dakota* (Washington: U.S. Department of the Interior, 1979), 53.

57 Schwieder, *Growing Up with the Town*, x, 108.

58 Kolbenschlag, *A Whirlwind Passes*, 18-19.

59 Miller, "In the Famine's Shadow," 126.

60 VanEpps-Taylor, *Forgotten Lives*, 135.

61 Nelson, *The Prairie Winnows Out Its Own*, 76-77; Riley, "Farm Women's Roles," 86-87.

62 Stanley H. Edmunds, "Well! What Do Ya Call That?": An Introduction to the Motor Age (1970), Stanley H. Edmunds Collection, CWS; Robert Orr, "A History of Aviation in South Dakota," (M.A. thesis, University of South Dakota, 1957), 24; Grant, *Down and Out on the Family Farm*, 13.

63 Carruth, "South Dakota: State without End," 335.

64 Nelson, *The Prairie Winnows Out Its Own*, 175.

65 Urbanek, *The Uncovered Wagon*, 14.

66 Miller, *Looking for History*, 8, 10-12, 16, 47.

67 Foss and Foss, *A Proud American*, 12-13, 19; "Reminiscences of Irene Mortenson Sargent," (1990), Edith Mortenson Delman Collection, CWS; Hasselstrom, *Windbreak: A Woman Rancher*, 232-33; Charles Rogers, *South Dakota's Challenges Since 1960* (Garretson, SD: Sanders Printing Co., 2011), 298; Stephen van Dulken, *Inventing the 19th Century: 100 Inventions that Shaped the Victorian Age* (New York: New York University Press, 2001); B. Zorina Khan, *The Democratization of Invention: Patents and Copyrights in American Economic Development, 1790-1920* (New York: Cambridge University Press, 2005).

68 All of the patents discussed here were found using Google's patent search engine.

69 Readers can search them at http://patft.uspto.gov/netahtml/PTO/search-bool.html using the state code SD in the inventor field. Unfortunately, patents issued between 1790 and 1975 are searchable only by issue date, patent number, and classification.

70 Lauck, *Prairie Republic*, 42.

71 Fite, "Observations by a Native Son," 468; Daniel Simundson, "The Yellow Press on the Prairie: South Dakota Daily Newspaper Editorials Prior to the Spanish-American War," *South Dakota History* 2, 3 (Summer 1972): 211-29; Brown and Willard, *The Black Hills Trails*, 486-89; Nelson, *After the West Was Won*, 84; Cochell and Beine, *Land of the Coyote*, 29; James Richard Smith, "Some Changing Features of a Regional Capital: Sioux Falls, South Dakota, 1920-1970," (Ph.D. diss., University of Nebraska, 1971), 132-34; Miller, *Looking for History*, 36-37.

72 *Will A. Beach Printing Co., 1889-1939*, William Beach Locke Collection, CWS.

73 Brooks, "Anticipating Mobility," 72; Mildred Fielder, *Railroads of the Black Hills* (Seattle: Superior Publishing Co., 1964), 70-78, 88.

74 Irving, Emmon, and Jaggar, *Economic Resources of the Northern Black Hills*, 54; Chai, *Hapa Girl*, 122; VanEpps-Taylor, *Forgotten Lives*, 72-73; South Dakota Board of Regents, *Foundation for the Future*, 11; Mandat-Grancey, *Cowboys and Colonels*, 268-69; Lincoln R. Page et al, *Pegmatite Investigations 1942-1945: Black Hills, South Dakota* (Washington: United States Government Printing Office, 1953), 4.

75 Irving, Emmon, and Jaggar, *Economic Resources of the Northern Black Hills*, 53, 95, 163-64; Brown and Willard, *The Black Hills Trails*, 489-90; Casey, *The Black Hills and Their Incredible Characters*, 136; Van Nuys, *The Family Band*, 225-26; David Wolff, "No Matter How You Do It, Fraud Is Fraud: Another Look at Black Hills Mining Scandals," *South Dakota History* 33, 2 (Summer 2003), 97-107; Page, *Pegmatite Investigations*, 5-6; Arthur E. Smith and Eric Fritzsch, "South Dakota," *Rocks & Minerals* 75 (May/June 2000): 156-69; T.V. Durkin, E. H. Holm, and B. A. Regynski, "South Dakota," *Mining Engineering* 49, 5 (May 1997), 73.

76 Irving, Emmon, and Jaggar, *Economic Resources of the Northern Black Hills*, 14; R. W. Stone et al, *Gypsum Deposits of the United States*, Geological Survey Bulletin No. 697, (Washington, D.C.: Government Printing Office, 1920), 42-43; J. G. Hutton, "South Dakota," in *Gypsum Deposits of the United States*, Geological Survey Bulletin No. 697, ed. R. W. Stone, et al (Washington, D.C.: Government Printing Office, 1920), 239-49.

77 Culp, *Letters from Tully*, 138.

78 Newton and Jenney, *Report on the Geology and Resources*, 324; Milton, *South Dakota: A Bicentennial History*, 154; P.D. Peterson, *Through the Black Hills and Bad Lands of South Dakota* (Pierre: J. Fred Olander Company, 1929), 165; Gray-Wood, "Resource Perceptions in the Black Hills," 15-16; Citibank, *South Dakota: The Business and Living Environment* (1981), Box 4, Dave Stenseth/EROS Collection, CWS.

79 Peterson, *Through the Black Hills and Bad Lands*, 57-59; Carrels, *Uphill against Water*, 6; D. B. Pratt, "Beet Sugar; South Dakota's New Industry," *The Black Hills Engineer* 15, 2 (1928): 65-80.

80 Berg, *South Dakota: Land of Shining Gold*, 77; Cash, *Working the Homestake*, ix-x, 55-56, 62-63, 80-99, 100-109.

81 Irving, Emmon, and Jaggar, *Economic Resources of the Northern Black Hills*, 58-59; Fielder, *Railroads of the Black Hills*, 69; Cash, *Working the Homestake*, 25; Mandat-Grancey, *Cowboys and Colonels*, 146-50.82 Irving, Emmon, and Jaggar, *Economic Resources of the Northern Black Hills*, 92-93; Norton, "Gold in the Black Hills," 2; Cash, *Working the Homestake*, 110; Durkin, Holm, and Regynski, "South Dakota," 73; E. H. Holm, T. Cline, Jr., M. Macy, and R. Fivecoate, "South Dakota," *Mining Engineering* 59, 5 (May 2007): 111; Thomas A. Loomis, "The Ross Hannibal Mine, Lawrence County, South Dakota," *Mineralogical Record* 30, 3 (May/June 1999), 199-206.

83 Mandat-Grancey, *Cowboys and Colonels*, 286; Casey, *The Black Hills and Their Incredible Characters*, 285; Kibbe, "Early Recollections of the Son of a Pioneer Newspaper Man," 334-35; "Dickensen's Café and Bakery," in Charles A. Smith, *A Comprehensive History of Minnehaha County, South Dakota*, 233-34 in Richard W. Dickenson Papers, CWS; Divorce Legislation in South Dakota, CWS.

84 Siberts and Wyman, *Nothing but Prairie and Sky*, 46-49; Fairchild and Wyman, *Frontier Woman*, 63-64.

85 Cochell and Beine, *Land of the Coyote*, 133-42; Lewis, *Nothing to Make a Shadow*, 36; Siberts and Wyman, *Nothing but Prairie and Sky*, 54, 59-61, 87, 94.

86 Siberts and Wyman, *Nothing but Prairie and Sky*, 90.

87 Ibid., 94-96, 105.

88 Ibid., 116-17, 124-26, 136; Fairchild and Wyman, *Frontier Woman*, 23-24, 101.

89 Schatz, *Longhorns Bring Culture*, 29; Siberts and Wyman, *Nothing but Prairie and Sky*, 141.

90 Schatz, *Longhorns Bring Culture*, 23-24, 44-45, 48.

91 Ibid., 67-75; Blasingame, *Dakota Cowboy*, 291, 315; Carruth, "South Dakota: State Without End," 333.

92 Siberts and Wyman, *Nothing but Prairie and Sky*, 31, 41, 47, 59, 67, 75, 112.

93 Schatz, *Longhorns Bring Culture*, 96-105; Fairchild and Wyman, *Frontier Woman*, 43; "In the Valley of the Jim: Story of the Dowdell Family" (1951), Dowdell Family Collection, CWS; Hasselstrom, *Windbreak: A Woman Rancher*, 168; Abourezk, *Advise and Dissent*, 73; Bob Lee, *Last Grass Frontier Volume II: The South Dakota Stockgrowers Heritage* (Sturgis: Black Hills Publishers, Inc., 1999), 1, 62.

94 VanEpps-Taylor, *Forgotten Lives*, 95; Karolevitz, *Challenge: The South Dakota Story*, viii; Miller, *Looking for History*, 96, 104, 116-19; VanEpps-Taylor, *Oscar Micheaux Dakota Homesteader*, 52; Carruth, "South Dakota: State Without End," 337; M. J. Andersen, *Portable Prairie: Confessions of an Unsettled Midwesterner* (New York: St. Martin's Press, 2005), 9; Nelson, *After the West Was Won*, 84; Miller, *Ghosts on a Sea of Grass*, 204.

95 VanEpps-Taylor, *Oscar Micheaux Dakota Homesteader*, 50-51.

96 South Dakota State Planning Board, *Mortgage Status of Farm Land in South Dakota* (1938), 7.

97 Ibid., 7, 20, 30, 32; A. E. Dahl, *Banker Dahl of South Dakota: An Autobiography* (Rapid City: Fenske Book Company, 1965), 52; Nelson, *The Prairie Winnows Out Its Own*, 5-7, 19-20.

98 Gooder Casey Land Co., *Southwestern South Dakota*.

99 Nelson, *After the West Was Won*, 32-33.

100 Gooder Casey Land Co., *Southwestern South Dakota*.

101 VanEpps-Taylor, *Oscar Micheaux Dakota Homesteader*, 70-72.

102 Robert E. Wright, "Corporate Citizens: South Dakota Chartermongering in the Early Twentieth Century," in *Plains Political Tradition: Essays on South Dakota Political Culture Volume 2*, ed. Jon Lauck, John E. Miller, and Donald C. Simmons, Jr. (Pierre:South Dakota State Historical Society Press, 2014); "Corporation Assessment Lists, 1909-1915," Roll 15/Volume 29, Records of the Internal Revenue Service, RG 58, NARA.

103 Weatherford, *A History of Women*, 4:413; Carruth, "South Dakota: State Without End," 335; Gilbert Fite, "The Transformation of South Dakota Agriculture: The Effects of Mechanization, 1939-1964," *South Dakota History* 19 (Fall 1989), 291; Miller, *Looking for History*, 120.

104 Doane Robinson, *History of South Dakota* (Indianapolis: B. F. Bowen, 1904), 1:481.

105 Ibid., 1:481-83.

106 Fairchild and Wyman, *Frontier Woman*, 54-55; Nelson, *After the West Was Won*, 65; "Telephone Was Only Luxury," *Lyman County Herald,* 25 Aug. 25 1955.

107 Cochell and Beine, *Land of the Coyote*, 109-120.

108 Nelson, *The Prairie Winnows Out Its Own*, 67-70, 71, 73.

109 Richard T. Read and David Rambow, "Hydrogen and Smoke: A Survey of Lighter-Than-Air Flight in South Dakota Prior to World War I," 18, 3 *South Dakota History* (2008): 132-51.

110 Read and Rambow, "Hydrogen and Smoke," 132-51.

111 Orr, "A History of Aviation in South Dakota," 5-7.

112 For additional information on the incident, see Clear Lake Balloon Incident, CWS.

113 Orr, "A History of Aviation in South Dakota," 15-30.

114 Ibid., 25-55.

115 Ibid., 86-102.

116 Ibid., 86, 106-17; S. Russell Halley to Nellie Zabel Willhite, June 22, 1939, Nellie Zabel Willhite Collection, CWS.

117 Foss and Foss, *A Proud American*, 30; Orr, "A History of Aviation in South Dakota," 57-59, 63.

118 Orr, "A History of Aviation in South Dakota," 64-79, 103; Foss and Foss, *A Proud American*, 31.

119 Orr, "A History of Aviation in South Dakota," 78; Nellie Zabel Willhite to Charles E. Planck, Oct. 30, 1941, Nellie Zabel Willhite Pilot's Log, Jacqueline Cochran to Nellie Zabel Willhite, Mar. 13, 1942, Nellie Zabel Willhite Collection, CWS.

120 Orr, "A History of Aviation in South Dakota," 57, 104, 132-36; Foss and Foss, *A Proud American*, 38; Smith, "Some Changing Features of a Regional Capital," 156-59.

121 W.K. Gray, A. A. Volk, A.M. Dreyer, M. L. White, and V. E. Montgomery, *South Dakota Economic and Business Abstract, 1939-1962* (Vermillion: Business Research Bureau, 1963), 56; Nelson, *The Prairie Winnows Out Its Own*, 121-23.

122 Thompson, *A New South Dakota History*, 231-32; Brown, "The Enduring Frontier," 29.

123 As quoted in Nelson, *The Prairie Winnows Out Its Own*, 147.

124 Sherwood Anderson, "Revolt in South Dakota," in *The Anxious Years: America in the Nineteen Thirties, a Collection of Contemporary Writings*, ed. Louis Filler (New York: Capricorn Books, 1963), 34-35; Stock, *Main Street in Crisis*, 12; Grant, *Down and Out on the Family Farm*, 23; Fite, "Observations by a Native Son," 458; Nelson, *The Prairie Winnows Out Its Own*, 120.

125 Beasley, "Life as a Hired Girl in South Dakota," 148-62.

126 Choate, "Debt, Drought, and Depression," 34.

127 Donald C. Simmons, Jr., "McGovern's Upbringing in South Dakota: The Making of a Political Mind," in *George McGovern: A Political Life, a Political Legacy*, ed. Robert P. Watson (Pierre: South Dakota State Historical Society Press, 2004), 1-2; Choate, "Debt,Drought, and Depression," 34; Grant, *Down and Out on the Family Farm*, 43; South Dakota State Planning Board, *Mortgage Status*, 13-15.

128 Grant, *Down and Out on the Family Farm*, 16-18; South Dakota State Planning Board and Hamlin County Planning Board, *Economic and Social Survey*, 46-52; Dahl, *Banker Dahl*, 24.

129 South Dakota State Planning Board, *Mortgage Status*, 18.

130 Grant, *Down and Out on the Family Farm*, 3, 17, 36-37; Choate, "Debt, Drought, and Depression," 36.

131 South Dakota State Planning Board, *Mortgage Status*, 18.

132 Nelson, *The Prairie Winnows Out Its Own,* 146, 165; Choate, "Debt, Drought, and Depression," 42.

133 Dahl, *Banker Dahl*, 81; Schwieder, *Growing Up with the Town*, 70; Anderson, "Revolt in South Dakota," 37; Choate, "Debt, Drought, and Depression," 38; Weatherford, *A History of Women*, 4:410; Herbert S. Schell, "Adjustment Problems in South Dakota," *Agricultural History* 14 (Apr. 1940): 71.

134 Grant, *Down and Out on the Family Farm*, 8, 9, 25, 29; South Dakota State Planning Board and Hamlin County Planning Board, *Economic and Social Survey*, 39.

135 Culp, *Letters from Tully*, 198-206.

136 Nelson, *The Prairie Winnows Out Its Own*, 178-79, 202; O'Brien, *Buffalo for the Broken Heart*, 6-7, 11; Gerald A. Doeksen, John Kuehn, and Joseph Schmidt, "Consequences of Decline and Community Economic Adjustment to It," in *Communities Left Behind: Alternatives for Development*, ed. Larry R. Whiting (Ames: Iowa State University Press, 1974), 32.

137 Schwieder, *Growing Up with the Town*, 67-68; Nelson, *The Prairie Winnows Out Its Own*, 134-44; Calvin L. Beale, "Quantitative Dimensions of Decline and Stability Among Rural Communities," in *Communities Left Behind: Alternatives for Development*, ed.

Little Business on the Prairie

Larry R. Whiting (Ames: Iowa State University Press, 1974), 5; Urbanek, *The Uncovered Wagon*, 59.

138 "Reminiscences of Irene Mortenson Sargent," (1990), Edith Mortenson Delman Collection, CWS.

139 Lisa Lindell, "'So Long as I Can Read'": Farm Women's Reading Experiences in Depression-Era South Dakota," *Agricultural History* (Fall 2009): 503-27; Andersen, *Portable Prairie*, 12-13; Schwieder, *Growing Up with the Town*, 72-73; Dorothy Schwieder, "South Dakota Farm Women and the Great Depression," *Journal of the West* 24 (Oct. 1985): 6-18.

140 Schwieder, *Growing Up with the Town*, 126.

141 Anderson, "Revolt in South Dakota," 34.

142 Ibid., 38-39.

Chapter 4

1 Lee, *Last Grass Frontier*, 1.

2 Arends, *The Central Dakota Germans*, 34; Peirce and Hagstrom, "South Dakota: State of Reluctant Change," 560; Donald C. Dahlin, "The 1982 Gubernatorial Election in South Dakota," in *Re-Electing the Governor: The 1982 Elections*, ed. Thad L. Beyle (New York: University Press of America, 1986), 281; Jon K. Lauck, *Prairie Republic: The Political Culture of Dakota Territory, 1879-1889* (Norman: University of Oklahoma Press, 2010), 168; H. Roger Grant, "Origins of a Progressive Reform: The Initiative and Referendum Movement in South Dakota," *South Dakota History* 3, 4 (Fall 1973): 390-407; RichBraunstein, *Initiative and Referendum Voting: Governing Through Direct Democracy in the United States* (New York: LFB Scholarly Publishing, 2004), 37-38, 41-42, 141; Thompson, *A New South Dakota History*, 204.

3 Robert Sam Anson, *McGovern: A Biography* (New York: Holt, Rinehart and Winston, 1972), 70.

4 Robert E. Burns and Herbert E. Cheever, Jr., "South Dakota: Conflict and Cooperation Among Conservatives," in *Interest Group Politics in the Midwestern States*, ed. Robert Hrebenar and Clive Thomas (Ames: Iowa State Press, 1993), 287; Richard Richardson, *Policy and Performance in American Higher Education* (Baltimore: Johns Hopkins University Press, 2009), 119-44; Schell, *History of South Dakota*, 370; Alan Clem, *Government by the People?: South Dakota Politics in the Last Third of the Twentieth Century* (Rapid City: Chiesman Foundation for Democracy, 2002), 17; Hoover, "South Dakota: An Expression of Regional Heritage," 202-3.

5 Karolevitz, *Challenge: The South Dakota Story*, v; Reese, *South Dakota*, vii.

6 Anson, *McGovern*, 69.

7 Burns and Cheever, "South Dakota: Conflict and Cooperation," 289.

8 John Gunther, *Inside U.S.A.* (New York: Harper & Brothers, 1947), 248.

9 "A Political Plot," Sioux Falls, 10 Oct. 1904, Jeannette L. Agrant Collection, CWS; Changing Social Patterns on the Lingering Frontier Records, CWS.

10 Burns and Cheever, "South Dakota: Conflict and Cooperation," 285.

11 Mary Lu Abbott, "South Dakota Surprises," *Houston Chronicle,* 10 Aug. 1986, 1.

12 Fite, "Observations by a Native Son," 469.

13 Karolevitz, *Challenge: The South Dakota Story*, 297.

14 As quoted in Anson, *McGovern*, 69.

15 Allan Mathews, "Agrarian Radicals: The United Farmers League of South Dakota," *South Dakota History* 3 (Fall 1973), 408-21; Simmons, "McGovern's Upbringing in South Dakota," 2; Valerie R. O'Regan and Stephen J. Stambough, "From the Grassroots: Building

the South Dakota Democratic Party," in *George McGovern: A Political Life, a Political Legacy,* ed. Robert P. Watson (Pierre: South Dakota State Historical Society Press, 2004), 38-43; Anson, *McGovern,* 69-74; Karolevitz, *Challenge: The South Dakota Story,* 299, 302.

16 Dehgan, *America in Quotations,* 52.

17 Simmons, *"McGovern's* Upbringing in South Dakota," 2.

18 Schell, *History of South Dakota,* 370; Department of Political Science and Government Research Bureau, *A White Paper Report: County Consolidation in South Dakota* (Vermillion: University of South Dakota, 1997), vi, 7-11, 37-38; State and Local Government Task Force, *Report to the South Dakota Legislature* (Pierre: 2005), 4.

19 South Dakota State Planning Board and Hamlin County Planning Board, *Economic and Social Survey,* 3, 14.

20 Clem, *Government by the People?,* i.

21 McLaird, "From Bib Overalls to Cowboy Boots," 475.

22 Fairchild and Wyman*, Frontier Woman,* 19.

23 Lamar, *Dakota Territory, 1861-1889,* 153-61; Abourezk, *Advise and Dissent,* 11.

24 Lyle M. Bender, "Tooling Up for Tomorrow's Job," *Journal of Farm Economics* 39, 5 (Dec. 1957), 1,698.

25 Peirce and Hagstrom, "South Dakota: State of Reluctant Change," 562; Alan Clem, *Prairie State Politics: Popular Democracy in South Dakota* (Washington, D.C.: Public Affairs Press, 1967), 73; Reese, *South Dakota,* 50; Amerson, *From the Hidewood,* x;Lauck, *Prairie Republic,* 14-15, 24-27, 40, 43; Schwieder, *Growing Up with the Town,* 124-25.

26 As quoted in Nelson, *After the West Was Won,* 15.

27 As quoted in Nelson, *After the West Was Won,* 42.

28 Hagerty, *Territory of Dakota,* 116.

29 Robert Higgs, *Crisis and Leviathan: Critical Episodes in the Growth of American Government* (New York: Oxford University Press, 1987).

30 Lamar, *Dakota Territory, 1861-1889,* 75; Clem, *Prairie State Politics,* 9-10, 134; Clem, *Government by the People?,* 24-28; Burns and Cheever, "South Dakota: Conflict and Cooperation," 288.

31 Clem, *Prairie State Politics,* 136.

32 Cochell and Beine, *Land of the Coyote,* 18.

33 Julia B. McGillycuddy, *McGillycuddy Agent: A Biography of Dr. Valentine T. McGillycuddy* (Stanford: Stanford University Press, 1941), 5.

34 Abourezk, *Advise and Dissent,* 200.

35 Vine Deloria, Jr., Collection, CWS.

36 Pickering, *Lakota Culture, World Economy,* xi-xiv, 5, 10, 14, 21, 24-25, 27, 33, 35-36, 44-51, 60-76, 96-103, 127-32, 136-39; Foss and Foss, *A Proud American,* 218; Terry L. Anderson, *Sovereign Nations or Reservations?: An Economic History of American Indians* (San Francisco: Pacific Research Institute for Public Policy, 1995).

37 Peirce and Hagstrom, "South Dakota: State of Reluctant Change," 566.

38 McGillycuddy, *McGillycuddy Agent,* 7.

39 Lawson, *Dammed Indians,* 27-29, 45-59; Jim Pollock, "Rebirth of a South Dakota Town," *South Dakota History* 19, 3 (Fall 1989): 342-61; "Sioux Nation Loses Land in South Dakota," *Canadian Mennonite,* 10 May 1999, 15; Andrea Cook, "Oglala Sioux Tribe Evicting Tribal Ranchers to Make Way for Bison Park," *Chadron Record,* 5 Dec. 2013.

40 Michael Lawson, "The Fractionated Estate: The Problem of American Indian Heirship," in *The Sioux in South Dakota History,* ed. Richmond L. Clow (Pierre: South Dakota Historical Society Press, 2007): 45-86.

41 Lawson, *Dammed Indians*, 39; Siberts and Wyman, *Nothing but Prairie and Sky*, 33; Don Southerton, "James R. Walker's Campaign Against Tuberculosis on the Pine Ridge Indian Reservation," in *The Sioux in South Dakota History,* ed. Richmond L. Clow (Pierre: South Dakota Historical Society Press, 2007): 141-56; Shirk and Wadia, *Kitchen Table Entrepreneurs*, 112.

42 McGillycuddy, *McGillycuddy Agent*, 12.

43 Joshua Garrett-Davis, "The Red Power Movement and the Yankton Sioux Industries Pork-Processing Plant Takeovers of 1975," in *The Sioux in South Dakota History*, ed. Richmond L. Clow (Pierre: South Dakota Historical Society Press, 2007): 271-304.

44 Collins and Mutschler, *A Doctor Among the Oglala*, 131, 148, 214, 239-44, 289-90, 297, 303.

45 Frazier, *On the Rez*, 28-31.

46 Schultz, *1,000 Places to See*, 655; Schell, *History of South Dakota*, 364; George Lazarus, "Dakota Beer Sales Go Flat for Miller," *Chicago Tribune*, 3 Feb. 1987; Norris, *Dakota: A Spiritual Geography*, 30; Peterson, *Storyville USA*, 213.

47 Miller, *Reservation "Capitalism,"* 94, 123; Harvard Project on American Indian Economic Development, *The State of the Native Nations: Conditions Under U.S. Policies of Self-Determination* (New York: Oxford University Press, 2008), 69-81; Pickering, *Lakota Culture, World Economy*, 17-18; Shirk and Wadia, *Kitchen Table Entrepreneurs*, 111; *25th Annual Report of the Employment Security Department of South Dakota* (1961),17; Frazier, *On the Rez*, 169-72, 250; Sebastian Braun, *Buffalo Inc.: American Indians and Economic Development* (Norman: Oklahoma University Press, 2008).

48 Miller, *Reservation "Capitalism,"* 113; Lisa Little Chief Bryan, *American Indian Entrepreneurs: Rosebud and Pine Ridge Reservations Case Studies* (Pablo, MT: Salish Kootenai College Press, 1999), 77; Frazier, *On the Rez*, 102-3; Shirk and Wadia, *Kitchen Table Entrepreneurs*, 106-29.

49 Shirk and Wadia, *Kitchen Table Entrepreneurs*, 109.

50 Frazier, *On the Rez*, 64.

51 Peterson, *Storyville USA*, 209-12, 215; Frazier, *On the Rez*, 59; U.S. Department of the Interior, Indian Arts and Crafts Board, *Native American Owned and Operated Arts and Crafts Businesses, Source Directory*, 1982-83 Edition, in Ben Reifel Collection, CWS.

52 Miller, *Reservation "Capitalism"*, 129.

53 Shirk and Wadia, *Kitchen Table Entrepreneurs*, 115.

54 Warren Bareiss, "Alternative Radio and Television in South Dakota: A Place Study of Public Service Electronic Media in the US," in *No News Is Bad News: Radio, Television and the Public*, ed. Michael Bromley (New York: Routledge, 2001), 229-30; Frazier, *On the Rez*, 51-52, 93, 108, 253; Bryan, *American Indian Entrepreneurs*, 77-78.

55 Rogers, *South Dakota's Challenges Since 1960*, 344; Allen Neuharth, "Open Letter to Mom: You CAN Go Home," *USA Today,* 22 June 1987, 8A; Bryan, *American Indian Entrepreneurs*, 91-93, 100; Frazier, *On the Rez*, 252-53.

56 Hernando de Soto, *The Mystery of Capital: Why Capitalism Triumphs in the West and Fails Everywhere Else* (New York: Basic Books, 2000).

57 David Benson, Aaron K. Lies, Albert A. Okunade, and Phanindra V. Wunnava, "Economic Impact of a Private Sector Micro-financing Scheme in South Dakota," *Small Business Economics* 36 (2011): 157-68; Collins and Mutschler, *A Doctor Among the Oglala*, 52; Steve Cocheo, "Justice Department Sues Tiny South Dakota Bank for Loan Bias," *ABA Banking Journal* (Jan. 1994), 6, 9.

58 Sandy Gerber, "Native CDFIs Work Toward a New Economic Reality in South Dakota," *Community Dividend* 3 (2008), 1, 6-8.

59 Carrels, *Uphill against Water*, xi, 24-26.

60 Johnson, *Highways and Byways*, 266.

61 Carrels, *Uphill against Water*, xiii.

62 Ibid., 25.

63 Ibid., 170.

64 Schell, *History of South Dakota*, 366.

65 Carrels, "South Dakota Farmers Reject a Free Lunch," 119-27.

66 Burns and Cheever, "South Dakota: Conflict and Cooperation," 290; Clem, *Government by the People?*, 17.

67 Clem, *Government by the People?*, 18.

68 "In the Valley of the Jim: Story of the Dowdell Family" (1951), Dowdell Family Collection, CWS.

69 Clem, *Government by the People?*, 19, 134-36.

70 Siberts and Wyman, *Nothing but Prairie and Sky*, 37.

71 John Painter, "Transitional Sioux Leader: Benjamin Reifel," in *South Dakota Leaders: From Pierre Chouteau, Jr., to Oscar Howe*, ed. Herbert T. Hoover and Larry J. Zimmerman (Vermillion: University of South Dakota Press, 1989), 331, 351; Ben Reifel Collection, CWS.

72 "South Dakota's New Executive Is Termed Second Will Rogers," Salt Lake City *Deseret News*, 16 Feb. 1933; Nelson, *The Prairie Winnows Out Its Own*, 139.73 Karolevitz, *Challenge: The South Dakota Story*, 302; Abourezk, *Advise and Dissent*, ix, 8, 17, 13-14, 20-21.

74 Abourezk, *Advise and Dissent*, x.

75 Riley, "Farm Women's Roles," 117; Lauck, *Prairie Republic*, 40-41.

76 Siberts and Wyman, *Nothing but Prairie and Sky*, 118.

77 Nancy T. Koupal, "Marietta Bones: Personality and Politics in the South Dakota Suffrage Movement," in *Feminist Frontiers: Women Who Shaped the Midwest*, ed. Yvonne J. Johnson (Kirksville, MO: Truman State University Press, 2010), 69-82.

78 Elizabeth Williams, "Agrarian Exponent: Emil Loriks," in *South Dakota Leaders: From Pierre Chouteau, Jr., to Oscar Howe*, ed. Herbert T. Hoover and Larry J. Zimmerman (Vermillion: University of South Dakota Press, 1989), 283-86; Choate, "Debt, Drought, and Depression," 35; Williams, "Agrarian Exponent," 287-90; Clem, *Government by the People?*, 18; Jeffrey M. Banks, "The Past, Present and Future of Anti-Corporate Farming Laws in South Dakota: Purposeful Discrimination or Permissive Protectionism?" *South Dakota Law Review* 49 (2004): 805-23; Kathryn Benz, "Saving Old McDonald's Farm After South Dakota Farm Bureau, Inc. v. Hazeltine: Rethinking the Role of the State, Farming Operations, the Dormant Commerce Clause, and Growth Management Statutes," *Natural Resources Journal* 46 (Summer 2006): 793-830.

79 Bill White, *America's Fiscal Constitution: Its Triumph and Collapse* (New York: PublicAffairs, 2014); Milton, *South Dakota: A Bicentennial History*, 128.

80 Karolevitz, *Challenge: The South Dakota Story*, 300.

81 Nelson, *The Prairie Winnows Out Its Own*, 142; Lauck, *Prairie Republic*, 52-56; Burns and Cheever, "South Dakota: Conflict and Cooperation," 286; Tom Daschle, "Reexamining the Life and Legacy of George McGovern," in *George McGovern: A Political Life, a Political Legacy*, ed. Robert P. Watson (Pierre: South Dakota State Historical Society Press, 2004), viii.

82 For examples, see the Gustave Otterness Collection, CWS.

83 Lee, *Last Grass Frontier*, 10.

84 Hasselstrom, *Windbreak: A Woman Rancher*, 141.

85 South Dakota State Planning Board and Hamlin County Planning Board, *Economic and Social Survey*, 30-31, 53; Grant, *Down and Out on the Family Farm*, 37, 48; Choate, "Debt, Drought, and Depression," 42.

86 Clem, *Prairie State Politics*, 57.

87 South Dakota State Planning Board and Hamlin County Planning Board, *Economic and Social Survey*, 13.

88 Reel 2, CWS; Sioux Falls Misc. Publications, CWS; William Beach Locke Collection, CWS.

89 Box 5, Northwest Bancorporation, Records of Member Banks, 1875-1985, GFL; Schwieder, *Growing Up with the Town*, 69-70, 141; Harl A. Dalstrom and Kay Calame Dalstrom, "'Back by Popular Demand!': Dancing in Small-Town South Dakota," *South Dakota History* 32, 4 (Winter 2002): 283-309; "Reminiscences of Irene Mortenson Sargent," (1990), Edith Mortenson Delman Collection, CWS; Nelson, *The Prairie Winnows Out Its Own*, 87.

90 Shawn Lay, ed. *The Invisible Empire in the West: Toward a New Historical Appraisal of the Ku Klux Klan of the 1920s* (Chicago: University of Illinois Press, 1992); Charles Rambow, "Ku Klux Klan in the 1920s: A Concentration on the Black Hills," *South Dakota History* 3 (Winter 1973): 63-81; Nelson, *The Prairie Winnows Out Its Own*, 91.

91 "No Disturbance as K.K.K. Holds Masked Parade," newspaper clipping, Ku Klux Klan Collection, CWS.92 David M. Chalmers, *Hooded Americanism: The History of the Ku Klux Klan* (Durham: Duke University Press, 1987), 142.

93 But there was a "Great Titan" in Sioux Falls as late as 1931. "Klansmen All, Greetings," *Tri-State Realm Official Bulletin* (St. James, Minnesota, Mar. 1931), Ku Klux Klan Collection, CWS.

94 Anson, *McGovern*, 6.

95 Lauck, *Prairie Republic*, 42.

96 As quoted in Ibid., 27.

97 Stanley H. Edmunds, "I Remember When," (c. 1970), Stanley H. Edmunds Collection, CWS.

98 Schwieder, *Growing Up with the Town*, 114; Lauck, *Prairie Republic*, 50; Bareiss, "Alternative Radio and Television," 219-42.

99 Schell, *History of South Dakota*, 366; Richard Polsky, *Boneheads: My Search for T. Rex* (San Francisco: Council Oak Books, 2011), 145; Peter Lawrence, *The Change Game: How Today's Global Trends Are Shaping Tomorrow's Companies* (London: Kogan Page Ltd., 2002), 119-20.

100 As quoted in Norris, "South Dakota: The Long Mile," 414.

101 Robert Putnam, "E Pluribus Unum: Diversity and Community in the Twenty-First Century," *Scandinavian Political Studies* 30, 2 (2007): 137-74.

102 John E. Miller, "Small Towns: Image and Reality," in *A New South Dakota History*, ed. Harry Thompson (Sioux Falls: Center for Western Studies, 2009), 185-86; John J. Usera, *Governing South Dakota: Government Meeting Future Challenges Roundtable* (Rapid City: Institute for South Dakota Leadership and Participation, 1999); Darrell D. Butterwick, "Economic Development in South Dakota," *South Dakota Business Review* 48, 4 (June 1990), 4; "Foundations are Popping Up Everywhere in South Dakota," *Independent Banker* 45, 1 (Jan. 1995), 46.

103 Peterson, *Through the Black Hills and Bad Lands*, 40.

104 Clem, *Prairie State Politics*, 86.

105 Charles Hillinger, "South Dakota Turns Cement to Cash at State-Owned Plant," *Los Angeles Times*, 24 Mar. 1986, E1; Reese, *South Dakota*, 43; Gilbert Fite, *Peter Norbeck:*

Prairie Statesman (Columbia: University of Missouri, 1948), 90-91; Rogers, *South Dakota's Challenges Since 1960*, 334; "No Longer Stuck in Cement," *Fedgazette* (May 2001): 13.

106 Fite, *Peter Norbeck: Prairie Statesman*, 89.

107 V. E. Montgomery and C. S. Van Doren, *The Economy of the West North Central Region of South Dakota* (Vermillion: Business Research Bureau, 1957), 58.

108 Fite, *Peter Norbeck: Prairie Statesman*, 91.

109 Reese, *South Dakota*, 42; Fite, *Peter Norbeck: Prairie Statesman*, 80-87, 92-93.

110 Sterling Evans, "Entwined in Conflict: The South Dakota State Prison Twine Factory and the Controversy of 1919-1921," *South Dakota History* 35, 2 (Summer 2005): 95-124.

111 Fite, *Peter Norbeck: Prairie Statesman*, 88.

112 A. A. Volk, *The Economy of the Black Hills Region of South Dakota* (Vermillion: Business Research Bureau, 1968), 27, 39, 41, 47; Earl O. Heady, "Foreword," in *Communities Left Behind: Alternatives for Development*, ed. Larry R. Whiting (Ames: Iowa State Press, 1974), vii; Beale, "Quantitative Dimensions of Decline," 11.

113 Stock, *Main Street in Crisis*, 206-10; Walter M. Kollmorgen and George F. Jenks, "Suitcase Farming in Sully County, South Dakota," *Annals of the Association of American Geographers* 48, 1 (Mar. 1958), 27-40.114 Berg, *South Dakota: Land of Shining Gold*, 148; Hasselstrom, *Roadside History*, 57, 71; Milton, *South Dakota: A Bicentennial History*, 113; Thompson, *A New South Dakota History*, 229; Chittick, *Growth and Decline, 1901-51*, 32; VanEpps-Taylor, *Forgotten Lives*, 100; Fite, "Transformation of South Dakota Agriculture," 280.

115 Nelson, *The Prairie Winnows Out Its Own*, 21-22.

116 Fite, "Transformation of South Dakota Agriculture," 280, 287; Grant, *Down and Out on the Family Farm*, 15.

117 Schell, *History of South Dakota*, 328.

118 Ibid., 320-21; Fite, "Transformation of South Dakota Agriculture," 288-90; Rogers, *South Dakota's Challenges Since 1960*, 298; Brokaw, *A Long Way From Home*, 69-77, 137.

119 Chittick, *Growth and Decline, 1901-51*, 13, 44-45; Schell, *History of South Dakota*, 330-31; Landis, *Growth and Decline, 1901-1933*, 3; Miller, *Looking for History*, 127-29; Beale, "Quantitative Dimensions of Decline," 20-21.

120 Riley, "Farm Women's Roles," 101; Miller, *Looking for History*, 131-33; Schwieder, *Growing Up with the Town*, 134.

121 Miller, *Looking for History*, 77, 81, 113; Montgomery and Van Doren, *Economy of the West North Central Region*, 26; Gray et al, *South Dakota Economic and Business Abstract*, 82.

122 Norris, *Dakota: A Spiritual Geography*, 28.

123 Dahl, *Banker Dahl*, 135, 227, 241; Casey, *The Black Hills and Their Incredible Characters*, 54, 76; Norris, *Dakota: A Spiritual Geography*, 27-28; Schwieder, *Growing Up with the Town*, 66; Schell, *History of South Dakota*, 327.

124 Dahl, *Banker Dahl*, 76.

125 Neil Miller, *In Search of Gay America: Women and Men in a Time of Change* (New York: Atlantic Monthly Press, 1989), 99.

126 Samuel H. Lea, "South Dakota Builds by Definite Program," *Nation's Business,* 18 Nov. 1912, 4; Lee, "Traveling the Sunshine State," 203; Reese, *South Dakota*, 68; Poth, *Transportation Rates*, 11-13.

127 Poth, *Transportation Rates*, 109.

128 Orr, "A History of Aviation in South Dakota," 129, 150-51, 159; Foss and Foss, *A Proud American*, 192, 200.

129 Poth, *Transportation Rates*, 13; Reese, *South Dakota*, 69.

130 Norris, *Dakota: A Spiritual Geography*, 30.

131 Orr, "A History of Aviation in South Dakota," 141.

132 Anon., "South Dakota Plans Nation's First Intrastate Air Service," *Fedgazette* (Mar. 1990), 5.

133 As quoted in Anson, *McGovern*, 88.

134 Foss and Foss, *A Proud American*, 207-9, 217, 220-21, 308; Lawson, *Dammed Indians*, 4; Schneiders, *Unruly River*, 23; Kate Parry, "South Dakota River Flooding Covers Nearly 1 Million Acres," *Minneapolis Star Tribune,* 22 Apr. 1986, 2B; Hasselstrom, *Roadside History*, 2; Frazier, *On the Rez*, 174-77, 182; Norris, "South Dakota: The Long Mile," 408; Bryan, *American Indian Entrepreneurs*, 25; Norris, *Dakota: A Spiritual Geography*, 35; Carrie Breitbach and Don Mitchell, "Growth Machines and Growth Pains: The Contradictions of Property Development and Landscape in Sioux Falls South Dakota," in *Making Space: Property Development and Urban Planning*, ed. Andrew MacLaran (London: Arnold, 2003), 216-17; South Dakota Department of Economic and Tourism Development, *Taxes!: A Businessman's Comparison* (Pierre: South Dakota Department of Economic and Tourism Development, 1975).135 Foss and Foss, *A Proud American*, 233; George A. Larson, "South Dakota's Soukup & Thomas Balloon and Airship Museum Houses a One-of-a-Kind Collection," *Aviation History* (May 1999), 66-68; http://flyprairiesky.com.

136 "Small South Dakota Company Flies High for the Holidays," *Tampa Bay Times,* 26 Nov. 1987, 13B; Benno Wymar, "South Dakota-Canadian Commercial Relations," *South Dakota Business Review* 53, 1 (Sept. 1994), 5; http://ravenind.com; http://www.forbes.com/sites/kathryndill/2014/03/18/americas-100-most-trustworthy-companies/2/.

137 Anson, *McGovern*, 90; Benz, "Saving Old McDonald's Farm," 798-99; Stock, *Main Street in Crisis*, 210; Randall M. Stuefen and De Vee Dykstra, "Growth, Diversification and In-Migration: South Dakota's Economic Awakening," *South Dakota Business Review* 56, 1 (Sept. 1997), 1.

138 Beale, "Quantitative Dimensions of Decline," 15; James Satterlee, *The New Community* (Brookings: South Dakota State University, 2002), 2.

139 U.S. Senate, *Impact of Interest Rates on the Small Business and Agricultural Sectors: Hearing before the Committee on Small Business* (Washington, DC: GPO, 1983). 25, 29.

140 Stock, *Main Street in Crisis*, 209.

141 Karolevitz, "The Human Dimension," 27.

142 "Funeral Services Held for Violet Uhden," *Wilmot Enterprise,* 29 Mar. 2012, 3.

143 Schell, *History of South Dakota*, 351-52.

144 U.S. Senate, *Impact of Interest Rates*, 3.

145 Ibid., 6, 17, 21.

146 Ibid., 29.

147 Ibid., 31.

148 Dahlin, "The 1982 Gubernatorial Election in South Dakota," 282; Jon D. Schaff, "A Clear Choice: George *McGovern* and the 1972 Presidential Race," in *George McGovern: A Political Life, a Political Legacy*, ed. Robert P. Watson (Pierre: South Dakota State Historical Society Press, 2004), 130.

149 Dahlin, "The 1982 Gubernatorial Election in South Dakota," 282-83; U.S. Senate, *Impact of Interest Rates*, 8, 40-41.

150 Burns and Cheever, "South Dakota: Conflict and Cooperation," 287; Frazier, *On the Rez*, 210; Andree Brooks, "Seeking the Real Deadwood," *New York Times,* 30 Aug. 1987, XX21; Dahlin, "The 1982 Gubernatorial Election in South Dakota," 283-85, 291.

151 Dahlin, "The 1982 Gubernatorial Election in South Dakota," 284; Poth, *Transportation Rates*, 108.

152 Except where otherwise noted, this section is based on Douglas J. Hajek, "South Dakota Takes Center Stage," *Northwestern Financial Review* (15 Sept. 2004), 13-16; Boxes 4, 11, 34, and 35, William J. Janklow Gubernatorial Papers, USD; Greg Redlin, "Citibank Comes to South Dakota: The Politics of Economic Change," (M.B.A. thesis, University of South Dakota, 2004); Robert E. Wright, "Wall Street on the Prairie: Citibank, South Dakota, and the Origins of Financial Deregulation," *Financial History* (Spring 2013), 24-26; Robert E. Wright, "Wall Street on the Prairie: How Financial Innovation and Regulation Cajoled Citibank into South Dakota," Museum of American Finance, New York, New York, 12 Mar. 2013; Phillip L. Zweig, *Wriston: Walter Wriston, Citibank, and the Rise and Fall of American Financial Supremacy* (New York: Crown, 1995), 679-83, 687-92, 710-11, 732-38.

153 Choate, "Debt, Drought, and Depression," 34.

154 Grant, "Origins of a Progressive Reform," 390-407.

155 Lauck, *Prairie Republic*, 41.156 Schell, *History of South Dakota*, 330; Fite, "Observations by a Native Son," 457-58; Brown, "The South Dakota Economy: A Historical Perspective," 4; Ralph Brown, "South Dakota Rankings on Wages, Personal Income and Gross State Product," *South Dakota Business Review* 59, 1 (Sept. 2000), 1, 4-8.

157 Business and Industry Round Table, *South Dakota*.

158 Anon., "South Dakota Business and Economic Activity, 1995-2000," *South Dakota Business Review* 58, 4 (June 2000): 6.

159 Breitbach and Mitchell, "Growth Machines and Growth Pains," 217.

160 "Michigan National Sets Switch of Credit Card Work to South Dakota," *Wall Street Journal,* 18 Sept. 1986, 1.

161 Breitbach and Mitchell, "Growth Machines and Growth Pains," 222-23.

162 Thomas F. Pogue, "Mounting Fiscal Pressures: How Can State and Local Governments Cope?" in *Economic Forces Shaping the Rural Heartland* (Kansas City: Federal Reserve Bank of Kansas City, 1996), 96.

163 Dahlin, "The 1982 Gubernatorial Election in South Dakota," 286-88.

164 Brown, "The South Dakota Economy: A Historical Perspective," 5; Dahlin, "The 1982 Gubernatorial Election in South Dakota," 293.

165 Daniel E. Cuff, "Security Pacific Plans Bank in South Dakota," *New York Times,* 4 May 1983, D4.

166 Breitbach and Mitchell, "Growth Machines and Growth Pains," 214-15; Schell, *History of South Dakota*, 355.

167 South Dakota Employment Security Department, *29th Annual Report of the Employment Security Department of South Dakota* (1965), 35.

168 Gray et al, *South Dakota Economic and Business Abstract*, 57.

169 Reese, *South Dakota*, 49.

170 Gray et al, *South Dakota Economic and Business Abstract*, 237, 242; Reese, *South Dakota*, 49-50.

171 Reese, *South Dakota*, 49; Page, *Pegmatite Investigations*, 1-3; Garland Gott, Don Wolcott, and C. Gilbert Bowles, *Stratigraphy of the Inyan Kara Group and Localization of Uranium Deposits, Southern Black Hills, South Dakota and Wyoming* (Washington, DC: U.S. GPO, 1974), 2; Schell, *History of South Dakota*, 331; Poth, *Transportation Rates*, 15; Citibank, *South Dakota: The Business and Living Environment* (1981), Box 4, Dave Stenseth/EROS Collection, CWS.

172 Business and Industry Round Table, *South Dakota*.

173 Lori Wilbur, "Governor's Economic Development Plan," Issue Memorandum 87-2 (May 1987), Janklow Papers, USD.

174 Business and Industry Round Table, *South Dakota*.

175 South Dakota Board of Regents, *Foundation for the Future*, 1.

176 Ibid., 1.

177 Business and Industry Round Table, *South Dakota*; Entrepreneur Press, *How to Start a Business in South Dakota*, 13.8; Butterwick, "Economic Development in South Dakota,"4; Matthew Lesko and Mary Ann Martello, "South Dakota," in *Lesko's Free Money for Entrepreneurs: How to Start or Expand a Business with Government Grants, Low Interest Loans, Contacts and Free Services* (Kensington, MD: Information USA, 2004), 151; David Fettig, "South Dakota Entrepreneur Program Hopes to Retain State's Youth," *Fedgazette* (Oct. 1994).

178 Butterwick, "Economic Development in South Dakota,"4; South Dakota Department of Labor, *South Dakota Works Hard!* (1989).179 Rob Hotakainen, "Twin Cities' Incinerated Solid Waste Has a Date with South Dakota in 1987," *Minneapolis Star Tribune,* 1 Nov. 1986, 1B; Linda Hasselstrom, *No Place Like Home: Notes from a Western Life* (Las Vegas: University of Nevada Press, 2009), 132-36.

180 Hasselstrom, *Roadside History*, 11.

181 "Coal Slurry Group Asks South Dakota to Delay Water Bill," *Wall Street Journal,* 6 Feb. 1984; Burns and Cheever, "South Dakota: Conflict and Cooperation," 288, 293.

182 Anon. "South Dakota Business and Economic Indices," *South Dakota Business Review* 49, 4 (June 1991), 3; Mark Drabenstott and Tim R. Smith, "The Changing Economy of the Rural Heartland," in *Economic Forces Shaping the Rural Heartland* (Kansas City: Federal Reserve Bank of Kansas City, 1996), 3-61; Wymar, "South Dakota-Canadian Commercial Relations," 4.

183 Pogue, "Mounting Fiscal Pressures," 78, 99.

184 Suzanne White, "Town and Gown, Analysis of Relationships: Black Hills State University and Spearfish, South Dakota, 1883 to 1991," (Ph.D. diss., Iowa State University, 1991), 124.

185 Robert Tosterud, Timothy Habbershon, Even Liahjell, "The 1993 South Dakota Family Business Survey: Preliminary Findings," *South Dakota Business Review* 51, 4 (June 1993), 1, 4-8.

186 Harold H. Wilde, "A Survey of the Attitudes of South Dakota Small Business Owners and/or Managers towards Social Responsibility Accounting," (Ph.D. diss., University of Nebraska, Dec. 1981), 9.

187 Robert Tosterud and Timothy Habbershon, "Rural Entrepreneurship: A Preliminary Study," *South Dakota Business Review* 50, 3 (Mar. 1992): 1-4.

Chapter 5

1 Brokaw, *A Long Way from Home*, 170.

2 Anon., "South Dakota Business and Economic Activity," 9; James H. Engeseth, "An Assessment of Formal Training in the Durable Goods Sector of South Dakota's Manufacturing Industry," (Ed.D. diss., University of South Dakota, 2006), 6; Phil Hunter and Marjorie Hunter, "Here Comes South Dakota," *New York Times,* 21 Feb. 1985, A20.

3 U.S. Senate, *Impact of Interest Rates*, 32.

4 Birzer, "Expanding Creative Destruction," 46; Schell, "Adjustment Problems in South Dakota," 67; Nelson, *The Prairie Winnows Out Its Own*, 181-82; Luke M. Muller, "Change of Scale in Upper Midwest Farms: A South Dakota Case Study," (M.A. thesis, South Dakota State University, 2005), 17-20; Judith Barjenbruch, "The First National Bank of Vermillion, 1875-1937," (M.A. thesis, University of South Dakota, 1975), 45; Kenneth Charles Dagel, "Ranchers' Adjustments to Drought in Western South Dakota, 1870-1990s: Creating

Sustainable Operations in a Marginal Environment," (Ph.D. diss., University of Nebraska, Lincoln, 1994).

5 Thompson, *A New South Dakota History*, 225-254.

6 Fairchild and Wyman, *Frontier Woman*, 103-6; McLaird, "From Bib Overalls to Cowboy Boots," 482.

7 Fairchild and Wyman, *Frontier Woman*, 50.

8 Schell, *History of South Dakota*, 327; Volk, *Economy of the Northeast Region*, 43; Grant, *Down and Out on the Family Farm*, 2, 4-5; Muller, "Change of Scale in Upper Midwest Farms," 61.9 Volk, *Economy of the Northeast Region*, 43; South Dakota State Planning Board and Hamlin County Planning Board, *Economic and Social Survey*, 2; 25th *Annual Report of the Employment Security Department of South Dakota* (1961), 17; Peterson, *Storyville USA*, 206.

10 Volk, *Economy of the Northeast Region*, 50; Roegiers and Weeldreyer, "South Dakota Sheep," 1, 4-6.

11 http://www.sdwinegrowers.com/index.php/site/wineries; Ann Grauvogl, *South Dakota: Pioneering the Future* (Encino, CA: Cherbo Publishing, 2006), 34; Head, *South Dakota: An Explorer's Guide*, 23; Don Jorgenson, "White Headed Robin Takes Flight," *Keloland.com*, 13 Oct. 2010; http://www.wineweb.com/scripts/wineryPg.cfm/43078/White-Headed-Robin-Winery/.

12 John Eligon, "Growing a Wine Destination in South Dakota," *New York Times,* 22 Oct. 2013.

13 "Orpheum Theater," CWS Reel 2.

14 Marjorie Platt and James Weisel, "Turning around the South Dakota Microbrewery," in *A Casebook on Corporate Renewal*, ed. Harlan Platt and Marjorie Platt (Ann Arbor: University Michigan Press, 2004), 312-18.

15 Polsky, *Boneheads* 66-67.

16 http://www.monkshouseofalerepute.com/brewery/4578982718; http://bitteresters brewhouse.com

17 Lawrence, *The Change Game*, 90-92.

18 Schatz, *Longhorns Bring Culture*, 18; David Miller, "Pioneering Black Hills Cattleman: James 'Scotty' Philip," in *South Dakota Leaders: From Pierre Chouteau, Jr., to Oscar Howe*, ed. Herbert T. Hoover and Larry J. Zimmerman (Vermillion: University of South Dakota Press, 1989), 249-57; Fairchild and Wyman, *Frontier Woman*, 11; Siberts and Wyman, *Nothing But Prairie and Sky*, 22, 83.

19 Robinson, *West from Fort Pierre*, 123-37; Braun, *Buffalo Inc.*, 61; O'Brien, *Buffalo for the Broken Heart*, 27, 29, 67-68.

20 O'Brien, *Buffalo for the Broken Heart*, 240-41.

21 Ibid., 36.

22 Ibid., 172.

23 Ibid., 9, 68.

24 Ibid., 12.

25 Ibid., 243.

26 Ibid., 114.

27 Fairchild and Wyman, *Frontier Woman*, 40-46; Nelson, *The Prairie Winnows Out Its Own*, 34-37; Cochell and Beine, *Land of the Coyote*, 50, 85.

28 Cochell and Beine, *Land of the Coyote*, 112, 123.

29 Norris, *Dakota: A Spiritual Geography*, 52-53; Grant, *Down and Out on the Family Farm*, 204; Ann Daum, *The Prairie in Her Eyes* (Minnesota: Milkweed Editions, 2001), 5.

30 Fairchild and Wyman, *Frontier Woman*, 2, 62.

31 Ibid., 3, 113.

32 Ibid., 57-58.

33 Ibid., 3.

34 Ibid., 3, 38, 60, 90-91; Riley, "Farm Women's Roles," 88.

35 Fairchild and Wyman, *Frontier Woman*, 5, 87-91, 112.

36 Well water was often "hard," suitable for drinking and cooking but not for washing, so cisterns were constructed to store rainwater for cleaning clothes, hair, and bodies.

37 Ibid., 50, 108-12; Amerson, *From the Hidewood*, 286-87; Berg, *South Dakota: Land of Shining Gold*, 145; Nelson, *The Prairie Winnows Out Its Own*, 71; Hasselstrom, *Windbreak: A Woman Rancher*, 9; "Reminiscences of Irene Mortenson Sargent," (1990), Edith Mortenson Delman Collection, CWS; Nelson, *After the West Was Won*, 57, 151.

38 Norris, *Dakota: A Spiritual Geography*, 22; Brokaw, *A Long Way from Home*, 50; Fairchild and Wyman, *Frontier Woman*, 21, 24, 53.

39 Ed Eisenbraun, "Creighton, South Dakota," in *Below the Line: Living Poor in America*, ed. Eugene Richards (Mount Vernon, NY: Consumers Union, 1987), 158-59.

40 Ibid., 162; Cochell and Beine, *Land of the Coyote*, 145; O'Brien, *Buffalo for the Broken Heart*, 144; Schell, *History of South Dakota*, 353; Van Nuys, *The Family Band*, xviii.

41 Schwieder, *Growing Up with the Town*, 15; Weatherford, *A History of Women*, 4:406; Linda Hasselstrom, *Feels Like Far: A Rancher's Life on the Great Plains* (New York: Lyons Press, 1999), 133; Glen C. Pulver, "New Avenues for Public Policy," in *Economic Forces Shaping the Rural Heartland* (Kansas City: Federal Reserve Bank of Kansas City, 1996), 111; Muller, "Change of Scale in Upper Midwest Farms," 23; Norris, *Dakota: A Spiritual Geography*, 4; Terry Nelson, "An Examination of Roles and Identities of the Farm Population Within Beadle, Brookings, Hamlin, Lake, and McCook Counties of South Dakota," (Ph.D. diss., South Dakota State University, 2001).

42 Carruth, "South Dakota: State without End," 336.

43 Berg, *South Dakota: Land of Shining Gold*, 74; Marcey Moss and James L. Satterlee, *South Dakota County Data Book* (Brookings: South Dakota State University, 2002), 18-20; Volk, *Economy of the Northeast Region*, 39; McLaird, "From Bib Overalls to Cowboy Boots," 460; Grant, *Down and Out on the Family Farm*, 204; Benno Wymar, "South Dakota-Japan Commercial Relations," *South Dakota Business Review* 52, 3 (Mar. 1994), 10-11.

44 Monte Olmsted, "Agriculture Conference Verses South Dakota Bankers about Economy," *Northwestern Financial Review,* 8 May 1999, 22-23; Muller, "Change of Scale in Upper Midwest Farms,"41-59; Hasselstrom, *Windbreak: A Woman Rancher,* 140, 148, 150, 171-73.

45 Cochell and Beine, *Land of the Coyote*, 92; Brokaw, *A Long Way from Home*, x, 16.

46 Urbanek, *The Uncovered Wagon*, 11.

47 Cochell and Beine, *Land of the Coyote*, 57; Mandat-Grancey, *Cowboys and Colonels*, 108-9; Robinson, *West from Fort Pierre*, 133; Weatherford, *A History of Women*, 4:410; "Nova Raberns Arrive in Oct., 1907," *Lyman County Herald,* 25 Aug. 1955.

48 Peterson, *Through the Black Hills and Bad Lands*, 53.

49 Reese, *South Dakota*, 90.

50 Anson, *McGovern*, 144.

51 Broom Tree Farm Records, CWS.

52 "Johnson Farms Tour," *Dakota Rural Action*, 25 July 2013; Andrew Shirley, "South Dakota Offers an Escape to EU Red Tape," *Farmers Weekly* (Oct. 2002).

53 Schell, "Adjustment Problems in South Dakota," 68; John E. Miller, "Eminent Horticulturalist: Niels Ebbesen Hansen," in *South Dakota Leaders: From Pierre Chouteau,*

Jr., to Oscar Howe, ed. Herbert T. Hoover and Larry J. Zimmerman (Vermillion: University of South Dakota Press, 1989), 271-80.

54 Fairchild and Wyman, *Frontier Woman,* 103.

55 Fite, *Peter Norbeck: Prairie Statesman,* 15-23, 24.56 South Dakota Department of State, *South Dakota and Foreign Trade* (1952), 2; St. Olaf Roller Mills, Box 2, Bessie Pettigrew Collection, CWS; Hagerty, *Territory of Dakota,* 94-96.

57 Lee, *Principle Over Party,* 10; Herzog, *Small World,* 56, 59, 62; Lawrence Cheever, *The House of Morrell* (Cedar Rapids: Torch Press, 1948), 143.

58 Cheever, *House of Morrell,* v-vii, ix, 5, 29, 35, 40, 55, 75, 143-72, 184-87; Reel 2, CWS; Sioux Falls Stock Yards Company, CWS.

59 Cheever, *House of Morrell,* 188-89, 194-95, 262-64; Smith, "Some Changing Features of a Regional Capital," 162; Bucklin, "Memoir of Frank Bloodgood," 123; Benno Wymar, "NAFTA and South Dakota – A Five Year Analysis," *South Dakota Business Review* 57, 4 (June 1999), 5.

60 Congress, *Ensuring Competitive and Open Agricultural Markets,* 2, 25-30, 80-93, 102-4.

61 Ibid., 90.

62 "South Dakota," *National Hog Farmer,* 15 May 1998, 23, 26; "Dakota Pork. Gateway. CoEv Magnetics. When Companies Pull Out of Communities, the Pain Runs Deep," *Sioux Falls Argus Leader,* 8 Jan. 2006, D1; Wymar, "South Dakota-Canadian Commercial Relations," 6; "This Date In History: Events of Local Interest," *Public Opinion* (2013).

63 "United Biscuit Company of America," BLHBS.

64 Reese, *South Dakota,* 156.

65 Manchester Biscuit Company, South Dakota Historical Marker. www.waymarking. com/waymarks/WMKJV_Manchester_Biscuit_Company; Wymar, "Foreign Investments and South Dakota," 5.

66 Hagerty, *Territory of Dakota,* 96.

67 Van Nuys, *The Family Band,* 148-50 n. 7; Alan Barkema and Mark Drabenstott, "Consolidation and Change in Heartland Agriculture," in *Economic Forces Shaping the Rural Heartland* (Kansas City: Federal Reserve Bank of Kansas City, 1996), 71-72; Ron Robinson, *Valley Queen Cheese: The Birth and Growth of an American Dream* (Sioux Falls: Ex Machina Publishing Company, 2006); Grauvogl, *South Dakota: Pioneering the Future,* 37; http://www.lakenorden.govoffice.com

68 Kathy Cobb, "Processing Plant Keeps Soybeans in South Dakota," *Fedgazette* 7, 3 (July 1995): 12; Wymar, "NAFTA and South Dakota," 4; Cobb, "Processing Plant," 12; Dan Schofer, "South Dakota: Great Faces, Great Places – and Great Value-Added Opportunities," *Rural Cooperatives* (Sept./Oct. 2007), 23.

69 Dan Schofer, "South Dakota: Great Faces, Great Places," 20-22; Phil Davies, "Labor's Changing Face," *Fedgazette* (Oct. 2013), 1.

70 Davies, "Labor's Changing Face," 5.

71 Douglas Clement, "Green Eggs ... and Ham," *Fed Gazette* (Mar. 2001), 12.

72 Hailey Higgins, "10,000 Eggs Donated to Feed South Dakota," *Keloland,* 22 Mar. 2012; Anon., "Donating Eggs by the Dozen," *KDLT News,* 22 Mar. 2012.

73 Grauvogl, *South Dakota: Pioneering the Future,* 34-35; William Neuman, "Food Companies Act to Protect Consumers from E. Coli Illness," *New York Times,* 15 July 2011; Clement, "Green Eggs ... and Ham," 12.

74 Dan Campbell, "South Dakota Turnaround," *Rural Cooperatives* (May/June 2002): 11-16.

75 "South Dakota Co-ops Merging," *Rural Cooperatives* (July/Aug. 2007): 36-37.

76 Schofer, "South Dakota: Great Faces, Great Places," 22.

77 Ibid., 23.78 "International Company Establishing Plant in Sioux Falls, S.D." *AGWEEK,* 7 Feb. 2013; Poth, *Transportation Rates,* 35; "Glanbia Nutritionals to Build Facility in Sioux Falls," *Directions* (Nov./Dec. 2012).

79 David L. Barkley, "Turmoil in Traditional Industry: Prospects for Nonmetropolitan Manufacturing," in *Economic Forces Shaping the Rural Heartland* (Kansas City: Federal Reserve Bank of Kansas City, 1996), 73.

80 "South Dakota Co-op Breaks Ground on New Ethanol Plant," *Oxy Fuel News,* 24 Apr. 2000, 1; http://www.dakotaethanol.com/lacp.html; Rogers, *South Dakota's Challenges Since 1960,* 313, 403; Grauvogl, *South Dakota: Pioneering the Future,* 57, 68; http://www.poet.com/history.

Chapter 6

1 Karolevitz, "The Human Dimension," 25.

2 Hasselstrom, *No Place Like Home,* 11-28; Gray et al., *South Dakota Economic and Business Abstract,* 215-16; Hagerty, *Territory of Dakota,* 93; Norris, "South Dakota: The Long Mile," 409; Hoover, "South Dakota," 46.

3 Gray et al., *South Dakota Economic and Business Abstract,* 215, 217; Citibank, *South Dakota: The Business and Living Environment* (1981), Box 4, Dave Stenseth/ EROS Collection, CWS; VanEpps-Taylor, *Forgotten Lives,* 64; Karolevitz, "The Human Dimension," 24; South Dakota Board of Regents, *Foundation for the Future,* 7; Berg, *South Dakota: Land of Shining Gold,* 77; Durkin, Holm, and Regynski, "South Dakota," 73; Holm, et al., "South Dakota," 112; Rogers, *South Dakota's Challenges Since 1960,* 297; Frazier, *On the Rez,* 228.

4 Hagerty, *Territory of Dakota,* 92.

5 "A Concise Exposition of the Advantages of the Sioux Falls Region for Settlement and Investment," 1886, Sioux Falls Misc. Publications, CWS.

6 Ibid.

7 George Banker Collection, CWS.

8 John N. Vogel, *Great Lakes Lumber on the Great Plains: The Laird, Norton Lumber Company in South Dakota* (Iowa City: University of Iowa Press, 1992); John N. Vogel, "Great Lakes Lumber on the Great Plains: The Laird, Norton Lumber Company in South Dakota," (Ph.D. diss., Marquette University, 1989).

9 Weatherford, *A History of Women,* 4:412; Robert E. Wright, *Fubarnomics: A Lighthearted, Serious Look at America's Economic Ills* (Amherst, NY: Prometheus, 2010), 69-82.

10 Culp, *Letters from Tully,* 34, 118-20, 220; VanEpps-Taylor, *Oscar Micheaux Dakota Homesteader,* 49; Carruth, "South Dakota: State Without End," 337; Brokaw, *A Long Way from Home,* 39, 42-43; Nelson, *After the West Was Won,* 86, 131; Miller, *Looking for History,* 181-82; Van Nuys, *The Family Band,* 56; Lewis, *Nothing to Make a Shadow,* 43; Peterson, *Storyville USA,* 208-9; Pollock, "Rebirth of a South Dakota Town," 343-44, 347-49; Frazier, *On the Rez,* 107, 122; "Operation Walking Shield Brings Homes to South Dakota," *National Mortgage News,* 11 Aug. 1997, 10.

11 Kathy Cobb, "These Are the Houses That Inmates Built," *Fedgazette* (Apr. 1998), 8.

12 O'Brien, *Buffalo for the Broken Heart,* 128, 130-31; Breitbach and Mitchell, "Growth Machines and Growth Pains," 216.

13 http://ronningcompanies.com/about-ronning.html; Grauvogl, *South Dakota: Pioneering the Future,* 100-02.

14 Grauvogl, *South Dakota: Pioneering the Future*, 104-05.15 Jeannette Kinyon, Lois Johnson, and Margaret Voels, *Prairie Architect, F.C.W. Kuehn: His Life and Work* (Sioux Falls: Center for Western Studies, 1984).

16 Alan K. Lathrop, "Designing for South Dakota and the Upper Midwest: The Career of Architect Harold T. Spitznagel, 1930-1974," *South Dakota History* 37, 4 (Winter 2007): 271-305.

17 Hagerty, *Territory of Dakota*, 93.

18 Fite, "Observations by a Native Son," 457.

19 South Dakota Board of Regents, *Foundation for the Future*, 10; Grauvogl, *South Dakota: Pioneering the Future*, 63; Sioux Falls Woolen Mill, Box 2, Bessie Pettigrew Collection, CWS.

20 Thomas L. Fawick to Nevis Fawick, Oct. 7, Dec. 31, 1922, Fawick Collection, CWS.

21 Eveyln Maguire King Collection, CWS.

22 Montgomery and Van Doren, *Economy of the West North Central Region*, 64; Schell, *History of South Dakota*, 331.

23 Bill Richards, "Prairie Promoter: Gov. Janklow Exhibits Strange Personal Style, But He Means Business," *Wall Street Journal,* 29 Mar. 1984, 1.

24 Peirce and Hagstrom, "South Dakota: State of Reluctant Change," 564; Richards, "Prairie Promoter," *Wall Street Journal,* 29 Mar. 1984, 1.

25 Marcia Brinkman, "Sioux Falls: Steady as She Grows," *Corporate Report* (Apr. 1976): 27-43, in Box 1, Dave Stenseth/EROS Collection, CWS.

26 Robert Whereatt, "Perpich Shrugs Off South Dakota Bid to Entice Business from Minnesota," *Minneapolis Star Tribune,* 5 May 1987, 5B.

27 *Sioux Falls Development Foundation, Directions,* (1976), 1, Box 1, Dave Stenseth/EROS Collection, CWS; Wymar, "Foreign Investments and South Dakota," 6.

28 *Horizons: Sioux Falls in the 1970s* (1971), Box 1; Folder 14, Box 4, Dave Stenseth/EROS Collection, CWS.

29 South Dakota Board of Regents, *Foundation for the Future*, 5.

30 Berg, *South Dakota: Land of Shining Gold*, 78.

31 Business and Industry Round Table, *South Dakota*; "South Dakota Seen As a Prime State for Manufacturing," *Wall Street Journal,* 10 June 1985, 1; "First in 'Manufacturing Climate' Study South Dakota Is Business Hot Spot," *Los Angeles Times,* 13 June 1985, 11; Barkley, "Turmoil in Traditional Industry," 16, 18; David E. Petzal, "Don Allen, Rifle Maker, Dies in South Dakota," *Field & Stream* 108, 5 (Sept. 2003); John Zent, "Dakota Rifles: American Best," *American Rifleman,* 17 Dec. 2010.

32 U.S. Census, *1992 Census of Manufactures: South Dakota*.

33 Wymar, "South Dakota-Canadian Commercial Relations," 5; Miller, *Looking for History*, 36; Barkley, "Turmoil in Traditional Industry," 13; South Dakota Board of Regents, *Foundation for the Future*, 9-10; Berg, *South Dakota: Land of Shining Gold*, 78.

34 Wymar, "NAFTA and South Dakota," 4; Wymar, "South Dakota-Canadian Commercial Relations," 6.

35 Michael Barrier, "A Man Who Sees No Limits on the South Dakota Prairie," *Nation's Business* 79, 3 (Mar. 1991), 16.

36 Barkley, "Turmoil in Traditional Industry," 20.

37 Miller, *In Search of Gay America*, 101; Lee, *Principle Over Party*, 13; Erling N. Sannes, "'Union Makes Strength': Organizing Teamsters in South Dakota in the 1930s," *South Dakota History* 18 (Spring/Summer 1988): 36-66.

38 Sioux Falls Personnel Association, *1985 Metro Sioux Falls Salary Survey* (Sioux Falls: Sioux Falls Personnel Association, 1985).

39 Susan R. Dana, "South Dakota Employment At Will Doctrine: Twenty Years of Judicial Erosion," *South Dakota Law Review* 49, 1 (2003): 47-66.

40 Breanna Fuss, "SD Named Cheapest Place to Live," *KDLT News*, 16 June 2013; Foss and Foss, *A Proud American*, 36; O'Brien, *Buffalo for the Broken Heart*, 22; South Dakota Board of Regents, *Foundation for the Future*, 9.

41 Engeseth, "An Assessment of Formal Training," 9, 152-54.

42 Berg, *South Dakota: Land of Shining Gold*, 78; Hoover, "South Dakota," 50; Schell, *History of South Dakota*, 355; Wymar, "South Dakota-Canadian Commercial Relations," 5.

43 Wymar, "NAFTA and South Dakota," 4; http://www.htch.com/career_siouxfalls.asp.

44 Wymar, "NAFTA and South Dakota," 4; Rogers, *South Dakota's Challenges Since 1960*, 392-93; "Daktronics," Folder 21, Box 4, Dave Stenseth/EROS Collection, CWS; Grauvogl, *South Dakota: Pioneering the Future*, 87; http://investor.daktronics.com/stockquote.cfm.

45 Mark Reilly, "TalentSoft Will Seek Talent on South Dakota Plains," *Minneapolis St. Paul Business Journal,* 30 July 1999, 8.

46 Bryan, *American Indian Entrepreneurs*, 12-15; http://bhecustomapparel.com.

47 http://sddsi.com/about/history/; Lawrence, *The Change Game*, 200; Grauvogl, *South Dakota: Pioneering the Future*, 96; http://www.cardinalcustomproducts.com/whoweare.html.

48 http://www.angus-palm.com/index.php/company-information/history.

49 Grauvogl, *South Dakota: Pioneering the Future*, 90-93; http://www.rainbowplay.com/about-rainbow/our-history/.

50 Grauvogl, *South Dakota: Pioneering the Future*, 94-95.

51 Ibid., 53; http://www.masabainc.com/about-us.

52 Norris, *Dakota: A Spiritual Geography*, 29.

53 Andrew Krmenec, "Manufacturing," in *The American Midwest: An Interpretive Encyclopedia*, ed. Richard Sisson, Christian Zacher, and Andrew Cayton (Bloomington: Indiana University Press, 2007), 148; Rob Grunewald, "South Dakota Leads District States in Manufactured Exports," *Fedgazette* (May 2001): 16; Grauvogl, *South Dakota: Pioneering the Future*, 50; Wymar, "South Dakota-Canadian Commercial Relations," 1, 4-8; Wymar, "NAFTA and South Dakota," 1, 4-7; Wymar, "South Dakota-Japan Commercial Relations," 10-11; Rob Grunewald and Aaron Richins, "Manufactured Exports Continued to Expand in 2011," *Fedgazette* (July 2012), 18-19; Ronald Wirtz, "Manufacturing an Uptick," *Fedgazette* (Oct. 2012), 1-7; Ronald Wirtz, "Made (again?) in the USA," *Fedgazette* (Oct. 2012), 7-9.

54 Gray et al., *South Dakota Economic and Business Abstract*, 159; Seventh Annual Meeting of the National Creamery Buttermakers' Association, Sioux Falls, Jan. 23 to 28, 1899, Sioux Falls Misc. Publications, CWS; Brown Drug Illustrated Catalog (1909) in Richard Rush Brown – Brown Drug Company Collection, CWS.

55 Minute Book of Brown Drug Company, Richard Rush Brown – Brown Drug Company Collection, CWS.

56 Smith, "Some Changing Features of a Regional Capital," 115, 147-49; *Horizons: Sioux Falls in the 1970s* (1971), Marcia Brinkman, "Sioux Falls: Steady as She Grows," *Corporate Report* (Apr. 1976): 27-43, Box 1, Dave Stenseth/EROS Collection, CWS; Wymar, "NAFTA and South Dakota," 4; http://www.vermillionedc.com/successstories/CaseStudiesDetail22.cfm?itemid=7.

57 Amund O. Ringsrud items, 1900-1914, JKH. 58 "Economic Census Comparative Statistics, South Dakota," *South Dakota Business Review* 58, 4 (June 2000), 11; Smith, "Some Changing Features of a Regional Capital," 38-53; *Horizons: Sioux Falls in the 1970s* (1971), Box 1, Dave Stenseth/EROS Collection, CWS; Peterson, *Storyville USA*, 204.

59 John Deere Plow Company, Sioux Falls Branch Collection, CWS.

60 Betty Nicholas Bowers, "Time in Amber in the Midlands," *New York Times,* 23 Nov. 1978, A23; Schwieder, *Growing Up with the Town,* 109.

61 Lewis, *Nothing to Make a Shadow,* 115; Nelson, *After the West Was Won,* 46; Fairchild and Wyman, *Frontier Woman,* 77, 90; Cochell and Beine, *Land of the Coyote,* 46.

62 Barkley, "Turmoil in Traditional Industry," 26-28; Bucklin, "Memoir of Frank Bloodgood," 113, 152-53; Reese, *South Dakota,* 114-15.

63 Philip. L. Gerber, ed., *Bachelor Bess: The Homesteading Letters of Elizabeth Corey, 1909-1919* (Iowa City: University of Iowa Press, 1990), 405-6, n.1; Andersen, *Portable Prairie,* 10; "Jolly Merchants: Low-Cost Loans Keeping Shoppers in South Dakota Town," *Tampa Bay Times,* 22 Dec. 1987, 10A; Orr, "A History of Aviation in South Dakota," 67.

64 Gerber, *Bachelor Bess,* 232, 330; Cochell and Beine, *Land of the Coyote,* 19; D.C. Doerr Collection: Look's Market, CWS.

65 U.S. Senate, *Impact of Interest Rates,* 3, 5.

66 Ibid., 5.

67 Ibid., 6; Schell, *History of South Dakota,* 354.

68 Anson, *McGovern,* 145n.

69 Nelson, *The Prairie Winnows Out Its Own,* 82.

70 http://www.1800usaband.com/page/view/8; Lawrence, *The Change Game,* 186, 210.

71 Bryan, *American Indian Entrepreneurs,* 3.

72 Miller, *Looking for History,* 125-26; http://www.trueyellow.com/EATING+PLACES/Harrold/South+Dakota/50/1/show.asp

73 VanEpps-Taylor, *Forgotten Lives,* 137; Schell, *History of South Dakota,* 357; Breitbach and Mitchell, "Growth Machines and Growth Pains," 215.

74 Schatz, *Longhorns Bring Culture,* 31; Siberts and Wyman, *Nothing but Prairie and Sky,* 79; Abourezk, *Advise and Dissent,* 13, 42; Wilder, *On the Way Home,* 11; Lewis, *Nothing to Make a Shadow.*

75 Montgomery and Van Doren, *Economy of the West North Central Region,* 65-66.

76 Volk, *Economy of the Northeast Region,* 62.

77 Dahl, *Banker Dahl,* 166, 195.

78 "South Dakota Firm to Add More Utah C-Stores," *The Enterprise,* 8 May 2000, 22.

Chapter 7

1 Dudley Nichols, *The Big Sky* (1952) as quoted in Dehgan, *America in Quotations,* 38.

2 Riley, "Farm Women's Roles," 109; Lewis, *Nothing to Make a Shadow,* 55, 144-46; Lee, "Traveling the Sunshine State," 203.

3 June Beecher and Priscilla Hillgren, "Footlights and Spotlights: A Journal of Sioux Falls Entertainment from 1870-1950," Final Draft, Sioux Falls Theater Collection, CWS.

4 Gerber, *Bachelor Bess,* lv; Dalstrom and Dalstrom, "Dancing in Small-Town South Dakota," 284-85; Miller, *Looking for History,* 192.

5 Volk, *Economy of the Northeast Region,* 69.

6 Weatherford, *A History of Women,* 4:412; Miller, *Looking for History,* 37.7 Entrepreneur Press, *How to Start a Business in South Dakota,* 13.3; Grauvogl, *South Dakota: Pioneering the Future,* 44; "The Traveler: Adventure and Festivities in South Dakota," *South Dakota Magazine* (Mar./Apr. 2011), 55-59; Head, *South Dakota: An Explorer's Guide;* Stanley H. Edmunds, "I Remember When," (c. 1970), Stanley H. Edmunds Collection, CWS; Brokaw, *A Long Way from Home,* 50; Polsky, *Boneheads* 124-25; Peterson, *Storyville USA,* 201.

8 Herzog, *Small World,* 53.

9   Yvette Cardozo and Bill Hirsch, "A Midwinter Night's Dream," *South Florida Sun-Sentinel,* 19 Jan. 1986, 1J.

10   "Reminiscences of Irene Mortenson Sargent," (1990), Edith Mortenson Delman Collection, CWS; Brokaw, *A Long Way from Home,* 121.

11   Head, *South Dakota: An Explorer's Guide,* 14-16, 22; Reese, *South Dakota,* 91; Wymar, "South Dakota-Japan Commercial Relations," 5, 11; Rosemary McCoy, "Austad's Keeps Swinging with Golfers," *Sioux Falls Argus Leader,* 8 Mar. 2005, A18.

12   Entrepreneur Press, *How to Start a Business in South Dakota,* 13.8; Head, *South Dakota: An Explorer's Guide,* 21.

13   "Family Mountain Biking in South Dakota," *Backpacker* 22, 5 (June 1994), 30; Miller, *Looking for History,* 82-84, 90.

14   Schultz, *1,000 Places to See,* 656-57; Dick Skuse, "South Dakota Boasts the World's Corniest Arena," *Toronto Star,* 12 July 1986, G11.

15   Peterson, *Storyville USA,* 202.

16   Ibid., 201-202.

17   Schultz, *1,000 Places to See,* 657; Dalstrom and Dalstrom, "Dancing in Small-Town South Dakota," 286.

18   VanEpps-Taylor, *Forgotten Lives,* 210-11; Eric Dregni, *Midwest Marvels: Roadside Attractions Across Iowa, Minnesota, the Dakotas, and Wisconsin* (Minneapolis: University of Minnesota Press, 2006), 259-339; "ICBM Returns to South Dakota," *American History* (Dec. 2001), 10-14; Schell, *History of South Dakota,* 326, 336-37; Rogers, *South Dakota's Challenges Since 1960,* 337; Miller, "Small Towns: Image and Reality," 188-89; Nelson, *After the West Was Won,* 48-50; Bucklin, "Memoir of Frank Bloodgood," 152; "Owen with Semi-Pro Club," *New York Times,* 14 Apr. 1949, 33; Abourezk, *Advise and Dissent,* 39; Dahl, *Banker Dahl,* 28.

19   Johnson, *Highways and Byways,* 276-77.

20   Reese, *South Dakota,* 82.

21   "Symbol," *New York Times,* 4 Oct. 1959, S17; Christopher Laingen, "Complex Feedbacks Among Human and Natural Systems and Pheasant Hunting in South Dakota, USA," (Ph.D. diss., University of Kansas, 2009), 7; Schultz, *1,000 Places to See,* 657-58.

22   Peirce and Hagstrom, "South Dakota: State of Reluctant Change," 566; Schultz, *1,000 Places to See,* 658; T. D. Griffith, "People of the Plains and Pines: Native Tourism in South Dakota," *Native Peoples* (Sept./Oct. 2006), 66-69; Cochell and Beine, *Land of the Coyote,* 55; Patricia Brooks, *Where the Bodies Are: Final Visits to the Rich, Famous & Interesting* (Guilford, CT: The Globe Pequot Press, 2002), 189-90; Griffith, "People of the Plains and Pines," 687-89; Polsky, *Boneheads* 87-88.

23   "Fire Razes Downtown Block in South Dakota Tourist Town," *New York Times,* 17 Dec. 1987, A223; Weatherford, *A History of Women,* 4:415; Kenneth Kellar, *Seth Bullock, Frontier Marshal* (Aberdeen: North Plains Press, 1972); Mitchel Whitington, *A Ghost in My Suitcase: A Guide to Haunted Travel in America* (Dallas: Atriad Press, 2005), 193-96; Brooks, *Where the Bodies Are,* 187-88; "Girls of the Gulch," *Deadwood Magazine* (1997); Andree Brooks, "Seeking the Real Deadwood," *New York Times,* 30 Aug. 1987, XX21; Yvette Cardozo and Bill Hirsch, "A Midwinter Night's Dream," *South Florida Sun-Sentinel,* 19 Jan. 1986, 1J; Reese, *South Dakota,* 92; William N. Thompson, *The International Encyclopedia of Gambling* (Santa Barbara: ABC-CLIO, 2010), 589-90; Schultz, *1,000 Places to See,* 654-55; Martin Mitchell, "Deadwood, South Dakota: Place and Setting Combine with Gambling and Historic Preservation," *American Geographical Society Focus on Geography* 51, 2 (Fall 2008): 26-33.

24   Miller, *Looking for History,* 195-205; Schultz, *1,000 Places to See,* 660-61.

25 As quoted in Miller, *Looking for History*, 197.

26 Schultz, *1,000 Places to See*, 661.

27 Stock, *Main Street in Crisis*, 211; Peterson, *Storyville USA*, 202.

28 Miller, *Looking for History*, 206-220.

29 Tom Lawrence, "John Thune, Er, 'Rested' Here," *Mitchell Daily Republic,* 21 Apr. 2011; Brokaw, *A Long Way from Home*, ix, 3.

30 Dehgan, *America in Quotations*, 52.

31 Rogers, *South Dakota's Challenges Since 1960*, 345-46, 348; Dregni, *Midwest Marvels*, 259; Marian Christy, "This Ladd's Got Spunk," *Boston Globe,* 23 Feb. 1986, 41; Ken Paulson and Paula Burton, "South Dakota Celebrities," *USA Today*, 22 June 1987, 11A.

32 Milton, *South Dakota: A Bicentennial History*, 149; VanEpps-Taylor, *Oscar Micheaux, Dakota Homesteader*; Berg, *South Dakota: Land of Shining Gold*, 78.

33 Karolevitz, *Challenge: The South Dakota Story*, 303; Rogers, *South Dakota's Challenges Since 1960*, 364, 370.

34 VanEpps-Taylor, *Forgotten Lives*, 148-49; Hoover, "South Dakota: An Expression of Regional Heritage," 195; Fite, "Observations by a Native Son," 469; Milton, *South Dakota: A Bicentennial History*, 9. See also Arthur Huseboe, *An Illustrated History of the Arts in South Dakota* (Sioux Falls: Center for Western Studies, 1989) for an assessment of South Dakota writers.

35 VanEpps-Taylor, *Forgotten Lives*, 88; Reese, *South Dakota*, 97; Lauck, *Prairie Republic*, 29; Fite, "Observations by a Native Son," 469; Milton, *South Dakota: A Bicentennial History*, 8-9.

36 Milton, *South Dakota: A Bicentennial History*, 151-53; Weatherford, *A History of Women*, 4:409; Jennifer Gerrietts, "South Dakota: The Literature State?" *Sioux Falls Argus Leader,* 27 Jan. 2013; Andersen, *Portable Prairie*; Charles Ealy, "Author Shares Memories of Her Life," Fredericksburg (Virginia) *Free-Lance Star,* 29 May 2005, F5; Patrick Hicks, ed., *A Harvest of Words: Contemporary South Dakota Poetry* (Sioux Falls: Center for Western Studies, 2010).

37 Milton, *South Dakota: A Bicentennial History*, 181.

38 John E. Miller, "From South Dakota Farm to Harvard Seminar: Alvin H. Hansen, America's Prophet of Keynesianism," *The Historian* 64 (Spring/Summer 2002), 604-22.

39 Weatherford, *A History of Women*, 4:407; Andersen, *Portable Prairie*, 16.

40 Weatherford, *A History of Women*, 4:418; Flyger, "An Invitation to South Dakota,"43; Miller, *Looking for History*, 50-63; Shirley Hoover Biggers, *American Author Houses, Museums, Memorials, and Libraries: A State-by-State Guide* (Jefferson, NC: McFarland and Co., 2000), 180; Schultz, *1,000 Places to See*, 655-56; Christine Woodside, "Little Libertarians on the Prairie," *Boston Globe,* 9 Aug. 2013.

41 Miller, *Looking for History*, 64-76; John Andrews, "Ten 'Must See' South Dakota Paintings," *South Dakota Magazine* (Jan./Feb. 2009); Milton, *South Dakota: A Bicentennial History*, 147; John R. Milton, ed. *The American Indian Speaks* (Vermillion: University of South Dakota, 1969), 193; Edward Welch, "The Making of a Legend: Oscar Howe," *High Plains Artist* (2013): 14-15.42 Brokaw, *A Long Way from Home*, 161; Rogers, *South Dakota's Challenges Since 1960*, 352; Larry Kitzel, "The Trombones of the Shrine to Music Museum (South Dakota)," (D.M.A. Thesis, University of Oklahoma, 1985); "Music Notes: A Plum Goes to South Dakota," *New York Times,* 8 July 1984, A18.

43 "Moreover: High Notes in South Dakota," *The Economist,* Jan. 16, 1999, 77.

44 Pagnamenta, *Prairie Fever*, xiii.

45 Mary Lu Abbott, "South Dakota Surprises," *Houston Chronicle,* 10 Aug. 1986, 1.

46 Lewis, *Nothing to Make a Shadow*, 138.

47 Cleophas O'Harra, *The White River Badlands* (Rapid City, S.D.: South Dakota School of Mines, 1920), 61-62; Newton and Jenney, *Report on the Geology and Resources*, 6; McDermott, *Journal of an Expedition to the Mauvaises Terres*, 1; Champ Clark, *The Badlands* (New York: Time-Life Books, 1974), 74-78.

48 Lewis, *Nothing to Make a Shadow*, 140; O'Harra, *The White River Badlands*, 70.

49 Lawrence, *The Change Game*, 184-85; Polsky, *Boneheads*, 5, 23, 57, 145, 161.

50 Lawrence, *The Change Game*, 184-85; Polsky, *Boneheads*, 22, 50, 61, 64-66, 158; Steve Fiffer, *Tyrannosaurus Sue: The Extraordinary Saga of the Largest, Most Fought Over T. Rex Ever Found* (New York: W. H. Freeman and Co., 2000), 13-14.

51 http://www.paleoadventures.com.

52 Fiffer, *Tyrannosaurus Sue*, xiii, 2, 17, 210; Polsky, *Boneheads,* 121-23, 160.

53 Rogers, *South Dakota's Challenges Since 1960*, 383-84; Joe Kafka, "South Dakota Town Supports Site for Fun and Profit: Excavations Reveal Mammoth Bone Cache," *Los Angeles Times,* 16 Aug. 1987, 4; http://www.mammothsite.com.

54 Lewis, *Nothing to Make a Shadow*, 11.

55 Lee, "Traveling the Sunshine State," 201.

56 Gooder Casey Land Co., *Southwestern South Dakota*.

57 Frazier, *On the Rez*, 136-37.

58 Johnson, *Highways and Byways*, 250-79.

59 Ibid., 263.

60 *Clason's So. Dakota Green Guide*, CWS.

61 Lee, "Traveling the Sunshine State," 198-200; Nelson, *The Prairie Winnows Out Its Own*, 79; Chris B. Nelson, "Life Along the Road: The Tourist Camp in South Dakota," *South Dakota History* 35, 4 (Winter 2005), 320.

62 Peterson, *Through the Black Hills and Bad Lands*, 48, 171.

63 Lee, "Traveling the Sunshine State," 210-11; Nelson, "Life Along the Road," 315-34.

64 "Coolidge Vacation to Start June 13," *New York Times,* 27 May 1927, 25.

65 Nelson, "Life Along the Road," 320; Lee, "Traveling the Sunshine State," 212-16.

66 Cash, *Working the Homestake*, 62; Peterson, *Through the Black Hills and Bad Lands*, 171; Nelson, "Life Along the Road," 320.

67 O'Harra, *The White River Badlands*, 147.

68 Ibid., 148.

69 Ibid.

70 Clark, *The Badlands*, 29.

71 As quoted in Gunther, *Inside U.S.A.*, 246.

72 As quoted in Clark, *The Badlands*, 27.

73 South Dakota State Planning Board and Hamlin County Planning Board, *Economic and Social Survey*, 14.

74 Ibid., 15-16.

75 O'Harra, *The White River Badlands*, 148.

76 Peterson, *Through the Black Hills and Bad Lands*, 40.77 Cassels, *Prehistoric Hunters*, 79-84; Gregory Little, ed. *The Illustrated Encyclopedia of Native American Mounds & Earthworks* (Memphis: Eagle Wing Books, 2009), 223.

78 Bryan, *American Indian Entrepreneurs*, 47-50; Business and Industry Round Table, *South Dakota*.

79 Schell, *History of South Dakota*, 332-33.

80 Reese, *South Dakota*, 69.

81 South Dakota Department of State, *South Dakota and Foreign Trade*, 3-4.

82 As quoted in Miller, *Looking for History*, 207.

83 "Come West! America's Different Vacation," *New York Times,* 26 Apr. 1964, XX19.

84 "South Dakota: Tourism Tax Expanded," *State Tax Review,* 24 Mar. 1997, 18.

85 Gray et al, *South Dakota Economic and Business Abstract*, 205.

86 Volk, *Economy of the Black Hills Region*, 73.

87 Andrew H. Malcolm, "Main Attraction Is Underground at South Dakota National Park," *Toronto Globe and Mail,* 17 Nov. 1984, 10.

88 Volk, *Economy of the Black Hills Region*, 75; Wymar, "South Dakota-Canadian Commercial Relations," 6.

89 U.S. National Park Service, *Wind Cave National Park*, 8-9, 12-15, 32.

90 Malcolm, "Main Attraction Is Underground," *Toronto Globe and Mail,* Nov. 17, 1984, 10.

91 U.S. National Park Service, *Wind Cave National Park*, 12, 32, 35-76.

92 Herb Conn and Jan Conn, *The Jewel Cave Adventure: Fifty Miles of Discovery Under South Dakota* (St. Louis: Cave Books, 1981), 33-37.

93 Andrew Yarrow, "Beneath South Dakota's Black Hills," *New York Times,* 9 Aug. 1987, A21.

94 Tom Fegely, "The Black Hills of South Dakota," Allentown *Morning Call,* 8 Mar. 1987, F01.

95 Reeve Bailey and Marvin Allum, *Fishes of South Dakota* (Ann Arbor: Museum of Zoology, University of Michigan, 1962), 7; Warren, *Preliminary Report of Explorations*, 104; Lewis, *Nothing to Make a Shadow*, 43.

96 Hagerty, *Territory of Dakota*, 49.

97 Bucklin, "Memoir of Frank Bloodgood," 138.

98 Bailey and Allum, *Fishes of South Dakota*, 5-11; "Missouri River, North and South Dakota," *Field & Stream* (Apr. 1999), 67.

99 As quoted in Lawson, *Dammed Indians*, 3.

100 Schneiders, *Unruly River*, 148, 154-55; Thomas C. Mack, "South Dakota's Role in Damming the Missouri River from 1915 to 1950," (M.A. Thesis, University of South Dakota, 2010).

101 Schneiders, *Unruly River*, 23; Berg, *South Dakota: Land of Shining Gold*, 36; Robinson, *West from Fort Pierre*, 276; Seth S. King, "Fall Recreation Spots on the Missouri," *New York Times,* 20 Sept. 1953, X21; Carrels, *Uphill Against Water*, 32.

102 Schneiders, *Unruly River*, 239.

103 Robinson, *West from Fort Pierre*, 276.

104 Carrels, *Uphill Against Water*, 206; Schneiders, *Unruly River*, 20; Conn and Conn, *Jewel Cave Adventure*, 98-99; "South Dakota: Two Heavyweights," *Outdoor Life* (May 1999): 98.

105 Mandat-Grancey, *Cowboys and Colonels*, 193; Casey, *The Black Hills and Their Incredible Characters*, 96-97.

106 Peterson, *Through the Black Hills and Bad Lands*, 167.107 William H. Over and Edward P. Churchill, *Mammals of South Dakota* (Vermillion: University of South Dakota, 1945), 1; Urbanek, *The Uncovered Wagon*, 97.

108 McDermott, *Journal of an Expedition to the Mauvaises Terres*, 60; "The New States: South Dakota's Capital," *New York Tribune,* 28 Apr. 1889, 24; Bucklin, "Memoir of Frank Bloodgood," 117; Warren, *Preliminary Report of Explorations*, 90; Duncan, *Blue Star*, 104; Col. James Clyman Collection, CWS; Siberts and Wyman, *Nothing but Prairie and Sky*, 12, 117, 124-25; Warren, *Preliminary Report of Explorations*, 91; Coleman, "The Missouri Valley of South Dakota," 94; Mandat-Grancey, *Cowboys and Colonels*, 307; Van Nuys, *The Family Band*, 118; Gilfillan, *Sheep*, 172-73; Gerber, *Bachelor Bess*, xlix; Robinson, *West*

from Fort Pierre, 305; Daum, *The Prairie in Her Eyes*, 133-36; Kenneth F. Higgins, Eilen Dowd Stukel, Judyann M. Goulet, and Douglas C. Backlund, *Wild Mammals of South Dakota* (Pierre: South Dakota Department of Game, Fish and Parks, 2000).

109 McDermott, *Journal of an Expedition to the Mauvaises Terres*, 57, 64; Warren, *Preliminary Report of Explorations*, 90-95; Siberts and Wyman, *Nothing but Prairie and Sky*, 48, 118; Fairchild and Wyman, *Frontier Woman*, 13, 74; Mandat-Grancey, *Cowboys and Colonels*, 310; Lewis, *Nothing to Make a Shadow*, 93; Nelson, *After the West Was Won*, 38-39.

110 Gilfillan, *Sheep*, 167.

111 Cochell and Beine, *Land of the Coyote*, 27-29; Gilfillan, *Sheep*, 95, 167; Hasselstrom, *No Place Like Home*, 20; Mandat-Grancey, *Cowboys and Colonels*, 305; Fairchild and Wyman, *Frontier Woman*, 21, 39; Van Nuys, *The Family Band*, 81; Bucklin, "Memoir of Frank Bloodgood," 149-50.

112 Siberts and Wyman, *Nothing but Prairie and Sky*, 48; Hasselstrom, *Windbreak: A Woman Rancher*, 122; Van Nuys, *The Family Band*, 127; "In the Valley of the Jim: Story of the Dowdell Family" (1951), Dowdell Family Collection, CWS; Warren, *Preliminary Report of Explorations*, 102; Gooder Casey Land Co., *Southwestern South Dakota*; Zimmerman, *Peoples of Prehistoric South Dakota*, 30.

113 McDermott, *Journal of an Expedition to the Mauvaises Terres*, 35, 37, 42, 46-47.

114 As quoted in Parker, "Early Explorations," 195.

115 "It Is Easier to Purchase a Minnesota Prairie Chicken in New York Than It Is in Winona," *New York Times,* 13 Oct. 1882, 4; Bucklin, "Memoir of Frank Bloodgood," 122.

116 Johnson, *Highways and Byways*, 275.

117 Oscar Godbout, "Wood, Field and Stream: Sharply Decreased Wetlands Threaten the Future of Waterfowl," *New York Times,* 6 Feb. 1964, 26; Amerson, *From the Hidewood*, 186-88; Frederic Remington, "Stubble and Slough in Dakota," in *The Collected Writings of Frederic Remington*, ed. Peggy Samuels and Harold Samuels (New York: Doubleday, 1979), 163; Paul Johnsgard, *Lewis and Clark on the Great Plains: A Natural History* (Lincoln: University of Nebraska Press, 2003), 35-61; Warren, *Preliminary Report of Explorations*, 103; Coleman, "The Missouri Valley of South Dakota," 94.

118 Warren, *Preliminary Report of Explorations*, 90; Over and Churchill, *Mammals of South Dakota*, 1; Herman, *Hunting and the American Imagination*, 203.

119   Richard Hummel, "Hunting," in *The American Midwest: An Interpretive Encyclopedia*, ed. Richard Sisson, Christian Zacher, and Andrew Cayton (Bloomington: Indiana University Press, 2007), 924-25; Zimmerman, *Peoples of Prehistoric South Dakota*, 30; Braun, *Buffalo Inc.*, 61.

120 VanEpps-Taylor, *Forgotten Lives*, 56.

121 Remington, "Stubble and Slough in Dakota," 163.122 Hasselstrom, *Roadside History*, 82; George Greenfield, "Rod and Gun," *New York Times*, 24 Nov. 1934, 12.

123 Siberts and Wyman, *Nothing but Prairie and Sky*, 112; Cochell and Beine, *Land of the Coyote*, 13.

124 Cochell and Beine, *Land of the Coyote*, 145.

125 George Abbott to John Krause, Aug. 5, 1902, George W. Abbott Collection, CWS.

126 Johnson, *Highways and Byways*, 276.

127   "It Is Easier to Purchase a Minnesota Prairie Chicken in New York Than It Is in Winona," *New York Times,* 13 Oct. 1882, 4; "The Destruction of Birds," *New York Times,* 17 Apr. 1898, 24.

128   Herman, *Hunting and the American Imagination*, 125-45, 154-55, 218-225 (quotation on 225); Foss and Foss, *A Proud American*, 23.

129 Lewis, *Nothing to Make a Shadow*, 86.

130 Kibbe, "Early Recollections of the Son of a Pioneer Newspaper Man," 326.

131 Culp, *Letters from Tully*, 23.

132 Cochell and Beine, *Land of the Coyote*, 68; Hagerty, *Territory of Dakota*, 49.

133 Robinson, *West from Fort Pierre*, 277; Remington, "Stubble and Slough in Dakota," 161.

134 Lewis, *Nothing to Make a Shadow*, 87.

135 Remington, "Stubble and Slough in Dakota," 160.

136 J. B. Barnes, "Something about Grouse – Confusion of Names, Varieties in the West," *New York Times,* 22 Nov. 1874, 9.

137 Culp, *Letters from Tully*, 234-35; Fred H. Dale, "Pheasants and Pheasant Populations," in *Pheasants in North America,* ed. Durward L. Allen (Harrisburg, PA: Stackpole Company, 1956), 1; Major L. Boddicker, "Bionomics of Mallophaga of Sharp-Tailed Grouse in South Dakota," (Ph.D. diss., South Dakota State University, 1972), 10, 13; Herman, *Hunting and the American Imagination*, 125-45, 154-55, 218-225; Vernon Van Ness, "Rod and Gun," *New York Times,* 27 Jan. 1933, 15.

138 Laingen, "Complex Feedbacks," 28, 30; J. B. Barnes, "Something About Grouse – Confusion of Names, Varieties in the West," *New York Times,* 22 Nov. 1874, 9; Dale, "Pheasants and Pheasant Populations," 2-4; "Coolidge Vacation to Start June 13," *New York Times,* 27 May 1927, 25; "Briefly Told," *New York Times,* 20 June 1885, 4; James W. Kimball, Edward L. Kozicky, and Bernard A. Nelson, "Pheasants of the Plains and Prairies," in *Pheasants in North America*, ed. Durward L. Allen (Harrisburg, PA: Stackpole Company, 1956), 204-07; Marten, "Culture of Pheasant Hunting," 89; Carolyn D. Burks, "Habitat Selection by the Ring-Necked Pheasant During the Breeding Season in Central South Dakota," (M.S. thesis, University of Wyoming, 1985), 1; "Minnehaha Brings Over Consignment for Fair Hill Farm," *New York Times,* 7 Jan. 1915, 14; Lincoln A. Werden, "Rod and Gun," *New York Times,* 30 Apr. 1932, 11; Vernon Van Ness, "Rod and Gun," *New York Times,* 6 Dec. 1933, 32; Lincoln A. Werden, "News of Wood, Field and Stream," *New York Times,* 2 Feb. 1943, 26; Gunther, *Inside U.S.A.,* 249.

139 Hoover, "South Dakota," 925; Marten, "Culture of Pheasant Hunting," 90; South Dakota State Planning Board and Hamlin County Planning Board, *Economic and Social Survey*, 17; Fairchild and Wyman, *Frontier Woman*, 79-80.

140 "Coolidge Vacation to Start June 13," *New York Times,* 27 May 1927, 25.

141 Peterson, *Through the Black Hills and Bad Lands*, 181.

142 Gunther, *Inside U.S.A.,* 249; Karolevitz, *Challenge: The South Dakota Story*, 237; George Greenfield, "Wood, Field and Stream," *New York Times,* 19 Feb. 1936, 26; "SayPheasants Eat Crops," *New York Times,* 25 Mar. 1928, 36; "Wisconsin to Aid Raising of Game," *New York Times,* 27 Aug. 1933, E6; Miller, *Looking for History*, 47.

143 Marten, "Culture of Pheasant Hunting," 90.

144 Ibid., 90.

145 Ibid., 101-2.

146 "Say Pheasants Eat Crops," *New York Times,* 25 Mar. 1928, 36.

147 Vernon Van Ness, "Rod and Gun," *New York Times,* 24 Oct. 1933, 29.

148 Harlan Miller, "Again Fortune Smiles on the Prairies," *New York Times,* 7 Oct. 1934, SM4.

149 George Greenfield, "Wood, Field and Stream," *New York Times,* 19 Feb. 1936, 26.

150 Kimball, Kozicky, and Nelson, "Pheasants of the Plains and Prairies," 208-11; Lincoln A. Werden, "Wood, Field and Stream," *New York Times,* 15 Nov. 1942, S8; Lincoln A. Werden, "News of Wood, Field and Stream," *New York Times,* 2 Feb. 1943, 26; Lincoln

A. Werden, "News of Wood, Field and Stream," *New York Times,* 2 Mar. 1943, 25; John Rendel, "Wood, Field and Stream," *New York Times,* 4 Mar. 1945, S2.

151 John Rendel, "Wood, Field and Stream," *New York Times,* 5 Oct. 1944, 18.

152 "Pheasants Fly to Navy Mess," *New York Times,* 28 Oct. 1945, 37; Marten, "Culture of Pheasant Hunting," 89; Burks, "Habitat Selection by the Ring-Necked Pheasant," 1; Gunther, *Inside U.S.A.,* 248-49.

153 Robert Dahlgren, *The Pheasant Decline* (Pierre: South Dakota Department of Game, Fish and Parks, 1967), 14.

154 Kimball, Kozicky, and Nelson, "Pheasants of the Plains and Prairies," 229, 261.

155 Raymond R. Camp, "Wood, Field and Stream," *New York Times,* 19 Apr. 1946, 23.

156 Raymond R. Camp, "Wood, Field and Stream," *New York Times,* 2 Oct. 1946, 38; Raymond R. Camp, "Wood, Field and Stream," *New York Times,* 8 Nov. 1946, 32.

157 "Three Die as Plane Hits Mountain in Virginia," *New York Times,* 21 Oct. 1946, 5.

158 "Monthly Calendar for the Tourist," *New York Times,* 29 Aug. 1948, X12; Peterson, *Storyville USA,* 203; Abourezk, *Advise and Dissent,* 36.

159 Raymond R. Camp, "News of Wood, Field and Stream," *New York Times,* 11 Apr. 1947, 21.

160 "There's Good Hunting in Those South Dakota Hills," *New York Times,* 21 Oct. 1948, 35; Reese, *South Dakota,* 88, 92, 110; Marten, "Culture of Pheasant Hunting," 88, 91, 98; "Pheasant Season Set," *New York Times,* 15 Aug. 1951, 41; John W. Randolph, "Wood, Field, and Stream: Surveys Indicate that Hunting in the U.S. Will be Better Than in 1955," *New York Times,* 12 Oct. 1956, 41; John W. Randolph, "Wood, Field, and Stream: Pheasant Hunters, Despite Unquestioned Abstemiousness, Found Prone to Gout," *New York Times,* 30 Nov. 1957, 30; Berg, *South Dakota: Land of Shining Gold,* 42; Orville Prescott, "Books of the Times," *New York Times,* 28 May 1947, 23.

161 Gunther, *Inside U.S.A.,* 248.

162 John W. Randolph, "Wood, Field and Stream: Preserve Hunters Cautioned Not to Get the Bird While Getting the Bird," *New York Times,* 29 Nov. 1959, S7; Robert Alden, "Advertising: Winchester Slates Big Drive," *New York Times,* 22 Sept. 1960, 44; Andrew G. Hopp, "South Dakota Pheasant Hunting Preserves," (M.S. thesis, South Dakota State University, 2007); South Dakota Department of Game, Fish, & Parks, *Private Shooting Preserve: 2012-13 Information Manual for Private Shooting Preserves* (Pierre: Division of Wildlife, 2012); Laingen, "Complex Feedbacks," 43-44; Oscar Godbout, "Wood, Field and Stream: State, National Reports on Prospects of Game Hunting are Optimistic," *New York Times,* 5 Oct. 1962, 59; Marten, "Culture of Pheasant Hunting," 88, 96, 109.163 James A. Loftus, "State Legislatures, Under Budget Pressure, Face Wide Range of Issues,' *New York Times,* 6 Jan. 1965, 22; Dahlgren, *Pheasant Decline,* 18.

164 Dahlgren, *Pheasant Decline,* 3-6, 30-31; Kimball, Kozicky, and Nelson, "Pheasants of the Plains and Prairies," 221, 229-30.

165 Dahlgren, *Pheasant Decline,* 7.

166 Ibid., 7, 11-15.

167 Ibid., 17.

168 Kimball, Kozicky, and Nelson, "Pheasants of the Plains and Prairies," 213-14; Oscar Godbout, "Wood, Field and Stream: Sharply Decreased Wetlands Threaten the Future of Waterfowl," *New York Times,* 6 Feb. 1964, 26; Jim Knight, "Ring-Necked Pheasant Management for Montana Landowners," in *Manage Your Land for Wildlife* (Bozeman: Montana State University Extension Publications, 2008); Burks, "Habitat Selection by the Ring-Necked Pheasant," 1, 100-15.

169 Dahlgren, *Pheasant Decline*, 18-19, 22, 38-39; Gordon Aldrich, Changing Social Patterns on the Lingering Frontier Records, CWS.

170 Marten, "Culture of Pheasant Hunting," 89; Dale, "Pheasants and Pheasant Populations," 20; Kimball, Kozicky, and Nelson, "Pheasants of the Plains and Prairies," 225; Laingen, "Complex Feedbacks," 35; Dahlgren, *Pheasant Decline*, 35, 40.

171 Kimball, Kozicky, and Nelson, "Pheasants of the Plains and Prairies," 256; Reese, *South Dakota*, 88; Dahlgren, *Pheasant Decline*, 32-33; South Dakota Department of Game, Fish, & Parks, *Private Shooting Preserve*.

172 Robert Sherrill, "High Noon on Capitol Hill," *New York Times,* 23 June 1968, SM7.

173 B. Drummond Ayres, Jr. "Politicians in Dakota Are Still Just Folks," *New York Times,* 30 Oct. 1970, 48.

174 Murray Chass, "Martin Denies That He Hit Man in Hotel," *New York Times,* 23 Nov. 1978, A23; Iver Peterson, "McGovern Fails in Attempt at Fourth Term as Senator," *New York Times,* 5 Nov. 1980, A21.

175 Marten, "Culture of Pheasant Hunting," 109; Kathryn Paulsen, "A Feast Day of Roast Corn Up in Michigan," *New York Times,* 5 June 1988, XX47; Burks, "Habitat Selection by the Ring-Necked Pheasant," 1; Verlyn Klinkenborg, "Keeping Iowa's Young Folks at Home After They've Seen Minnesota," *New York Times,* 9 Feb. 2005, A22; Eric Schmitt, "Cheney Mixes Jokes with Tough Talk," *New York Times,* 20 Feb. 2002, A11; Eric Schmitt, "Democrats Provided Edge on Detainee Vote," *New York Times,* 12 Nov. 2005, A11; Elisabeth Bumiller, "Bush and Cheney Still Side by Side But ..." *New York Times,* 21 Nov. 2005, A19; Charles Fergus, "Cheney's Accident Holds Lessons for All Hunters," *New York Times,* 18 Feb. 2006, D6.

176 Marten, "Culture of Pheasant Hunting," 109; Laingen, "Complex Feedbacks," 3.

177 Marten, "Culture of Pheasant Hunting," 89; Kimball, Kozicky, and Nelson, "Pheasants of the Plains and Prairies," 227, 253-54.

178 Laingen, "Complex Feedbacks," 3.

179 Reese, *South Dakota*, 110.

180 Head, *South Dakota: An Explorer's Guide*, 180; Reese, *South Dakota*, 49; Laingen, "Complex Feedbacks," 3, 8.

181 Gray et al., *South Dakota Economic and Business Abstract*, 205; Foss and Foss, *A Proud American*, 212; Higgins et al, *Wild Mammals of South Dakota*; Reese, *South Dakota*, 88-89.

182 Reese, *South Dakota*, 87.

183 "South Dakota: Black Hills Gobblers," *Outdoor Life* (Mar. 1999), 93; Jim Zumbo, "South Dakota's Merriam's Turkeys," *Outdoor Life* (Mar. 2005).184 Bob Schrank, "A Dove Affair in South Dakota," *Minneapolis Star Tribune,* Sept. 14, 1986, 19C.

185 Bob Schrank, "South Dakota Dreamin' Pays Off," *Minneapolis Star Tribune,* Sept. 21, 1986, 7B.

186 "South Dakota: Riverfront Property," *Outdoor Life* (Nov. 1999): 84-85; Jerome Robinson, "South Dakota Geese," *Field & Stream* 96, 8 (Dec. 1991), 24-26.

187 Herman, *Hunting and the American Imagination*, 154-90; Schwieder, *Growing Up with the Town*, 3; Raymond R. Camp, "Wood, Field and Stream," *New York Times,* 8 Nov. 1946, 32; Reese, *South Dakota*, 87-89; Lee, "Traveling the Sunshine State," 219-20; "South Dakota Pheasant Hunts," *New York Times,* 20 Oct. 2000, E43; "South Dakota Pheasant Hunts," *New York Times,* 27 Oct. 2000, E47; http://wing-and-clay.blacksdirectories.com/display_company.cgi?company_id=2477&final_cat1=&final_cat2=&final_cat3=&final_cat4=&from_index=Y; Tatiana Boncompagni, "Shooting for a New Generation," *New York Times,* 9 Jan. 2004, F2.

188 Dahlgren, *Pheasant Decline*, 34.

189 Peter H. Lewis, "Why Compaq is Getting Down in the Trenches," *New York Times,* 17 Nov. 1991, F8; Gavin Ehringer, *100 Best Ranch Vacations in North America* (Guilford, CT: Globe Pequot Press, 2004), 116-17.

190 Bob Schrank, "Lean Year in South Dakota, But the Best Is Yet to Come," *Minneapolis Star Tribune,* Nov. 9, 1986, 19C; Schell, *History of South Dakota*, 353; Kimball, Kozicky, and Nelson, "Pheasants of the Plains and Prairies," 249; Keith E. Severson and F. Robert Gartner, "Problems in Commercial Hunting Systems: South Dakota and Texas Compared," *Journal of Range Management* 25, 5 (Sept. 1972): 342-45; Anon., "South Dakota's Version of the Deer Hunt Going to the Birds," *Fedgazette* (Jan. 2000), 10; Laingen, "Complex Feedbacks," 59-60.

191 Joseph Bruchac, "A Taxidermist's Dream Comes True," *Modern Taxidermist Magazine*, in Walter Heldt Collection, CWS.

192 Gunther, *Inside U.S.A.*, 249.

193 Chai, *Hapa Girl*, 68.

194 Laura K. Ringling, "Benson v. State: Road Hunting Tradition Upheld at the Expense of South Dakota Property Owners," *South Dakota Law Review* 52, 2 (2007): 417-43.

195 See, for example, HOPE, *Human Trafficking: Realities and Facts* (Watertown, SD: 2014).

Chapter 8

1 Dakota Bankers Association, 1934, as quoted in Karen Knepper, "100 Years of Banking in the Dakotas," *Commercial West*, 30 June 1984, 12.

2 By the late 1990s, agriculture and ag services accounted for only about 9% of earnings in the state. The service sector accounted for just under 24%, government about 17%, retail and wholesale trade about 16%, manufacturing about 14%, and finance and construction about 6% each. Mining provided the less than 1% residue. Anon., "South Dakota Business and Economic Activity," 9.

3 A point well documented by Augustana College professor of history, political science, and economics Ole Tonning in Chapter 23 of his unpublished manuscript, "The Upper Mississippi Basin: The Land That God Forgot, But Man Found," [1952], in the Ole O. Tonning Collection, CWS.4 George W. Nash, "Education," in *History of South Dakota,* by Doane Robinson (Indianapolis: B. F. Bowen, 1904), 1:470-71; Milton, *South Dakota: A Bicentennial History*, 163; Lewis, *Nothing to Make a Shadow*, 100.

5 Nash, "Education," 1:472; Schell, *History of South Dakota*, 334.

6 "Reminiscences of Irene Mortenson Sargent," (1990), Edith Mortenson Delman Collection, CWS.

7 Norma C. Wilson and Charles L. Woodard, ed. *One-Room Country School: South Dakota Stories* (Brookings: South Dakota Humanities Foundation, 1998); Flyger, "An Invitation to South Dakota,"43.

8 Nelson, *The Prairie Winnows Out Its Own*, 97; Beasley, "Life as a Hired Girl in South Dakota," 150; Fairchild and Wyman, *Frontier Woman*, 33; Dahl, *Banker Dahl*, 13-14; "Reminiscences of Irene Mortenson Sargent," (1990), Edith Mortenson Delman Collection, CWS; Flyger, "An Invitation to South Dakota,"43; Cochell and Beine, *Land of the Coyote*, 60-61.

9 William L. Raymond, "Out State Bonds as Investments: North Dakota – South Dakota," *Barron's,* June 15, 1925, 5; Reese, *South Dakota*, vii; Lawrence, *The Change Game*, 211;

Volk, *Economy of the Northeast Region*, 16; Wuthnow, *Remaking the Heartland,* 268; O'Brien, *Buffalo for the Broken Heart*, 111; U.S. Senate, *Impact of Interest Rates*, 41.

10 Hagerty, *Territory of Dakota*, 5.

11 Pogue, "Mounting Fiscal Pressures," 99; Brokaw, *A Long Way from Home*, 98.

12   Sylvia Jane Street, "Implementation of Planned Change: The South Dakota Modernization Process," (Ed.D. diss., University of South Dakota, 1994), 2.

13 Huntsinger, "Pioneering Black Hills Sheepman," 262.

14   Susan Warmuth, "School/Business Partnerships in South Dakota Elementary Schools," (Ed. diss., University of South Dakota, 1998).

15 Berg, *South Dakota: Land of Shining Gold*, 152.

16 Fairchild and Wyman, *Frontier Woman*, 33-34.

17 Ibid., 34.

18 Ibid., 51.

19 "Reminiscences of Irene Mortenson Sargent," (1990), Edith Mortenson Delman Collection, CWS.

20 Dahl, *Banker Dahl*, 8-9.

21 Schwieder, *Growing Up with the Town*, 95.

22 Cash, *Working the Homestake*, 71-78.

23 Entrepreneur Press, *How to Start a Business in South Dakota*, 13.7; Engeseth, "An Assessment of Formal Training," 146-47; Anon., "Inmates Wire South Dakota Schools for the Future," *Rural Telecommunications* 17, 1 (Jan./Feb. 1998), 10; Kathy Cobb, "Legislation Aims to Ease Path for New Technology," *Fedgazette* (July 1997), 7; Monty Robinson, "Students' and Employers' Perceptions of Technology and Technology Education in South Dakota," (Ed.D. diss., University of South Dakota, 2008).

24 Richardson, *Policy and Performance*, 119-44.

25   Grauvogl, *South Dakota: Pioneering the Future*, 39; Richardson, *Policy and Performance*, 126.

26 Fite, "Observations by a Native Son," 468.

27 Dahl, *Banker Dahl*, 233.

28 U.S. Senate, *Impact of Interest Rates*, 30.

29 Ibid., 32.30 VanEpps-Taylor, *Forgotten Lives*, 190; Smith, "Some Changing Features of a Regional Capital," 60, 62-63.

31 W. Franklin Jones, *Concrete Investigation of the Material of English Spelling with Conclusions Bearing on the Problem of Teaching Spelling* (Vermillion: University of South Dakota, 1913), 25-26.

32 LaDell Swiden and Mary DeVries, *South Dakota Exports* (Brookings: South Dakota State University, 1989); "Dr. James King," *Sioux Falls Argus Leader,* 10 Apr. 2012.

33 Carruth, "South Dakota: State without End," 333.

34 Van Nuys, *The Family Band*, 112.

35 Hoover, "South Dakota," 49; De Lorme W. Robinson, "Physicians and the Practice of Medicine," in *History of South Dakota* by Doane Robinson (Indianapolis: B. F. Bowen, 1904), 1:476-77.

36 Robinson, "Physicians and the Practice of Medicine," 1:480; Amerson, *From the Hidewood*, 127-48; Rogers, *South Dakota's Challenges Since 1960*, 352; Dalstrom and Dalstrom, "Dancing in Small-Town South Dakota," 290.

37 James Marten, "A Medical Entrepreneur Goes West: Father William Kroeger in South Dakota, 1893-1904," *South Dakota History* 21 (Winter 1991): 333-61; http://thomas.loc.gov/cgi-bin/query/z?r110:S09SE8-0037.

38 Hoover, "South Dakota," 49; Smith, "Some Changing Features of a Regional Capital," 58-60, 136-38; Robert E. Van Demark, Sr., ed. *Reminiscences of Irene Fisher Coon, R.N., about the Early History of Orthopaedic Nursing at Sioux Valley Hospital with Historical Origins of the Crippled Children's Hospital and School* (Sioux Falls: Center for Western Studies, 1992).

39 Institute for South Dakota Leadership and Participation, *The Future of Health Care in South Dakota Roundtable Report* (2000), 1-2; Grauvogl, *South Dakota: Pioneering the Future*, 47; Sarah Mahoney and Susan Coenen, "25 Happiest, Healthiest Cities in America," *Prevention Magazine* (2013); Breitbach and Mitchell, "Growth Machines and Growth Pains," 227-28.

40 For an overview of healthcare in South Dakota, see Thompson, *A New South Dakota History*, 423-50. Schell, *History of South Dakota*, 358; Bank of New York brief, c. 1985, William Janklow Papers, USD; Michael J. Myers and Dennis A. Johnson, "De Facto South Dakota Healthcare Reform: An Emerging 'Managed Competition Model'," *South Dakota Business Review* 50, 4 (June 1992): 1, 4-5.

41 U.S. Senate, *Rural Health Care Crisis: Hearings before the Committee on Finance* (Washington: U.S. GPO, 1990), 2.

42 Ibid., 35.

43 Hoover, "South Dakota," 49; Bank of New York brief, c. 1985, William Janklow Papers, USD.

44 Entrepreneur Press, *How to Start a Business in South Dakota*, 13.7.

45 U.S. Senate, *Rural Health Care Crisis*, 30.

46 Stock, *Main Street in Crisis*, 211; Institute for South Dakota Leadership and Participation, *The Future of Health Care*, 2; Pogue, "Mounting Fiscal Pressures," 99; U.S. Senate, *Rural Health Care Crisis*, 3; Myers and Johnson, "De Facto South Dakota Healthcare Reform," 1, 4-5; Grauvogl, *South Dakota: Pioneering the Future*, 48.

47 U.S. Senate, *The Role of Nursing Homes In Today's Society*, Hearing Before the Special Committee on Aging, United States Senate, Aug. 29, 1983, 98th Cong., 1st Sess., (Washington: GPO, 1984).

48 "Sanford Buys Hematech, Inc.," *KELO-Land News*, 4 Jan. 2013; Grauvogl, *South Dakota: Pioneering the Future*, 48.49 http://sdtbc.com/clients/graduates/.

50 South Dakota Board of Regents, *Foundation for the Future*, 3; http://www.researchparkatsdstate.com/about-us.html; "Mitchell, S.D. Named a Smart21 Community," *Community Dividend* (Jan. 2014), 8.

51 Karolevitz, *Challenge: The South Dakota Story*, 298; Marcia Brinkman, "Sioux Falls: Steady as She Grows," *Corporate Report* (Apr. 1976): 37-41, in Box 1, Dave Stenseth/EROS Collection, CWS; Schell, *History of South Dakota*, 333.

52 Suzanne Malich, "Signals from Space Become Pictures at South Dakota Rural Data Center," *Los Angeles Times*, 29 June 1986, A35. For a history of the first twenty-five years of EROS, see Rebecca L. Johnson, *What It Took: A History of the USGS Data Center* (Sioux Falls: Center for Western Studies, 1998).

53 Robert Gillette, "South Dakota Offers Lower Costs in Atom Smasher Race," *Los Angeles Times*, 2 July 1987, B42.

54 Grauvogl, *South Dakota: Pioneering the Future*, 86; Dan Daly, "Knology Will Be New Name for PrairieWave," *Rapid City Journal*, 9 Feb. 2008; Evelyn M. Rusli, "Wow Buys Knology for $750 Million," *New York Times*, 18 Apr. 2012.

55 Miller, *In Search of Gay America*, 102-4; Bryan, *American Indian Entrepreneurs*, 29; Lawrence, *The Change Game*, 197-98; Grauvogl, *South Dakota: Pioneering the Future*, 56.

56 Doane Robinson, *History of South Dakota*, 1:473-74.

57 Driscoll, *Pioneer Banking History*, 9, 17.

58 Barjenbruch, "The First National Bank of Vermillion," iii-iv; Grauvogl, *South Dakota: Pioneering the Future*, 72.

59 Dana R. Bailey, *History of Minnehaha County, South Dakota* (1899), 433, Co-operative Savings and Loan Association to Whom It May Concern, Nov. 24, 1894, in George W. Abbott Collection, CWS.

60 Building and Loan Auditor of Oklahoma, "Union Savings Association, Sioux Falls S.D.," (Nov. 1910), George W. Abbott Collection, CWS.

61 Charles S. Hughes to L. B. Bauer, Oct. 28, 1910, George W. Abbott Collection, CWS.

62 H. M. Malone to J. D. Lankford, May 13, 1911, George W. Abbott Collection, CWS.

63 W. H. Roddle to George Abbott, July 14,1910, May 19, 1911, George Abbott to W. H. Roddle, July 18, 1910, George W. Abbott Collection, CWS.

64 Box 3, Northwest Bancorporation, Records of Member Banks, 1875-1985, GFL; Barjenbruch, "The First National Bank of Vermillion," v, 1-12.

65 Boxes 3 and 5, Northwest Bancorporation, Records of Member Banks, 1875-1985, GFL; Driscoll, *Pioneer Banking History*, 10-15.

66 Boxes 3 and 6, Northwest Bancorporation, Records of Member Banks, 1875-1985, GFL.

67 Box 6, Northwest Bancorporation, Records of Member Banks, 1875-1985, GFL.

68 Boxes 1 and 3, Northwest Bancorporation, Records of Member Banks, 1875-1985, GFL.

69 Lamar, *Dakota Territory, 1861-1889*, 210; Barjenbruch, "The First National Bank of Vermillion," 29; "Corporation Assessment Lists, 1909-1915," Roll 15/Volume 29, Records of the Internal Revenue Service, RG 58, NARA; Dahl, *Banker Dahl*, 25; Eugene White, "The Political Economy of Banking Regulation, 1864-1933," *Journal of Economic History* 42 (Mar. 1982): 38.

70 Robinson, *History of South Dakota*, 1:475.

71 Driscoll, *Pioneer Banking History*, 9; Robinson, *History of South Dakota*, 1:473-75.

72 Barjenbruch, "The First National Bank of Vermillion," 75; Driscoll, *Pioneer Banking History*, 18-19, 21; Hendrickson, "Public Career of Richard F. Pettigrew," 101-6; Dahl, *Banker Dahl*, 42, 46; Harold Chucker, *Banco at Fifty: A History of Northwest Bancorporation, 1929-1979* (Minneapolis: Banco, 1979).

73 Urbanek, *The Uncovered Wagon*, 29; Siberts and Wyman, *Nothing but Prairie and Sky*, 30, 131; Van Nuys, *The Family Band*, 88; O'Brien, *Buffalo for the Broken Heart*, 49-53.

74 Nelson, *The Prairie Winnows Out Its Own*, 10; Dahl, *Banker Dahl*, xiv, 19-22, 34, 68.

75 South Dakota State Planning Board, *Mortgage Status*, 8.

76 Dahl, *Banker Dahl*, 199.

77 Barjenbruch, "The First National Bank of Vermillion," 79-80; Dahl, *Banker Dahl*, 8, 10.

78 Dahl, *Banker Dahl*, 10-11.

79 Ibid., 16, 19-21, 25.

80 Ibid., 25-33.

81 Ibid., 36-39, 64-65, 77, 87-88.

82 Ibid., 90-91, 169.

83 Ibid., 92-95, 102-4.

84 Ibid., 81, 100-101, 106, 111-12, 118.

85 Ibid., 121.

86 Ibid., 122.

87 Ibid., 178.

88 Ibid., 44, 52-53, 62.

89 Ibid., 124.

90 Ibid., 146.

91 Ibid., 195.

92 Ibid., 248-49.

93 Ibid., 167, 183-84, 200-202.

94 Ibid., 218-21, 230.

95 Gray et al, *South Dakota Economic and Business Abstract*, 248; Dahl, *Banker Dahl*, 259-60; http://sd.findacase.com/research/wfrmDocViewer.aspx/xq/fac.19791224_0006. SD.htm/qx.

96 U.S. Senate, *Impact of Interest Rates*, 11, 15-16.

97 Ibid., 33-35.

98 Ibid., 52.

99 Ibid., 51.

100 Bill Wagner, "He Knows How Things Are Done on the Farm," *ABA Banking Journal*, Nov. 1984, 37-39.

101 "Norwest Corp. Sets Plan to Consolidate Its South Dakota Banks," *Wall Street Journal*, 4 June 1984, 1.

102 John Spiegel, Alan Gart, and Steven Gart, *Banking Redefined: How Super-regional Powerhouses Are Reshaping Financial Services* (Chicago: Irwin Professional Publishing, 1996), 179-96.

103 "South Dakota Bank is First to Benefit as USDA Offers Streamlined Guarantee," *National Mortgage News*, 5 Apr. 1999, 22; http://research.fdic.gov/bankfind/index.html.104 Grauvogl, *South Dakota: Pioneering the Future*, 77; "South Dakota's Dacotah Bank Plans N.D. Foray," *Northwestern Financial Review*, 20 Nov. 1999, 26.

105 Grauvogl, *South Dakota: Pioneering the Future*, 78; http://research.fdic.gov/bankfind/index.html.

106 Sharon Gerrie, "South Dakota Company Opens Bank in Las Vegas," *Las Vegas Business Press*, 9 Aug. 1999, 3.

107 http://research.fdic.gov/bankfind/index.html.

108 Gray et al, *South Dakota Economic and Business Abstract*, 245-49.

109 "Laurentian Capital Begins Talks to Buy South Dakota Insurer," *Wall Street Journal*, 4 Mar. 1985, 1; Grauvogl, *South Dakota: Pioneering the Future*, 74-75; Joseph Frazier Wall, *Policies and People: The First Hundred Years of the Bankers Life, Des Moines, Iowa* (Englewood Cliffs, N.J.: Prentice Hall, 1979), 53.

110 Joe P. Kirby, *Western Surety Company: One of America's Oldest Bonding Companies* (Sioux Falls, 2012).

111 Grauvogl, *South Dakota: Pioneering the Future*, 79.

112 Lawrence, *The Change Game*, 198-99, 211; "Overview of Aman Collection Service, Inc." *Bloomberg Businessweek*.

113 http://heggcompanies.com/about-us/.

114 Daniel G. Worthington and Peter M. Williams, "Retirement Planning with South Dakota Trusts," *Trusts & Estates* (Sept. 1997), 74-86, 93.

115 Zachary R. Mider, "Moguls Rent South Dakota Addresses to Dodge Taxes Forever," *Bloomberg News*, 27 Dec. 2013.

116 "The New States: South Dakota's Capital," *New York Tribune*, 28 Apr. 1889, 24.

117 Grant, *Down and Out on the Family Farm*, 8; McDermott, *Journal of an Expedition to the Mauvaises Terres*, 69-70; Siberts and Wyman, *Nothing but Prairie and Sky*, 93; Stanley H. Edmunds, "I Remember When," (c. 1970), Stanley H. Edmunds Collection, CWS;

Abourezk, *Advise and Dissent*, 40; Mitchell, "Deadwood, South Dakota," 30; Head, *South Dakota: An Explorer's Guide*, 16.

118 Rogers, *South Dakota's Challenges Since 1960*, 338-39; William V. Ackerman, "Indian Gaming in South Dakota: Conflict in Public Policy," *American Indian Quarterly* 33, 2 (Spring 2009), 260, 265-70.

119 Ackerman, "Indian Gaming in South Dakota," 275-58; Norris, "South Dakota: The Long Mile," 413; Thompson, *International Encyclopedia of Gambling*, 589-90; Grauvogl, *South Dakota: Pioneering the Future*, 44; Lawrence, *The Change Game*, 119-20.

Chapter 9

1 Fortune cookie fortune, Hibachi Grill and Supreme Buffet, Sioux Falls, S.D., 30 Oct. 2013.

2 Nelson, Higbee, and Steinken, *The Spirit of an American Entrepreneur.*

3 Brown, "The South Dakota Economy: A Historical Perspective," 1.

4 Banks, "The Past, Present and Future of Anti-Corporate Farming Laws."

5 Karolevitz, *Challenge: The South Dakota Story.*

6 Breitbach and Mitchell, "Growth Machines and Growth Pains," 214.

7 Karolevitz, *Challenge: The South Dakota Story*, ix.

8 Business and Industry Round Table, *South Dakota*; Karolevitz, *Challenge: The South Dakota Story*, 297-98.

9 Business and Industry Round Table, *South Dakota.*

10 Hagerty, *Territory of Dakota*, 58.11 Business and Industry Round Table, *South Dakota*; Hans-Peter Kohler, "The Effect of Hedonic Migration Decisions and Region-Specific Amenities on Industrial Location: Could Silicon Valley Be in South Dakota?" *Journal of Regional Science* 37, 3 (1997): 379-94.

12 Butterwick, "Economic Development in South Dakota,"1.

13 Van Nuys, *The Family Band*, xi.

14 Milton, *South Dakota: A Bicentennial History*, 3.

15 Ibid., 4.

16 Business and Industry Round Table, *South Dakota.*

17 Yvette Cardozo and Bill Hirsch, "A Midwinter Night's Dream," *South Florida Sun-Sentinel*, 19 Jan. 1986, 1J.

18 Ken Paulson and Paula Burton, "South Dakota Celebrities," *USA Today*, 22 June 1987, 11A; Marcia Brinkman, "Sioux Falls: Steady as She Grows," *Corporate Report* (Apr. 1976): 31 in Box 1, Dave Stenseth/EROS Collection, CWS 30454.

19 Flyger, "An Invitation to South Dakota,"43.

20 Lawrence, *The Change Game*, 5.

21 Kohler, "Effect of Hedonic Migration Decisions?" 380.

22 Brokaw, *A Long Way from Home*, 21.

23 Andersen, *Portable Prairie*, 31.

24 Norris, *Dakota: A Spiritual Geography*, 26; Milton, *South Dakota: A Bicentennial History*, 3.

25 Hagerty, *Territory of Dakota*, 93-94.

26 Patrick M. Garry, Candice J. Spurlin, and Derek A. Nelsen, "Wind Energy in Indian Country: A Study of the Challenges and Opportunities Facing South Dakota Tribes," *South Dakota Law Review* 54, 3 (2009): 448-59; Rogers, *South Dakota's Challenges Since 1960*, 297-305, 308; Norris, "South Dakota: The Long Mile," 410.

27 Business and Industry Round Table, *South Dakota.*

28 Robert Tosterud, "Venture Capital and South Dakota Economic Development," *South Dakota Business Review* 50, 2 (Dec. 1991), 1, 7-12, 16.

29 John E. Miller, "Small Towns: Image and Reality," 183; Wymar, "South Dakota-Canadian Commercial Relations," 8; Jim Dawson, "South Dakota Going Underground to Lure Research Dollars," *Physics Today* (Dec. 2005), 30.

30 Rogers, *South Dakota's Challenges Since 1960*, 405-409; Hoover, "South Dakota: An Expression of Regional Heritage," 186; Blayne N. Grave, "Carbon Capture and Storage in South Dakota: The Need for a Clear Designation of Pore Space Ownership," *South Dakota Law Review* 55, 1 (2010): 72-98.

31 Dulgunn Batbold, "The Unnatural Trend in Natural Disasters," *Fedgazette* (Jan. 2013), 13-14.

32 As quoted in Schell, *History of South Dakota*, 365.

33 Neil J. Ericksen, "A Tale of Two Cities: Flood History and the Prophetic Past of Rapid City, South Dakota," *Economic Geography* 51, 4 (Oct. 1975): 305-20; Nelson, *After the West Was Won*, 37; Hoover, "South Dakota: An Expression of Regional Heritage," 188.

34 Phil Davies, "The Beetle and the Damage Done," *Fedgazette* (Jan. 2013), 9-12; Larry M. Gigliotti, "Hunter's Concerns About Chronic Wasting Disease in South Dakota," *Human Dimensions of Wildlife* 9 (2004): 233-35; "Conservationists Win Wetlands Battle in South Dakota," *International Wildlife* 30, 3 (May/June 2000): 7.

35 Joe Mahon, "The Disappearing Act," *Fedgazette* (July 2013), 10-11; Gray-Wood, "Resource Perceptions in the Black Hills," 22; McLaird, "From Bib Overalls to Cowboy Boots," 480.36 Gray-Wood, "Resource Perceptions in the Black Hills," 51-52; Schell, *History of South Dakota*, 333.

37 Thomas V. Durkin, Robert D. Townsen, and Michael D. Cepak, "South Dakota Gold Mining: Regulations and Environmental History," *Mining Engineering* 50, 4 (Apr. 1998): 27-32.

38 Chai, *Hapa Girl*, 120.

39 Paula Woessner, "New Credit Union Promotes Financial Access on Pine Ridge Reservation," *Community Dividend* (Jan. 2013), 4.

40 Chris McGreal, "Obama's Indian Problem," *The Guardian,* 10 Jan. 2010; Peter Harriman, "Tribal Gaming Revenue Hits Record High," *Sioux Falls Argus Leader,* 10 Apr. 2014; Algernon Austin, "Native Americans and Jobs," *Economic Policy Institute,* 17 Dec. 2013; http://www.epi.org/publication/bp370-native-americans-jobs/.

41 Bryan, *American Indian Entrepreneurs*, 25.

42 Jennifer Malkin and Johnnie Aseron, *Native Entrepreneurship in South Dakota: A Deeper Look* (CFED, 2006), 5, 11-12, 29, 39-42, 49-50; Duane Champagne, "Tribal Capitalism and Native Capitalists: Multiple Pathways of Native Economy," in *Native Pathways: American Indian Culture and Economic Development in the Twentieth Century*, ed. Brian Hosmer and Colleen O'Neill (Boulder: University Press of Colorado, 2004), 320-21; Harvard Project on American Indian Economic Development, *The State of the Native Nations*, 117-21; Miller, *Reservation "Capitalism"*, 3, 113, 129; Collins and Mutschler, *A Doctor Among the Oglala*; Shirk and Wadia, *Kitchen Table Entrepreneurs*; Peterson, *Storyville USA*; Pickering, *Lakota Culture, World Economy*; Frazier, *On the Rez*, 169-70, 220; Bryan, American Indian Entrepreneurs; Kenneth Provost, "American Indian Entrepreneurs: A Case Study," (Ph.D. diss., South Dakota State University, 1991); Champagne, "Tribal Capitalism and Native Capitalists," 317-18; Michael J. Francisconi, *Kinship, Capitalism, Change: The Informal Economy of the Navajo, 1868-1995* (New York: Routledge, 1998), 81-98, 103-5; Bryan, *American Indian Entrepreneurs*, 4, 35-36, 111;

Frazier, *On the Rez*, 194; Ahna Minge and Andrew Twite, "Making Surety Bonds a Surer Thing for Native Contractors," *Community Dividend* (Jan. 2014), 1, 6-7.

43 Karolevitz, *Challenge: The South Dakota Story*, 301.

44 Shirk and Wadia, *Kitchen Table Entrepreneurs*, 115.

45 Miller, *Reservation "Capitalism"*, 119.

46 Provost, "American Indian Entrepreneurs," 55-61, 105, 141; Robert J. Tosterud and Joseph H. Sykora, "South Dakota High Schoolers: Business Attitudes and Ambitions," *South Dakota Business Review* 52, 3 (Mar. 1994), 8-10.

47 Miller, *Reservation "Capitalism,"* 49-70; Harvard Project on American Indian Economic Development, *The State of the Native Nations*, 26, 44-47, 112. For other examples of tribal economic success see Frazier, *On the Rez*, 78-79, 85-86, 252-53. The characteristics of successful individual Indian entrepreneurs are very similar to the population at large: appropriate education, experience, and social skills. See Provost, "American Indian Entrepreneurs"; Champagne, "Tribal Capitalism and Native Capitalists," 322-23.

48 Hoover, "South Dakota," 47; Davies, "Labor's Changing Face," 1-11.

49 Miller, *In Search of Gay America*, 102; Mandat-Grancey, *Cowboys and Colonels*, 326.

50 Bucklin, "Memoir of Frank Bloodgood," 132.

51 John W. Ravage, *Black Pioneers: Images of the Black Experience on the North American Frontier* (Salt Lake City: University of Utah Press, 1997), 102.52 Siberts and Wyman, *Nothing but Prairie and Sky*, 18-19.

53 Elizabeth Lapovsky Kennedy, "'But We Would Never Talk About It'": The Structures of Lesbian Discretion in South Dakota, 1928-1933," in *Inventing Lesbian Cultures in America*, ed. Ellen Lewin (Boston: Beacon Press, 1996), 34.

54 Abourezk, *Advise and Dissent*, 65; VanEpps-Taylor, *Forgotten Lives*, 165; Brokaw, *A Long Way from Home*, 191-93.

55 Brokaw, *A Long Way from Home*, 190.

56 VanEpps-Taylor, *Forgotten Lives*, 137-39, 182-88.

57 Chai, *Hapa Girl*, 51, 59, 124.

58 Ibid., 2, 64-65, 182, 196, 206.

59 Ibid., 8.

60 Ibid., 61, 84.

61 Ibid., 73.

62 Ibid., 119-20; Hasselstrom, *Roadside History*, 5; VanEpps-Taylor, *Forgotten Lives*, 207.

63 Rogers, *South Dakota's Challenges Since 1960*, 378-82; Brown, "The South Dakota Economy: A Historical Perspective," 5; Business and Industry Round Table, *South Dakota*; "Free Exchange: Down Towns: When Cities Start to Decline, Economic Diversity Is the Thing That Can Save Them," *Economist,* 17 Aug. 2013, 64.

64 Dahl, *Banker Dahl*, 241.

65 Marcia Brinkman, "Sioux Falls: Steady as She Grows," *Corporate Report* (Apr. 1976): 27-43, in Box 1, Dave Stenseth/EROS Collection, CWS.

66 Barkley, "Turmoil in Traditional Industry," 33.

67 Grauvogl, *South Dakota: Pioneering the Future*, 65.

68 Robert E. Wright, "On the Economic Efficiency of Organizations: Toward a Solution of the Efficient Government Enterprise Paradox," *Essays in Economic and Business History* 25 (Apr. 2007): 143-54; John Christopher Fine, "How Being Business Friendly Benefits South Dakota," *Epoch Times,* 23 Oct. 2013.

69 Schell, *History of South Dakota*, 354.

70 Breitbach and Mitchell, "Growth Machines and Growth Pains," 229; Hasselstrom, *Roadside History*, 2; Business and Industry Round Table, *South Dakota*; Erik Eckholm, "Gang Violence Grows on an Indian Reservation," *New York Times,* 14 Dec. 2009, A14; Peirce and Hagstrom, "South Dakota: State of Reluctant Change," 566; Yvette Cardozo and Bill Hirsch, "A Midwinter Night's Dream," *South Florida Sun-Sentinel,* 19 Jan. 1986, 1J; Chai, *Hapa Girl*, 123-45; State and Local Government Task Force, *Report to the South Dakota Legislature*, 5.

71 Breitbach and Mitchell, "Growth Machines and Growth Pains," 217.

72 Ibid., 225; Norris, *Dakota: A Spiritual Geography*, 35; Entrepreneur Press, *How to Start a Business in South Dakota*, 13.7.

73   John Hudak, "Dispatch from Colorado: The Interesting Case of Marijuana Entrepreneurs," *Brookings,* 22 May 2014: http://www.brookings.edu/blogs/fixgov/posts/2014/05/22-marijuana-legalization-colorado-entrepreneurship-hudak.

74 Mark Keenan, "Due Process, Garnishment and Attachment, and Section 1983: South Dakota Attorneys and Their Clients Are at Risk," *South Dakota Law Review* 32 (1987): 264-80.

75 Joyce Hazeltine, *Domestic Business Corporations* (Office of the South Dakota Secretary of State, 1992), 9-10.76 George T. Solomon, ed., *National Survey of Entrepreneurial Education*, 3rd ed. (Washington: U.S. Small Business Administration, 1986), 5:11, 395-96; Grauvogl, *South Dakota: Pioneering the Future*, 33.

77 Chai, *Hapa Girl*, 146, 169; Abbigail A. Meeder, "Entrepreneurial Activity by Women in Rural South Dakota," (M.A. thesis, South Dakota State University, 2007), 1-2, 15, 33, 46.

78 Meeder, "Entrepreneurial Activity by Women in Rural South Dakota," 34-39, 49, 53.

79 Bryan, *American Indian Entrepreneurs*, 25.

80 Meeder, "Entrepreneurial Activity by Women in Rural South Dakota," 41, 56, 59; Phillip A. Kauffman, "Identifying Variables and Policy Prescriptions That Contribute to Female Entrepreneurial Success in Rural South Dakota," (M.A. thesis, South Dakota State University, 2007), iv, 41, 55; Barkley, "Turmoil in Traditional Industry," 33.

81 South Dakota Board of Regents, *Foundation for the Future*, 2.

82 Bank of New York brief, c. 1985, William Janklow Papers, USD.

83 Satterlee, *The New Community*, 1; Breitbach and Mitchell, "Growth Machines and Growth Pains," 223; Entrepreneur Press, *How to Start a Business in South Dakota*, 13.1.

84 Entrepreneur Press, *How to Start a Business in South Dakota*, 13.2.

85 Lawrence, *The Change Game*, 44-57.

86 Norris, "South Dakota: The Long Mile," 415; Norris, *Dakota: A Spiritual Geography*, 36; Grant, *Down and Out on the Family Farm*, 3.

87 Nelson, *The Prairie Winnows Out Its Own*, 149-50.

88 Ibid., 190-91.

89 Ibid., 185.

90   Choate, "Debt, Drought, and Depression," 42; Kimball, Kozicky, and Nelson, "Pheasants of the Plains and Prairies," 258; "Enterprise Kicks off Eighth Year of 50 Million Tree Pledge," 25 Apr. 2013. http://www.enterpriseholdings.com/press-room/enterprise-kicks-off-eighth-year-of-50-million-tree-pledge-seeds-living-legacy-to-honor-heroes-of-flight-93.html; Peter Carrels, "Fertilized by Ethanol: The Prairie Blooms Cash," *Prairie Fire: The Progressive Voice of the Great Plains* (Dec. 2008); Peter Carrels, "Who Will Make the Case to Preserve Prairie?" *Prairie Fire: The Progressive Voice of the Great Plains* (Oct. 2013).

91 Nelson, *After the West Was Won*, 144; Norris, "South Dakota: The Long Mile," 410; Yonas Hamda, "Analysis of Farm Programs Payments in South Dakota: 1990-2001," (M.S. thesis, South Dakota State University, 2004), 92.

Sources Consulted

Archival Collections

BLHBS: Baker Library, Harvard Business School, Boston, Massachusetts United Biscuit
    Company of America, Lehman Brothers Collection, Contemporary Business Archives

CWS: Center for Western Studies, Augustana College, Sioux Falls, South Dakota
    CWS Microfilm Reel 2
    George W. Abbott Collection, CWS 30001
    Jeannette L. Agrant Collection, CWS 30004
    George Banker Collection, CWS 30015
    Nathan Brenneise, Hardships Blessings Opportunities: A History of the Brenneise
        Family (1979), CWS 30029
    Richard Rush Brown – Brown Drug Company Collection, CWS 20031
    Changing Social Patterns on the Lingering Frontier Records, CWS 30037
    Clason's So. Dakota Green Guide, CWS 39000.40
    Clear Lake Balloon Incident, CWS 30039
    Col. James Clyman Collection, CWS 30040
    D.C. Doerr Collection: Look's Market, CWS 30053
    Edith Mortenson Delman Collection, CWS 30047
    Vine Deloria Jr. Collection, CWS 30048
    Richard W. Dickenson Papers, CWS 30050
    Divorce Legislation in South Dakota, CWS 30052
    Dowdell Family Collection, CWS 30094
    Stanley H. Edmunds Collection, CWS 30057
    Fawick Collection, CWS 30548
    John Deere Plow Company, Sioux Falls Branch Collection, CWS 20012
    Walter Heldt Collection, CWS 30088
    Evelyn Maguire King Collection CWS 39000.054
    Ku Klux Klan Collection, CWS 20013
    William Beach Locke Collection, CWS 30124
    Frank Moody Mills Collection, CWS 30142
    Gustave Otterness Collection, CWS 30162
    Bessie Pettigrew Collection, CWS 30171
    Ben Reifel Collection, CWS 30374
    Sioux Falls Miscellaneous Publications, CWS 39000.010
    Sioux Falls Stock Yards Company CWS 20036
    Sioux Falls Theater Collection, CWS 20065
    Dave Stenseth/EROS Collection, CWS 30454
    Ole O. Tonning Collection, CWS 30224
    Nellie Zabel Willhite Collection, CWS 30235

GFL: Gale Family Library, Minnesota Historical Society, St. Paul, Minnesota Northwest
    Bancorporation, Records of Member Banks, 1875-1985

JKH: James K. Hosmer Special Collections Library, Hennepin County Library, Minneapolis
    Central Library, Minneapolis, Minnesota Amund O. Ringsrud materials

NARA: National Archives and Records Administration, Washington, DC Records of the
    Internal Revenue Service, Record Group 58

USD: Archives and Special Collections, University of South Dakota, Vermillion, South Dakota
    William J. Janklow Gubernatorial Papers

Articles, Book Chapters, Dissertations, Theses, and Working Papers

Ackerman, William V. "Indian Gaming in South Dakota: Conflict in Public Policy." *American Indian Quarterly* 33, 2 (Spring 2009): 253-79.

Adovasio, J. M. and David Pedler. "The People of North America." In *North American Archaeology*, ed. Timothy R. Pauketat and Diana DiPaolo Loren. Malden, MA: Blackwell Publishing, 2005.

Ames, Kenneth M. "Tempo and Scale in the Evolution of Social Complexity in Western North America: Four Case Studies." In *North American Archaeology*, ed. Timothy R. Pauketat and Diana DiPaolo Loren. Malden, MA: Blackwell Publishing, 2005.

Anderson, Sherwood. "Revolt in South Dakota." In *The Anxious Years: America in the Nineteen Thirties, a Collection of Contemporary Writings*, ed. Louis Filler. New York: Capricorn Books, 1963.

Andrews, John. "Ten 'Must See' South Dakota Paintings." *South Dakota Magazine* (Jan./Feb. 2009).

Anonymous, "Conservationists Win Wetlands Battle in South Dakota." *International Wildlife* 30, 3 (May/June 2000).

_____. "Economic Census Comparative Statistics, South Dakota." *South Dakota Business Review* 58, 4 (June 2000).

_____. "Exploration: South Dakota," *Oil & Gas Journal* (Mar. 1, 1993).

_____. "Family Mountain Biking in South Dakota," *Backpacker* 22, 5 (June 1994).

_____. "Foundations are Popping up Everywhere in South Dakota." *Independent Banker* 45, 1 (Jan. 1995).

_____. "Girls of the Gulch." *Deadwood Magazine* (1997).

_____. "Glanbia Nutritionals to Build Facility in Sioux Falls." *Directions* (Nov./Dec. 2012).

_____. "Lincoln Territory (South Dakota)." In *Declarations of Independence: Encyclopedia of American Autonomous and Secessionist Movements*, ed. James L. Erwin. Westport, CN: Greenwood Press, 2007.

_____. "ICBM Returns to South Dakota." *American History* (Dec. 2001), 10-14.

_____. "Inmates Wire South Dakota Schools for the Future." *Rural Telecommunications* 17, 1 (Jan./Feb. 1998).

_____. "Missouri River, North and South Dakota." *Field & Stream* (Apr. 1999).

_____. "Mitchell, S.D. Named a Smart21 Community." *Community Dividend* (Jan. 2014).

_____. "No Longer Stuck in Cement." *FedGazette* (May 2001).

_____. "South Dakota: Black Hills Gobblers." *Outdoor Life* (Mar. 1999).

_____. "South Dakota Business and Economic Activity, 1995-2000." *South Dakota Business Review* 58, 4 (June 2000).

_____. "South Dakota Business and Economic Indices." *South Dakota Business Review* 49, 4 (June 1991).

_____. "South Dakota Co-ops Merging." *Rural Cooperatives* (July/Aug. 2007): 36-37.

_____. "South Dakota Plans Nation's First Intrastate Air Service." *Fedgazette* (Mar. 1990).

_____. "South Dakota: Riverfront Property." *Outdoor Life* (Nov. 1999).

_____. "South Dakota: Two Heavyweights." *Outdoor Life* (May 1999).

_____. "South Dakota's Version of the Deer Hunt Going to the Birds." *Fedgazette* (Jan. 2000).

_____. "The Traveler: Adventure and Festivities in South Dakota." *South Dakota Magazine* (Mar./Apr. 2011).

_____. "This Date in History: Events of Local Interest." *Public Opinion* (2013).

Bampoky, Catherine, Luisa Blanco, Aolong Liu, and James E. Prieger. "Economic Growth and the Optimal Level of Entrepreneurship." Working Paper, 17 July 2013.

Banks, Jeffrey M. "The Past, Present and Future of Anti-Corporate Farming Laws in South Dakota: Purposeful Discrimination or Permissive Protectionism?" *South Dakota Law Review* 49 (2004): 805-23.

Bareiss, Warren. "Alternative Radio and Television in South Dakota: A Place Study of Public Service Electronic Media in the US." In *No News Is Bad News: Radio, Television and the Public*, ed. Michael Bromley. New York: Routledge, 2001.

Barjenbruch, Judith. "The First National Bank of Vermillion, 1875-1937." M.A. thesis, University of South Dakota, 1975.

Barkema, Alan and Mark Drabenstott. "Consolidation and Change in Heartland Agriculture." In *Economic Forces Shaping the Rural Heartland*. Kansas City: Federal Reserve Bank of Kansas City, 1996.

Barkley, David L. "Turmoil in Traditional Industry: Prospects for Nonmetropolitan Manufacturing." In *Economic Forces Shaping the Rural Heartland*. Kansas City: Federal Reserve Bank of Kansas City, 1996.

Barrier, Michael. "A Man Who Sees No Limits on the South Dakota Prairie." *Nation's Business* 79, 3 (Mar. 1991).

Batbold, Dulguun and Rob Grunewald, "Bakken Activity: How Wide is the Ripple Effect?" *Fedgazette* (July 2013).

Beale, Calvin L. "Quantitative Dimensions of Decline and Stability among Rural Communities." In *Communities Left Behind: Alternatives for Development*, ed. Larry R. Whiting. Ames: Iowa State Press, 1974.

Beasley, Maurine Hoffman. "Life as a Hired Girl in South Dakota, 1907-1908: A Woman Journalist Reflects." *South Dakota History* 12, 2 (Summer 1982): 147-62.

Bender, Lyle M. "Tooling Up for Tomorrow's Job." *Journal of Farm Economics* 39, 5 (Dec. 1957): 1,698-1,704.

Benson, David, Aaron K. Lies, Albert A. Okunade, and Phanindra V. Wunnava. 'Economic Impact of a Private Sector Micro-financing Scheme in South Dakota." *Small Business Economics* 36 (2011): 157-68.

Benz, Kathryn. "Saving Old McDonald's Farm After South Dakota Farm Bureau, Inc. v. Hazeltine: Rethinking the Role of the State, Farming Operations, the Dormant Commerce Clause, and Growth Management Statutes." *Natural Resources Journal* 46 (Summer 2006): 793-830.

Birzer, Bradley J. "Expanding Creative Destruction: Entrepreneurship in the American Wests." *Western Historical Quarterly* 30, 1 (Spring 1999): 45-63.

Boddicker, Major L. "Bionomics of Mallophaga of Sharp-Tailed Grouse in South Dakota." Ph.D. diss., South Dakota State University, 1972.

Bohi, Charles W. and H. Roger Grant. "Country Railroad Stations of the Milwaukee Road and the Chicago & North Western in South Dakota." *South Dakota History* 9, 1 (Winter 1978): 1-23.

Bonilla, Carlton L. "A South Dakota Rendezvous: The Sturgis Motorcycle Rally and Races." *South Dakota History* 28, 3 (1998): 123-43.

Bozell, John R. "Culture, Environment, and Bison Populations on the Late Prehistoric and Early Historic Central Plains." *Plains Anthropologist* 40, 152 (1995): 145-63.

_____. "Fauna from the Hulme Site and Comments on Central Plains Tradition Subsistence Variability." *Plains Anthropologist* 36, 136 (June 1991): 229-52.

Breitbach, Carrie and Don Mitchell. "Growth Machines and Growth Pains: The Contradictions of Property Development and Landscape in Sioux Falls, South Dakota." In *Making Space: Property Development and Urban Planning*, ed. Andrew MacLaran. London: Arnold, 2003.

Brooks, Allyson. "Anticipating Mobility: How Cognitive Processes Influenced the Historic Mining Landscape in White Pine, Nevada and the Black Hills of South Dakota." Ph.D. diss., University of Nevada, Reno, 1995.

Brown, Ralph J. "South Dakota Rankings on Wages, Personal Income and Gross State Product." *South Dakota Business Review* 59, 1 (Sept. 2000).

_____. "The South Dakota Economy: A Historical Perspective." *South Dakota Business Review* 46, 4, (June 1988).

Brown, Richard Maxwell. "The Enduring Frontier: The Impact of Weather on South Dakota History and Literature." *South Dakota History* 15, 1 (Spring 1985): 26-57.

Bucklin, Steven J., ed. "'Pioneer Days of South Dakota': The Memoir of Frank Bloodgood." *South Dakota History* 29, 2 (Summer 1999): 113-54.

Burks, Carolyn D. "Habitat Selection by the Ring-Necked Pheasant during the Breeding Season in Central South Dakota." M.S. thesis, University of Wyoming, 1985.

Burns, Robert E. and Herbert E. Cheever, Jr. "South Dakota: Conflict and Cooperation among Conservatives." In *Interest Group Politics in the Midwestern States*, ed. Robert Hrebenar and Clive Thomas. Ames: Iowa State University Press, 1993.

Butterwick, Darrell D. "Economic Development in South Dakota." *South Dakota Business Review* 48, 4 (June 1990).

Campbell, Dan. "South Dakota Turnaround." *Rural Cooperatives* (May/June 2002): 11-16.

Carrels, Peter. "Fertilized by Ethanol: The Prairie Blooms Cash." *Prairie Fire: The Progressive Voice of the Great Plains* (Dec. 2008).

_____. "South Dakota Farmers Reject a Free Lunch." In *Reopening the Frontier*, ed. Ed Marston. New York: Island Press, 1989.

_____. "Who Will Make the Case to Preserve Prairie?" *Prairie Fire: The Progressive Voice of the Great Plains* (Oct. 2013).

Carruth, Hayden. "South Dakota: State without End." In *These United States: Portraits of America from the 1920s*, ed. Daniel H. Borus. Ithaca: Cornell University Press, 1992.

Champagne, Duane. "Tribal Capitalism and Native Capitalists: Multiple Pathways of Native Economy." In *Native Pathways: American Indian Culture and Economic Development in the Twentieth Century,* ed. Brian Hosmer and Colleen O'Neill. Boulder: University Press of Colorado, 2004.

Choate, Jean. "Debt, Drought, and Depression: South Dakota in the 1930s." *Journal of the West* (Oct. 1992): 33-44.

Clement, Douglas. "Green Eggs ... and Ham." *Fed Gazette* (Mar. 2001).

Cleworth, Marc. "Artesian-Well Irrigation: Its History in Brown County, South Dakota, 1889-1900." *Agricultural History* 15, 4 (Oct. 1941): 195-201.

Cobb, Kathy. "Legislation Aims to Ease Path for New Technology." *Fedgazette* (July 1997).

_____. "Processing Plant Keeps Soybeans in South Dakota." *Fedgazette* (July 1995).

_____. "These Are the House That Inmates Built." *Fedgazette* (Apr. 1998).

Cocheo, Steve. "Justice Department Sues Tiny South Dakota Bank for Loan Bias." *ABA Banking Journal* (Jan. 1994).

Coleman, John. "The Missouri Valley of South Dakota: Its Human Geography at Euroamerican Contact." Ph.D. diss., Indiana University, 1968.

Conzen, Michael P. "Understanding Great Plains Urbanization through the Lens of South Dakota Townscapes." *Journal of Geography* 109 (Jan.-Feb. 2010): 3-17.

Craig, Mary. "The Black Hills Passion Play at Spearfish, South Dakota." M.A. thesis, University of Wyoming, 1952.

Dagel, Kenneth Charles. "Ranchers' Adjustments to Drought in Western South Dakota, 1870-1990s: Creating Sustainable Operations in a Marginal Environment." Ph D. diss., University of Nebraska, Lincoln, 1994.

Dahlin, Donald C. "The 1982 Gubernatorial Election in South Dakota." In *Re-Electing the Governor: The 1982 Elections*, ed. Thad L. Beyle. New York: University Press of America, 1986.

Dale, Fred H. "Pheasants and Pheasant Populations." In *Pheasants in North America*, ed. Durward L. Allen. Harrisburg, PA: Stackpole Company, 1956.

Dalstrom, Harl A. and Kay Calame Dalstrom. "'Back by Popular Demand!': Dancing in Small-Town South Dakota." *South Dakota History* 32, 4 (Winter 2002): 283-309.

Dana, Susan R. "South Dakota Employment At Will Doctrine: Twenty Years of Judicial Erosion." *South Dakota Law Review* 49, 1 (2003): 47-66.

Daschle, Tom. "Reexamining the Life and Legacy of George McGovern." In *George McGovern: A Political Life, a Political Legacy*, ed. Robert P. Watson. Pierre: South Dakota State Historical Society Press, 2004.

Davies, Phil. "Labor's Changing Face." *Fedgazette* (Oct. 2013).

_____. "The Beetle and the Damage Done." *Fedgazette* (Jan. 2013).

Davies, Phillips G. "Touring the Welsh Settlements of South Dakota, 1891." *South Dakota History* 10, 3 (Summer 1980): 223-40.

Dawson, Jim. "South Dakota Going Underground to Lure Research Dollars." *Physics Today* (Dec. 2005).

Doeksen, Gerald A., John Kuehn, and Joseph Schmidt. "Consequences of Decline and Community Economic Adjustment to It." In *Communities Left Behind: Alternatives for Development*, ed. Larry R. Whiting. Ames: Iowa State University Press, 1974.

Drabenstott, Mark and Tim R. Smith. "The Changing Economy of the Rural Heartland." In *Economic Forces Shaping the Rural Heartland*. Kansas City: Federal Reserve Bank of Kansas City, 1996.

Durkin, Thomas V., E. H. Holm, and B. A. Regynski. "South Dakota." *Mining Engineering* 49, 5 (May 1997).

Durkin, Thomas V., Robert D. Townsen, and Michael D. Cepak. "South Dakota Gold Mining: Regulations and Environmental History." *Mining Engineering* 50, 4 (Apr. 1998): 27-32.

Eisenbraun, Ed. "Creighton, South Dakota." In *Below the Line: Living Poor in America*, ed. Eugene Richards. Mount Vernon, NY: Consumers Union, 1987.

Ellis, Clyde. "Five Dollars a Week to Be 'Regular Indians': Shows, Exhibitions, and the Economics of Indian Dancing, 1880-1930." In *Native Pathways: American Indian Culture and Economic Development in the Twentieth Century*, eds. Brian Hosmer and Colleen O'Neill. Boulder: University Press of Colorado, 2004.

Engeseth, James H. "An Assessment of Formal Training in the Durable Goods Sector of South Dakota's Manufacturing Industry." Ed.D. diss., University of South Dakota, 2006.

Ericksen, Neil J. "A Tale of Two Cities: Flood History and the Prophetic Past of Rapid City, South Dakota." *Economic Geography* 51, 4 (Oct. 1975): 305-20.

Evans, Sterling. "Entwined in Conflict: The South Dakota State Prison Twine Factory and the Controversy of 1919-1921." *South Dakota History* 35, 2 (Summer 2005): 95-124.

Fettig, David. "South Dakota Entrepreneur Program Hopes to Retain State's Youth." *Fedgazette* (Oct. 1994).

Fite, Gilbert. "South Dakota: Some Observations by a Native Son." *South Dakota History* 4, 4 (Fall 1974): 455-70.

————. "The Transformation of South Dakota Agriculture: The Effects of Mechanization, 1939-1964." *South Dakota History* 19 (Fall 1989): 278-305.

Flyger, D. L. "An Invitation to South Dakota." *Countryside and Small Stock Journal* 82, 2 (Mar./Apr. 1998).

Frison, George. "Clovis, Goshen, and Folsom: Lifeways and Cultural Relationships." In *Megafauna and Man: Discovery of America's Heartland*, ed. Larry Agenbroad, Jim Mead, and Lisa Nelson. Hot Springs: Mammoth Site of Hot Springs and Northern Arizona University, 1990.

Garrett-Davis, Joshua. "The Red Power Movement and the Yankton Sioux Industries Pork-Processing Plant Takeovers of 1975." In *The Sioux in South Dakota History*, ed. Richmond L. Clow. Pierre: South Dakota Historical Society Press, 2007.

Garry, Patrick M., Candice J. Spurlin, and Derek A. Nelsen. "Wind Energy in Indian Country: A Study of the Challenges and Opportunities Facing South Dakota Tribes." *South Dakota Law Review* 54, 3 (2009): 448-59.

Gerber, Sandy. "Native CDFIs Work Toward a New Economic Reality in South Dakota." *Community Dividend* 3 (2008).

Gigliotti, Larry M. "Hunter's Concerns about Chronic Wasting Disease in South Dakota." *Human Dimensions of Wildlife* 9 (2004).

Goering, Orlando J. and Violet Miller Goering. "Keeping the Faith: Bertha Martinsky in West River South Dakota." *South Dakota History* 25, 1 (Spring 1995): 37-48.

Grant, H. Roger. "Origins of a Progressive Reform: The Initiative and Referendum Movement in South Dakota." *South Dakota History* 3, 4 (Fall 1973): 390-407.

Grave, Blayne N. "Carbon Capture and Storage in South Dakota: The Need for a Clear Designation of Pore Space Ownership." *South Dakota Law Review* 55, 1 (2010): 72-98.

Grayson, Donald and David Meltzer. "A Requiem for North American Overkill." *Journal of Archaeological Science* 30 (2003): 585-93.

Gray-Wood, Carrie E. "Resource Perceptions in the Black Hills of Custer County, South Dakota: Fifty Years of Change." M.A. thesis, South Dakota State University, 2007.

Greene, Lance and Mark R. Plane, "Introduction." In *American Indians and the Market Economy, 1775-1850*, ed. Lance Greene and Mark R. Plane. Tuscaloosa: University of Alabama Press, 2010.

Griffith, T. D. "People of the Plains and Pines: Native Tourism in South Dakota." *Native Peoples* (Sept./Oct. 2006).

Grunewald, Rob. "South Dakota Leads District States in Manufactured Exports." *Fedgazette* (May 2001).

Grunewald, Rob and Aaron Richins. "Manufactured Exports Continued to Expand in 2011." *Fedgazette* (July 2012).

Grunewald, Rob and Dulguun Batbold. "Bakken Stands Out in Comparison with Other Shale Drilling Areas." *Fedgazette* (Jan. 2014).

Guthrie, R. Dale. "Late Pleistocene Faunal Revolution – A New Perspective on the Extinction Debate." In *Megafauna and Man: Discovery of America's Heartland*, ed. Larry Agenbroad, Jim Mead, and Lisa Nelson. Hot Springs: Mammoth Site of Hot Springs and Northern Arizona University, 1990.

Hamburg, James F. "Railroads and the Settlement of South Dakota during the Great Dakota Boom, 1878-1887." *South Dakota History* 5, 2 (Spring 1975): 165-78.

Hamda, Yonas. "Analysis of Farm Programs Payments in South Dakota: 1990-2001." M.S. thesis, South Dakota State University, 2004.

Hannus, L. Adrien. "The Lange-Ferguson Site: A Case for Mammoth Bone-Butchering Tools." In *Megafauna and Man: Discovery of America's Heartland*, ed. Larry Agenbroad, Jim Mead, and Lisa Nelson. Hot Springs: Mammoth Site of Hot Springs and Northern Arizona University, 1990.

———. "The Lange/Ferguson Site -- An Event of Clovis Mammoth Butchery with the Associated Bone Tool Technology: The Mammoth and Its Track." Ph.D. diss., University of Utah, 1985.

Heady, Earl O. "Foreword." In *Communities Left Behind: Alternatives for Development*, ed. Larry R. Whiting. Ames: Iowa State University Press, 1974.

Hendrickson, Kenneth Elton, Jr. "The Public Career of Richard F. Pettigrew of South Dakota, 1848-1926." Ph.D. diss., University of Oklahoma, 1962.

Henning, Dale R. "The Evolution of the Plains Village Tradition." In *North American Archaeology*, ed. Timothy R. Pauketat and Diana DiPaolo Loren. Malden, MA: Blackwell Publishing, 2005.

Hofsommer, Don L. "Boosterism and Townsite Development along the Minneapolis & St. Louis Railroad in South Dakota." *Journal of the West* 42, 4 (Fall 2003): 8-16.

———. "The Watertown Express and the 'Hog and Human': M&StL Passenger Service in South Dakota, 1884-1960." *South Dakota History* 3 (Spring 1973): 127-55.

Holm, E. H., T. Cline, Jr., M. Macy, and R. Fivecoate. "South Dakota." *Mining Engineering* 59, 5 (May 2007).

Hoover, Herbert T. "South Dakota: An Expression of Regional Heritage." In *Heart Land: Comparative Histories of the Midwestern States,* ed. James H. Madison. Bloomington: Indiana University Press, 1988.

———. "South Dakota." In *The American Midwest: An Interpretive Encyclopedia*, ed. Richard Sisson, Christian Zacher, and Andrew Cayton. Bloomington: Indiana University Press, 2007.

———. "The Arrival of Capitalism on the Northern Great Plains: Pierre Chouteau, Jr. and Company." In *South Dakota Leaders: From Pierre Chouteau, Jr., to Oscar Howe*, ed. Herbert T. Hoover and Larry J. Zimmerman. Vermillion: University of South Dakota Press, 1989.

Hopp, Andrew G. "South Dakota Pheasant Hunting Preserves." M.S. thesis, South Dakota State University, 2007.

Hummel, Richard. "Hunting." In *The American Midwest: An Interpretive Encyclopedia*, ed. Richard Sisson, Christian Zacher, and Andrew Cayton. Bloomington: Indiana University Press, 2007.

Huntsinger, Jami. "Pioneering Black Hills Sheepman: Myron John Smiley." In *South Dakota Leaders: From Pierre Chouteau, Jr., to Oscar Howe*, ed. Herbert T. Hoover and Larry J. Zimmerman. Vermillion: University of South Dakota Press, 1989.

Hutton, J. G. "South Dakota." In *Gypsum Deposits of the United States*, Geological Survey Bulletin No. 697, ed. R. W. Stone et al. Washington, D.C.: Government Printing Office, 1920.

Jennewein, J. Leonard. "Ben Ash and the Trail Blazers." *South Dakota Historical Collections and Report* 25 (1950).

Karolevitz, Robert F. "The Human Dimension." In *Communities Left Behind: Alternatives for Development*, ed. Larry R. Whiting. Ames: Iowa State University Press, 1974.

Karr, Landon, Alan Outram, and L. Adrien Hannus. "Open-area Excavations at the Mitchell Prehistoric Indian Village, South Dakota (A.D. 1000-1150): New Interpretations of Site Function from Interdwelling Areas." *Journal of Field Archaeology* 36, 4 (2011): 281-88.

Kauffman, Phillip A. "Identifying Variables and Policy Prescriptions That Contribute to Female Entrepreneurial Success in Rural South Dakota." M.A. thesis, South Dakota State University, 2007.

Keenan, Mark. "Due Process, Garnishment and Attachment, and Section 1983: South Dakota Attorneys and Their Clients Are at Risk." *South Dakota Law Review* 32 (1987): 264-80.

Kennedy, Elizabeth Lapovsky. "'But We Would Never Talk About It'": The Structures of Lesbian Discretion in South Dakota, 1928-1933." In *Inventing Lesbian Cultures in America*, ed. Ellen Lewin. Boston: Beacon Press, 1996.

Kibbe, Lynus. "Early Recollections of the Son of a Pioneer Newspaper Man of South Dakota and Dakota Territory." *South Dakota Historical Collections and Report* 25 (1950).

Kimball, James W., Edward L. Kozicky, and Bernard A. Nelson. "Pheasants of the Plains and Prairies." In *Pheasants in North America*, ed. Durward L. Allen. Harrisburg, PA: Stackpole Company, 1956.

Kitzel, Larry. "The Trombones of the Shrine to Music Museum (South Dakota)." D.M.A. thesis, University of Oklahoma, 1985.

Knepper, Karen. "100 Years of Banking in the Dakotas." *Commercial West*, 30 June 1984, 12-15.

Knight, Jim. "Ring-Necked Pheasant Management for Montana Landowners." In *Manage Your Land for Wildlife*. Bozeman: Montana State University Extension Publications, 2008.

Kohler, Hans-Peter. "The Effect of Hedonic Migration Decisions and Region-Specific Amenities on Industrial Location: Could Silicon Valley Be in South Dakota?" *Journal of Regional Science* 37, 3 (1997): 379-94.

Kollmorgen, Walter M. and George F. Jenks. "Suitcase Farming in Sully County, South Dakota." *Annals of the Association of American Geographers* 48, 1 (Mar. 1958): 27-40.

Koupal, Nancy T. "Marietta Bones: Personality and Politics in the South Dakota Suffrage Movement." In *Feminist Frontiers: Women Who Shaped the Midwest,* ed. Yvonne J. Johnson. Kirksville, MO: Truman State University Press, 2010.

Krier, Daniel and William J. Swart. "The Commodification of Spectacle: Spectators, Sponsors and the Outlaw Biker Diegesis at Sturgis." *Critical Sociology* (May 2014): 1-21.

Krmenec, Andrew. "Manufacturing." In *The American Midwest: An Interpretive Encyclopedia*, ed. Richard Sisson, Christian Zacher, and Andrew Cayton. Bloomington: Indiana University Press, 2007.

Laingen, Christopher. "Complex Feedbacks Among Human and Natural Systems and Pheasant Hunting in South Dakota, USA." Ph.D. Diss., University of Kansas, 2009.

Larson, George A. "South Dakota's Soukup & Thomas Balloon and Airship Museum Houses a One-of-a-Kind Collection." *Aviation History* (May 1999).

Lathrop, Alan K. "Designing for South Dakota and the Upper Midwest: The Career of Architect Harold T. Spitznagel, 1930-1974." *South Dakota History* 37, 4 (Winter 2007): 271-305.

Lawrence, Diana M., et al. "Mitochondrial DNA of Protohistoric Remains of an Arikara Population from South Dakota: Implications for the Macro-Siouan Language Hypothesis." *Human Biology* 82, 2 (Apr. 2010): 157-78.

Lawson, Michael. "The Fractionated Estate: The Problem of American Indian Heirship." In *The Sioux in South Dakota History*, ed. Richmond L. Clow. Pierre: South Dakota Historical Society Press, 2007.

Lee, Shebby. "Traveling the Sunshine State: The Growth of Tourism in South Dakota, 1914-1939." *South Dakota History* 19, 2 (Summer 1989): 194-223.

Lesko, Matthew and Mary Ann Martello. "South Dakota." In *Lesko's Free Money for Entrepreneurs: How to Start or Expand a Business with Government Grants, Low Interest Loans, Contacts and Free Services*. Kensington, MD: Information USA, 2004.

Lindell, Lisa. "'So Long as I Can Read'": Farm Women's Reading Experiences in Depression-Era South Dakota." *Agricultural History* (Fall 2009): 503-27.

Loomis, Thomas A. "The Ross Hannibal Mine, Lawrence County, South Dakota." *Mineralogical Record* 30, 3 (May/June 1999): 199-206.

Mack, Thomas C. "South Dakota's Role in Damming the Missouri River from 1915 to 1950." M.A. thesis, University of South Dakota, 2010.

Mahon, Joe. "The Disappearing Act." *Fedgazette* (July 2013).

Marceaux, P. Shawn and Timothy K. Perttula. "Negotiating Borders: The Southern Caddo and Their Relationships with Colonial Governments in East Texas." In *American Indians and the Market Economy, 1775-1850*, ed. Lance Greene and Mark R. Plane. Tuscaloosa: University of Alabama Press, 2010.

Marten, James. "A Medical Entrepreneur Goes West: Father William Kroeger in South Dakota, 1893-1904." *South Dakota History* 21, 4 (Winter 1991): 333-61.

_____. "'We Always Looked Forward to the Hunters Coming': The Culture of Pheasant Hunting in South Dakota." *South Dakota History* 29, 2 (Summer 1999): 87-112.

Martin, Paul S. "Who or What Destroyed Our Mammoths?" In *Megafauna and Man: Discovery of America's Heartland*, ed. Larry Agenbroad, Jim Mead, and Lisa Nelson. Hot Springs, SD: Mammoth Site of Hot Springs and Northern Arizona University, 1990.

Mathews, Allan "Agrarian Radicals: The United Farmers League of South Dakota." *South Dakota History* 3, 4 (Fall 1973): 408-21.

McLaird, James D. "From Bib Overalls to Cowboy Boots: East River/West River Differences in South Dakota." *South Dakota History* 19, 4 (Winter 1989): 454-91.

Meeder, Abbigail A. "Entrepreneurial Activity by Women in Rural South Dakota." M.A. thesis, South Dakota State University, 2007.

Miller, David. "Pioneering Black Hills Cattleman: James 'Scotty' Philip." In *South Dakota Leaders: From Pierre Chouteau, Jr., to Oscar Howe*, ed. Herbert T. Hoover and Larry J. Zimmerman. Vermillion: University of South Dakota Press, 1989.

Miller, John E. "Eminent Horticulturalist: Niels Ebbesen Hansen." In *South Dakota Leaders: From Pierre Chouteau, Jr., to Oscar Howe*, ed. Herbert T. Hoover and Larry J. Zimmerman. Vermillion: University of South Dakota Press, 1989.

_____. "From South Dakota Farm to Harvard Seminar: Alvin H. Hansen, America's Prophet of Keynesianism." *The Historian* 64 (Spring/Summer 2002): 603-22.

_____. "Small Towns: Image and Reality." In *A New South Dakota History*, ed. Harry F. Thompson. Sioux Falls: Center for Western Studies, 2009.

Miller, Kerby A. "In the Famine's Shadow: An Irish Immigrant from West Kerry to South Dakota, 1881-1979." In *Fleeing the Famine: North American and Irish Refugees, 1845-1851*, ed. Margaret Mulrooney. New York: Praeger, 2003.

Minge, Ahna and Andrew Twite. "Making Surety Bonds a Surer Thing for Native Contractors." *Community Dividend* (Jan. 2014).

Mitchell, Lynn Marie. "William Richard Cross, Photographer on the Nebraska-South Dakota Frontier." *South Dakota History* 20, 4 (Winter 1990): 81-95.

Mitchell, Martin. "Deadwood, South Dakota: Place and Setting Combine with Gambling and Historic Preservation." *American Geographical Society Focus on Geography* 51, 2 (Fall 2008): 26-33.

Mitton, Todd. "The Wealth of Subnations: Geography, Institutions, and Within-Country Development." Working Paper, Mar. 25, 2013.

Muller, Luke M. "Change of Scale in Upper Midwest Farms: A South Dakota Case Study." M.A. thesis, South Dakota State University, 2005.

Myers, Michael J. and Dennis A. Johnson. "De Facto South Dakota Healthcare Reform: An Emerging 'Managed Competition Model.'" *South Dakota Business Review* 50, 4 (June 1992).

Nash, George W. "Education." In *History of South Dakota* by Doane Robinson. Indianapolis: B. F. Bowen, 1904.

Nelson, Chris B. "Life along the Road: The Tourist Camp in South Dakota." *South Dakota History* 35, 4 (Winter 2005).

Nelson, Terry. "An Examination of Roles and Identities of the Farm Population within Beadle, Brookings, Hamlin, Lake, and McCook Counties of South Dakota." Ph.D. diss., South Dakota State University, 2001.

Newton, Cody. "Business in the Hinterlands: The Impact of the Market Economy on the West-Central Great Plains at the Turn of the 19th Century." In *American Indians and the Market Economy, 1775-1850*, ed. Lance Greene and Mark R. Plane. Tuscaloosa: University of Alabama Press, 2010.

Norris, Kathleen. "South Dakota: The Long Mile." In *These United States: Original Essays by Leading American Writers on Their State Within the Union,* ed. John Leonard. New York: Thunder's Mouth Press, 2004.

Olson, Gary D. "Norwegian Immigrants in Early Sioux Falls: A Demographic Profile." *Norwegian-American Studies* 36 (2011): 45-84.

Olsson, Ola and Christopher Paik. "A Western Reversal since the Neolithic? The Long-Run Impact of Early Agriculture." University of Warwick Working Papers Series No. 139, June 2013.

O'Regan, Valerie R. and Stephen J. Stambough. "From the Grassroots: Building the South Dakota Democratic Party." In *George McGovern: A Political Life, a Political Legacy,* ed. Robert P. Watson. Pierre: South Dakota State Historical Society Press, 2004.

Orr, Raymond. "The Reservation of Common Secrets: Pain and Profit in the Making of the American Indian World." Unpublished ms., 2014.

Orr, Robert. "A History of Aviation in South Dakota." M.A. thesis, University of South Dakota, 1957.

Painter, John. "Transitional Sioux Leader: Benjamin Reifel." In *South Dakota Leaders: From Pierre Chouteau, Jr., to Oscar Howe,* ed. Herbert T. Hoover and Larry J. Zimmerman. Vermillion: University of South Dakota Press, 1989.

Palais, Hyman. "A Study of the Trails to the Black Hills Gold Fields." *South Dakota Historical Collections and Report* 25 (1950).

Parker, Donald. "Early Explorations and Fur Trading in South Dakota." *South Dakota Historical Collections and Report* 25 (1950).

Pauketat, Timothy. "The Forgotten History of the Mississippians." In *North American Archaeology,* ed. Timothy R. Pauketat and Diana DiPaolo Loren. Malden, MA: Blackwell Publishing, 2005.

Peirce, Neal and Jerry Hagstrom. "South Dakota: State of Reluctant Change." In *The Book of America: Inside Fifty States Today.* New York: W. W. Norton, 1983.

Petzal, David E. "Don Allen, Rifle Maker, Dies in South Dakota." *Field & Stream* 108, 5 (Sept. 2003).

Pickering, Kathleen. "Articulation of the Lakota Mode of Production and the Euro-American Fur Trade." In *The Fur Trade Revisited: Selected Papers of the Sixth North American Fur Trade Conference*, ed. Jennifer Brown, W. J. Eccles, and Donald P. Heldman. East Lansing: Michigan State University Press, 1991.

Plane, Mark R. "'Remarkable Elasticity of Character': Colonial Discourse, the Market Economy, and Catawba Itinerancy, 1770-1820." In *American Indians and the Market Economy, 1775-1850*, ed. Lance Greene and Mark R. Plane. Tuscaloosa: University of Alabama Press, 2010.

Platt, Marjorie and James Weisel. "Turning Around the South Dakota Microbrewery." In *A Casebook on Corporate Renewal,* ed. Harlan Platt and Marjorie Platt. Ann Arbor: University Michigan Press, 2004.

Pogue, Thomas F. "Mounting Fiscal Pressures: How Can State and Local Governments Cope?" In *Economic Forces Shaping the Rural Heartland*. Kansas City: Federal Reserve Bank of Kansas City, 1996.

Pollock, Jim. "Rebirth of a South Dakota Town." *South Dakota History* 19, 3 (Fall 1989): 342-61.

Pratt, D. B. "Beet Sugar; South Dakota's New Industry." *The Black Hills Engineer* 15, 2 (1928): 65-80.

Provost, Kenneth. "American Indian Entrepreneurs: A Case Study." Ph.D. diss., South Dakota State University, 1991.

Pulver, Glen C. "New Avenues for Public Policy." In *Economic Forces Shaping the Rural Heartland*. Kansas City: Federal Reserve Bank of Kansas City, 1996.

Putnam, Robert. "E Pluribus Unum: Diversity and Community in the Twenty-First Century." *Scandinavian Political Studies* 30, 2 (2007): 137-74.

Rambow, Charles. "Ku Klux Klan in the 1920s: A Concentration on the Black Hills." *South Dakota History* 4,1 (Winter 1973): 63-81.

Read, Richard T. and David Rambow. "Hydrogen and Smoke: A Survey of Lighter-Than-Air Flight in South Dakota Prior to World War I." 18, 3 *South Dakota History* (1998): 132-51.

Redlin, Greg. "Citibank Comes to South Dakota: The Politics of Economic Change." M.B.A. thesis, University of South Dakota, 2004.

Remington, Frederic "Stubble and Slough in Dakota." In *The Collected Writings of Frederic Remington*, ed. Peggy Samuels and Harold Samuels. New York: Doubleday, 1979.

Riley, Glenda. "Farm Women's Roles in the Agricultural Development of South Dakota." *South Dakota History* 13, 1 (Spring 1983): 83-121.

Ringling, Laura K. "Benson v. State: Road Hunting Tradition Upheld at the Expense of South Dakota Property Owners." *South Dakota Law Review* 52, 2 (2007): 417-43.

Ritterbush, Lauren W. "Drawn by the Bison: Late Prehistoric Native Migration into the Central Plains." *Great Plains Quarterly* 22 (Fall 2002): 259-70.

Robinson, DeLorme W. "Physicians and the Practice of Medicine." In *History of South Dakota* by Doane Robinson. Indianapolis: B. F. Bowen, 1904.

Robinson, Jerome. "South Dakota Geese." *Field & Stream* 96, 8 (Dec. 1991): 24-26.

Robinson, Monty. "Students' and Employers' Perceptions of Technology and Technology Education in South Dakota." Ed.D. diss., University of South Dakota, 2008.

Robinson, Will G. "Board of Indian Commissioners Report, 1880." *South Dakota Historical Collections and Report* 32 (1964).

_____. "Digest of the Report of the Commissioner of Indian Affairs, 1877." *South Dakota Historical Collections and Report* 32 (1964).

_____. "Our Indian Problem." *South Dakota Historical Collections and Report* 25 (1950).

_____. "Recollections of an Adventurous Life as Told by Dennis Moran to Will G. Robinson." *South Dakota Historical Collections and Report* 24 (1949).

_____. "Report of the Commissioner of Indian Affairs, 1880." *South Dakota Historical Collections and Report* 32 (1964).

Roegiers, Charles and Sandy Weeldreyer. "South Dakota Sheep." *South Dakota Business Review* 47, 2 (Dec. 1988).

Roper, Donna C. "Documentary Evidence for Changes in Protohistoric and Early Historic Pawnee Hunting Practices." *Plains Anthropologist* 37, 141 (1992): 353-66.

Sannes, Erling N. "'Union Makes Strength': Organizing Teamsters in South Dakota in the 1930s." *South Dakota History* 18, 1, 2 (Spring/Summer 1988): 36-66.

Schaff, Jon D. "A Clear Choice: George McGovern and the 1972 Presidential Race." In *George McGovern: A Political Life, a Political Legacy*, ed. Robert P. Watson. Pierre: South Dakota State Historical Society Press, 2004.

Schell, Herbert S. "Adjustment Problems in South Dakota." *Agricultural History* 14, 2 (Apr. 1940): 65-74.

Schneiders, Robert. "Missouri River." In *The American Midwest: An Interpretive Encyclopedia*, ed. Richard Sisson, Christian Zacher, and Andrew Cayton. Bloomington: Indiana University Press, 2007.

Schofer, Dan. "South Dakota: Great Faces, Great Places – and Great Value-Added Opportunities." *Rural Cooperatives* (Sept./Oct. 2007).

Schwieder, Dorothy. "South Dakota Farm Women and the Great Depression." *Journal of the West* 24 (Oct. 1985): 6-18.

Severson, Keith E. and F. Robert Gartner. "Problems in Commercial Hunting Systems: South Dakota and Texas Compared." *Journal of Range Management* 25, 5 (Sept. 1972): 342-45.

Shirley, Andrew. "South Dakota Offers an Escape to EU Red Tape." *Farmers Weekly* (Oct. 2002).

Simmons, Donald C., Jr. "McGovern's Upbringing in South Dakota: The Making of a Political Mind." In *George McGovern: A Political Life, a Political Legacy*, ed. Robert P. Watson. Pierre: South Dakota State Historical Society Press, 2004.

Smith, Arthur E. and Eric Fritzsch. "South Dakota." *Rocks & Minerals* 75 (May/June 2000): 156-69.

Smith, James Richard. "Some Changing Features of a Regional Capital: Sioux Falls, South Dakota, 1920-1970." Ph.D. diss., University of Nebraska, 1971.

Southerton, Don. "James R. Walker's Campaign against Tuberculosis on the Pine Ridge Indian Reservation." In *The Sioux in South Dakota History*, ed. Richmond L. Clow. Pierre: South Dakota Historical Society Press, 2007.

Stone, R. W., et al. *Gypsum Deposits of the United States*. Geological Survey Bulletin No. 697. Washington, D.C.: Government Printing Office, 1920.

Street, Sylvia Jane. "Implementation of Planned Change: The South Dakota Modernization Process." Ed.D. diss., University of South Dakota, 1994.

Strezewski, Michael. "'These Indians Appear to Be Wealthy': Economy and Identity During the Late Fur-Trade Period in the Lower Great Lakes." In *American Indians and the Market Economy, 1775-1850*, ed. Lance Greene and Mark R. Plane. Tuscaloosa: University of Alabama Press, 2010.

Stuefen, Randall M. and De Vee Dykstra. "Growth, Diversification and In-Migration: South Dakota's Economic Awakening." *South Dakota Business Review* 56, 1 (Sept. 1997).

Tosterud, Robert. "Venture Capital and South Dakota Economic Development." *South Dakota Business Review* 50, 2 (Dec. 1991).

Tosterud, Robert and Joseph H. Sykora. "South Dakota High Schoolers: Business Attitudes and Ambitions." *South Dakota Business Review* 52, 3 (Mar. 1994).

Tosterud, Robert and Timothy Habbershon. "Rural Entrepreneurship: A Preliminary Study." *South Dakota Business Review* 50, 3 (Mar. 1992).

Tosterud, Robert, Timothy Habbershon, and Even Liahjell. "The 1993 South Dakota Family Business Survey: Preliminary Findings." *South Dakota Business Review* 51, 4 (June 1993).

Vogel, John N. "Great Lakes Lumber on the Great Plains: The Laird, Norton Lumber Company in South Dakota." Ph.D. diss., Marquette University, 1989.

Wagner, Bill. "He Knows How Things Are Done on the Farm." *ABA Banking Journal* (Nov. 1984): 37-39.

Warmuth, Susan. "School/Business Partnerships in South Dakota Elementary Schools." Ed.D. diss., University of South Dakota, 1998.

Welch, Edward. "The Making of a Legend: Oscar Howe." *High Plains Artist* (2013): 14-15.

White, Eugene. "The Political Economy of Banking Regulation, 1864-1933." *Journal of Economic History* 42, 1 (Mar. 1982): 33-40.

White, Suzanne. "Town and Gown, Analysis of Relationships: Black Hills State University and Spearfish, South Dakota, 1883 to 1991." Ph.D. diss., Iowa State University, 1991.

White Hat, Albert and Travis Whirlwind Soldier. "Panel V: Revitalizing Economies, Preserving Cultures & Protecting the Environment: Striking the Balance in South Dakota & Indian Country." *Great Plains Natural Resources Journal* 7, 1 (Fall 2002).

Wilde, Harold H. "A Survey of the Attitudes of South Dakota Small Business Owners and/or Managers towards Social Responsibility Accounting." Ph.D. diss., University of Nebraska, 1981.

Wilkinson, Kenneth P. "Consequences of Decline and Social Adjustment to It." In *Communities Left Behind: Alternatives for Development*, ed. Larry R. Whiting. Ames: Iowa State University Press, 1974.

Williams, Elizabeth. "Agrarian Exponent: Emil Loriks." In *South Dakota Leaders: From Pierre Chouteau, Jr., to Oscar Howe*, ed. Herbert T. Hoover and Larry J. Zimmerman. Vermillion: University of South Dakota Press, 1989.

Wilson, Norma C. and Charles L. Woodard, eds. *One-Room Country School: South Dakota Stories*. Brookings: South Dakota Humanities Foundation, 1998.

Wirtz, Ronald. "Made (again?) in the USA." *Fedgazette* (Oct. 2012).

_____. "Manufacturing an Uptick." *Fedgazette* (Oct. 2012).

Woessner, Paula. "New Credit Union Promotes Financial Access on Pine Ridge Reservation." *Community Dividend* (Jan. 2013).

Wolff, David A. "No Matter How You Do It, Fraud Is Fraud: Another Look at Black Hills Mining Scandals." *South Dakota History* 33, 2 (Summer 2003): 91-119.

Worthington, Daniel G. and Peter M. Williams. "Retirement Planning with South Dakota Trusts." *Trusts & Estates* (Sept. 1997).

Wright, Robert E. "Corporate Citizens: South Dakota Chartermongering in the Early Twentieth Century." In *Plains Political Tradition: Essays on South Dakota Political Culture,* Volume 2, ed. Jon Lauck, John E. Miller, and Donald C. Simmons, Jr. Pierre: South Dakota State Historical Society Press, 2014.

_____. "On the Economic Efficiency of Organizations: Toward a Solution of the Efficient Government Enterprise Paradox," *Essays in Economic and Business History* 25 (Apr. 2007): 143-54.

_____. "Wall Street on the Prairie: Citibank, South Dakota, and the Origins of Financial Deregulation," *Financial History* (Spring 2013): 24-26.

_____. "Wall Street on the Prairie: How Financial Innovation and Regulation Cajoled Citibank into South Dakota," Museum of American Finance, New York, New York, 12 Mar. 2013.

Wymar, Benno. "Foreign Investments and South Dakota." *South Dakota Business Review* 55, 3 (Mar. 1997).

_____. "NAFTA and South Dakota – A Five Year Analysis." *South Dakota Business Review* 57, 4 (June 1999).

_____. "South Dakota-Canadian Commercial Relations." *South Dakota Business Review* 53, 1 (Sept. 1994).

_____. "South Dakota-Japan Commercial Relations." *South Dakota Business Review* 52, 3 (Mar. 1994).

Zumbo, Jim. "South Dakota's Merriam's Turkeys." *Outdoor Life* (Mar. 2005).

Books

Abel, Annie, ed. *Chardon's Journal at Fort Clark*. Pierre: Department of History, State of South Dakota, 1932.

Abourezk, James. *Advise and Dissent: Memoirs of South Dakota and the U.S. Senate*. Chicago: Lawrence Hill Books, 1989.

Acemoglu, Daron and James A. Robinson. *Why Nations Fail: The Origins of Power, Prosperity, and Poverty*. New York: Crown, 2012.

Amerson, Robert. *From the Hidewood: Memories of a Dakota Neighborhood*. St. Paul: Minnesota Historical Society Press, 1996.

Andersen, M. J. *Portable Prairie: Confessions of an Unsettled Midwesterner*. New York: St. Martin's Press, 2005.

Anderson, Terry L. *Sovereign Nations or Reservations?: An Economic History of American Indians*. San Francisco: Pacific Research Institute for Public Policy, 1995.

Anson, Robert Sam. *McGovern: A Biography*. New York: Holt, Rinehart and Winston, 1972.

Arends, Shirley Fischer. *The Central Dakota Germans: Their History, Language, and Culture*. Washington: Georgetown University Press, 1989.

Bailey, Reeve and Marvin Allum. *Fishes of South Dakota*. Ann Arbor: Museum of Zoology, University of Michigan, 1962.

Banner, Stuart. *How the Indians Lost Their Land: Law and Power on the Frontier*. Cambridge, MA: Harvard University Press, 2005.

Baumol, William, Robert Litan, and Carl Schramm. *Good Capitalism, Bad Capitalism, and the Economics of Growth and Prosperity*. New Haven: Yale University Press, 2007.

Berg, Francie. *South Dakota: Land of Shining Gold*. Hettinger, ND: Flying Diamond Books, 1982.

Biggers, Shirley Hoover. *American Author Houses, Museums, Memorials, and Libraries: A State-by-State Guide*. Jefferson, NC: McFarland and Co., 2000.

Biolsi, Thomas. *Organizing the Lakota: The Political Economy of the New Deal on the Pine Ridge and Rosebud Reservations*. Tucson: University of Arizona Press, 1992.

Blasingame, Ike. *Dakota Cowboy: My Life in the Old Days*. New York: G. P. Putnam's Sons, 1958.

Braun, Sebastian. *Buffalo Inc.: American Indians and Economic Development*. Norman: Oklahoma University Press, 2008.

Braunstein, Rich. *Initiative and Referendum Voting: Governing Through Direct Democracy in the United States*. New York: LFB Scholarly Publishing, 2004.

Brokaw, Tom. *A Long Way from Home: Growing Up in the American Heartlcnd*. New York: Random House, 2002.

Brooks, Patricia. *Where the Bodies Are: Final Visits to the Rich, Famous & Interesting*. Guilford, CT: The Globe Pequot Press, 2002.

Brown, Jesse and A. M. Willard. *The Black Hills Trails: A History of the Struggles of the Pioneers in the Winning of the Black Hills*. Rapid City: Rapid City Journal Company, 1924.

Bryan, Lisa Little Chief. *American Indian Entrepreneurs: Rosebud and Pine Ridge Reservations Case Studies*. Pablo, MT: Salish Kootenai College Press, 1999.

Business and Industry Round Table. *South Dakota: Final Report*. Oct. 1988.

Carrels, Peter. *Uphill against Water: The Great Dakota Water War*. Lincoln: University of Nebraska Press, 1999.

Casey, Robert J. *The Black Hills and Their Incredible Characters: A Chronicle and a Guide*. Indianapolis: Bobbs-Merrill Co., 1949.

Cash, Joseph H. *Working the Homestake*. Ames: Iowa State University Press, 1973.

Cassels, E. Steve. *Prehistoric Hunters of the Black Hills*. Boulder: Johnson Hills, 1986.

Chai, May-lee. *Hapa Girl*. Philadelphia: Temple University Press, 2007.

Chalmers, David M. *Hooded Americanism: The History of the Ku Klux Klan*. Durham: Duke University Press, 1987.

Cheever, Lawrence. *The House of Morrell*. Cedar Rapids: Torch Press, 1948.

Child, Brenda J. *Boarding School Seasons: American Indian Families, 1900-1940*. Lincoln: University of Nebraska Press, 1998.

Chittick, Douglas. *Growth and Decline of South Dakota Trade Centers, 1901-51*. Brookings: South Dakota State College, Rural Sociology Department Bulletin 448, May 1955.

Chucker, Harold. *Banco at Fifty: A History of Northwest Bancorporation, 1929-1979*. Minneapolis: Banco, 1979.

Clark, Champ. *The Badlands*. New York: Time-Life Books, 1974.

Clem, Alan. *Government by the People?: South Dakota Politics in the Last Third of the Twentieth Century*. Rapid City: Chiesman Foundation for Democracy, 2002.

_____. *Prairie State Politics: Popular Democracy in South Dakota*. Washington, D.C.: Public Affairs Press, 1967.

Cochell, Shirley and George Beine. *Land of the Coyote*. Ames: Iowa State University Press, 1972.

Collins, Cary C. and Charles V. Mutschler, eds. *A Doctor among the Oglala Sioux Tribe: The Letters of Robert H. Ruby, 1953-1954*. Lincoln: University of Nebraska Press, 2010.

Conn, Herb and Jan Conn. *The Jewel Cave Adventure: Fifty Miles of Discovery under South Dakota*. St. Louis: Cave Books, 1981.

Crawford, Lewis. *The Medora-Deadwood Stage Line*. Bismarck: Capital Book Company, 1925.

Culp, Estella Bowen. *Letters from Tully: A Woman's Life on the Dakota Frontier*. Boulder: Johnson Books.

Dahl, A. E. *Banker Dahl of South Dakota: An Autobiography*. Rapid City: Fenske Book Company, 1965.

Dahlgren, Robert. *The Pheasant Decline*. Pierre: South Dakota Department of Game, Fish and Parks, 1967.

Daum, Ann. *The Prairie in Her Eyes*. Minnesota: Milkweed Editions, 2001.

Dehgan, Bahman, ed. *America in Quotations*. Jefferson, NC: McFarland & Co., 2003.

Department of Political Science and Government Research Bureau. *A White Paper Report: County Consolidation in South Dakota*. Vermillion: University of South Dakota, 1997.

de Soto, Hernando. *The Mystery of Capital: Why Capitalism Triumphs in the West and Fails Everywhere Else.* New York: Basic Books, 2000.

Dregni, Eric. *Midwest Marvels: Roadside Attractions Across Iowa, Minnesota, the Dakotas, and Wisconsin.* Minneapolis: University of Minnesota Press, 2006.

Driscoll, Robert E. *The Black Hills of South Dakota: Its Pioneer Banking History.* New York: Newcomen Society in North America, 1951.

Dugan, Mark. *The Making of Legends: More True Stories of Frontier America.* Athens: Ohio University Press, 1997.

Duncan, Kunigunde. *Blue Star: The Story of Corabelle Fellows: Teacher at Dakota Missions, 1884-1888.* St. Paul: Minnesota Historical Society Press, 1990.

Easterly, William. *The Elusive Quest for Growth: Economists' Adventures and Misadventures in the Tropics.* Cambridge: MIT Press, 2001.

Ehringer, Gavin. *100 Best Ranch Vacations in North America.* Guilford, CT: Globe Pequot Press, 2004.

Entrepreneur Press. *How to Start a Business in South Dakota.* New York: Entrepreneur Media, 2004.

Fairchild, Grace and Walker D. Wyman. *Frontier Woman: The Life of a Woman Homesteader on the Dakota Frontier.* River Falls: University of Wisconsin-River Falls Press, 1972.

Fernandez-Shaw, Carlos M. *The Hispanic Presence in North America from 1492 to Today.* New York: Facts on File, 1991.

Fielder, Mildred. *Railroads of the Black Hills.* Seattle: Superior Publishing Co., 1964.

Fiffer, Steve. *Tyrannosaurus Sue: The Extraordinary Saga of the Largest, Most Fought Over T. Rex Ever Found.* New York: W. H. Freeman and Co., 2000.

Fite, Gilbert. *Peter Norbeck: Prairie Statesman.* Columbia: University of Missouri, 1948.

Flake, Lester D., John W. Connelly, Thomas R. Kirschenmann, and Andrew J. Lindbloom. *Grouse of Plains and Mountains: The South Dakota Story.* Pierre: South Dakota Department of Game, Fish and Parks, 2010.

Foss, Joe and Donna Wild Foss. *A Proud American: The Autobiography of Joe Foss.* New York: Pocket Books, 1992.

Francisconi, Michael J. *Kinship, Capitalism, Change: The Informal Economy of the Navajo, 1868-1995.* New York: Routledge, 1998.

Frazier, Ian. *On the Rez.* New York: Farrar, Straus, and Giroux, 2000.

Gallay, Alan. *The Indian Slave Trade: The Rise of the English Empire in the American South, 1670-1717.* New Haven: Yale University Press, 2002.

Garoogian, David. *Weather America: A Thirty-Year Summary of Statistical Weather Data and Rankings,* 2nd ed. Lakeville, CT: Grey House Publishing, 2001.

Gerber, Philip. L. ed., *Bachelor Bess: The Homesteading Letters of Elizabeth Corey, 1909-1919.* Iowa City: University of Iowa Press, 1990.

Gilfillan, Archer B. *Sheep: Life on the South Dakota Range.* St. Paul: Minnesota Historical Society Press, 1993.

Gooder Casey Land Co. *Southwestern South Dakota: A Booklet Descriptive of the Country along the New Extension of the C. M. & St. P. Railway between Chamberlain and the Famous Black Hills.* Chamberlain: Gooder Casey Land Co., [1910].

Gott, Garland, Don Wolcott, and C. Gilbert Bowles. *Stratigraphy of the Inyan Kara Group and Localization of Uranium Deposits, Southern Black Hills, South Dakota and Wyoming.* Washington, DC: Government Printing Office, 1974.

Grant, Michael Johnston. *Down and Out on the Family Farm: Rural Rehabilitation in the Great Plains, 1929-1945.* Lincoln: University of Nebraska Press, 2002.

Grauvogl, Ann. *South Dakota: Pioneering the Future.* Encino, CA: Cherbo Publishing, 2006.

Gray, W.K., A. A. Volk, A.M. Dreyer, M. L. White, and V. E. Montgomery. *South Dakota Economic and Business Abstract, 1939-1962.* Vermillion: Business Research Bureau, 1963.

Greene, Jerome A. *Fort Randall on the Missouri, 1856-1892.* Pierre: South Dakota State Historical Society Press, 2005.

Gunther, John. *Inside U.S.A.* New York: Harper & Brothers, 1947.

Gwartney, James, Robert Lawson, and Joshua Hall. *Economic Freedom of the World: 2013 Annual Report.* Montreal: Fraser Institute, 2013.

Hagerty, Frank. *The Territory of Dakota: The State of North Dakota; the State of South Dakota.* Aberdeen: Daily News Print, 1889.

Hall, Philip S. *To Have This Land.* Vermillion: University of South Dakota Press, 1991.

Harvard Project on American Indian Economic Development. *The State of the Native Nations: Conditions Under U.S. Policies of Self-Determination.* New York: Oxford University Press, 2008.

Hasselstrom, Linda. *Feels Like Far: A Rancher's Life on the Great Plains.* New York: Lyons Press, 1999.

_____. *No Place Like Home: Notes from a Western Life.* Las Vegas: University of Nevada Press, 2009.

_____. *Roadside History of South Dakota.* Missoula, MT: Mountain Press Publishing Co., 1994.

_____. *Windbreak: A Woman Rancher on the Northern Plains.* Berkeley, CA: Barn Owl Books, 1987.

Hazeltine, Joyce. *Domestic Business Corporations.* Pierre: Office of the South Dakota Secretary of State, 1992.

Head, Marion. *South Dakota: An Explorer's Guide.* Woodstock, VT: Countryman Press, 2009.

Herman, Daniel. *Hunting and the American Imagination.* Washington: Smithsonian Institution Press, 2001.

Herzog, Brad. *Small World: A Microcosmic Journey.* New York: Pocket Books, 2004.

Hicks, Patrick, ed. *A Harvest of Words: Contemporary South Dakota Poetry.* Sioux Falls: Center for Western Studies, 2010.

Higgins, Kenneth F., Eilen Dowd Stukel, Judyann M. Goulet, and Douglas C. Backlund. *Wild Mammals of South Dakota.* Pierre: South Dakota Department of Game, Fish and Parks, 2000.

Higgs, Robert. *Crisis and Leviathan: Critical Episodes in the Growth of American Government.* New York: Oxford University Press, 1987.

Hodges, Graham Russell Gao. *Taxi!: A Social History of the New York City Cabdriver.* New York: New York University Press, 2007.

HOPE. *Human Trafficking: Realities and Facts.* Watertown, SD: 2014.

Huseboe, Arthur R. with Arthur Amiotte. *An Illustrated History of the Arts in South Dakota.* Sioux Falls: Center for Western Studies, 1989.

Institute for South Dakota Leadership and Participation. *The Future of Health Care in South Dakota Roundtable Report.* 2000.

Irving, J. D., S. F. Emmon, and T. A. Jaggar, Jr. *Economic Resources of the Northern Black Hills.* Washington, D.C.: Government Printing Office, 1904.

Johnsgard, Paul. *Lewis and Clark on the Great Plains: A Natural History.* Lincoln: University of Nebraska Press, 2003.

Johnson, Clifton. *Highways and Byways of the Rocky Mountains.* New York: MacMillan Co., 1910.

Johnson, Rebecca L. *What It Took: A History of the USGS EROS Data Center.* Sioux Falls: Center for Western Studies, 1998.

Jones, W. Franklin. *Concrete Investigation of the Material of English Spelling with Conclusions Bearing on the Problem of Teaching Spelling.* Vermillion: University of South Dakota, 1913.

Karolevitz, Robert. *Challenge: The South Dakota Story.* Sioux Falls: Brevet Press, 1975.

Keating, Raymond J. *Small Business Survival Index 2009: Ranking the Policy Environment for Entrepreneurship Across the Nation.* Oakton, VA: Small Business & Entrepreneurship Council, 2009.

Kellar, Kenneth. *Seth Bullock, Frontier Marshal.* Aberdeen: North Plains Press, 1972.

Khan, B. Zorina. *The Democratization of Invention: Patents and Copyrights in American Economic Development, 1790-1920.* New York: Cambridge University Press, 2005.

Kinyon, Jeannette, Lois Johnson, and Margaret Voels. *Prairie Architect, F.C.W. Kuehn: His Life and Work.* Sioux Falls: Center for Western Studies, 1984.

Kirby, Joe P. *Western Surety Company: One of America's Oldest Bonding Companies.* Sioux Falls, 2012.

Kolbenschlag, George. *A Whirlwind Passes: Newspaper Correspondents and the Sioux Indian Disturbances of 1890-1891.* Vermillion: University of South Dakota Press, 1990.

Laffer, Arthur B., Stephen Moore, and Jonathan Williams. *Rich States, Poor States: ALEC-Laffer State Economic Competitiveness Index,* 4th ed. 2011.

Lamar, Howard. *Dakota Territory, 1861-1889: A Study of Frontier Politics.* New Haven: Yale University Press, 1956.

Landes, David, Joel Mokyr, and William Baumol. *The Invention of Enterprise: Entrepreneurship from Ancient Mesopotamia to Modern Times.* Princeton: Princeton University Press, 2010.

Landis, Paul H. *The Growth and Decline of South Dakota Trade Centers, 1901-1933.* Brookings: South Dakota State College of Agriculture, 1933.

Lauck, Jon. *Prairie Republic: The Political Culture of Dakota Territory, 1879-1889.* Norman: University of Oklahoma Press, 2010.

Lawrence, Peter. *The Change Game: How Today's Global Trends Are Shaping Tomorrow's Companies.* London: Kogan Page Ltd., 2002.

Lawson, Michael. *Dammed Indians: The Pick-Sloan Plan and the Missouri River Sioux, 1944-1980.* Norman: University of Oklahoma Press, 1982.

Lay, Shawn, ed. *The Invisible Empire in the West: Toward a New Historical Appraisal of the Ku Klux Klan of the 1920s.* Chicago: University of Illinois Press, 1992.

Lee, Bob. *Last Grass Frontier: The South Dakota Stockgrowers Heritage.* Vol. 2. Sturgis: Black Hills Publishers, Inc., 1999.

Lee, R. Alton. *Principle Over Party: The Farmers' Alliance and Populism in South Dakota, 1880-1900.* Pierre: South Dakota State Historical Society Press, 2011.

Lewis, Faye C. *Nothing to Make a Shadow.* Ames: Iowa State University Press, 1971.

Lippincott, Kerry. *A Late Prehistoric Period Pronghorn Hunting Camp in the Southern Black Hills, South Dakota: Site 39FA23.* Pierre: South Dakota Archaeological Society, 1996.

Little, Gregory, ed. *The Illustrated Encyclopedia of Native American Mounds & Earthworks.* Memphis: Eagle Wing Books, 2009.

Maddison, Angus. *The World Economy: A Millennial Perspective.* Paris: OECD, 2002.

Malkin, Jennifer and Johnnie Aseron. *Native Entrepreneurship in South Dakota: A Deeper Look*. CFED, 2006.

Mandat-Grancey, Edmont. *Cowboys and Colonels: Narrative of a Journey Across the Prairie and Over the Black Hills of Dakota*. Translated by William Conn. Philadelphia: J. B. Lippincott Co., 1963.

McClintock, John S. *Pioneer Days in the Black Hills: Accurate History and Facts Related by One of the Early Day Pioneers*. Deadwood: John S. McClintock, 1939.

McDermott, John Francis, ed. *Journal of an Expedition to the Mauvaises Terres and the Upper Missouri in 1850 by Thaddeus A. Culbertson*. Washington: Smithsonian Institution, 1950.

McGillycuddy, Julia B. *McGillycuddy Agent: A Biography of Dr. Valentine T. McGillycuddy*. Stanford: Stanford University Press, 1941.

Milanovic, Branko. *The Haves and the Have-Nots: A Brief and Idiosyncratic History of Global Inequality*. New York: Basic Books, 2011.

Miller, Donald C. *Ghosts on a Sea of Grass: Ghost Towns of the Plains*. Missoula, MT: Pictorial Histories Publishing Company, 1990.

Miller, John E. *Looking for History on Highway 14*. Pierre: South Dakota State Historical Society Press, 2001.

Miller, Neil. *In Search of Gay America: Women and Men in a Time of Change*. New York: Atlantic Monthly Press, 1989.

Miller, Robert J. *Reservation "Capitalism": Economic Development in Indian Country*. New York: Praeger, 2012.

Milton, John. *South Dakota: A Bicentennial History*. New York: W. W. Norton and Co., 1977.

_____. ed. *The American Indian Speaks*. Vermillion: University of South Dakota, 1969.

Montgomery, V. E. and C. S. Van Doren. *The Economy of the West North Central Region of South Dakota*. Vermillion: Business Research Bureau, 1957.

Moss, Marcey and James L. Satterlee. *South Dakota County Data Book*. Brookings: South Dakota State University, 2002.

Murray, David. *Indian Giving: Economies of Power in Indian-White Exchanges*. Amherst: University of Massachusetts Press, 2000.

Nelson, Mark, Paul Higbee, and Ken Steinken. *The Spirit of an American Entrepreneur: Succeeding in Family Business*. Sioux Falls: Mark Nelson, 2009.

Nelson, Paula M. *After the West Was Won: Homesteaders and Town-Builders in Western South Dakota, 1900-1917*. Iowa City: University of Iowa Press, 1986.

_____. *The Prairie Winnows Out Its Own: The West River Country of South Dakota in the Years of Depression and Dust*. Iowa City: University of Iowa Press, 1996.

Newton, Henry and Walter P. Jenney. *Report on the Geology and Resources of the Black Hills of Dakota, with Atlas*. Washington, D.C.: Government Printing Office, 1880.

Norris, Kathleen. *Dakota: A Spiritual Geography*. New York: Ticknor and Fields, 1993.

Norton, James J. *Gold in the Black Hills, South Dakota, and How New Deposits Might Be Found*. U.S. Department of the Interior, Geological Survey Circular 699, 1969.

O'Brien, Dan. *Buffalo for the Broken Heart: Restoring Life to a Black Hills Ranch*. New York: Random House, 2001.

O'Harra, Cleophas. *The White River Badlands*. Rapid City: South Dakota School of Mines, 1920.

Oswald, John. *Printing in the Americas*. New York: Gregg Publishing Company, 1937.

Over, William H. and Edward P. Churchill. *Mammals of South Dakota*. Vermillion: University of South Dakota, 1945.

Page, Lincoln R., et al. *Pegmatite Investigations 1942-1945: Black Hills, South Dakota.* Washington, D.C.: Government Printing Office, 1953.

Pagnamenta, Peter. *Prairie Fever: British Aristocrats in the American West, 1830-1890.* New York: W. W. Norton and Co., 2012.

Perkins, Edwin J. *Wall Street to Main Street: Charles Merrill and Middle-Class Investors.* New York: Cambridge University Press, 1999.

Peterson, Dale. *Storyville USA.* Athens: University of Georgia Press, 1999.

Peterson, Fred W. *Homes in the Heartland: Balloon Frame Farmhouses of the Upper Midwest, 1850-1920.* Lawrence: University Press of Kansas, 1992.

Peterson, P.D. *Through the Black Hills and Bad Lands of South Dakota.* Pierre: J. Fred Olander Company, 1929.

Pickering, Kathleen Ann. *Lakota Culture, World Economy.* Lincoln: University of Nebraska Press, 2000.

Piott, Steven. *Giving Voters a Voice: The Origins of the Initiative and Referendum in America.* Columbia: University of Missouri Press, 2003.

Polsky, Richard. *Boneheads: My Search for T. Rex.* San Francisco: Council Oak Books, 2011.

Poth, L. A. *Transportation Rates, Products Transported, and Trade Barriers Important to South Dakota.* Vermillion: University of South Dakota, 1950.

Powell, Benjamin. *Making Poor Nations Rich: Entrepreneurship and the Process of Economic Development.* Stanford: Stanford University Press, 2008.

Professional Soil Scientists Association of South Dakota. *Soil, the Basis of Life: Houdek, South Dakota's State Soil.* 1999.

Rath, George. *The Black Sea Germans in the Dakotas.* Freeman, SD: Pine Hill Press, 1977.

Ravage, John W. *Black Pioneers: Images of the Black Experience on the North American Frontier.* Salt Lake City: University of Utah Press, 1997.

Reese, M. Lisle, ed. *South Dakota: A Guide to the State,* 2nd ed. New York: Hastings House, 1952.

Richardson, Richard. *Policy and Performance in American Higher Education.* Baltimore: Johns Hopkins University Press, 2009.

Robinson, Doane. *History of South Dakota.* Indianapolis: B. F. Bowen, 1904.

Robinson, James M. *West from Fort Pierre: The Wild World of James (Scotty) Philip.* Los Angeles: Westernlore Press, 1974.

Robinson, Ron. *Valley Queen Cheese: The Birth and Growth of an American Dream.* Sioux Falls: Ex Machina Publishing Company, 2006.

Rogers, Charles. *South Dakota's Challenges Since 1960.* Garretson, SD: Sanders Printing Co., 2011.

Ross-Nazzal, Jennifer M. *Winning the West for Women: The Life of Suffragist Emma Smith DeVoe.* Seattle: University of Washington Press, 2011.

Sanger, William W. *The History of Prostitution: Its Extent, Causes, and Effects Throughout the World.* New York: Harper and Brothers, 1858.

Satterlee, James. *The New Community.* Brookings: South Dakota State University, 2002.

Schatz, August. *Longhorns Bring Culture.* Boston: Christopher Publishing House, 1961.

Schell, Herbert. *History of South Dakota,* 4th ed. Pierre: South Dakota State Historical Society Press, 2004.

Schneiders, Robert. *Unruly River: Two Centuries of Change Along the Missouri.* Lawrence: University of Kansas Press, 1999.

Schultz, Patricia. *1,000 Places to See in the USA and Canada Before You Die.* New York: Workman Publishing, 2007.

Schwieder, Dorothy. *Growing Up with the Town: Family and Community on the Great Plains.* Iowa City: University of Iowa Press, 2002.

Shane, Scott. *The Illusions of Entrepreneurship: The Costly Myths that Entrepreneurs, Investors, and Policy Makers Live By.* New Haven: Yale University Press, 2008.

Shirk, Martha and Anna Wadia. *Kitchen Table Entrepreneurs: How Eleven Women Escaped Poverty and Became Their Own Bosses.* New York: Westview Press, 2002.

Siberts, Bruce and Walker D. Wyman. *Nothing but Prairie and Sky: Life on the Dakota Range in the Early Days.* Norman: University of Oklahoma Press, 1954.

Sides, W. Hampton. *Stomping Grounds: A Pilgrim's Progress through Eight American Subcultures.* New York: William Morrow and Co., 1992.

Sioux Falls Personnel Association. *1985 Metro Sioux Falls Salary Survey.* Sioux Falls: Sioux Falls Personnel Association, 1985.

Solomon, George T., ed. *National Survey of Entrepreneurial Education*, 3rd ed. Washington: U.S. Small Business Administration, 1986.

Spiegel, John, Alan Gart, and Steven Gart. *Banking Redefined: How Superregional Powerhouses Are Reshaping Financial Services.* Chicago: Irwin Professional Publishing, 1996.

State and Local Government Task Force. *Report to the South Dakota Legislature.* Pierre: 2005.

Stock, Catherine. *Main Street in Crisis: The Great Depression and the Old Middle Class on the Northern Plains.* Chapel Hill: University of North Carolina Press, 1992.

Stone, R. W. *Coal Near the Black Hills, Wyoming-South Dakota.* Washington: U.S. Geological Survey Bulletin 499, 1912.

Swiden, LaDell and Mary DeVries. *South Dakota Exports.* Brookings: South Dakota State University, 1989.

Thompson, Harry F., ed. *A New South Dakota History*, 2nd ed. Sioux Falls: Center for Western Studies, 2009.

Thompson, William N. *The International Encyclopedia of Gambling.* Santa Barbara: ABC-CLIO, 2010.

United States Chamber of Commerce and the National Chamber Foundation. *Enterprising States: Recovery and Renewal for the 21st Century.* 2011.

United States National Park Service. *Wind Cave National Park, South Dakota.* Washington: U.S. Department of the Interior, 1979.

Urbanek, Mae. *The Uncovered Wagon.* Denver: Sage Books, 1958.

Usera, John J. *Governing South Dakota: Government Meeting Future Challenges Roundtable.* Rapid City: Institute for South Dakota Leadership and Participation, 1999.

Van Demark, Robert E., Sr., ed. *Reminiscences of Irene Fisher Coon, R.N., about the Early History of Orthopaedic Nursing at Sioux Valley Hospital with Historical Origins of the Crippled Children's Hospital and School.* Sioux Falls: Center for Western Studies, 1992.

Van Dulken, Stephen. *Inventing the 19th Century: 100 Inventions that Shaped the Victorian Age.* New York: New York University Press, 2001.

VanEpps-Taylor, Betti. *Forgotten Lives: African Americans in South Dakota.* Pierre: South Dakota Historical Society Press, 2008.

_____. *Oscar Micheaux, Dakota Homesteader, Author, Pioneer Film Maker: A Biography.* Rapid City: Dakota West Books, 1999.

Van Nuys, Laura Bower. *The Family Band: From the Missouri to the Black Hills, 1881-1900.* Lincoln: University of Nebraska Press, 1961.

Vogel, John N. *Great Lakes Lumber on the Great Plains: The Laird, Norton Lumber Company in South Dakota.* Iowa City: University of Iowa Press, 1992.

Volk, A. A. *The Economy of the Black Hills Region of South Dakota.* Vermillion: Business Research Bureau, 1968.

_____. *The Economy of the Northeast Region of South Dakota.* Vermillion: University of South Dakota, 1967.

Wall, Joseph Frazier. *Policies and People: The First Hundred Years of the Banker's Life, Des Moines, Iowa.* Englewood Cliffs, N.J.: Prentice Hall, 1979.

Warren, Gouverneur K. *Preliminary Report of Explorations in Nebraska and Dakota, in the Years 1855-'56-'57.* Washington, DC: Government Printing Office, 1875.

Weatherford, Doris ed., *A History of Women in the United States: State-by-State Reference.* Danbury, CT: Grolier Academic Reference, 2004.

White, Bill. *America's Fiscal Constitution: Its Triumph and Collapse.* New York: PublicAffairs, 2014.

Whitington, Mitchel. *A Ghost in My Suitcase: A Guide to Haunted Travel in America.* Dallas: Atriad Press, 2005.

Wilder, Laura Ingalls. *On the Way Home: The Diary of a Trip from South Dakota to Mansfield, Missouri, in 1894.* New York: Harper & Row, 1962.

Willey, P. *Prehistoric Warfare on the Great Plains: Skeletal Analysis of the Crow Creek Massacre Victims.* New York: Garland, 1990.

Wills, Jocelyn. *Boosters, Hustlers, and Speculators: Entrepreneurial Culture and the Rise of Minneapolis and St. Paul, 1849-1883.* St. Paul: Minnesota Historical Society Press, 2005.

Wright, Robert E. *Corporation Nation.* Philadelphia: University of Pennsylvania Press, 2014.

_____. *Fubarnomics: A Lighthearted, Serious Look at America's Economic Ills.* Amherst, NY: Prometheus, 2010.

Wuthnow, Robert. *Remaking the Heartland: Middle America Since the 1950s.* Princeton: Princeton University Press, 2011.

Zimmerman, Larry J. *Peoples of Prehistoric South Dakota.* Lincoln: University of Nebraska Press, 1985.

Zweig, Phillip L. *Wriston: Walter Wriston, Citbank, and the Rise and Fall of American Financial Supremacy.* New York: Crown, 1995.

Government Documents

South Dakota Board of Regents. *Foundation for the Future: The Future Fund.* 1989.

South Dakota Department of Economic and Tourism Development. *Taxes!: A Businessman's Comparison.* 1975.

South Dakota Department of Game, Fish, & Parks. *Private Shooting Preserve: 2012-13 Information Manual for Private Shooting Preserves.* 2012.

South Dakota Department of Labor. *South Dakota Works Hard!* 1989.

South Dakota Department of State. *South Dakota and Foreign Trade.* 1952.

South Dakota Employment Security Department. *29th Annual Report of the Employment Security Department of South Dakota.* 1965.

South Dakota State Planning Board. *Mortgage Status of Farm Land in South Dakota.* 1938.

South Dakota State Planning Board and Hamlin County Planning Board. *Economic and Social Survey of Hamlin County.* 1937.

U.S. Census Bureau. *1992 Census of Manufactures: South Dakota.* 1992.

U.S. Congress. Senate. Committee on the Judiciary. *Ensuring Competitive and Open Agricultural Markets: Are Meat Packers Abusing Market Power?* 107th Cong., 2d Sess. 23 Aug. 2002.

U.S. Congress. Senate. *Impact of Interest Rates on the Small Business and Agricultural Sectors: Hearing before the Committee on Small Business.* Washington, DC: Government Printing Office, 1983.

U.S. Congress. Senate. *Rural Health Care Crisis: Hearings before the Committee on Finance.* 1990.

U.S. Congress. Senate. Special Committee on Aging. *The Role of Nursing Homes in Today's Society.* 98th Cong., 1st Sess., 29 Aug. 1983.

U.S. Department of the Interior. Indian Arts and Crafts Board. *Native American Owned and Operated Arts and Crafts Businesses, Source Directory.* 1982-83 Edition.

U.S. National Park Service. *Wind Cave National Park, South Dakota.* Washington: U.S. Department of the Interior, 1979.

Newspapers and News Periodicals (Printed or Online)

AGWEEK
American Rifleman
Barron's
Bloomberg Businessweek
Bloomberg News
Boston Globe
Bulletin of the American Meteorological Society (BAMS)
Canadian Mennonite
Chadron Record
Chicago Tribune
CNBC.com
Dakota Rural Action
Deseret News [Salt Lake City]
Economist, The
Enterprise, The
Epoch Times
Free-Lance Star [Fredericksburg, VA]
Guardian, The
Houston Chronicle
KDLT News.com [Sioux Falls]
Keloland.com [Sioux Falls]
Las Vegas Business Press
Lewiston Daily Sun
Los Angeles Times
Lyman County Herald
Minneapolis Star Tribune
Minneapolis St. Paul Business Journal
Mitchell Daily Republic
Morning Call [Allentown, PA]
National Hog Farmer
National Mortgage News
Nation's Business

New York Times
New York Tribune
Northwestern Financial Review
Oxy Fuel News
Rapid City Journal
Sioux Falls Argus Leader
South Florida Sun-Sentinel
State Tax Review
Tampa Bay Times
Time
Toronto Globe and Mail
Toronto Star
USA Today
Wall Street Journal
Wilmot Enterprise

Websites

BHE Custom Apparel: http://bhecustomapparel.com
Bitter Esters Brewhouse: http://bitterestersbrewhouse.com
Brookings: http://www.brookings.edu
Cardinal Industries, Inc.: http://www.cardinalcustomproducts.com
Dakota Ethanol: http://www.dakotaethanol.com
Daktronics: http://investor.daktronics.com
Dependable Sanitation, Inc.: http://sddsi.com
Economic Policy Institute: http://www.epi.com
Enterprise Holdings: http://www.enterpriseholdings.com
Federal Deposit Insurance Corporation: http://www.fdic.gov
Find A Case: http://sd.findacase.com
Forbes: http://www.forbes.com
Google Patents: http://www.google.com
Hegg Companies: http://heggcompanies.com
Hutchinson Technology: http://www.htch.com
Lake Norden: http://www.lakenorden.govoffice.com
Mammoth Site of Hot Springs, South Dakota, Inc.: http://mammothsite.com
Masaba Mining Equipment: http://www.masabainc.com
Monks House of Ale Repute: http://www.monkhouseofalerepute.com
Paleoadventures: http://www.paleoadventures.com
POET: http://www.poet.com
Prairie Sky, Inc.: http://flyprairiesky.com
Rainbow Play Systems, Inc.: http://www.rainbowplay.com
Raven Industries: http://ravenind.com
ResearchPark at South Dakota State University: http://www.researchparkatsdstate.com
Ronning Companies: http://ronningcompanies.com
South Dakota Governor's Office of Economic Development: http://www.sdreadytowork.com
South Dakota Technology Business Center: http://sdtbc.com
South Dakota Winegrowers Association: http://www.sdwinegrowers.com
Taylor Music: http://www.1800usaband.com

TaxProf Blog: http://taxprof.typepad.com
THOMAS/Library of Congress: http://thomas.loc.gov/home/thomas.php
True Yellow: True Interactive Yellow Page Directories, Inc.: http://www.trueyellow.com
U.S. Patent and Trademark Office: http://patft.uspto.gov
Vermillion Economic Development: http://www.vermillonedc.com
Waymarking: http://www.waymarking.com
Wine Web: http://www.wineweb.com
Worthington Industries: http://www.angus-palm.com

Index

losses incurred by, 199; disintermediation and, 99; employment practices of, 199; failure of, 193, 196-99; fraudulent practices of, 196; funding from available to start ups, 210; governance of, 199-200; Great Depression and, 194; home mortgages and, 193; importance of, 200; loans made by, 193, 196-97; mergers of, 201; Minnesota and, 197; practices of in South Dakota, 193, 196; practices of, 198-200; private banks, 196; regulation of in South Dakota, 193-200; robberies of, 196; size of, 200; South Dakota and, 192-202; stockholders in, 197; suicides associated with, 197; unit banking in South Dakota, 195-96. *See also* credit and creditors
Banquet, The (NGO), 85
Bar T Ranch, 59
barbers and barber shops, 36, 44, 47, 49, 50, 213
barley, 113, 113, 125
Barrison (theater), 149
bars. *See* saloons
baseball: equipment, 141; hall of fame (South Dakota), 152; Major Leaguers in South Dakota, 174; Pheastival, 174; popularity of in South Dakota, 152
basketball, 86, 145, 215
bass (fish), 166, 178
Baum, Frank, 156
Baumgartner, Felix, 96
Beach Printing, 54

Beach, Will A., 54
Beadle County, 91, 113
Beadle, William, 87
beads, beaders, and beading, 18, 21, 25, 47, 79, 80, 213
bears, 17, 157, 167-68, 180
beauty schools and shops, 51, 215
beaver, 17, 21-22, 167, 180
Beef Products, Inc., 124
beef, 60, 107, 122-25, 144
beekeeping, 117
Belgium, 128
Belk, John T., 90
Belle Fourche Creamery, 34
Belle Fourche Dam, 57
Belle Fourche Hospital, 34
Belle Fourche Roundup, 33
Belle Fourche, 33, 56, 86, 119, 122, 141, 194, 202
Ben Blair: The Story of a Plainsman (book), 155
Benevolent and Protective Order of Elks, 86
Bennett, James Gorden, 59
Bennett, Sandy, 114
Benny, Jack, 149, 151
bentonite, 107
Beresford Bancorp, 202
Berheim, Don, 119-20
Berheim, Helen, 119-20
Berry, Tom, 83
beryl, 55, 107
beryllium, 107
Beutner, August, 143
BHE Custom Apparel, 139
BHE Industries, 139
bicycles and bicyclists, 53, 151, 188
Big Bat (Indian entrepreneur), 81
Big Sioux River, 20, 26, 98, 158; discovery of by French, 23; falls of, 23, 162, *163;* rock polishing and, 128
Big Stone Canning, 96
Big Stone Lake, 23

Big Stone State Bank, 104
Bigfoot (Sasquatch), 154, 208
Billings, Montana, 202
Billion, Henry, 145
Billiter, E. D., 66
biofuel, 126, 132, 209, 221
Biolsi, Thomas, 42-43
Bismarck, North Dakota, 31, 67, 209
Bismark Bock (beer), 114
bison: bones of sold to factories, 36; chips of used as fuel, 36; demise of great herds of 42; effigy etching of pictured, *20;* fences used to enclose, 129; furniture made from hides of, 132; herd of pictured, *115;* hunting of 157, 162, 169; Indians and, 17-22, 78-79, 167; privatization of 115-16; ranching of, 79, 116; replacement of by cattle on Northern Plains, 40; robes made from skins of, 25; taxidermy of, 180; tourism and 164, 167. *See also* Buffalo Commons
Bitter Esters Brewhouse, 115
Black and Yellow Trail, 51-52
black ferrets, 168
Black Hills Caverns, 165
Black Hills Embroidery, 139
Black Hills FiberCom, 191
Black Hills Glass and Mirror Company, 147-48
Black Hills Institute of Geological Research, 158
Black Hills Motor Classic. *See* Sturgis Rally and Races
Black Hills Passion Play, 3

by microfinance institutions, 81-82; begetting of more entrepreneurship, 213-14; debauched examples of, 1-2; economic effects of, 6-7; education and, 185, 219; examples of serial, 50-51, 193-94, 200-1; examples of, 36; exploitative, 60, 218; exporting spirit of to the rest of the United States, 221; good varieties of, 207; immigration and, 216; importance of for Indians, 79-80; importance of property rights to, 81; importance of to South Dakota's economy, 2-4; incentives for, 218-21; innovative and, 207; marijuana and, 218; outlook for in South Dakota, 220; pheasant hunting and, 172-75; replicative examples of, 112-13, 207, 219; scholars of, 185; social aspects of, 213-14; Sturgis Rally and Races and, 1. *See also* entrepreneurs; *and specific types of entrepreneurs and specific individuals' names*

environmental quality, 210
Epiphany (town), 187-88
Equitable Fidelity and Title Guaranty Company, 193-94
Ericksen, Neil, 211
Erickson, Myron, 140
Erie Canal, 27
Erkonen, Bob, 97, 200
Ernest Orlando Lawrence (award), 156. *See also* Lawrence, Ernest
Estonia, 10

ethanol, 126, 132, 209, 221. *See also* biofuels
Etta Mine, 55
Euroamericans: construction of "Sioux" tribe by, 21; direct contact of with Indians, 22; economic freedom of, 76; failure of to see environment in pristine state, 167; first contact of with Indians via trade, 21; force Indian students to labor as domestic servants, 43; government policies of threaten Indian lives, property, and prosperity, 78; governments of deny Indians basic civil rights protections, 41; ignorance of Indians' plight, 43; immigrants and, 214-16; imperialism of, 44; incentives faced by, 44; Indian boarding schools run by, 43; interest in photographs of Indians, 37; lease of Indian land by, 79; lives and properties of generally protected by government, 41, 77-78, 82-83; medicinal treatments of, 186-88; migration patterns of into the Great Plains, 27; policies of toward Indians, 42-43; population of, 26; prejudices of against Indians, 76-77; provisioning of Indians by, 34; trading networks of, 21; trafficking of female Indians and, 31; transformation of the nature of South Dakota's economy by,

40; treatment of Indians by, 212; use of bison by, 167; use of cattle by, 167; as Wasichu, 21. *See also* Indians; South Dakotans
European Union, 120
Evans and Hornick Freight Lines, 31
Evarts, 33
Executive Suite (book and TV series), 156
exploitative entrepreneurs and entrepreneurship, 6-8, 19, 22, 30, 32, 42, 43, 66, 218. *See also* entrepreneurs; entrepreneurship
Fairchild, Grace, 117, 184
Fairchild, Shiloh, 74, 117
Fairmont Food Company, 143-44
Fall River County, 87, 107
Falls Park, 162, *163*
Fannie Mae. *See* Federal National Mortgage Loan Association
Fantle, Charles, *146*
Fantle, Sam, *146*
Fantle's Department Store, *146*, 146
Fantus Company, 107
Fargo, North Dakota, 87, 201, 209
Farm Holiday Association, 73
farm: assembly of equipment used on, 107; bankruptcies, 4, 116-17; crisis of the 1980s, 4, 96, 116-17, 210; equipment stores, 49; implement dealers, 96; incomes, 68-69, 90-91; ownership of, 44; subsidies, 73; tenancy, 86, 90-91; vertical integration of, 144. *See also* agriculturalists; farmers; farming; farms

First Nations Oweesta Corporation, 82
First State Bank, 46
First Western Bank, 202
Fischer Brothers, 144
fish, 19, 21, 38, 106, 117, 127, 138, 144, 165-67. *See also* fishing and fishers; *and names of specific fish species*
Fisher, Marie, 96-97
fishing and fishers, 19, 38, 79, 94, 111, 117, 138, 151, 162, 163, 165-67, 170, 178-80. *See also* fish
Fite, Gilbert, 103, 131, 185
Flandreau (town), 23, 43, 124
Flandreau Indian Reservation, 41
Flathead Reservation, 214
flax tow mill, 38
flax, 36, 38, 113, 125
Floren, Myron, 157
florists and flowers, 92, 157, 159
flour mills, 38, 56, 93, 107, 121, 135
Flower Girl (perfume), 141
Flyger, D. L., 209
food: processing, 121-27; safety, 124-25. *See also* flour mills
Forbes (magazine), 96
Ford Brothers' Indian Oil (patent medicine), 141
Ford, Henry, 6
foreclosures, 61, 68-69, 117, 129, 193, 197, 198
Forester Park (Yankton), 215
Fort Pierre, 23, 24, 25, 30, 144
Fort Randall, 23, 26, 31, 39
Fort Sill Indian Center, 157
Fort Thompson Mounds, 162
Forward Sioux Falls (NGO), 106

Foss, Joe: airport named for, 67; aviation company of, 94; economic development programs of, 95; governorship of, 11, 94-95; transportation and other infrastructure improvements sought by, 94-95; as war hero, 11; as young hunter, 170; youth of, 52, 170
Foss, Olouse, 52
Fossett, Steve, 95
foundry, 33
Four Bands Community Fund, 82
Four Heads Stout (beer), 114
foxes, 1, 26, 168, 175, 180
France and French, 23-24, 37, 119, 128, 133, 167, 182, 214
Franklin, Benjamin, 6
Fraser Institute, 8
Fraser, James Earle, 157
Frazier, Ian, 159
free enterprise system, 1, 72, 103
Freedom Group, 136
freelance writing, 118
Freeman, 182, 209
freighter (wagon), *34*
Fremar Farmers Cooperative, 125
Fremont, Elkhorn & Missouri River Railroad, 32, 39
French Canadians, 37
French, Grace Ann, 157
Frog In Your Throat (patent medicine), 141
Fuller, William, 157
fur trade and fur traders, 22, 25, 28; British, 24; exploitation of Indians by, 42; French, 23-24
furbearers, 178. *See also names of specific animal species*

furniture, furniture manufacturers, and furniture stores, 29, 92, 96, 132, 143
Future Fund (government program), 107
Galiano, Henry, 158
Galley Proof (business), 190
gambling, 30-32, 151, 153; entrepreneurship and, 206; South Dakota and, 205-6. *See also* casinos; poker
game wardens, 170, 172, 173
Gandy Dancer Brew Works, 114-15
garbage and collection of, 47, 109, 140
gardens, gardeners, and gardening, 29, 59, 70, 117, 119, 157, 159, 166
Garland, Hamlin, 155
Garretson, 162, *190*, 190, 198
Garryowen (town), 38
Gary, Indiana, 211
gasoline and fuel stations, 47, 70, 79, 92, 154, 160, 162, 206
Gates, Bill, 6
Gateway (company), 138-39
gathering (subsistence strategy), 18, 22, 40, 117. *See also* fishing and fishers; hunting; trapping
gays and lesbians, 93, 214, 215
Geddes, 100
geese, 38, 144, 168-69, 170, 178, 179
Gehl (company), 140
Gem Theater, 30
gemstones, 127
General Electric (GE), 140
general stores, 32, 36, 46-49, 143, 144
Genesis Innovation, 219

International Harvester, 47, 91

International Vinegar Museum, 152

invasive species, 166, 172, 211

Iowa, 26-28, 46, 64, 91, 95, 131-33, 141, 169, 170, 177, 183, 187, 191, 204

Ipswich, 65

Ireland and Irish, 27, 37-38, 121, 125, 156

Irene (town), 119, *120*

Iroquois, 19

Irving, Washington, 15

Isabel (town), 127

Izaak Walton League, 86

jackalope, 168

Jake's (restaurant), 153

James River Irrigation Company, 40

James River Valley: fertility of, 82; fishing in, 166; hunting in, 170; irrigation aqueduct of, 82; precipitation levels of, 82, 113; river of, 26, 38, 115

Janklow, William, 76, 78, 90; 1982 election of, 104; attempts of to lure businesses to South Dakota, 103; boosterism of, 137; critics of economic policies of, 100, 103; critique of federal government regulations by, 101; economic development programs of, 97-98, 106; Indians and, 212; influence of on Minnesota public policies, 221; re-election of, 97-98; seduction of Citibank by, 98-104

Japan, 10, 118, 151, 172, 221

Jasper, Minnesota, 52

Jauron, Gerald, 166

JDS Industries, 142

Jefferson, Thomas, 24, 29, 75, 217

Jensen, Joe, 179

Jewel Cave Corporation, 165

Jewel Cave, 164-65

jewelers and jewelry, 46, 49, 80, 92, 147-48

Jews, 37, 216

Jim Leighton (steamboat), 45

Jimmy Barnett Orchestra, 150

Job Service of South Dakota, 108

Jobs, Steve, 6

Joe Foss airfield (Sioux Falls), 67, 130

Joe, Belinda, 78

John Birch Society, 74

John Deere (company), 46, 140, 143

John Morrell and Company, 44, 121-22, 137-38

Johns Hopkins University, 83

Johnson family, 120

Johnson, Annie Fellow, 182

Johnson, Charlie, 120

Johnson, Clifton, 159

Johnson, Gustav, 48

Johnson, Jerry, 200

Johnson, Oscar, 4

Johnson, Tim, 73, 83

Jolson, Al, 149

Jones Ranch, 34

Jones, Abraham Lincoln, 53

Jones, January, 154

Jones, John B. Sr., 44

Jones, W. Franklin, 185-86

Kadoka, 46-47, 63-64, 74, 86, 160, 196

Kampeska, Lake, 179

Kane, Richard C., 102

Kansas City Royals, 139

Kansas City, Missouri, 102, 139

Kansas, 115, 186

Karen (people), 124

Karolevitz, Robert, 207

Kassel (town), 38

Kauffman Stadium (Kansas City), 139

keiretsu (type of business organization), 22

Kennebec, 84

Kennedy, John F., 119

Kentucky, 27

Keyes, Hazel, 64

Keystone (town), 55, 163, 180

Keystone Land and Cattle Company, 59

KILI Radio, 81

Kilkenny, Ireland, 125

Kilmer, Val, 79

Kimball *Graphic* (newspaper), 54

Kimball, 54, 64, 76, 117, 152

King, James, 186

King, Lena, 117

Kingsbury County, 113, 156

Kirby family, *203*

Kirby, Joe, 144, 204

kitsch, 150, 154

Kiwanis Club, 86

Kneip, Richard F., 85

Knights of Labor (NGO), 137

Knights of Pythias Lodge (NGO), 86

Knology (company), 191

Kohler, Hans-Peter, 209

Kolsrud, David, 125

Kovacecich, Richard, 201

Kraft Foods, 123

Krause, Herbert, 155

Kroeger, Father William, 187

Ku Klux Klan (1920s), 86-87

Kuehn, Frank Charles William, 131

Kuwait Stock Exchange, 139

Rapid City Regional
Hospital, 188
Rapid City: air force
base of, 93; banks and
banking in, *192*, 197-
200; bison industry of,
116; business incubators
in, 219; caves located
near, 165; celebrities
association with, 154-
57; cement plant of,
88; cheese industry
of, 123; commercial
airline services in, 94;
denizens of as tourists,
151; distance of from
Pierre, 129; distrust of
outsiders by denizens of,
74; early connection of
with aeronautics, 64-66;
early entrepreneurship
in, 32-33; early
newspapers in, 37; early
population of, 32; early
transportation system of,
39; embroidery industry
of, 139; entrepreneurship
in, 148, 219; financial
institutions of, 103;
first railroad to, 30;
flooding in, 65, 210-11;
flour milling in, 93;
freight bound for, *34*;
gay bars in, 93, 215;
growth of, 93; healthcare
system of, 188; high tech
sector of, 190; Indian
artists of, 162; Indian
entrepreneurs of, 80-81;
interest rates in, 201; job
placement services in,
108; life insurance sector
in, 202; light pollution
in, 15; lumber industry
of, *56*, 93; manufacturing
sector of, 132-33, 136;
meatpacking in, 122;
missile silos near, 102;
motorcycle rallies

in, 2; old governor's
house moved to, 129;
population of, 9, 109,
200; prominent people
of, 199; railroads in,
45; ranches near, 93;
retail sector of, 93, 143,
147-48; scenery of, 159;
size and location of, 45;
Stratobowl of, 95; think
tanks in, 88; tourism
industry of, 93, 154, 160;
transportation system
of, 93-94; vocational-
technical institutes in,
108; wholesale sector of,
93. *See also* Black Hills
Raptor's Nest Inn, 158
rattlesnakes, 168
Raven Industries, *95*,
95-96
Reagan, Ronald, 98
real estate: agents, 44, 46,
47, 204; companies, 27;
prices, 61, 68-69, 127,
138, 198; sector, 110,
202, 219-20; speculation
in, 36, 60, 141; taxation
of, 217
Reardon, Thomas M., 101
Rebeccahs (NGO), 86
Reclamation State Bank of
Newell, 194
Recordak (microfilm
machine), 198
recreation halls, 47. *See
also* dances and dance
halls; pool halls and
leagues
Red Bull Stratos (balloon),
96
Red Owl Stores, 48
Redfield, 151, 195
redhorse (fish), 166
REDI Fund, 108
referendum (ballot), 72
Regulation Q, 99
Reifel, Benjamin, 83
Reinbold and Company, 55

Remington (firearms
manufacturer) , 136, 170
Remington, Frederic,
170-71
Renner Field, *67*, 67
REO Speedwagon, 152
replicative entrepreneurs
and entrepreneurship:
blended with exploitative
entrepreneurship, 30;
definition of, 7; farmers
as, 112; homesteaders
as, 34; immigrants as,
37-38; incentives of, 6;
in Dakota Territory, 32;
Indians as 17, 19, 22,
79; in early Minnesota,
28; in early Sioux Falls,
29; in early South
Dakota, 42, 44, 52; in
South Dakota today,
207; pioneer farmers
as, 27; ranchers as,
33; sod-busting as an
example of, 35. *See
also* entrepreneurs;
entrepreneurship
Republican Party: divisions
within, 75; domination of
South Dakota politics by,
10, 30, 72, 75; members
of caught gambling, 205;
policies of, 88, 101, 194;
reasons for popularity of
in South Dakota, 72-73,
97; social conservatism
of, 11
restaurants, 47-48, 49, 51,
70, 92, 154, 162, 164, 206
retailers, retailing, and
the retail sector, 27,
30, 46, 79, 92-93,
180, 192; attributes
of successful, 144-45;
bankruptcies among,
145; entrepreneurs
of, 146-48; extension
of credit by, 144;

Little Business on the Prairie

amenities found in, 188; high tech sector of, 189-90; homeless denizens of, 218; hospitals in, 130; Indian mound sites in and near, *20*, 162; institutions of higher education in, 185; intercity bus routes emanating from, 46; interest rates in, 201; inventors in, 52-53; job placement services in, 108; Ku Klux Klan in, 87; labor relations in, 122; labor relations in, 137; life insurers in, 202-3; light pollution in, 15; manufacturing sector of, 132-34, 136; meatpacking industry in, 121-22, 137; medical research industry of, 186; methane production in, 126; musicians of, 150; national plowing contest held in, 119; need for street railway in, 46; Northern League baseball team of, 152; Norwegian population of, 37; nursing home industry of, 189; pedagogical entrepreneurs in, 186; penitentiary in, 129, 131, 144; pink quartzite of, 127-28; POET and, 126; population growth of, 9, 109; post office of, 101-2; printing industry of, 54; private equity real estate industry in, 204; productivity of workforce of, 102-3, 134-35; quality of healthcare system of, 188; quarries of, 127; quartzite of, 130; railroads in, 45; rainfall in, 45; Raven Industries and, *95*; reasons it attracted Citibanks's credit card business, 101-3; reputation of as show town, 149; retail sector of, 93, 143, *146*, 146; Senate committee hearing held in, 122; Sioux Empire and, 191; social organizations in, 86; taxes in, 106, 134-35; taxidermy in, 180; telecommunications industry of, 191; telephone system of, 102; theaters of, 131, 149; time zone of, 102; trading area of, 122, 132, 141-43; transformation of, 207; transportation costs in, 217; transportation system of, 93-94; unionized workers of, 74; vacancy rates in, 98; visit of John F. Kennedy to, 119; vocational-technical institutes in, 108; wages in, 102-3; wholesaling sector of, 141-42; workers compensation company headquartered in, 204; workforce of, 101-2

Sioux Transit, 46
Sioux Valley Hospital, 188
Sisseton Indian Reservation, 41
Sisseton, 21, 23, 123, 155
Sisseton-Wahpeton Federal Credit Union, 82
Sitting Bull Crystal Cave, 165
Sitting Bull, 152
skunks, 167
Slaughter, Enos, 174
Small Business Administration (SBA), 97, 139, 185

Small Business Innovation Research program, 219
smallpox, 22-23, 42, 186
Smart21 Community, 190
Smiley, Myron J., 33-34, 183
Smiley-Gay Hardware Company, 34
Smith, Adam, 11
Smith, Henry Weston, 153
Smith, Mr. (homesteader), 35
Smithfield Foods, 122
snipe, 178
snowmobiles and snowmobiling, 142, 153
soap and soap factories, 30, 38
Social Security, 156, 213, 221
sod busting, 35
Sodak Gaming, 206
soddies (houses), 35
soils, 35, 121. *See also* houdek
solar energy, 209
Solum, Burdette, 201
Son of the Middle Border, A (book), 155
SONIFI Solutions, 191
Soprano, Tony, 7
sorghum, 113
Sotheby, 158-59
Soukup and Thomas International Balloon and Airship Museum, 95
Sousa, John Philip, 149
South Dakota: 1980 federal census and, 104; ability of to attract entrepreneurs, 220; ability of to attract workers, 220; access to financial capital and, 9; acres of taken up by pioneer farmers during Great Dakota Boom, 34; Adam Smithian nature of economy of, 11;

African American entrepreneurs in, 50-51; agricultural development of, 26, 42; agricultural equipment manufacturing in, 140; agricultural industry of, 4, 109-20; agricultural subsidies received by farmers in, 10, 112; air quality in, 13-15, 62, 75, 95; airline industry and, 65-68, 94; airplane entrepreneurs of, 64-68; altitude of above sea level, 210; amusement entrepreneurs in, 119, 150, 215; archeological riches of, 162; architects of, 131, 195; attempts of by government to lure businesses to, 103; at-will employment doctrine of, 137; automobiles in, 51; ballooning in, 95-96; bank failures in, *192*, 193, 196-97; bankers of and Citibank episode, 101; banking industry of, 182; banking practices in, 196; banking regulations of, 199-200; banks of, 99-101, 192-202, 210; baseball and, 152; beauty of touted in books, 159; believed unsuitable for Euroamerican-style agriculture, 26; bicentennial of, 207; biggest challenge facing, 221; biological threats to tourism industry of, 211; bison in, 115-16, *115*; boosterism in, 61, 208; brain drain from, 96; branch banking in, 195; branch manufacturing

in, 136; breweries in, 114; building moving industry of, 129; business climate in, 10, 50, 138; business conditions on reservations of, 213; business culture of, 11; business friendliness of, 9, 110; businesses of face challenges, 208-21; careers of politicians of, 76; cattle ranching industry of, 58-60, 114; celebrities associated with, 154-57; challenges faced by, 16, 207-21; challenges facing agriculturalists of, 113; change in, 208; chartermongering efforts of, 62; civil rights record of, 215; climate and disappearance of megafauna of, 17; climate of, 11-15, 61-62, 68-69, 95, 113, 116, 151, 161, 175-76, 187, 189, 209, 210-11; college graduation rates in, 183-84; companies operating in, 106; company size and, 220; competition of for Citibank's credit card business, 99; computers and, 191; conflated with North Dakota by some, 209; conservative political elements in, 75; construction in, *110*; construction industry of, 127-30; cooperative enterprises in, 125; corporate sector of, 11, 27, 62; cost of doing business in, 102; cost of living in, 103; costs of potential

industrialization of, 211; court rulings in, 137; credit card industry of, 98-104, 205; crime in, 137, 218; critics of, 100, 103; crop prices in, 97, 118; crop yields in, 97, 113; crops primarily planted in, 113-14; cultural zones of, 45; culture and politics of, 74-75; current model of government economic activism in, 90-91; dearth of capital in, 209-10; dearth of credit facilities on reservations of, 213; debt collection in, 204, 218; degree of ethnic bigotry in, 214-16; degree of racial animosity in, 214-16; democratic nature of, 83; Democratic party in, 73, 97; democratic political culture of, 10; Democrats of as outsiders, 73; dependence of government of on gambling revenues, 205-6; depopulation of, 104, 221; dinosaur fossil hunting in, 153, 157-59; disintermediation and, 99; diversification of economy of, 109-12, 216; divided into two geographically by the Missouri River, 41; droughts in, 14, 20, 40, 48, 221; dust bowls in, 68, 221; dynamic nature of economy of, 208; dynamic small business sector of, 50; early capitalists in, 25; early corn cultivation in, 18; early ethnic diversity of, 37-38; early

of, 108-9; government bureaucracy of, 76; government debt in, 217; government of, 2, 76, 109; government revenues of, 98; government-ownership of railroads in, 98; grasslands of, 11; health of denizens of, 15, 186, 188; health tourism in, 187-88; healthcare costs in, 103, 189; healthcare in rural middle of, 189; healthcare industry of, 186-89; healthy amenities in, 188; heavy manufacturing in, 136; high income jobs and, 109; high school graduation rates in, 183-84; higher education system of, 185; history of ballooning in, 64; history of, 208; hog numbers in, 114; hollowing out of rural areas of, 221; homeownership in, 86; homey charm of, 114; homosexuality in, 215; hospitality of workers in, 162-63; hotel industry of, 163-64; houses of early Euroamerican settlers of, 35; hunting and fishing in, 138; hunting in, 165-81; hunting tourism in, 168, 179-80; illicit drugs in, 218; illiteracy rate in, 183; image of, 4, 208-9; immigration into, 214; importance of manufacturing to economy of, 135-36; importance of service sector to economy of, 182; importance of tourism industry to

economy of, 161, 164, 207; income equality of compared to Western Europe, 9-10; incomes in, 9, 98; increasing ethnic diversity of, 214-16; incubation of entrepreneurs in, 9; independent banks of, 201; Indian cultures of, 212; Indian Reservations of, 9; Indian segregation policies of, 215; Indians of immiserated by federal government policies, 212; industrial breakdown of economy of, 106; industrial machinery and equipment manufacturing in, 136; industrial workers of, 137; industries of, 4, 62; infrastructure of, 9; injection molded parts manufacturing in, 140; innovative entrepreneurs and entrepreneurship in, 6-7, 19, 22, 27, 37-39, 42, 52, 57, 70, 77, 114, 119, 138, 143, 185, 190, 199, 207, 213, 218-19; insects in, 15; institutions of higher education in, 185; interest rates in, 96-97, 99-101, 200-1; Knights of Labor and, 137; Ku Klux Klan in, 87; labor force of, 122-23, 142; labor relations in, 137; labor unions and, 74; lakes of, 179; as land of general consensus, 73; as land of infinite variety, 73; laws of changed to lure Citibank to Sioux Falls, 101, 104; laws of, 218; legislature of, 76; libertarian political

elements in, 11, 75; licensed pilots in, 94; limestone in soils of and pheasant fecundity, 176; limited wealth redistribution in, 85; literacy rates in, 53-54; lobbying of federal government by state legislatures of, 112; location of, 151, 208-9; long-term trends in economy of, 207; machine politics anathema in, 73; major economic sectors in, 110; manufacture of electronic signage in, 139; manufacturing climate of, 135; manufacturing employment in, 133, 135-36; manufacturing entrepreneurs of, 136-37; manufacturing industry of, 107, 110, 112, 127, 131-41; manufacturing of disk drives in, 139; manufacturing value added in, 134; meaning of, 72; mechanization of agricultural sector of, 113; megalithic structures of, 152; meritocratic nature of, 39; migration from, 69; military assets located in, 93, 102; mining equipment manufacturing in, 140; mining industry of, 110, 110, 212; missile silos in, 93; mortgage loans made by government of, 197; mottoes of towns in, 151; as Mount Rushmore State, 4; movies made in, 155; musicians of, 150; national parks of, 151;

government and small
business by, 84-85,
100; tests faced by,
207; uniqueness of
political views of, 75;
use of relief by during
Great Depression,
69; views of proper
sphere of government,
85; views of toward
federal government
initiatives, 85; views
of toward government
indebtedness, 85;
voluntarism of, 87-88;
voter participation rates
of, 76, 83; willingness
of to experiment, 90;
work ethic of, 44, 50,
102-3, 124, 137, 149;
workforce of, 220; zeal
of for education, 182-84.
See also South Dakota;
*and specific companies,
names, places, etc.*
South Korea, 8, 118
soybeans, 45, 112-15, 118,
120, 123-25
Spain, 24
Spanish American War
(1898), 59
Spearfish Canyon, 55
Spearfish, 3, 32, 65, 79,
108, 160, 194, 202;
economy of, 109-10
Spink County, 36, 53, 113
Spirit Mound, 162
*Spirit of an American
Entrepreneur, The*
(book), 207
Spitznagel, Harold, *130*, 131
sporting goods stores, 29,
180
Spotted Eagle, Roselyn,
79-80
Spotted Tail Reservation.
See Rosebud Indian
Reservation

*Springfield
[Massachusetts]
Republican*, 40
Springfield, 129, 195
Springview (town), 48
squash (vegetable), 18, 19
squirrels, 117, 168, 178
St. Lawrence, 60
St. Louis Cardinals, 174
St. Louis Fur Company, 24
St. Louis, Missouri, 11, 27,
28, 64, 102
St. Luke's (hospital), 188
St. Olaf Roller Mill, 121
St. Olaf, Minnesota, 184
Stabler family, 50, 164-65
Stage Barn Crystal Cave,
163
stagecoach companies and
lines, 28, 30, 34, 146,
208. *See also names of
specific companies*
Stalin, Josef, 7
Standing Rock Indian
Reservation, 41
Stanford Achievement
Tests (SATs), 183
Starboy Enterprises, 80
State (theater), 149
State Bank and Trust
Company, 195
State Banking and Trust
Company, 141, 195
State Banking Commission,
200
State Brand Board, 85
State Capital Annex, 130
steam tractors, 91. *See also*
tractors
steamboats and
steamships, 25-28, 31,
34, 42, 45, 208. *See
also names of specific
steamboats*
Stebbins Fox and Co., 194
Stein, Walter, 158
Stenseth, David, 191
stock growers. *See* ranchers
Stock, Catherine, 44

Stockman's Bar, 174
Stoppelmoor, Cheryl, 154
Storla, 37
Stratobowl, 95
Stroh, Dan, 189
Sturgis Rally and Races,
1-2, *3*, 218
Sturgis, 1-3, 32, 50, 136,
160, 200, 202, 218
subsistence hunting. *See*
hunting, cooking pot
variety of
suckers (fish), 166
Sue (Tyrannosaurus rex),
158
suffrage and suffragist
movement, 39, 84
sugar, sugar beets, and
sugar refineries, 33, 36,
56-57, 107, 114, 123
Sully County, 38
sunfish, 166
sunflowers, 18, 19, 45, 113,
114
Supreme Court of South
Dakota, 200
surety business, 193
swans, 168-69
Swedes, 37
sweet clover, 113
Swift (meatpacker), 122
Swift Eagle (airplane).
See Wamblee Ohanka
(airplane)
swimming and swimming
pools, 69, 160, 166
Sword and Dagger Ranch,
33
Sylvan Lake Lodge, 131
Syndicate Building, *203*
tack shops, 29, 36. *See also*
horses, horse dealers,
and horse stables
Taft, William Howard, 75
tailors, 29, 32, 92
Taiwan, 8, 118, 141
TalentSoft, 139
TAN Ranch, 59
tapirs, 17

turkeys (birds), 70, 123, 124, 144, 159, 168, 178

TV. *See* televisions, TV networks, and TV shows

Twin Disc Clutch Company, 132

Two Kettles (people), 22

Tyrannosaurus rex, 153, 158

Tyson (meatpacker), 125

U&I Sugar Beet Factory, 33

U.S. Chamber of Commerce, 10

U.S. Comptroller of the Currency, 99, 200

U.S. Department of Agriculture, 139, 201, 221

U.S. Department of the Interior, 80, 139, *190*

U.S. Federal Aviation Administration, 140

U.S. Geological Survey, *190*, 190

U.S. Gypsum Company, 56

U.S. News and World Report (periodical)*, 216*

U.S. Post Office, 191

U.S. Senate, 200

U.S. Supreme Court (SCOTUS), 99, 200

U.S.-Dakota War of 1862, 28

Uhden, Violet, 96

Ukraine, 221

Ulry-Talbert Company, 146

Uncle Sam Mine, 57

undertakers, 47-49

Unemployment Insurance Fund, 107

Union County, 38, 136, 143

Union Savings Association, 193

United Airlines, 173

United Biscuit, 123

United Family Farmers (UFF), 82-83

United Farmers League, 73

United Kingdom. *See* Britain, British, United Kingdom, England, English, Wales, and Welsh

United Sioux Tribes Conference, 76-77

United States, economic future of, 221. *See also* federal government; *and names of specific agencies, departments, etc.*

University of Colorado, 186

University of Minnesota, 156, 184

University of Pennsylvania, 131

University of Sioux Falls, 185

University of South Dakota (USD), 81, 127, 154-55, 182, 185, 189, 200, 208, 216

University of Wisconsin, 156

Unkowapi (business), 80

uranium, 107

Urethane Soy Systems, 124

USA Today, 81

USS South Dakota (battleship), 173

Utah, 10, 139, 148, 158

Valley Queen Cheese, 123

Valley Springs, 125

Van Demark Clinic, 188

vanadium, 57, 107

Vance, Earl T., 66

varmints, 178. *See also the names of specific animal species*

Vaudeville acts, 149

Vega, 76

venture capital and venture capitalists, 209-10, 219

VeraSun, 126

Verendrye Monument, 23

Vermillion River, 26, 166

Vermillion: banks in, 194; Bower family of, 39, 118; distribution center in, 142; early history of, 26, 29, 45; entrepreneurs in, 50-51, 140; floods in, 129; Indian archeological site near, 162; museum in, 157; racism in 215; technology corridor of, 190, 219; workforce of, 142. *See also* University of South Dakota

Vermont, 9, 10

Veterans Administration Medical Center, 130

Veterans Administration, 221

Viborg, 114, 156

Vienna (town), 49

Vietnam and Vietnamese, 108, 214

Vilas, 49, 61

Virginia, 27, 173

viticulture, 114

Vivian (town), 13

Volcker, Paul, 99, 105

Volga (town), 65, 124, 132

Wagner (town), 38, 66, 78

Wahpekute (tribe), 21

Wahpeton (tribe), 21

Wakeman, Richard, 77

Wall (town), 153, 168, 202

Wall Drug, 153-54

Wall Street Journal, 153

Wall Street, 71, 209

walleye (fish), 138, 166, 167, 180. *See also* sauger

Walter family, 125

Walter, Tim, 125

Wamblee Ohanka (airplane), 65

wampum, 25

Wanamingo, Minnesota, 126

War of 1812, 24

Ward, Charles, 65

Ward, Warren Albert, 64

Wardall, Alonzo, 39

Wulf, Frank, 64
Wylie Park/Storybook
    Land, 156
Wyoming Stage Company,
    30
Wyoming, 2, 8, 10, 81, 109,
    125, 158, 209, 218
Yankton (tribe), 22, 78
Yankton College, 156
Yankton Indian
    Reservation, 41
Yankton: authors from,
    155-56; aviation industry
    and, 65; banks in, 193,
    201; credit card industry
    of, 103; damming of the
    Missouri River and, 92,
    167; early economy of,
    38-39; early newspapers
    in, 37; early settlement
    of, 29; as early trading
    post, 26; Enterprise
    Institute in, 219;
    entrepreneurs in, 51;
    famous personages who
    lived in or visited, 157,
    215; Gurney Nursery
    of, 121; hospitals in,
    188; industrial crystal
    plant in, 127; inventors
    from, 52; meatpacking
    industry of, 121-22;
    population density
    of, 45; racism in, 215;
    staging area for Black
    Hills gold rush, 34;
    transportation system
    of, 30-31
Yanktonai (people), 22-23,
    157
Yellowstone National Park,
    52
YMCA, 86
Z Bell Ranch, 59
Zell, Sam, 204
Ziebach County, 153
Ziebach, Frank M., 37
Zietlow, J. L. W., 63

zones: climatic, 113;
    economic, 45; time, 102;
    zoning laws, 211-12